**HISTORICAL DICTIONARIES
OF WARS, REVOLUTION, AND CIVIL UNREST
Edited by Jon Woronoff**

1. *Afghan Wars, Revolutions, and Insurgencies*, by Ludwig W. Adamec. 1996.

   British Civil Wars, by Ian Roy. Forthcoming.

   World War II: Europe and the Mediterranean, by Anne Wells and D. Clayton James. Forthcoming.

Dictionary of Afghan Wars, Revolutions, and Insurgencies

Ludwig W. Adamec

Historical Dictionaries of
Wars, Revolution, and Civil Unrest, No. 1

The Scarecrow Press, Inc.
Lanham, Md., & London
1996

SCARECROW PRESS, INC.

Published in the United States of America
by Scarecrow Press, Inc.
4720 Boston Way
Lanham, Maryland 20706

4 Pleydell Gardens, Folkestone
Kent CT20 2DN, England

British Cataloguing-in-Publication Information Available

Library of Congress Cataloging-in-Publication Data

Adamec, Ludwig W.
    Dictionary of Afghan wars, revolutions, and insurgencies / Ludwig W.
Adamec
        p.   cm. — (Historical dictionaries of wars, revolutions, and civil
unrest ; no. 1)
    Includes bibliographical references.
    ISBN 0-8108-3232-1 (cloth : alk. paper)
    1. Afghanistan—History—Dictionaries. 2. Afghanistan—History,
Military—Dictionaries. I. Title. II. Series.
DS356.A26   1996
958.1'003—dc20
                                                            96-35600
                                                            CIP

ISBN 0-8108-3232-1 (cloth : alk.paper)

To Rahella

CONTENTS

EDITOR'S FOREWORD

It is indeed appropriate that this new series of *Historical Dictionaries of War, Revolution, and Civil Unrest* should start with a volume on the Afghan wars. For it covers not just one of a few wars but an endless chain of full-fledged wars and lesser actions stretching over two-and-a-half centuries and continuing to the present day. First there are the wars during which rather small and obscure tribes carved out and then expanded an empire. Then come three Anglo-Afghan wars during which this seemingly vulnerable and vincible force held its own against the world's largest and most voracious empire. After only relative calm, the warfare resumed with Afghans taking on an even more aggressive Soviet Union. It ends, in this book but not in the field, with the Afghans fighting one another.

Few nations have as warlike a past and present. Perhaps for that reason the Afghans have become such good warriors. Or it may be the other way around. For they have maintained a reputation as a "martial race" well beyond the period when the British Empire sought such people for its colonial armies and sometimes avoided them during its colonial conquests. That knowledge was not shared by the men in the Kremlin, or initially by the Soviet military, because it was assumed that in the modern era martial qualities were inadequate when pitted against sophisticated weaponry, and that poorly armed guerrilla fighters could not possibly defeat heavily armed soldiers backed by airplanes, artillery, and — if necessary — chemical arms. They were wrong. But these qualities, once an advantage, have since become a horrible drawback as Afghans take on one another in a bitter free-for-all.

This *Dictionary of Afghan Wars, Revolutions, and Insurgencies* is far from the only book on the subject. These wars have fascinated many authors and there are numerous studies. But it is the only one that includes information on all of the wars. And it is the only one that provides essential data in such a handy format. There are entries on the wars and campaigns, on the generals and sometimes diplomats, on tactics and logistics, and on weapons. In the introduction and dictionary there is also useful background material on how the wars got started, and why, and how they were concluded. More diffusely, there is a description of the Afghan warrior with his qualities and defects. The chronology provides a broad overview. And the bibliography, which is in many ways unique, directs readers toward countless other books that can round out their understanding.

This volume was written by Ludwig W. Adamec, a specialist not only on contemporary Afghanistan but earlier periods as well. He has traveled widely in the region and served briefly as head of the Afghanistan Branch of the Voice of America, but otherwise spent most of his time as a professor of Near and Middle Eastern studies. He presently teaches at the University of Arizona. Dr. Adamec has written extensively on Afghanistan and nearby countries, including works on diplomatic history, foreign affairs, and a who's who. He is also the author of the *Historical Dictionary of Afghanistan*. This book offers further insight into the crucial aspects of an intriguing society.

Jon Woronoff
Series Editor

PREFACE

Alphabetization and Spellings. Names beginning with "Abdul" (A. *'abd-al*, meaning servant or slave), followed by one of the names of Allah (God), as, for example, Abdul Rahman (Servant of the Merciful) or Abdul Karim (Servant of the Bountiful), form a unit and should not be taken as first and last names. Abdul Rahman (pronounced and often written Abdur Rahman) will therefore be found under "A" not "R." Compounds with Allah, like Habibullah (Habib Allah) or Amanullah (Aman Allah), will be found in alphabetical order under its compound version. If the name Muhammad is followed only by one other name, like Muhammad Isma'il or Muhammad Nadir, the name will be found under "M." Titles, like General, Shah (King), or Khan (Chief) are not counted in the alphabetization.

This volume describes major wars as well as revolts, skirmishes, and smaller armed actions. To maintain the narration in dictionary format, a major war was described in several entries and under subheadings discussing the objectives, causes, costs, lessons, and various aspects of a particular war. Cross-references, including "q.v." (*quod vide*, "which see") will refer the reader to related topics.

Statistics. Population statistics are estimates for the prewar (1979) period, unless otherwise indicated. No complete census has been taken in Afghanistan, and estimates of the Afghan population vary from 13 to 15.5 million. The numbers of casualties, body counts, and so forth, in armed conflicts are only approximations and often exaggerated according to the bias of the source. British official accounts often did not list casualties from causes other than enemy fire. Most of our sources on the Anglo-Afghan wars are British, and even official accounts vary as to the number of casualties.

Illustrations. A number of photographs are included in this work, but the greater part of illustrations consist of drawings from British illustrated newspapers. They are the artist's conception of events and individuals and therefore not exact reproductions. Some stereotyping can be discerned in depicting the Afghans, Indian soldiers, and European officers. It has been necessary to reduce and adapt the maps, plans, and plates to fit the format of this publication. This was often accomplished at a loss in quality and legibility, but it was felt that the illustrations would enhance the usefulness of this book and the author hopes that his readers will agree.

ILLUSTRATIONS

Maps

Plans

Plates

ABBREVIATIONS AND ACRONYMS

A.	Arabic
ADA	Air Defense Artillery
A.D.C.	Aide de Camp
AGSA	Afghan Security Service
A.I.G.	Afghan Interim Government
AN	Antonov Soviet Aircraft
APC	Armored Personnel Carrier
AR	*The Life of Abdur Rahman*
Bn(s).	Battalion(s)
Bde.	Brigade
BM	Ballistic Missile
Brig.	Brigade
Coy.	Company
D.	Dari, the Farsi of Afghanistan
Div.	Division
DRA	Democratic Republic of Afghanistan
Fd. Coy.	Field Company
GAZ	*Historical and Political Gazetteer of Afghanistan,* by Adamec, vols. 1–6
GHQ	General Headquarters
G.S.O.	General Staff Organization
Harakat	Harakat-i Inqilab-i Islami of Muhammadi
HBAA	*Handbook of the Afghan Army*
Hizb (H)	Hizb-i Iskami of Hekmatyar
Hizb (K)	Hizb-i Islami of Khales
HQ	Headquarters
IFV	Infantry Fighting Vehicle
IL	Ilyushin Soviet Aircraft
ILN	*Illustrated London News*
IOR	India Office Records
IRA	Islamic Republic of Afghanistan

ISI	Inter-Services Intelligence
Ittihad	Ittihad-i Islami Barayi Azadi-yi Afghanistan of Sayyaf
Jabha	Jabha-yi Milli Najat-i Afghanistan of Mujaddidi
Jam'iat	Jam'iat-i Islami of Rabbani
KAM	Workers' Intelligence Service
KHAD	State Intelligence Service
LCSFA	Limited Contingent of Soviet Forces in Afghanistan
LWA	Ludwig W. Adamec
MI	Soviet Aircraft
MIG	Soviet Fighter Aircraft
MR	Military Report
MRL	Multiple Rocket Launcher
MRD	Motorized Rifle Division
NCO	Noncommissioned Officers
NWFP	North-West Frontier Province of India, now Pakistan
OA (1,2,3)	Official Account (of First, Second, or Third Anglo-Afghan War)
Obs.	Obsolete
P.	Pashtu
PDPA	People's Democratic Party of Afghanistan
PFM	"Butterfly" Mine
PIN	*Penny Illustrated Newspaper*
PP Col.	Parliamentary Papers Collection
P&S	Political and Secret
Q.v.	(*Quod vide*) Which see
Regts.	Regiments
RFA	Artillery
RGA	Artillery
SAM	Surface-to-Air Missile
S&M	Sappers and Miners
Spetsnaz	Special Operations Forces
Sqn.	Squadron (Sqdn.)
SU	(Sukhoi) Fencer Bombers
TU	(Tupelov) Badger Bombers
WAD	State Intelligence Service

ACKNOWLEDGMENTS

It is my pleasant duty to express my thanks to various institutions and individuals who have provided sources necessary for completion of this project. Much of the historical information about the three Anglo-Afghan wars was gleaned from the archives of the Oriental and India Office Collection of the British Library in London, England. Official Accounts of Afghan wars, maps, and illustrations from Crown copyright documents appear with permission of the Controller of Her Majesty's Stationery Office. Illustrations from the *Illustrated London News*, the *Penny Illustrated Newspaper*, the *Penny Pictorial News*, and the *Graphic* were acquired from the Newspaper Library of the British Library.

Ms. Atefa Rawan, librarian at the University of Arizona, was helpful in ferreting out bibliographical sources.

My thanks also go to Mr. Alain Marigo, a noted French cartographer, who provided maps of Kabul and Afghanistan. Mr. Marigo and the Centre de Recherches et d'Etudes Documentaire sur l'Afghanistan (CEREDAF) in Paris, France, provided a number of photos of the *mujahedin* war against the Soviet/Kabul forces. Several of the photo journalists whose works are presented in this publication died during the last years of the war or are still missing. Plate 11 is by Shah Bazgar (d. 1989); Plate 13 by S. Thiollier (d. 1990); Plate 15 by Edouard De Pazzi; Plate 16 by Thierry Niquet (still missing). One photo was provided by MAHAZ (Plate 12); others are from Afghanistan Today, Plate 14 and 18; and one is from *Jam'iat*, Plate 17. Plate 5 is by John Burke (1839) from the IOL. I also want to thank Mr. Etienne Gille, Ms. Sylvie Heslot, Ms. Vera Marigo, and all their colleagues of CEREDAF, whose *Les Nouvelles d'Afghanistan* has been an important source for my research.

This volume was produced as a camera-ready copy – to the extent that it conforms to a professional typesetting job, I am indebted to suggestions of the editorial staff of Scarecrow Press.

INTRODUCTION

Afghanistan is the creation of a martial race who revolted against Persian domination of its mountain fastness and destroyed Safavid rule (1501–1732) at the Battle of Gulnabad in 1722. The Afghans occupied much of Persia, but were not able to maintain themselves on the Iranian plateau and eventually were forced to yield to Nadir Shah Afshar (1736–47, q.v.), founder of the short-lived Afsharid dynasty (1736–95). Appreciating the martial value and intractable nature of the Afghan tribes and the geographical barriers preventing easy passage to the riches of India, Nadir Shah enlisted Afghan tribes to his colors rather than trying to destroy them. Nadir invaded India, humbled the Moghul emperor, and sacked Delhi, his capital; in the end the erratic military genius fell prey to a plot by his own officers.

The leaderless Persian army was in a state of disarray, which permitted Ahmad Khan, the barely 23-year-old chief of the Sadozai clan of the Abdali tribe, to step into the power vacuum. He proclaimed Afghan independence from Persia and was elected king, assuming the title "Ahmad Shah Durrani" (1747–73, q.v.). His Abdali clansmen henceforth became known as the Durrani tribe. He captured a convoy with revenue from India valued at 20,000.000 rupees (about £1,000.000), which enabled him to consolidate his power and win the support of the most powerful tribes.

Rather than becoming an absolute monarch in the Persian tradition, Ahmad Shah established a system of military feudalism that succeeded in welding the Afghan tribes into a highly efficient force. He confirmed the Durrani chiefs in possession of the Kandahar area with the sole obligation of providing a requisite number of troops (*see* DURRANI, LAND TENURE). The Durrani chiefs were given the highest offices in the young state, and his own clan, the Sadozai, were elevated to the status of royal clan. Ahmad Shah adopted a council of nine influential Afghan chiefs who shared in the responsibility of decisions but left all real authority with the young king.

Discussing the character of the Afghan king, a British historian stated:

> The country, now termed Afghanistan, had merely consisted of a congeries of petty states, ruled by tyrannical Chiefs, who were frequently at war with one another. Later, it became provinces of great empires

which were ruled by foreign conquerors and their descendants. Later again, it was a dismembered country, with its provinces held by three neighboring states. Now, for the first independent state, ruled by a monarch whose high descent and warlike qualities made him peculiarly acceptable to his aristocratic and virile Chiefs, as well as to his warlike subjects in general. (Sykes, I, 367)

Ahmad Shah succeeded as founder of modern Afghanistan because he proved himself as a military genius. He quickly captured Kabul, Ghazni, and Peshawar and in December 1747 embarked on the first of eight invasions of India (*see* AHMAD SHAH). The territorial conquests generated booty and revenues that assured him the loyalty of the unruly chiefs. He added Kashmir, Sind, and the Western Panjab (q.v.) to his domain and founded an empire that extended from eastern Persia to northern India and from the Amu Daria (q.v.) to the Indian Ocean. He began the unification of the Afghan heartland with an army of 12,000 men, and by the time he invaded the Panjab in January 1748, he commanded a force of 30,000 tribesmen, including Qizilbash, Hazaras (qq.v.), Khorasanians, and others who flocked to his colors. A setback at the Battle of Manupur (q.v., March 11, 1748), where the Afghans met an imperial army of 60,000 men, was avenged with the capture of Lahore. Ahmad Shah outflanked the defensive perimeter of the city by crossing the Indus River at midnight with a force of 10,000 horsemen and attacking the camp of Hayatullah Khan, the Moghul governor of this strategic city. Ahmad Shah agreed to make peace and accepted the Indus River as his eastern border. A year later (1749), following his third invasion of India, Ahmad Shah turned west to capture the Province of Herat and advanced into Khorasan (q.v.). In 1757 the Afghan king occupied Delhi, which resulted in indiscriminate slaughter and plunder when a group of Ahmad Shah's soldiers was attacked by a mob. *Khutba* (Friday sermon) was read in the name of Ahmad Shah, making him the de facto head of the Empire of Delhi. He did not remain but bestowed the sultanate of Hindustan upon Alamgir II.

He destroyed an enemy army near Sirhind, estimated at 80,000 men, and defeated the powerful Maratha confederation at the Battle of Panipat (January 14, 1761) (qq.v.). The booty was said to have included 22,000 men and women, 50,000 horses, 500 elephants, 200,000 oxen, several thousand camels, artillery, and an enormous amount of jewelry and cash; but geopolitical factors militated against an Afghan conquest of northern India. Afghan territorial possessions had reached their largest extent, and Ahmad Shah's lines of communication to India were overextended. Therefore, he had to resort to indirect rule, appointing governors over the newly acquired provinces. But as soon as the victorious army returned to Afghanistan, the newly conquered areas were in revolt.

A new socioreligious nation, the Sikhs (q.v.), emerged in the Panjab and, in spite of suffering fearful massacres, was able to deprive the Afghans of their dream of replacing the Moghul Empire of India. Barely 70 years later the British East India Company (q.v.), which had obtained a charter for exploration and commerce of Bengal in 1600, had become the dominant power in India. In the pursuit of never-ending acquisitions of territory and the search for the "scientific frontier" to close the Afghan "gateway to India," the stage was set for three Anglo-Afghan wars.

The wars of Ahmad Shah Durrani served two major objectives: liberation of the Afghan heartland and consolidation of the newly created state. The martial energies generated in the unification of the country inevitably found their release in the search for a new frontier and booty. The multitude of tribal and ethnic groups were able to set aside their mutual suspicions and join in the common enterprise.

Ahmad Shah carefully prepared his Indian campaigns: he would invite a provincial governor to submit, promising rewards or high office, thus winning his alliance against his previous master. Some, like Ali Muhammad Khan, governor of Sirhind, chose to withdraw as the easier solution to the dilemma of choosing sides; others, to their regret, left the decision to the battlefield. If met by opposition, Ahmad Shah ordered the immediate execution of any natives prowling in the vicinity of his camp to secure the secrecy of his movements. He counted on speed to take the enemy by surprise, attacking in the early hours of the morning. He permitted an irregular rabble to engage the enemy and then attacked, trying to encircle the enemy or push him against some geographical barrier — a river or mountain — and order his right and left wings to attack. Initially, he still lacked artillery and a regular army, and the tribes fought under their own chiefs. But size required organization, and Ahmad Shah appointed his most trusted *sardar* (chief) with the position of commander in chief (*sipah salar* or *sardar-i sardaran*) to be responsible for the organization, equipment, and training of troops and for the planning and conduct of campaigns. Heavy guns were captured, and eventually the Afghans learned the art of casting cannon from a mixture of brass and copper. At the Battle of Panipat (q.v.), Ahmad Shah employed a cannon, almost 15 feet in length with a bore of about 9 inches, capable of launching balls of about 40 pounds.

Gradually, a regular army (*askar-i munazzam*) was established, supported by the much larger, irregular tribal levies (*askar-i ghair munazzam* or *khawanin sawaran*). Three-fourths of the army were cavalrymen, armed with matchlocks and swords or spears — only a few had more modern firearms. Shields, daggers, axes, and various small weapons were used in close combat. Eventually, Ahmad Shah's arsenal of heavy guns increased, cannons were drawn by horses or camels, sometimes by elephants. The elephant was the "tank" of traditional warfare — used in battle to break the lines of the enemy or to carry the heavy artillery. Although useful in India, the pachyderm was difficult to "fuel" in the deserts and mountains of Afghanistan. The irregular tribal army was composed of tribesmen who joined for a particular campaign, or of levies from various tribes, whose chiefs were to provide tribal cavalry corresponding to the size of their fiefs. Some tribal forces were maintained for the protection of the frontiers or collection of revenues. (*See* AHMAD SHAH, MILITARY ADMINISTRATION.) Toward the end of his rule Ahmad Shah's army was estimated at 120,000, 40,000 of whom constituted the regular army. But only a small part of the army was employed in individual battles. Camp followers greatly increased these numbers, which gave rise to hyperbolic accounts by native historians of cataclysmic battles involving hundreds of thousands of troops.

Ahmad Shah's death marked the end of foreign conquests. His son Timur Shah (1773–93, q.v.) was more scholarly inclined and lacked the military genius of his father. He moved the Afghan capital to Kabul, away from the center of Durrani power to a location that was strategically better suited for control of the eastern provinces. He established a bodyguard of some 12,000 clansmen of his Ishaqzai tribe, which he augmented with a division of 12,000 *qizilbash* troops. Thus he was able to limit the power of the feudal forces and their powerful chiefs. A campaign into Sind in 1779, although victorious, could not prevent the eventual loss of this province, and a campaign into the north reaffirmed Afghan control of the northern provinces but left Balkh virtually independent. Revolts in Khorasan and Peshawar were only barely suppressed. Shah Zaman (1793–1800, q.v.), one of 23 recognized sons of Timur, succeeded to power, but was embroiled in internecine warfare with his brothers and was finally blinded and forced into exile in India. The Panjab was definitely lost to Ranjit Singh (q.v.), king of the new Sikh nation. Civil war between Timur's sons led to the demise of the Sadozai branch of the Durranis and the emergence of the Barakzai/Muhammadzai branch under Amir Dost Muhammad Khan (1826–38 and 1842–63, q.v.).

In the nineteenth century, European rivalry for commerce and empire quickly extended to the Middle East. In 1798 the Napoleonic invasion of Egypt temporarily established a French foothold in this strategic area, which

Britain feared as an important step in a move against India. Russia moved into Central Asia, and by the end of the nineteenth century the czar's influence extended to the Amu Daria (q.v.). The British East India Company became an ally of Ranjit Singh and thus extended its influence to the borders of Afghanistan.

In 1826 Dost Muhammad, first of the Muhammadzai rulers, ascended the throne. He wanted an alliance with India and hoped to regain Peshawar, which had been lost to the emerging Sikh nation under Ranjit Singh. Lord Auckland (q.v.), the British governor general of India, chose an alliance with the Sikh ruler instead and decided to restore Shah Shuja (q.v.) to the Afghan throne. The presence of a purported Russian agent at Kabul (*see* VITKEVICH) and Dost Muhammad's hostility to the Sikh ruler were the reasons for India's declaration of war (*see* SIMLA MANIFESTO). A tripartite treaty was signed in July 1838 between Shah Shuja, Ranjit Singh, and Lord Auckland, and the "Army of the Indus" invaded Afghanistan (qq.v.). The invaders met with little resistance, Shah Shuja was restored to the Kabul throne, and Dost Muhammad was forced into Indian exile. But it was soon apparent that the Sadozai ruler needed protection to keep himself in power, and the British army became a force of occupation. The families of British officers came to Kabul, and thousands of Indian camp followers engaged in the lucrative business of importing from India the necessities of colonial life. But all was not well. The occupation was costly, and retrenchments demanded a reduction in subsidies (or bribes) to tribal chiefs, which had the effect of turning them against the invaders. On November 2, 1841 Kabul rose in rebellion, and a mob stormed the British mission and killed all its members, including Alexander Burnes (q.v.), its head. Muhammad Akbar (q.v.), a son of Dost Muhammad, together with a number of chiefs, now rallied his forces and increasingly threatened the occupiers. The British were forced to negotiate a retreat, which only few of the 16,000 troops and camp followers survived. (*See* CAPITULATION, TREATY OF, and DEATH MARCH.) Britain felt it necessary to have its martial reputation restored and in 1842 sent in General George Pollock (q.v.), who wreaked vengeance on Kabul, laying torch to the covered bazaar and permitting plunder that destroyed much of the the city. (*See* FIRST ANGLO-AFGHAN WAR.) The British forces left, and Amir Dost Muhammad returned in 1843 to rule Afghanistan until he died a natural death 20 years later. The "Signal Catastrophe" of the war inclined the British government to abandon its search for a "scientific" frontier and pursue a policy of "masterly inactivity," which was to leave Afghanistan to the Afghans. But a generation later the advocates of a "forward policy," to counter Russian moves in Central Asia, succeeded in being heard.

Amir Shir Ali (1863–79, q.v.), a son of Amir Dost Muhammad, had ascended the Afghan throne after eliminating a number of rivals. He gained British recognition in 1869 and was invited to meet Viceroy Lord Mayo in Ambala, India. (*See* AMBALA CONFERENCE.) Shir Ali was worried about Russian advances in Central Asia and wanted British guarantees from Russian aggression and recognition of his son, Abdullah Jan, as crown prince and his successor. But the viceroy was willing to give only presents of 600,000 rupees and a few pieces of artillery, and would not offer any guarantees from Russian attack. Disappointed, he was receptive when General Kaufman (q.v.), the Russian governor general at Tashkent, made overtures, promising what Britain was not willing to give. Major-General Stolietoff (q.v.) arrived in Kabul on July 22, 1878, with the charge to draft a treaty of alliance with the Afghan ruler. Britain was now alarmed and sent General Neville Chamberlain (q.v.) to lead a military mission to Kabul. Arrange-ments had been made with the independent tribes on the frontier for the mission's escort of one thousand troops, but when he reached the border, Chamberlain was prevented from entering Afghan territory. Britain chose this "insult" as a *casus belli* and dispatched an army under General Sir Frederick Roberts (q.v.), which entered Kabul on July 24, 1879. Shir Ali fled north in the hope of receiving Russian support. No help was forthcoming and the amir died of natural causes in Mazar-i Sharif on February 21, 1879. (*See* SECOND ANGLO-AFGHAN WAR.)

Britain recognized Shir Ali's son Yaqub Khan (q.v.) as amir (Abdullah Jan, the crown prince, had preceded his father in death) and concluded with him the Treaty of Gandomak (q.v.) on May 26, 1879. Louis Cavagnari (q.v.) was established as British envoy at Kabul, and history repeated itself when after only six weeks in Kabul, mutinous troops whose pay was in arrears stormed the British mission and assassinated the envoy and his staff. Yaqub Khan resigned in October 1879, leaving the field to his brother, Muhammad Ayub, and his cousin Abdur Rahman Khan.

This ushered in a new era in Afghan history under Amir Abdur Rahman (1880–1901, q.v.) and a complete reorganization of the state, including the armed forces. Abdur Rahman, the oldest son of Amir Muhammad Afzal Khan (1866–67), had fought his uncle Amir Shir Ali (q.v.) in 1864 and was forced to flee to the court of the amir of Bukhara. He returned to Afghanistan in 1866 and defeated Amir Shir Ali, but rather than assume power himself, placed his father, Afzal Khan, on the Afghan throne. Forced into exile again, Abdur Rahman spent 11 years in Samarkand and Tashkent in the newly acquired Russian province of Turkestan. The "Iron Amir," as he came to be known to history, used his time well. He was able to acquaint himself with the relatively modern technology of the Russian army and, in discussions with General Kaufman, gained an insight into the Western imperialist mind, which saw its "manifest destiny" in the conquest of the Asian continent. Not overly burdened by tradition, he realized that the survival of Afghanistan depended on borrowing from the enemy the military technology that was superior to anything Afghanistan could muster. After the death of Amir Shir Ali in February 1879, Abdur Rahman Khan returned to Afghanistan. Kaufman had provided him with some 200 breech-loading rifles and some money; he borrowed 2,000 sovereigns from merchants to purchase horses and equipment and moved south. He issued a proclamation, saying, "I have not come to fight Afghans who are true believers, but to make *ghaza*" (war). But he did not expressly state that he was going to fight the British army of occupation. (AR, 173)

The British government feared a repetition of the debacle of the first Anglo-Afghan war, and on March 14, 1880, the secretary of state for India sent a telegram to the viceroy, urging that it was

> necessary to find, without delay, some Native authority to which we can restore Northern Afghanistan, without risk of immediate anarchy, on our evacuation of Kabul not later than next autumn, and, if possible, earlier. No prospect of finding in country any man strong enough for this purpose. I therefore advocate early public recognition of Abdur Rahman as legitimate heir of Dost Mahomed, and open deputation of Sirdars with British concurrence to offer him throne of Afghanistan, as sole means of saving country from anarchy.

Thereupon, the viceroy dispatched Lepel Griffin (q.v.), the chief political officer at Kabul, to inquire as to the *sardar*'s (prince's) objectives. Negotiations culminated on July 22, 1880, in the grudging recognition of Abdur Rahman as "Amir of Kabul and its Dependencies," in spite of the fact that he had entered Afghanistan with the assistance of Russia. In an attempt at divide and rule, the London government intended to sever Herat and Kandahar from Kabul control, but the 35-year-old *sardar* had set his aim at the reunification of Afghanistan. The return of Abdur Rahman Khan had encouraged resistance elsewhere, while he was consolidating his power in northern Afghanistan, *ghazis* (q.v.) began to attack British bases in the south. Sir Percy Sykes tells the story of one battle at Ahmad Khel on April 19, 1880:

> The Afghan cavalry charged, and at first, on the left flank, threw back the 19th Bengal Lancers, who had to charge uphill to meet them. Meanwhile the Afghan footmen pressed on with such fanatical valour,

that neither the guns firing nor the heavy fire of the infantry seemed able
to stop their rush. The situation became critical. However the arrival of
further troops at the front and the steady fire of the guns and infantry,
which moved down the *Ghazis* by hundreds, finally broke their charge.
(*See* AHMAD KHEL, BATTLE OF.) (Sykes, 131)

A British officer remarked, "I saw only two Afghans ask for mercy, and
one cannot help admiring their reckless bravery." (Sykes, 132)

The British position at Kandahar was "unsatisfactory." Lieutenant
General J. M. Primrose (q.v.) faced a serious problem of logistics — his long
lines of communication came under increasing attack, and Ayub Khan, son
of Amir Shir Ali and a contender to the Afghan throne, was said to be
preparing for an attack on the city.

Primrose sent Brigadier General G.R.S. Burrows (q.v.) with a brigade
of some 2,500 men to strengthen the forces of the British appointed
governor, most of whose soldiers deserted to the army of Ayub Khan. The
ensuing Battle of Maiwand (*see* MAIWAND, BATTLE OF) resulted in the
annihilation of the 66th British-Indian regiment. Kandahar came under
siege, and the British garrison, some 3,000 strong, withdrew into the walled
city, expelling the Afghan population of about 15,000.

The viceroy was alarmed. He sent a telegram to the secretary of state,
reporting that

> General Burrows has been seriously defeated by Ayub Khan. Primrose
> has vacated cantonments at Kandahar and retired to citadel. We are
> pushing forward reinforcements already on their way, as quickly as
> possible, and sending large additional reinforcements from India. It may
> be necessary to anticipate despatch of troops from England intended for
> this season's reliefs. (PP, L/P&S/20/MEMO/2)

It was left to General Sir Frederick Roberts to avenge the defeat at
Maiwand and to come to the relief of the Kandahar garrison.

Abdur Rahman quickly consolidated his power and set out to eliminate
his rivals: on August 11 he occupied Kabul, and on September 22, 1881, he
defeated Ayub Khan at Kandahar and then proceeded to take Herat.

The two Anglo-Afghan wars led the British-Indian general staff to
reassess the lessons learned from its confrontation with the Afghans. In the
secret *Handbook of Kandahar Province, 1933*, officers were told:

> Never surrender, when in a tight corner as it will merely lead to a
> degrading and barbarous death. A vigorous offensive at the right
> moment is the best policy; it may snatch victory from an apparently

hopeless situation. Never relax precautions, the Afghans and the tribesmen will invariably punish a tactical error or lack of precautions. Do not allow Afghans to enter small military posts; they are very observant, and will soon spot the weak points in the defence.

History provides numerous examples of the price paid for lack of alertness and for taking insufficient precautions, such as failures to piquet heights; neglect to adopt perimeter camps, and faulty siting camps; movements up and down *nalas* [dry riverbeds], instead of along spurs; columns being overtaken by darkness, before protective measures could be adopted; employment of detachments too weak for their tasks. Never hesitate or remain inactive, or take purely defensive measures — they stimulate the Afghans in a remarkable manner. Be prepared for Afghan rushes — they are most notable for the fury with which they start, as for the rapidity with which they die away.

Afghans will hold a position with the utmost determination until their front is penetrated or their flank is turned — then they suddenly retire in the utmost disorder. Do unto the Afghans as they do unto you. Never make terms with the Afghans, unless they can be compelled to observe these terms.

Don't pay bribes to conceal weakness and pay cash on delivery only and never in advance. Punishment must be stern and drastic — inflict the heaviest possible casualties, followed by destruction of villages and the confiscation of livestock, grain, fodder, and fuel. The Afghans thoroughly appreciate and respect the enemy who can and does punish and then makes friends again.

A somewhat racist assessment of the "Afghan character" describes Afghans as a blend of "virtue and vice":

They are hardy, brave, proud, simple in their mode of living, frank, prepared to die in accordance with their code of honour yet faithless and treacherous; generous to a degree yet devoured by greed for money; capable of great endurance and of feats of energy but constitutionally lazy.

They are capable of strong personal attachments but never forget a wrong. Hospitality is part of their creed. A host will defend a guest at the risk of his life, but he may have little scruples against revealing his guest's future movements to others.

> The pure Afghan tribes [meaning Pashtuns], no matter what their
> internal jealousies may be, will resist outside interference as strenuously
> now and in the future, as they have done in the past.

The Soviet expeditionary army had to learn these lessons a hundred years
later.

Afghan irregular tribal forces (*lashkars*, q.v.) were generally more
effective than Afghan regulars. They excelled in guerrilla warfare, showing
considerable bravery and determination. During the first Anglo-Afghan war
the ranks of tribal forces were quickly increased with the addition of an
unpaid reserve, called *alijaris* (q.v.), forming a formidable force of about
100,000 men. Of these the Durrani, Ghilzai (qq.v.), and transborder Afghans
were the most intrepid fighters. They were rapidly assembled by the sound
of drums that quickly covered the entire tribal belt, including the Afghans on
the British side of the border. In response to a call for holy war (*jehad*, q.v.),
an Afghan ruler could fire the martial spirit of the tribes and induce them to
temporarily resolve their feuds and vendettas. Tribal pride and competition
with others made them perform heroic deeds. The major weakness of tribal
lashkars was that they preferred to fight close to home and carried
provisions for a limited number of days, after which time they had to return
to their homes. The British were at times able to snatch victory from defeat,
when the Afghans dispersed to carry their plunder back to their areas and
were cut off by a relatively small force.

Before the advent of aerial warfare the deserts and mountains of
Afghanistan were a formidable barrier to an invader. *Registan,* the "Country
of Sand," and a waterless desert on the southern border of Afghanistan with
India (now Pakistan), and the difficult mountain passes to the east were the
graveyards of many an Englishman. British troops were able to occupy the
major cities on the periphery of the mountainous core, and Kabul, Ghazni,
Kandahar, and Herat could be occupied while the Afghans retreated into the
mountains. Problems of logistics would quickly emerge; the lines of supply
would be cut, small forces of the invader would be destroyed, and with
success the attacks would become increasingly brazen. Eventually, the
British occupiers had to decide to take a stand and fight to the end — as in
the first Afghan war; or treat with the most prominent of the Afghan *sardars*
to ensure a dignified withdrawal to India. Britain chose the latter alternative.

Abdur Rahman concluded an agreement with the British government,
by which Britain guaranteed him protection from unprovoked Russian aggression, provided he permitted Britain to conduct his foreign relations. He
obtained a subsidy in money and materiel to strengthen the defenses of his
country. Abdur Rahman considered this treaty an alliance between equals,

and, having protected his northern borders, he kept the British at arm's length, never allowing them to gain any influence in the country under the aegis of their common defense. He formulated a "buffer-state policy," which aimed at playing off Afghanistan's imperialist neighbors against each other. This policy served Afghanistan well until the end of World War II, when changed conditions required new approaches in the conduct of Afghan foreign policy. Afghanistan's northern and eastern boundaries were demarcated during the amir's tenure, including the Durand Line (1893), which he accepted under "duress" in the Durand Agreement (q.v.).

The Iron Amir used whatever taxes he could raise and the subsidy from the British-Indian government to purchase weapons from India. He also set up workshops to manufacture ammunition and small arms. The military reforms under Amir Dost Muhammad and Amir Shir Ali were not continued because of the chaos following their rule, and Amir Abdur Rahman had to start from the beginning. His major objectives were to unify the country and ward off foreign aggressors. The Iron Amir declared to a council of elders:

> The forces I am going to raise are intended only for the protection of Afghanistan in the event of a foreign invasion. You know your country is situated like a village between the two governments of the infidels, each of which is ambitious to invade and take Afghanistan. You must, therefore, be prepared for a time of emergency so as to safeguard yourself from invasion. If you fail to provide for such an event, you will then have to contend with the fate of your brethren in India, who, you know well, have no power over their wives. You will then all become women yourselves, with no influence over your families. (Kakar, 96)

Abdur Rahman set about creating an army that was initially officered by persons of little status, but eventually he also recruited the sons of notables (*khanzada*), and eventually Durranis of his own Muhammadzai clan who constituted a privileged elite. Within 10 years he had organized an army of some 60,000 and by the end of his reign his army probably amounted to 100,000 men, no fewer than a hundred years later. With the exception of most Hazara and Qizilbash, Shi'a minorities, all ethnic communities were represented in the army, and the *Ghilzai*, although traditional rivals of the Durranis, formed the largest component (Kakar, 97). Amir Abdur Rahman organized his regular army according to the British model into infantry (*piyada*), cavalry (*sawara*), and artillery (*topkhana*) branches. Royal bodyguards were enlisted that included in addition to sections of the Durranis of Kandahar also the sons of notables of the non-Pushtun community. The irregular army consisted of the feudal cavalry (*sawara-i kushada* or *sawara-*

i khudaspa), raised from feudal *khans* in lieu of payment of revenues. Tribes and ethnic groups were levied at a certain ratio for temporary service, whereas soldiering in the regular army was a lifetime profession.

With the defeat of his rival Ayub Khan at Kandahar (*see* KANDAHAR, BATTLE OF) and the capture of Herat, Abdur Rahman had reunited Afghanistan under his resolute rule and was recognized by Britain as "Amir of Afghanistan and its Dependencies." This ended wars with Afghanistan's neighbors, except for the Panjdeh Incident of 1885, in which Russia was able to annex the Panjdeh oasis (*see* PANJDEH INCIDENT). The Iron Amir now turned to the task of eliminating the last pockets of autonomous rule. In a very vicious and protracted war, he pacified the Hazarajat (*see* HAZARA WARS), and in 1895–96 he turned against Kafiristan (q.v.), an area which Islam had not yet penetrated and converted the Kafirs, whose country became henceforth known as Nuristan, from *nur*, light, meaning the country enlightened by the spark of Islam. *See* KAFIR WAR.

Abdur Rahman was keenly aware of his predecessors' policies. He felt that during their administration "nearly every mullah and *khan* (chief) considered himself independent, and they gave themselves the airs of princes and prophets." He wanted to be the unchallenged master of his realm and considered the Ghilzai a threat. In his biography, *The Life of Abdur Rahman* (compiled by Sultan Mahomed Khan), he states:

> The Ghilzais had very influential chiefs, with a considerable number of fighting men. These khans or chiefs, as well as their armies, were very cruel and harsh to the subjects, their cruelties, their unlimited authority, their excessive taxation, their robberies and plunderings, their attacks on the caravans, their constant warfare with each other, the wholesale slaughter of humanity in general, were well known to the people. . . . It was natural, therefore, that I, who was the least likely person in the world to allow such misbehaviour under my very eyes, should be hated by them, and that every possible attempt would be made to upset my rule. (AR, I, 250)

Therefore, the amir stopped all the government allowances to Ghilzai chiefs and clergy (*ulama*) with the result that the Ghilzais staged a major uprising in 1886–87 that was suppressed only with great difficulty. (*See* GHILZAI and ABDUL KARIM.)

By the time Amir Abdur Rahman died, he had created a strong, centralized state with borders recognized by his neighbors and an army that freed the ruler from dependence on the tribes. The government passed into the hands of his first son, Habibullah, without any challenge or major domestic or foreign wars during his reign.

Amir Habibullah (1901–19, q.v.) ordered a general amnesty and permitted many to return from foreign exile. His outstanding achievements were in the fields of education and diplomacy. He set up the beginnings of a modern system of education, employing members of the clergy (*ulama*) in the elementary levels and Afghan and foreign teachers in Habibia College, a high school patterned in part on the British Indian system. He also permitted publication of a modern newspaper, the *Siraj al-Akhbar*, edited by Sardar Mahmud Tarzi, which became quickly an important organ expressing Afghan nationalist sentiments and solidarity with the Islamic world.

The British government was not satisfied with some of the provisions of the agreements concluded with Amir Abdur Rahman, and therefore wanted to force certain changes before it recognized the new amir. London maintained that the agreements were with the *person* of the amir, not the State of Afghanistan, and therefore the agreements had to be renegotiated with his successor. In spite of severe pressures, Habibullah did not yield. In December 1904 he finally agreed to meet in Kabul with Louis W. Dane (q.v.), foreign secretary of the government of India. The result was a complete victory for Habibullah when Britain was forced to renew the agreements concluded with Amir Abdur Rahman in the form of a treaty (March 1905), which recognized Habibullah's title, "Independent King of the State of Afghanistan and Its Dependencies." (*See* ANGLO-AFGHAN TREATY OF 1905.)

A crisis in relations with British India occurred when Habibullah learned that Afghanistan's neighbors had concluded the Anglo-Russian Convention of 1907 (q.v.). This agreement divided Afghanistan (and Iran) into spheres of influence with provisions for "equality of commercial opportunity" in Afghanistan for Russian and British traders and the appointment of commercial agents in Kabul. The amir was invited to ratify the agreement, but he refused and the convention was never implemented.

The outbreak of World War I posed another crisis in foreign relations: in spite of warnings not to do so from the viceroy of India, Amir Habibullah received a German-Ottoman mission at Kabul. He met with members of the Hentig-Niedermayer expedition (q.v.) and initialed the draft of a secret treaty of friendship and military assistance with Germany to provide for the eventuality of an Allied defeat. Germany could not deliver, and Britain promised a handsome reward for Afghan neutrality; therefore, a realistic appraisal of the situation prompted the Afghan ruler to stay out of the war. But Britain showed itself miserly and, once the crisis was over, wanted to continue its exclusive control of Afghanistan. The "war party" at his court felt that the amir had failed to take advantage of a unique opportunity of winning independence from Britain and his enemies conspired to depose him. He was assassinated on February 20, 1919, while he was on a hunting trip at Kala Gosh in Laghman.

Sardar Amanullah, eldest son of Habibullah, ascended the throne in February 1919 after a short palace coup against his uncle Nasrullah Khan. King Amanullah (1919–29, q.v.) decided to win his country's independence, if necessary by means of war. He made it known that he wanted to base his relations with Britain on a new foundation. On March 3, 1919 he wrote to Lord Chelmsford, the viceroy of India, that the "usurpers" (Sardar Nasrullah) had abdicated and the "free Government of Afghanistan" was prepared to conclude such treaties as may be useful to our government and yours.

On the occasion of a royal *darbar* (audience) on April 13, 1919, Amanullah showed himself more belligerent, announcing to an assembly of dignitaries

> ... I have declared myself and my country entirely free, autonomous and independent both internally and externally. My country will hereafter be as independent a state as the other states and powers of the world are. No foreign power will be allowed to have a hair's breadth of right to interfere internally and externally with the affairs of Afghanistan, and if any ever does I am ready to cut its throat with this sword. (Adamec, 1974, 47)

He turned to the British agent and said, "Oh Safir, have you understood what I have said?" The British agent replied, "Yes, I have." The government of India was at a loss to decide whether it should accept this fait accompli. Having declared the previous agreements concluded with the "person" of the amir, India could not deny the need for a new treaty with King Amanullah. Therefore, the viceroy merely thanked Amanullah for the information that he was acknowledged as amir "by the populace of Kabul and its surroundings" and used the mourning for Amir Habibullah's assassination as an excuse for not discussing any new agreements.

Amanullah was ready for action. On March 11 he announced to the Afghan envoy in India that "the Government of Afghanistan hopes by the grace of God, within a short time, to have itself counted as one of the most well-known and honorable Governments in the world." On May 1, 1919 he sent Saleh Muhammad, the commander in chief, to Dakka, Muhammad Nadir (the subsequent king) moved to Khost, and Abdul Quddus, the prime minister, proceeded to Kandahar. (qq.v.) Two days later Afghan pickets stopped a group of Khaibar Rifles escorting a caravan from moving into disputed territory between Landi Khana and Torkham. The British tribal militia withdrew. A *farman* (royal decree) by King Amanullah advised the frontier tribes that Hindus and Muslims in India were in revolt and that Saleh had advanced to the border for the protection of Afghanistan.

The first hostile action began on May 4, when Afghan troops occupied Bagh (q.v.), a hamlet on the British side of the border, and cut the water supply to Landi Kotal. On May 5 the Indian government decided to stop demobilization of all combatant forces in India and recalled all British officers of the Indian army. In Peshawar the situation deteriorated rapidly. A force of some eight thousand holy warriors had gathered, ready to march on the cantonment, and it was only with great difficulty that the British commissioner, Sir George Roos-Keppel, had the walled city surrounded and cut the supplies of water, electricity, and food. A British messenger demanding the surrender of the Afghan postmaster in Peshawar was the only casualty. (*See* THIRD ANGLO-AFGHAN WAR.)

As so often in the past, the Indian government felt that war was the only way to save face, but London feared that an attack on one of the few remaining independent Muslim states would have serious repercussions elsewhere. It requested information as to what kind of armistice the Afghans wanted. Although there was no widespread rebellion in India, the situation was nevertheless serious. Pashtun soldiers of the British Khaibar Rifles deserted in large numbers, and tribes on the North-West Frontier prepared for *jehad*. London eventually authorized an invasion of Afghanistan and occupation of Jalalabad, but warned India "you will not have forgotten [the] lessons of history, that we have not so much to fear from [the] Afghan regular Army as from the irregular tribesmen and their constant attacks on our isolated camps and lines of communications." (Adamec, 1967, 116) In the meantime the Indian government considered such far-fetched measures as approaching the sultan/caliph of the defeated Ottoman Empire to prohibit *jehad* and "disowning those by whom it may be proclaimed."

While the frontier at Dakka became stabilized, Nadir Khan invaded Waziristan and advanced toward Thal, and Roos-Keppel, chief commissioner of the North-West Frontier, warned that all the Khurram border tribes seemed likely to rise "unless we have success against Nadir Khan shortly." John Maffey, the chief political officer with the field force, worried that an invasion of Afghanistan might leave no one to settle with, and he was greatly relieved when he heard that King Amanullah was ready to negotiate. He felt that "our peace terms can then be presented as an ultimatum" and added, "This time we shall have got the Afghan really cold,

I hope." But caution prevailed. In view of the uncertainties of war, its repercussions in the Islamic world, and the possibility of widespread revolt by the Frontier Afghans, Denys Bray, foreign secretary to the government of India, favored peace. He recalled that the Indian government considered releasing Afghanistan from British tutelage as a reward for Amir Habibullah's neutrality in World War I.

The war had not led to any great territorial conquests: the British captured Dakka in the east and Spin Boldak in the south, but the British defenses on the Waziristan and Zhob frontier had collapsed and the situation in the Afghan tribal belt was critical. After aerial bombings of Jalalabad and Kabul, the Indian government agreed to make peace. A cease-fire was declared on June 3, and an Afghan delegation arrived in Rawalpindi on July 25 to begin peace negotiations, which resulted in a British declaration that the treaty and an appended letter "leave Afghanistan officially free and independent in its internal and external affairs." (Ibid., 183) (*See also* ANGLO-AFGHAN TREATY OF 1919; 1921; and MUSSOORIE CONFERENCE.)

As a result of the short war that won Afghanistan's independence from British tutelage, King Amanullah became a national hero. Relations with Britain eventually normalized, and Afghanistan established relations with the major states in the world.

King Amanullah was a reformer, he believed that his was an "era of the pen, not the sword," and he embarked on a series of social reforms that were to modernize Afghanistan and started the process toward the emancipation of women. He opened his country to foreign influences, permitting the establishment of embassies in Kabul, and sent students in large numbers abroad. Politically, he followed the policy of Amir Abdur Rahman by playing off his powerful neighbors against each other while inviting German experts in large numbers to help in the task of developing the country. He saw himself as the "Democratic King," drafting a modern constitution, greatly expanding the Afghan system of education, and building a new capital at Darulaman (*Dar al-Aman*), including a monumental parliamentary building. In the 10 years of his rule, he was able to create a cadre of "Young Afghans," who became his major supporters. His modernist tendencies were reinforced after a journey to European capitals in 1927–28 and meetings with Reza Shah of Iran and Mustafa Atatürk of Turkey. But reaction to his social reforms, such as the permission for women to discard the veil and participate in the public life of the country, was growing. A tribal revolt, the Khost Rebellion (q.v.) in 1924–25, was suppressed only with great difficulty; and a general revolt in 1928–29 led to the ouster of the Reformer King and the establishment of Habibullah Kalakani (q.v.), the "Son of a Water Carrier" (*Bacha-i Saqqau*) on the Afghan throne for a violent seven-months rule.

Two factors prevented Kalakani from consolidating his rule: he was a Tajik and not a member of the dominant Pashtun majority; and he had a reputation as a bandit. He found some £750,000 when he captured the Arg (royal palace, q.v.), which enabled him to win the temporary adherence of the major tribes. But they soon defected and joined Nadir Khan, one of King Amanullah's generals in the third Anglo-Afghan war, who defeated the dwindling forces of Habibullah Kalakani, and ascended the Afghan throne on October 15, 1929.

Nadir Shah (1929–1933) and his son Zahir Shah (1933–1973) (qq.v.) were, like King Amanullah, of the royal Muhammadzai clan of the Durranis and therefore acceptable to the Pashtun tribes. Nadir Shah began the process of consolidation during his short reign, a task that was greatly accelerated during the reign of his successor. The new monarchs did not have to fight any foreign wars. They devoted themselves to the task of greatly expanding the system of education and creating a modern army that was able to reduce the once formidable power of the tribes.

The Afghan army was organized according to the Western model into the *qaul-i urdu* (corps), *firqa* (division), *ghund* (brigade), *kandak* (battalion), toli (company), and *baluk* (platoon, troop). To this was added the *shahi-firqa* (guards division). (*See* ARMY, AFGHAN.) Cavalry, artillery, pioneer and signal divisions were set up as well as a fledgling air force, reorganized from King Amanullah's reign. In addition to the regular army, irregular tribal forces were levied. Initially, the army also performed police functions; small units were stationed in provincial centers with large garrisons in the major towns.

After Nadir Shah was assassinated in November 1933, a council of his brothers served as advisers to the young king. Muhammad Hashim became prime minister (1929–46), followed by Shah Mahmud (1946–53), after whom the position was held by Zahir Shah's cousin Muhammad Daud (1953–63) (qq.v.). The gradual modernization of the Afghan army was greatly accelerated under Muhammad Daud, and the Soviet Union became the principal supplier of weapons and military technology to Afghanistan. Already during the reign of King Amanullah, the Soviet Union provided some pilots and technical support for the creation of an Afghan air force (*see* AIR FORCE, AFGHAN). The Soviet Union had a concession for air service from Kabul to Moscow, which was, however, not renewed by Amanullah's successors. But the times seemed to have changed in the 1950s, and Soviet assistance again became necessary when it was not forthcoming from the West.

World War II resulted in the end of the colonial empires of Britain and France, and India became independent in 1947. In Kabul this was seen as the opportunity to reclaim territory Britain had annexed on Afghanistan's eastern and southern borders. The Afghan government demanded that the Pashtuns of the North-West Frontier Province of India be given the choice to vote for independence rather than merely for inclusion in India or the newly created State of Pakistan. This choice was not given, and Afghanistan's relations with Pakistan remained cool from the start and turned frequently hostile.

The beginning of the cold war further strained relations with Pakistan. The American government sought allies in its policy of containment of the Soviet Union and readily succeeded in 1955 to win Turkey, Iraq, Iran, and Pakistan in an alliance called the Baghdad Pact (later renamed Central Treaty Organization [CENTO]). Afghanistan was tacitly left in the Soviet sphere and the Indian subcontinent was to be defended at the Khaibar Pass rather than the Amu Daria, Afghanistan's northern border. A 1949 study for the U. S. Defense Department's joint chiefs of staff said: "Afghanistan is of little or no strategic importance to the United States .... Its geographic location coupled with the realization by Afghan leaders of Soviet capabilities presages Soviet control of the country whenever the international situation so dictates." (Bradsher, 20)

Afghanistan was not to receive the promise of help in case of Russian aggression that Britain was willing to offer in the past; therefore, there was no alternative to coexisting with Afghanistan's powerful neighbor. Afghan policy was well summarized in 1932 by Sir Richard Maconachie, the British minister in Kabul:

> King Nadir Shah's foreign policy, as stated by himself and the Prime Minister, is one of quietism. Since the demands of internal reconstruction will absorb the whole resources of the Government for many years to come, such friendly relations as will insure against aggression from without are to be maintained with all foreign powers; there is to be no interference in areas beyond the Afghan frontiers, and Amanullah Khan's "irredentist" attitude towards Russian Turkestan on the one side, and India, on the other, is to be definitely abandoned. (Adamec, 1974, 201)

It was therefore natural that Afghanistan would drift into the neutralist camp of Asian and African countries led by Jawaharlal Nehru, Josef Broz Tito, Abdul Gamal Nasser, and others. Buffer-state politics seemed no longer possible, and the concept of peaceful coexistence and "positive neutrality" seemed the only possible course. Kabul observed the United States arming of Pakistan with considerable alarm, but efforts to obtain weapons from the West met with a cool response. Thus, like Egypt, the Afghan government turned to the Soviet Union for military assistance.

A turning point occurred in December 1955, when Nikita Khrushchev and Nikolai Bulganin came to Kabul. The Russians supported Afghanistan in the "Pashtunistan" dispute (q.v.) and offered massive aid, which the United States was not willing to match. Among the projects financed was a network of roads, connecting to the Soviet Union, including the famous Salang tunnel and the air base at Bagram (q.v.). Until the Marxist coup of 1978, the Soviet Union had provided $1,265 million in economic assistance compared to the United States' $532.87 million. Soviet military aid amounted to $1,250 million, and 3,725 Afghan military personnel went to the Soviet Union for training; only 20 Afghans were enrolled in American military institutions in 1978. In addition some 5,000 Afghan students received academic training, and some 1,600 obtained technical education in Soviet institutions. In 1955 President Daud convened a *loya jirga* (q.v.) to approve his acceptance of Soviet aid (Bradsher, 26ff.). Some observers noted that foreign students who attended Western educational institutions tended to become leftists, whereas those studying in Eastern bloc countries tended to become disenchanted with the Soviet system. But students in military academies were carefully segregated from civilian life, and it is not clear to what extent they were influenced by Soviet ideology. Western scholars were largely ignorant of developments in the Afghan armed forces. Unlike Afghan politicians, journalists, and members of the urban bureaucracy, military officers kept aloof of the social functions attended by foreigners and little of substance pertaining to the armed forces was published in Kabul. With the Soviet weapons arrived advisers and experts, who were in close daily contact with their counterparts in the Afghan services. No matter whether they were Marxists or not, it was not lost on the officers' corps that they had the capacity to stage a successful coup.

Afghanistan was one developing country where the United States did not try to outdo the Soviet Union in competitive assistance. Soviet aid was largely in low-interest loans as compared to outright American gifts, but it was nevertheless welcome to provide the means for Afghanistan's ambitious developmental projects. The Soviet Union and Afghanistan were natural trading partners. Afghanistan could offer one item of export that was much in demand in the Soviet Union — natural gas, which could not be sold elsewhere at the time. Furthermore, a barter trade in goods made it possible to import goods for which no hard currency was available. The massive foreign aid that also came from other European and Middle Eastern countries made it possible to establish the beginnings of a native small industry and to greatly expand Afghanistan's system of education. There is no question that there was considerable economic improvement and some prosperity, which, however, did not equally benefit all segments of society. With heightened expectations and the experiment with democracy after 1963, voices began to be heard in public that attacked the *ancien régime* and demanded the establishment of alternative political systems.

The expansion of the secular educational system in Afghanistan led to the emergence of an elite group of young Afghans who became the principal protagonists in a political dialogue between secular leftists and radical Islamists. The People's Democratic Party of Afghanistan (PDPA) was a Marxist party founded on January 1, 1965 by 27 original members who elected Nur Muhammad Taraki and Babrak Karmal (qq.v.) as their leaders. They began a process of secret recruitment of followers in the army, the bureaucracy, and schools that was soon challenged by an Islamist reaction, headed by Sayyid Musa Tawana, Ghulam Muhammad Niazi, and Burhan-uddin Rabbani, (qq.v.), all professors at the school of theology at Kabul University who were disciples of Hasan al Banna, the founder of the Muslim Brotherhood in Egypt.

The conflict between the radical Left and Islamists seemed decided in favor of the former when, in July 1973, Muhammad Daud, a cousin of King Zaher, staged a palace coup and transformed Afghanistan into a republic. President Daud was a military man who had served as military governor in important provinces and as commander of the central forces and minister of defense, interior, and prime minister. He felt that he had the loyalty of the armed forces and was supported by Pashtun nationalists and modernist reformers who felt the development of the country would be best served by a strongman as the head of state. Babrak Karmal's wing of the PDPA, commonly called *Parcham* (q.v.), supported the coup, and some of its members were appointed to government positions. Members of the Islamist opposition were jailed or sought asylum abroad and the government took a decided turn to the left. At the same time the nucleus of an Islamist guerrilla force formed with support from Pakistan and staged limited operations into Panjshir, which did not seriously threaten the regime. President Daud eventually decided to disengage himself from the leftist embrace; he dismissed many of his leftist supporters, reestablished correct neighborly relations with Pakistan, and sought support from oil-rich states. His moves came too late: on April 27, 1978 (7 Saur 1357), in a rare move of unity,

Parcham and *Khalq*, the two wings of the PDPA, staged a successful coup, which led to the establishment of the "Democratic Republic of Afghanistan" (DRA).

This marked the end of continuous peace since the third Anglo-Afghan war, and the beginning of a civil war and a war of liberation when the Soviet Union intervened to support the faltering Marxist regime.

By the 1970s the Afghan government had a force of 90,000 to 100,000 men, about the same number it traditionally counted, but modernized and equipped with Soviet weapons and an air force of some 7,000 men. Corps headquarters existed in Kabul, home of the central forces; Kandahar, the second corps; and Gardez, the third corps, which served as regional headquarters.

Into the 1980s the tactical organization of the Afghan army was as follows:

11	Infantry divisions
3–4	Mechanized brigades
2	Mountain infantry brigades
2–3	Commando brigades
1	Paratroop brigade/regiment
1	Artillery brigade

Assorted combat support and service support regiments
Equipment included:
500–600 Light and medium tanks
400–500 APC/IFV
450 Artillery pieces, 100-mm or greater
100 120-, 160-mm mortars
50 BM-13, BM-16 MRLs (McMichael, 45)

The air force was organized into 7 air regiments as follows:

3 Fighter sqns. with MIG-21s
3 Fighter-bomber sqns. with SU-7s and SU-22s
4 Fighter-bomber sqns. with IL-28 light bombers
2 Transport sqns. with AN-2s, AN-26sIL-14s
3-4 Helo sqns. with Mi-4s, Mi-8s, and Mi-17s
2 Independent helo sqns. with Mi-24s
1 Training sqn.

Total aircraft amounted to 140–170 fighters and 45–60 helicopters. (McMichael, 46)

In addition there were the *sarandoy* (q.v.), a paramilitary police force of the ministry of interior, which operated in the provinces; combat units of KHAD (later WAD, q.v.), the state security service (later ministry); a paramilitary border brigade; and the militias, recruited from tribes and ethnic minorities.

This considerable arsenal was further strengthened after 1980 with the Soviet intervention in Afghanistan. (*See* LIMITED CONTINGENT OF SOVIET FORCES IN AFGHANISTAN; and SOVIET INTERVENTION/ INVASION.)

With the weapons at their disposal, the nascent resistance movement did not seem a serious threat to the Kabul government. The Kabul government had the backing of one of the superpowers, and in late December 1979, the Soviet intervention appeared to tilt the odds strongly in the regime's favor.

After about 60 years of peace in Afghanistan, a new, destructive civil war began soon after the Marxist coup, followed in 1980 by a war of liberation against the Soviet occupation, and again a civil war after the departure of Soviet forces. The victorious *mujahedin*, "holy warriors," as they called themselves, began a struggle for power that has not been resolved to this day. The *mujahedin* prevailed over the combined Soviet/Kabul forces for a number of reasons:

The nature of Afghan geography. The country's terrain, its mountains and deserts, offered a ready refuge from an invading army and staging areas for guerrilla attacks. The Soviet political leadership (members of the Soviet general staff now claim they were against the intervention) probably felt that with control of Afghanistan's airspace, its forces could overcome the disadvantages of the Afghan terrain. Unlike the Vietcong in Vietnam, the *mujahedin* did not have the protection of large forests, but they were able to move at night to cross open terrain and find shelter in rugged mountain terrain to avoid detection. *Muhajedin* groups usually operated in territory they knew well, which facilitated the movement of troops and supplies. McMichael points out "Most mountain valleys will not permit the movement of more than a division-sized formation. As the main valley narrows or as units move off into side-canyons, the command is split and there is no room for manoeuvre. Flanks are very difficult to secure; it is all but impossible to maintain contact with units to the left and right." The few roads make surprise impossible, and often there is only one vehicular approach, and once a unit has been blocked, it has nowhere to go until it is relieved (McMichael, 23). Helicopters and ground attack aircraft had to fly at low altitudes, and when the *mujahedin* acquired Blowpipe and stinger shoulder-launched anti-aircraft missiles, the Soviet command had to resort to less effective high-altitude bombing.

The availability of an abundance of manpower. The *mujahedin* had a considerable reservoir of manpower, some locally obtained and considerable numbers recruited from the refugee camps in Peshawar. About 3,500,000 Afghan refugees lived in camps in Pakistan, constituting a ready pool of recruits. In the latter part of the war, they were able to put 80,000 to 100,000 in the field, but not all those were active combatants at any one time. This often exceeded the number of recruits available to the Kabul government. A common *mujahedin* complaint was that there were not enough weapons for the number of fighters available. Defections from the Afghan government forces replenished the ranks of the *mujahedin* with trained military personnel who often carried their weapons with them.

The existence of a safe haven in Pakistan. The *mujahedin* found a ready haven in Pakistan that permitted rotation of manpower, training, procurement of materiel, and political organization. In order to prevent a proliferation of parties and, no doubt, with an eye to control them, the Pakistan government required refugees to register with one of six, later seven, parties. The leaders were responsible for controlling their followers, providing logistical support, and acting as a coordinating council. These parties were loosely divided into two groups: the moderates headed by Sayyid Ahmad Gailani, Muhammad Nabi Muhammadi, and Sebghatullah Mujaddidi; and the radical Islamists of Gulbuddin Hekmatyar, Burhanuddin Rabbani, Muhammad Yunus Khales, and, somewhat later, Abdul Rauf Sayyaf (qq.v.). The leaders and their representatives were able to travel abroad to explain their cause and solicit materiel support. Journalists were taken into the field to witness guerrilla activities against Soviet and Kabul forces.

Recourse to Islam as a political ideology. Islam was a powerful ideology and rallying point of the *mujahedin.* They called their war a *jehad* (holy war) against an infidel invader, and their religion provided the enthusiasm and willingness to die for a sacred cause, with booty for the victor and instant Paradise for the fallen *mujahed.* Muslims are brothers and war between them is illegal; therefore, each party accused the other of having strayed from Islam and become *kafirs* (unbelievers). Even the Kabul government of Taraki represented its campaign against its Islamist opponents (whom it called the *ikhwan al-shayatin,* the brotherhood of devils) as a *jehad* and had its council of clergy issue a *fatwa* (legal decision) to this effect, thus legitimizing the war against the rebels. But with the Soviet intervention the issue became clear: it was viewed by many Afghans and their supporters as a war of good versus evil, and the stigma of fighting on the wrong side was a powerful incentive to desert. As powerful an ideology as it was when faced with the Soviet enemy, Islam did not provide political unity, and from the beginning of the war, some leaders' aspirations to political power led to clashes between *mujahedin* organizations.

Tactical advantage of guerrilla warfare. *Mujahedin* enjoyed the tactical advantage of the classical guerrilla war, they held the initiative. Initially, they operated in small units against "targets of opportunity," outlying posts that were weakly defended. Their system of intelligence was excellent; they were usually well informed of Soviet and government troop movements and they were able to disperse quickly after hit-and-run attacks. The Soviet forces were not prepared for counterinsurgency, and were forced into defensive stronghold positions from where they conducted great sweeps but could count on few great victories that would be an indication of progress in the pacification of the country. Their tanks and heavy armor were of little use away from the few lines of communication. Originally employed to garrison strategic points, towns, and lines of communication, with the assumption that regime forces would bear the brunt of the combat, Soviet forces were inevitably drawn into search-and-destroy missions that did not produce the desired results. (*See* PANJSHIR, SOVIET OFFENSIVES.) The "Limited Contingent of Soviet Forces in Afghanistan" (LCSFA) (q.v.) entered Afghanistan to assist the people against "foreign aggressors," but its soldiers soon realized that the local population saw them as aggressors rather than liberators. While the *mujahedin* initially controlled little territory, they had the support of the majority of the people and eventually held much of the rural areas.

Confrontation with heterogeneous and unmotivated enemy. In his study of the LCSFA, entitled *Inside the Soviet Army in Afghanistan,* Alexander Alexiev highlights certain inherent weaknesses. He states that the army was divided into two distinct groups: the occupation forces and the counterinsurgency forces. About 80 percent of the total troops consisted of the former; they included most of the regular motorized rifle and tank units and performed primarily security and support duties. They were ethnically mixed, received relatively little training, and included undesirable elements. In spite of considerable efforts at political indoctrination, they were poorly motivated, riven by ethnic and sectarian conflicts, drug addicts, and corrupt. Discrimination, hazing, and beating of soldiers by their officers was rampant. The conscripted Soviet soldier wanted to survive his term without getting into harm's way.

Foreign military and diplomatic support was probably the most important factor in turning the tide in the war. During the early period of the war, the *mujahedin* obtained their weapons from defectors or captured them from their Soviet/Kabul enemy. When friendly states realized that the Afghans were willing to fight in the face of apparently overwhelming odds, they began to provide significant amounts of assistance. At first supplies of Soviet weapons from Egypt and China were clandestinely channeled to the *mujahedin*, but soon more sophisticated weapons arrived. In 1981 President Sa'dat declared at a press conference that the United States "told me, 'Please open your stores for us so that we can give the Afghanis the armaments they need to fight' and I gave them the armaments." (Bradsher, 223) In July 1984 the U.S. House of Representatives' appropriations committee approved $50 million in clandestine aid to the Afghan *mujahedin*; and in April 1985 President Reagan signed a national security directive that provided for assistance "by all available means." U.S. support in 1987 reached $680 million and contributions by the European Community and Arab states increased this amount to over $1 billion a year. Introduction of the stinger missile (q.v.) ended Soviet aerial supremacy. On the diplomatic front, the American government announced the suspension of wheat exports to the USSR and called for a boycott of the 1980 Olympic Games in Moscow. The sanctions were supported by the majority of European states. The United Nations General Assembly in 1980 voted 104 to 18 with 18 abstentions for a resolution that "strongly deplored" the "recent armed intervention" in Afghanistan and demanded the "total withdrawal of foreign troops" from the country. This became a yearly event, and it was telling on the prestige and image of the Soviet Union. In the end, international isolation, the costs of the war, and growing casualties compelled the new Soviet leadership to withdraw its troops from Afghanistan.

In February 1989 Soviet troops completed their withdrawal from Afghanistan claiming losses of over 13,000 dead and 35,000 wounded; Afghan losses according to the Kabul government amounted to some 243,900 soldiers and civilians killed. Some Western observers claim a toll of about one million casualties.

Soviet operational and strategic lessons of the war in Afghanistan, pertaining primarily to force structure and operational art, were summarized by one expert as follows:

The importance of improved small unit capability for independent action;
The importance of command of the air and neutralization of enemy air defense;
The use of helicopters, airborne, and heliborne forces including special forces (not just Spetsnaz) for aerial and ground operations;
Better training and logistics for unconventional wars;
The importance of morale and unit cohesion;
The need for better intelligence assessments;

The need to learn how to fight defensively;
Strategies for winning small wars: denial of cities to the enemy. (Blank, 1990)

The *mujahedin* captured Kabul on April 25, 1992, and the struggle for power between the *mujahedin* began. In late 1994 the major protagonists were Gulbuddin Hekmatyar's *hizb-i Islami* and Burhanuddin Rabbani's *jam'iat-i Islami*. A third force emerged in north-central Afghanistan, headed by the *Junbish-i Milli-i Islami* of General Abdul Rashid Dostum, and in November 1994 the *Taleban* (q.v.) began their spectacular conquest of a greater part of western and southern Afghanistan. At the time of this writing, a tactical alliance pits all parties against Rabbani, who is holding on to Kabul and northeastern Afghanistan. There is as yet no indication as to which of the leaders will succeed to become the future ruler of Afghanistan.

An explanation for the present stalemate in the civil war of the *mujahedin* may be found in economic, ethnic, regional, and social factors. None of the major contenders for power has the means to maintain a large army and bureaucracy. The days of generous foreign support of the *mujahedin* are gone, and the leaders have to rely on the income from local taxation, tolls, narcotics trafficking, or from raiding of neighboring groups. Rabbani, by virtue of controlling the capital and an emaciated state bureaucracy, has been able to benefit from international donations and loans and the fact that he controls Afghanistan's central bank and the printing of money. Taxes and mining provide only a limited amount of support, utilized primarily by local commanders. Dostum inherited the resources of northern Afghanistan and may enjoy some support from neighboring Uzbekistan. The *Taleban*, no doubt, receive foreign support, primarily from Islamist groups in Pakistan and the Gulf. They have conquered enough territory to derive some benefit from taxation. As to the Hazaras, they subsist, as they have for ages, in the mountainous heartland of central Afghanistan. They are protected in their environment with virtually no opportunity to expand their domain.

Ethnic factors have contributed to the division into autonomous spheres in which the Hazaras, Tajiks, Uzbeks, and Pashtuns predominate. Potentially, there is the danger that expansionism by some may turn into a war between the nationalities. In such a case, the various ethnic and sectarian groups may receive open support from Afghanistan's neighbors.

Regional factors have become increasingly important. In the war against the Soviet/Kabul government, the *mujahedin*, like the tribal armies of yesteryear, operated in their home territories. They knew their areas better than the enemy and had their roots in the local soil. Certain core areas exist, Hazarajat, Panjshir, Nuristan, and north-central Afghanistan in which local forces, now well armed, dominate. This fragmentation of power will make it difficult to reunify the country.

Social factors militating against the centralization of power are the existence of tribalism, sectarian separatism, and what seems to be an innate individualism of the Afghan people, which is suppressed under the banner of Islam, if faced with a foreign aggressor, but reemerges as soon as the danger is gone. There exists a general distrust of central authority, which is reinforced by the politicization of the hitherto quiescent rural population.

Except for the few who benefit from the status quo, the vast majority of Afghan people are tired of war. There are two possibilities for reuniting the country: through conquest by one of the major contenders for power — a process that may take another decade; or through mediation, with the help of the United Nations and moral, political, and financial support from the major powers. At the time of this writing it is not yet clear which of the alternatives will end the vicious circle of war.

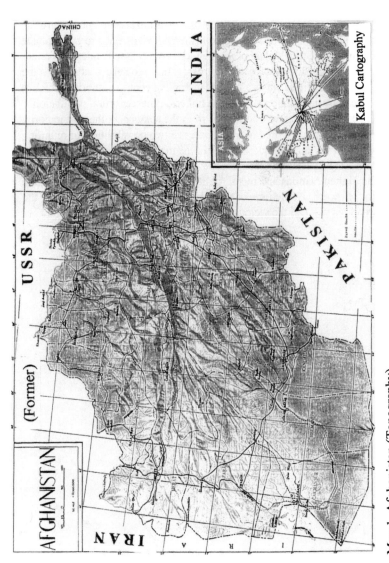

Map 1. Afghanistan (Topography)

THE DICTIONARY

A.B.C. Abbreviation for atomic, biological, and chemical agents used as weapons or weapons warheads. Several authors claim that the Soviet forces in Afghanistan used rockets with "toxic smoke and harassing agents" during the Herat uprising in March 1979 and later sporadically elsewhere. Blood, blister, and nerve agents as well as napalm were said to have been delivered by aircraft, rockets, artillery, and other means. The primary motive behind the use of chemical weapons may have been to use the battlefield as a testing ground (McMichael).

ABD AL–. *See* **ABDUL.**

ABDUL AZIZ KHAN, KANDAK MISHAR. Son of Ghulam Haidar Charkhi. In third Anglo-Afghan war was employed at the Asmar front, commanding Afghan troops in Arandu on October 1919, and refused British demands to move back across Afghan border, as required by the cease-fire agreement, saying that he had not received any orders to do so from King Amanullah. Promoted to Ghund Mishar in June 1920.

ABDUL KARIM. A Ghilzai mulla of the Andar section who was the son of Din Muhammad, the famous mulla Mushk-i Alam (q.v.). Amir Abdur Rahman gave him the title *Khan-i-Ulum* (Chief of [religious] Sciences), but he became disaffected when the amir ended the virtual autonomy enjoyed by the Ghilzai tribes and imposed taxes on hitherto exempt lands. He was one of the leaders of the Ghilzai Rebellion of 1886–87, and called for a *jehad* against the amir. The rebellion was suppressed with great difficulty. It was the last of three uprisings of this tribe in the nineteenth century. *See also* GHILZAI; and GHILZAI REBELLION.

ABDUL QUDDUS. A nephew of Amir Dost Muhammad (q.v.) and general who shared Amir Abdur Rahman's (q.v.) exile in Bukhara and Samarkand. On their return, he assisted the amir in extending his power over Afghanistan. He captured Herat from Ayub Muhammad Khan, son of Amir Shir Ali (qq.v.), in 1881 with a small force of 400 cavalry and 400 infantry soldiers and two mountain guns, and in 1890–93 he pacified the Hazarajat (*see* HAZARA WARS). Amir Habibullah gave him the title *Itimad-ud-Daula* (Confidence of the State) and appointed him prime minister. He was confirmed in this position by King Amanullah. In the third Anglo-Afghan war Abdul Quddus commanded the Kandahar front. A British officer characterized him as "a Tory of the most crusted type in politics, and an apostle of Afghanistan for the Afghans." His descendants, who were prominent in Afghan government, adopted his title, "Etemadi," as their family name.

ABDUL RAHIM KHAN, GENERAL SARDAR. Known as "Jarnel-i Lang." Employed in Kabul with household troops in 1917. In 1918 in charge of Jalalabad military district, and subsequently governor. In command of Afghan troops at Dakka, where he was forced to give way to British forces in third Anglo-Afghan war (q.v.).

ABDUL RAHMAN, AMIR (ABDUR RAHMAN, 1880–1901). Amir of Afghanistan, the oldest son of Amir Muhammad Afzal Khan, who assumed the Kabul throne at the end of the second Anglo-Afghan war. He fought his uncle Amir Shir Ali in 1864 and was forced to flee to the court of the amir of Bukhara. Returning to Afghanistan in 1866, he defeated Amir Shir Ali and recognized his father, Afzal Khan, as the new king. Three years later Amir Shir Ali regained the throne, and Abdur Rahman was forced into exile, spending some 10 years in Bukhara, Tashkent, and Samarkand. After the death of Amir Shir Ali in February 1879, Abdur Rahman Khan returned to Afghanistan. On his way south he gathered a large army. The British occupation force feared a repetition of the debacle of the first Anglo-Afghan war (q.v.) and, on July 22, 1880, grudgingly recognized Abdur Rahman as "Amir of Kabul and its Dependencies," in spite of the fact that he had come with Russian support. In September 1881 the amir took possession of Kandahar, defeating the forces of Ayub Khan. With the capture of Herat, Abdur Rahman was the undisputed ruler of Afghanistan.

Abdur Rahman concluded an agreement with the British government, in which Britain guaranteed him protection from unprovoked Russian aggression, provided he permitted Britain to conduct his foreign relations. He obtained a subsidy in money and materiel to strengthen the defenses of his country. Abdur Rahman considered this treaty an alliance between equals, and, having protected his northern borders, he kept the British at arm's length, never allowing them to gain any influence in the country under the aegis of their common defense. He formulated a "buffer-state policy," which aimed at playing off Afghanistan's imperialist neighbors against each other. This policy served Afghanistan well until the end of World War II, when changed conditions required new approaches in the conduct of Afghan foreign policy. Afghanistan's northern and eastern boundaries were demarcated during the amir's tenure, including the Durand Line (1893), which he accepted under "duress" in the Durand Agreement (q.v.).

ABDUL RAHMAN, CAMPAIGNS. The future Afghan king learned his trade as a military commander at an early age. His father, Muhammad Afzal Khan, was governor of Balkh and appointed Abdur Rahman, who was then about 13 years old, subgovernor of Tashqurghan (now called Khulm), a flourishing town and district in Afghan Turkestan. He became a pupil of General Shir Muhammad Khan, a Scot formerly named Campbell, who was captured at the Battle of Kandahar (qq.v.) and converted to Islam. Abdur Rahman Khan succeeded him as commander of the army of Balkh. He defeated the Uzbek chiefs of Qataghan and Badakhshan and forced them to renew their loyalty to Kabul. He helped to place his father on the Kabul throne in 1866 and supported his uncle, Muhammad Azim in his accession in 1867. He was the most obstinate rival of Amir Shir Ali Khan, defeating the amir's superior forces in encounters at Sayyidabad (1866), Qalat (1867), and the Panjshir Pass (1867), but was eventually forced into exile.

To capture a fortified position, Abdur Rahman first tried diplomacy, appealing to the defenders to avoid the bloodshed of fellow Muslims and promising leniency. Lured into a trap, when the spiritual leader of the Mirs of Qataghan invited him to dinner, he took his host prisoner and, dividing his force of some 1,600 *sowars* (cavalry) and two guns into small units, defeated an enemy of 10,000. When he returned from exile, the troops that had assembled to prevent his crossing into Afghanistan melted away. He proclaimed, "I inform you that I have come to release the country of Faiza from the hands of the English. If I succeed in doing so peacefully, well and good, otherwise we shall have to fight." (AR, 174) As he moved slowly south, his forces continued to grow, and Sir Lepel Griffin, the political officer with the British expeditionary forces at Kabul, initiated negotiations that led to Abdur Rahman's recognition as "Amir of Kabul." A final challenge to his power was Ayub Khan's capture of Kandahar in August 1881, when Abdur Rahman took to the field and decisively defeated his rival.

Having eliminated most of his major rivals, Amir Abdur Rahman proceeded to quell local revolts. He defeated Sayyid Mahmud of Kunar in 1881 and took direct control of Maimana in 1883. The Shinwari revolt was suppressed in 1883, and the Ghilzai Rebellion was crushed in 1886–87. The Iron Amir's last rival, his cousin Ishaq Khan, was defeated at the Battle of Ghaznigak in 1888. Government control of the Hazarajat was achieved by 1893 after a long series of wars (*see* HAZARA WARS), and Kafiristan was the last area integrated into the State of Afghanistan (*see* KAFIR WAR). When Amir Habibullah succeeded to the throne in 1901, the entire country was pacified.

ADMINISTRATIVE DIVISIONS. Since the time Timur Shah (q.v., 1773–93) made it his capital, Kabul was the center of the kingdom, and princes ruled more or less autonomously in the provinces. Major provinces headed by princes included Kandahar, Herat, Afghan Turkestan, and Qataghan and Badakhshan. Amir Abdur Rahman centralized government, and Nadir Shah divided the country into seven provinces.

As a result of the Constitution of 1964, Afghanistan was divided into 26 provinces (*wilayat*), each with a provincial center (*markaz*) that is graded according to importance into first, second, or third grade; Kabul, Ghazni, Gardez, Jalalabad, Mazar-i-Sharif, Herat, and Kandahar are first-grade administrative centers. They were headed by a governor (*wali*), as the executive officer, responsible to the Ministry of Interior in Kabul. In addition, each province had representatives of various departments at the administrative center who reported directly to Kabul. There were also a number of subprovinces (*loy woluswali*), which have since been absorbed into provinces. Each province is subdivided into districts (*woluswali*), with an administrator called *woluswal*, who is responsible to his supervising governor and may himself be in charge of one or more subdistricts (*alaqadari*). The administrator of a subdistrict (*alaqadar*), resides in a major village and is responsible to all his supervising administrators. Districts are divided into four grades, depending on population. In the 1970s the 27 provinces were divided into six subprovinces, 175 districts, and 118 subdistricts. Villages and rural subdivisions or (*qarya*), are headed by a village headman (*qarya-dar*, *malik*, or *arbab*) who acts as a link between the rural population

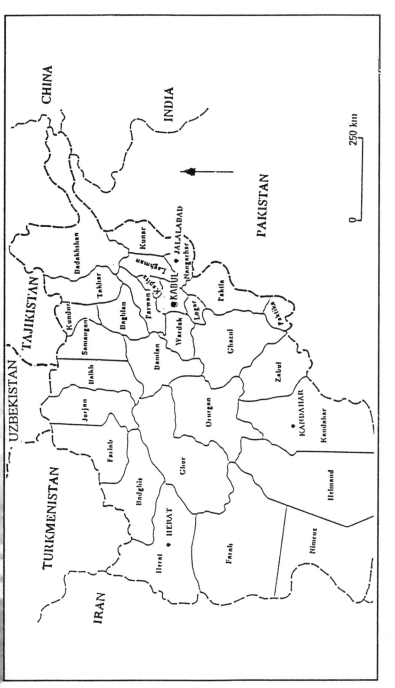

Map 2. Afghanistan (Administrative Divisions)

and the district chief. Cities are divided into wards, or *nahiya*.

Province	Area	Population	Wols.	Alaq.	Center
Badakhshan	48,176	484,000	5	7	Faizabad
Badghis	21,854	247,000	4	1	Qala-i-Nau
Baglan	17,165	486,000	5	4	Baghlan
Balkh	11,833	570,000	7	3	Mazar-i Sharif
Bamian	17,411	285,000	4	2	Bamian
Farah	58,834	356,000	8	2	Farah
Fariab	22,274	547,000	7	5	Maimana
Ghazni	32,797	701,000	10	12	Ghazni
Ghor	38,658	341,000	5	1	Chagh-charan
Helmand	61,816	570,000	8	4	Lashkargah
Herat	50,245	685,000	11	1	Herat
Jozjan	25,548	642,000	5	6	Shiberghan
Kabul	4,583	1,372,000	8	4	Kabul
Kandahar	49,430	699,000	11	4	Kandahar
Kunduz	7,926	575,000	5	1	Kunduz
Laghman	7,227	387,000	4	1	Mehterlam
Logar	4,409	424,000	3	3	Pul-i-Alam
Maidan (1)	9,699	310,000	4	4	Kota-i Ashro
Nangarhar (2)	18,636	786,000	17	14	Jalalabad
Nimruz	41,347	112,000	3	1	Zaranj
Oruzgan	28,756	483,000	8	-	Tirinkot
Paktia (3)	17,772	706,000	11	21	Gardez
Parwan	5,911	418,000			Charikar
Kapisa	5,358	366,000			Mahmud Raqi
Samangan	16,640	275,000	3	2	Aibak
Takhar	12,325	528,000	6	5	Taloqan
Zabul	17,298	181,000	5	3	Qalat

(1) Also called Wardak. (2) Including Kunar. (3) Including Paktika.

(Groetzbach, 1990)

In the late 1970s the Afghan government estimated the Afghan population at 15.5 million. Since the defeat of the Marxist government in April 1992, the central government has ceased to exist and the Afghan countryside is under the control of local commanders and warlords, while the capital is under siege. The *Jam'iat* of Professor Rabbani controls Kabul and large portions of northeastern Afghanistan, General Abdul Rashid Dostum controls the north-central provinces, the newly emerged forces of the *Taleban* (qq.v.) control the western and southern area, and various parties or coalitions control the area between Kabul and the Pakistan border.

AFGANTSY (Sing. AFGANETS). Soviet veterans of the Afghan war (1980–89) who were mostly conscripts in a war that did not enjoy popular support. According to a recent study, about 750,000 served in troop units in Afghanistan from 1979 to 1989. Casualties included about 15,000 dead, 50,000 wounded — about 11,500 of whom remained invalids — 330 missing in action, and 18 defectors. (Galeotti) They felt neglected and their needs ignored. About a quarter of the veterans are organized in the "afganets movement" with the support of a Council of Soldiers' Mothers and Widows. Afgantsy in the highest military posts during 1979–91 include Marshal Sokolov, defense minister, 1984–87, and first deputy prime minister, 1984-85; Marshal D. Akhromeev, chief of general staff, 1984–88; General Lobov, chief of general staff and commander in chief of the Warsaw Pact, 1991; Colonel General Grachev, first deputy minister, 1991; General V. Varennikov, commander of ground forces, 1989–91; and General Yu Maximov, commander of strategic rocket forces, 1985–90s. (Galeotti) Some observers see the Afgantsy as a "new force" of conservative nationalists who may have an impact on the future political life of Russia. *See also* LIMITED CONTINGENT OF SOVIET FORCES IN AFGHANISTAN.

AFGHAN FOREIGN RELATIONS. Afghanistan's relations with her neighbors were always influenced by the fact that the territory inhabited by the Afghans was the "gateway" to the Indian subcontinent. The power that controlled the tribes and the passes leading south and east would not encounter any great physical obstacles in the conquest of the subcontinent and its fabulous riches. Mahmud of Ghazni (988–1030), Tamerlane (Timur-e Lang, 1370–1405), and Nadir Shah Afshar (q.v., 1736–47) crossed the Afghan passes for the propagation of Islam, for

glory, and for booty. It is therefore not surprising that Ahmad Shah
Durrani (q.v., 1747-73), the founder of the State of Afghanistan, saw it
his manifest destiny to create an empire that included a large portion of
northern India. He invaded India eight times and defeated the powerful
Maratha confederation at the Battle of Panipat (qq.v.), north of Delhi,
in 1761. But by the turn of the century, the gradual northwest expansion
of British influence resulted in a confrontation between Britain and
Afghanistan, which was to continue into the twentieth century.
Afghanistan's foreign relations can be divided into five major periods:
First, the expansionist period, which lasted from 1747 to 1800; second,
the period of foreign conflict, from 1800 to 1880, which involved
Afghanistan in hostilities with Persia and the rising Sikh nation in the
Panjab as well as with Britain and Russia; third, the period of defensive
isolationism and "buffer-state" politics, initiated by Amir Abdur
Rahman (1880–1901) and continued by Amir Habibullah (1901–1919)
until his death; fourth, the period of defensive neutralism, which opened
Afghanistan to foreign influences and lasted until after World War II
when Britain's departure from India ushered in a new era of peaceful
coexistence that, nevertheless, ended with the Marxist coup in 1978 and
Soviet intervention. The final, fifth, period was one of close cooperation
with the Soviet Union, ending in the war of the 1980s and the
subsequent civil war.

During the expansionist period Afghan rulers conquered territories
north of the Hindu Kush and east of the Indus River, but internecine
fighting among the Durrani *sardars* (princes and chiefs) and the
emergence of new players in the "Great Game" in Central Asia made the
Afghan Empire a short-lived enterprise. When in 1798 Zaman Shah
invited the Marquess Wellesley, governor of Bengal (1798–1805), to
join him in a campaign against the Maratha confederacy of northwestern
India, Wellesley sought Persian assistance "to keep Zaman Shah in
perpetual check." The period of foreign conflict saw the emergence of
the Sikh nation under Ranjit Singh (q.v.), who wrested the Panjab from
the Afghans. Britain feared the appearance of a French mission in
Tehran in 1807 and the Russian territorial gains in the Caucasus a threat
to India. Therefore, in 1808 the British governor general, Lord Minto,
sent Mountstuart Elphinstone (q.v.) to Peshawar to conclude a treaty of
friendship and common defense against Franco-Persian attacks. Shah
Shuja-ul-Mulk (q.v.), who had ascended the Kabul throne, agreed to
prohibit Frenchmen from entering his realm in exchange for military
support. This treaty as well as others concluded between Britain and

Fath Ali Shah, the ruler of Persia, were "inoperative" almost as soon as they were ratified. Shah Shuja was ousted in 1810 and, after an interval of internecine fighting, the Muhammadzai branch of the Durranis replaced the Sadozai rulers.

Dost Muhammad (q.v.), a capable ruler, succeeded to the throne in 1826. He wanted British friendship, but also wanted to regain Peshawar from Ranjit Singh, whose forces had conquered Multan in 1810, Kashmir in 1819, and Peshawar in 1823. But Lord Auckland, governor-general of British India (1836–42), favored a forward policy; he concluded the Tripartite Agreement of July 1838 (qq.v.) with Ranjit Singh and Shah Shuja to restore the shah to the Kabul throne. Dost Muhammad's negotiations with a purported Russian envoy and the amir's hostility to the Sikh ruler were the *casus belli*, and the Simla Manifesto of 1838 (q.v.), issued by the British-Indian government, constituted the declaration of war. The "Army of the Indus," as it was proudly called, invaded Afghanistan in what came to be known as the first Anglo-Afghan war (q.v.). Once installed on the Kabul throne, Shah Shuja was unable to consolidate his power even with British support. Afghan tribal forces attacked isolated outposts, and on November 2, 1841, the British Political Officer Alexander Burnes and his staff were assassinated. The British forces were forced to negotiate an ignominious retreat, which resulted in the virtual annihilation of the British-Indian forces. *See* FIRST ANGLO-AFGHAN WAR; CAPITULATION, TREATY OF; and DEATH MARCH.

This extraordinary setback for Britain led to the restoration of Dost Muhammad to the throne (1842–63). Like Shah Shuja, he had been in Indian exile and his return to Kabul began the rule of the Muhammadzai (q.v.) dynasty, a collateral branch of the Sadozai, which lasted until 1973. The British-Indian government resigned itself to a period of "masterly inactivity," which left Afghanistan to revert to civil war following the succession of Amir Shir Ali in 1863. But the search for a "scientific" frontier and the desire to fill a "power vacuum" in Afghanistan led to a return to a forward policy. Baluchistan came under British control in 1879, and the Indian government had to decide where its boundary with Afghanistan should be — the crest of the Hindu Kush, the Amu Daria, or the tribal belt of the northwestern frontier? Lacking any direct control over Afghanistan, Britain wanted envoys stationed at Herat and Kabul who could guard Indian interests in those vital areas. Amir Shir Ali was willing to forge an alliance with Britain, but he wanted protection from Russian aggression, a subsidy in weapons and funds, and British recognition of his son, Abdullah Jan, as his successor (*see* AMBALA CONFERENCE) . When he could not obtain a clear commitment from Britain, he listened to the overtures of General Kaufman, the Russian governor-general of Turkestan Province, and permitted a mission under General Stolietoff (q.v.) to proceed to Kabul. The Russians gave the not quite ironclad promise "that if any foreign enemy attacks Afghanistan and the Amir is unable to drive him out. . . the Russian Government will repel the enemy either by means of advice or by such other means as it may seem proper."

The British government now insisted that the amir receive a mission, headed by General Neville Chamberlain. Shir Ali asked for a postponement of the mission, but the mission proceeded in spite of the wishes of the amir. When it was stopped at the Afghan frontier, Britain presented an ultimatum; on January 8, 1879, British troops occupied Kandahar in the start of the second Anglo-Afghan war (q.v.). The promised Russian support was in the form of "advice," namely, that the amir should make his peace with the British. Shir Ali felt betrayed; he was forced to flee and died two months later near Mazar-i Sharif.

His son Yaqub Khan succeeded to the throne at the cost of ceding territory to British India in the Treaty of Gandomak and permitting Sir Pierre Louis Cavagnari (qq.v.) to come to Kabul to head a permanent British mission. History repeated itself when Cavagnari and his staff were massacred in Kabul. General Sir Frederick Roberts, son of General Sir Abraham Roberts, the commander of Shah Shuja's forces during the first Anglo-Afghan war, occupied Kabul. (qq.v.) In the meantime, other contenders for the Kabul throne came to the fore. Ayub Khan, another son of Amir Shir Ali, wiped out General Burrows' forces in the Battle of Maiwand (1880) (qq.v.), and Abdur Rahman Khan, a grandson of Amir Dost Muhammad, entered Afghanistan after 11 years in Central Asian exile. To avoid disaster and to extricate their forces from Afghanistan, the British found it advisable to recognize Abdul Rahman as amir of "Kabul and its Dependencies." Amir Abdul Rahman (q.v., 1880–1901) was quick to eliminate all rivals to his power. He united the country, initiated domestic reforms, and formulated a foreign policy that served Afghanistan well until World War I. He fashioned a cautious alliance with Britain, which obligated Britain to defend Afghanistan from unprovoked Russian aggression and strengthened his power with aid in money and arms. Abdur Rahman agreed to conduct his relations with foreign powers through the intermediary of the British government. Having protected himself from the danger in the north, the amir formulated a policy that was to prevent Britain from gaining influence within his domain under the aegis of their common defense. This policy rested on the following triad: militant assertion of independence, defensive isolationism, and a balancing of the pressures by the two imperialist neighbors.

The "Iron Amir" considered his agreement with Britain an alliance between equals in which the two partners contributed to their common defense. He permitted the establishment in Kabul of a British agency, headed by an Indian Muslim whose sphere of activity was strictly limited, but refused to accept British military advisers and declined an offer of British help in extending the Indian rail system into Afghanistan. Although in 1893 he accepted under "duress" the Durand Line (*see* DURAND AGREEMENT), which cut large portions of Pashtun territory from the Afghan state, he did not assist in the complete demarcation of the border and continued to lay claim to the free "unadministered" tribal belt, which he saw as a buffer between Afghanistan and India. When Britain made punitive expeditions into this area, the Afghan ruler supported the tribes with shipments of arms and granted fugitives from India shelter in his domain. Amir Abdur Rahman was on a state visit in India in 1885 when Russian troops moved into the Panjdeh oasis. (*See* PANJDEH INCIDENT.) The fact that Britain did not assist him against Russian aggression convinced him that he could only rely on himself.

Amir Habibullah (q.v., 1901–19) continued the policy of his father. He resisted British demands for modifications of the agreements concluded with Amir Abdur Rahman and succeeded in 1905 in obtaining a treaty that confirmed all the existing provisions (*see* ANGLO-AFGHAN TREATY OF 1905). Two years later, Amir Habibullah visited India for talks with the governor-general, Lord Minto, unaware of the fact that at the same time Russia and Britain had concluded the Anglo-Russian Convention of 1907 (q.v.). The amir never permitted Russia the commercial privileges expected under the convention and made sure that his imperialist neighbors would not solve the "Afghanistan Question" at the cost of his independence. The situation was drastically changed during World War I when both the Central Powers and the Allies vied for the support of the Afghan ruler. The Hentig-Niedermayer expedition (q.v., Aug. 1915–May 1916) was able to conclude a treaty with the amir, but could not provide any tangible support in funds and weapons. Therefore, Habibullah remained neutral, hoping to win rich rewards and complete independence from Britain; but when these expectations were not realized, he paid for the failure of his policy with his life. Amir Habibullah was assassinated on the night of February 19–20, 1919, at Kalla Gush in Laghman Province. Amanullah Khan ascended the throne over the rival claims of his uncle, Nasrullah Khan, and his brother, Inayatullah Khan.

King Amanullah (1919–29, he adopted the title of king in 1926) demanded a new treaty from British India that would recognize Afghanistan's absolute independence. When the Indian government was reluctant to comply, he started military action that resulted in the third Anglo-Afghan war of 1919 (q.v.). With India in semirevolt and British forces demobilized after the European war, the British government did not find this an opportune time to wage war and agreed to a peace treaty at Rawalpindi (August 8, 1919, *see* ANGLO-AFGHAN TREATY OF 1919). It took another three months of negotiations at Mussoorie (Mussoorie Conference, April 17 – July 18, 1920, q.v.) and almost one year of talks at Kabul, Jan. 1, 1921 – Dec. 2, 1921, before normal, neighborly relations were established. (*See* ANGLO-AFGHAN TREATY OF 1921.) By that time Amanullah had established diplomatic relations with the Soviet Union, Turkey, Persia, and Italy and had modified Abdur Rahman's policy to end the isolation of his country. A contemporary of Reza Shah of Iran and Kemal Ataturk of the young Turkish Republic, Amanullah initiated such drastic social reforms that he was ousted in a wave of reaction after a 10-year period of tenuous rule. Next followed the chaotic 10-months rule of a "lowly" Tajik, Habibullah Kalakani (Jan. 18 – Nov. 3, 1929, q.v.), called "The Son of a Water Carrier" (*Bacha-e Saqqau*) by his friends and   "Amir Habibullah Ghazi, Servant of the Religion of the Messenger of God" (*Khadem-i Din Rasul Allah*), by his followers after his coronation.

The new dynasty of Muhammad Nadir Shah (1929–33) and his son Muhammad Zahir Shah (1933–73) (qq.v.) continued Afghanistan's traditional policy of foreign relations but now tried to enlist Germany as a "third power" in obtaining the technical and political support that the Afghan rulers did not dare to accept from their neighbors. Economic and cultural collaboration between Afghanistan and Germany was greatly expanded, and Germans were soon the largest European community in the country. But the deterioration of the political situation in Europe and the outbreak of World War II ended any possibility that the economic cooperation might evolve into political collaboration. Afghanistan remained neutral during the war.

The end of the war created an entirely new situation: the Soviet Union, although severely battered, acquired nuclear technology and emerged as a superpower, and Britain, in spite of her victory, was forced to relinquish her hold on India in 1947. During the short reign of King Amanullah, Afghanistan's border with the Soviet Union was open to commercial relations, and regular air service to Tashkent existed, but his successors maintained a closed-border policy. Keeping Afghanistan's border to the north closed was criticized in Moscow as inconsistent with friendly "neighborly" relations. Soviet demands for a "normalization" of relations could not be ignored, but it was hoped in Kabul that the United States would fill the vacuum left by the British and serve as a balancing force against the Soviet Union.

The United States formally recognized Afghanistan in August 1934, but did not have an accredited representative in Kabul until 1942, when it appeared possible that the German advance into the Caucasus might make it impossible to maintain a link to the Soviet Union through western Iran. In spite of its status as an independent state, Washington considered Afghanistan within the British sphere of influence and not very important in terms of international trade. With the onset of the cold war during the Truman administration and the policy of containment of communism under John Foster Dulles, secretary of state under President Eisenhower, the Afghan government might have entered into an alliance with the United States if it could have been given explicit guarantees of protection from Soviet attack.

The U.S. government had never been willing to give that kind of guarantee; a possible Soviet advance was to be stopped at the Khaibar Pass, not north of the Hindu Kush. The Baghdad Pact (subsequently renamed in 1959 the Central Treaty Organization, CENTO) united in 1955 Turkey, Iraq, Iran, and Pakistan, with Britain as the representative of the West and the United States as the sponsor and "paymaster." The alliance inherited the legacy of regional disputes between Middle Eastern neighbors and upset the balance of powers.

A turning point occurred in December 1955, when Nikita Khrushchev and Nikolai Bulganin came to Kabul. The Soviets supported Afghanistan in the "Pashtunistan" dispute (q.v.) and offered massive aid, which the United States was unwilling to match. The government of Prime Minister Muhammad Daud (q.v.), in spite of its misgivings, turned to the Soviet Union for the weapons it could not obtain from the West.

The weapons arrived with Soviet advisers and experts, and thousands of Afghans went to the Soviet Union for military training. Graduates from Afghan institutes of higher education won fellowships to foreign universities, including the USSR, and there emerged a growing cadre of military officers, students, and technocrats with leftist and republican, if not pro-Russian, sympathies. When Sardar Muhammad Daud on July 17, 1973 staged a coup against his cousin, the king, he counted the Left (and Parchamis, q.v.) among his supporters. Five years later a Marxist coup ended the "aristocratic" republic and established the Democratic Republic of Afghanistan. Its alliance with the Soviet Union and the subsequent war, which Soviet intervention in 1979 turned into a war of liberation, resulted in the eventual Soviet withdrawal in 1989 and a "simmering" civil war with no end in sight. *See also* SOVIET-AFGHAN RELATIONS.

AFGHANIS/ARABS. Radical Islamists called Afghanis, mostly of Arab nationality, but also from other Muslim countries, who gained fighting experience in the war in Afghanistan and returned to their countries with the intention of toppling their governments and establishing an "Islamic State." They are said to include some 5,000 Saudis, 3,000 Yemenis, 2,000 Egyptians, 2,800 Algerians, 400 Tunisians, 370 Iraqis, 200 Libyans, some Jordanians (James Bruce), as well as citizens of other Muslim countries. They are a serious threat to the military regime in Algeria and also have started terrorist activities in Egypt and are fighting as volunteers in regional wars from Bosnia to Kashmir and the Philippines.

AFGHAN SECURITY SERVICE. After the Saur Revolt, the Taraki government established a security service, named AGSA (*Da Afghanistan da Gatay da Satanay Edara*, Afghanistan Security Service Department), which was headed by Asadullah Sarwari from May 1978 until August 1979. After his accession to power, Hafizullah Amin renamed the service KAM (*Da Kargarano Amniyyati Mu'asasa*, Workers' Security Institution). Within a week of their assumption of power on December 27, 1979, the Parchami regime purged the security service of Khalq supporters and renamed it KHAD (*Khedamat-i Ettela'at-i Daulati*, State Information Service). It was headed by Dr. Najibullah (q.v.) before he succeeded to the position of general secretary of the PDPA in 1986 and president of Afghanistan. Najibullah upgraded KHAD to ministerial status; hence its acronym WAD

(*Wizarat-i Ettela'at-i Daulati*, Ministry of State Security). WAD was subsequently headed by General Ghulam Faruq Yaqubi. The organization is said to have controlled from 15 thousand to 30 thousand operatives, organized on the KGB model, with its own military units, including a national guard. Its task appeared to be similar to that of the KGB: 1. Detecting and eradicating domestic political opposition. 2. Subverting armed resistance. 3. Penetrating opposition groups abroad. 4. Providing military intelligence to the armed forces. It is said to have been set up with the assistance of Soviet and East German intelligence officers.

Yaqubi did not survive the downfall of the Marxist regime. Former Afghan prisoners have accused WAD and its predecessors of torture, intimidation, and murder. Burhanuddin Rabbani (q.v.) started his own security service, which was also popularly called KHAD.

AFGHANS, METHODS OF FIGHTING. British-Indian manuals on the third Anglo-Afghan war describe the Afghans as masters of guerrilla warfare: "They do not await assault, but follow a retiring enemy relentlessly and with utmost boldness. They show great skill in cutting off detachments and in laying ambushes for isolated bodies of troops. They are, however, deficient in some important military qualities. They lack steadfastness in adversity and lose heart when subjected to reverses. They have little cohesion and concerted action on their part cannot be expected. Their forces (*lashkars*) are brought to, and kept in, the field by the exertions of their religious leaders, and each man fights as he pleases. Time is lost owing to lengthy discussions which often precede military action or declaration of policy. Mutual jealousies or blood feuds, which are sunk on occasions. . . , are apt to reappear during prolonged operations." This was written in 1925, but it was valid also for the *mujahedin*, fighting the Soviet and Kabul government forces in the 1980s. *See also* GUERRILLA WARFARE.

AFRIDI. A Pashtu-speaking tribe that is located in the area of the Khaibar Pass, just beyond the Afghan border. Herodotus, the Greek historian, mentions the "Aprytae," a member of the tribe of Osman who called himself "God's Creature" (*afrideh-ye khoda*). Some Afghan scholars consider him the eponymic ancestor of the Afridis. For centuries, the Afridis saw themselves as the "guardians" of the gate to India, and invaders since ancient times have found it preferable to pay for passage rather than fight their way through the Khaibar. At times, Afridis entered the services of Afghan rulers, primarily as bodyguards and tribal militia. In conflicts between Afghanistan and British India, they supported the Afghans, although they could not resist the temptation to loot the Afghan arsenal when the British bombed Jalalabad in 1919. In the 1960s the Afridis were said to be able to muster an armed force of 50,000 men. A British officer described them as "wiry, shaven-headed, full-bearded, Pashtu-speaking hillmen of uncertain origin." (Ridgway) During the 1980s the Kabul government attempted to enlist Afridis into a militia to attack the supply lines of the *mujahedin*, and the Afridis accepted their pay but did not perform their assigned functions.

At the end of the third Anglo-Afghan war, Sir Hamilton Grant, chief commissioner of the North-West Frontier, complained to the viceroy of India that "the constant raiding by Afridi gangs into the Peshawar District is sorely discrediting our administration. It is astounding that such a state of affairs should be possible with the number of troops we have got in the Peshawar Valley and shows how very difficult it would be to make any military operation of trans-frontier area really successful." He added that only subjugation of the Afridis would help, but this would be "a most formidable and undesirable undertaking." (G.C.)

AHMAD KHEL, BATTLE OF. A battle on April 19, 1880 between the Bengal regiments, commanded by General Sir Donald Steward (q.v.), and an army of 15,000 Ghilzais, some Durranis, and a force of some 4,000 ill-equipped *ghazis* in which the Afghan forces were eventually defeated. Steward was on his way from Kandahar to Kabul to replace General Roberts (q.v.) when at Ahmad Khel, about 20 miles from Ghazni, he came on a strong force of *ghazis*. His forces included the Bengal division, consisting of two infantry brigades commanded by Brigadier Generals Hughes and Barter, and the cavalry brigade commanded by Brigadier General Palliser. There were also the horse and field artillery with cavalry and infantry escort, as well as six squadrons of Indian cavalry, Bengal Lancers, the elite 60th Rifles, and Gurka and Sikh infantries. His two 40 pounders and two 6.3-inch howitzers took up a mile of the road, "each gun with twenty yoke of oxen trudging slowly along." (Heathcote, 1980) A horde of Hazaras moved behind the British force, plundering and wreaking vengeance on Pashtun villages. A larger force of several thousand hostile *ghazis* marched day by day parallel with the British flank. Steward did not seek battle, but when he reached the vicinity of Ahmad Khel his road was

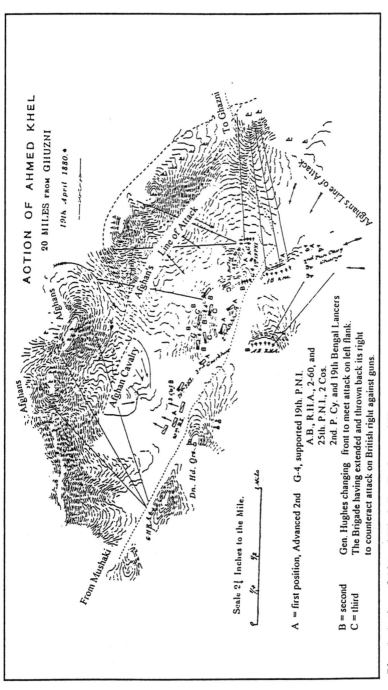

Plan 1. Action of Ahmad Khel. By Forbes and Hensman

ACTION OF AHMED KHEL

20 MILES FROM GHUZNI

19th April 1880.

Scale 2¼ Inches to the Mile.

A = first position, Advanced 2nd   G-4, supported 19th. P.N.I.
A.B, R.H.A., 2-60, and
25th. P.N.I., 2 Cos.
2nd. P. Cy. and 19th Bengal Lancers

B = second   Gen. Hughes changing   front to meet attack on left flank.
The Brigade having extended and thrown back its right
C = third   to counteract attack on British right against guns.

To Ghazni

Afghan's Line of Attack

Line of Attack

Afghans

Afghan Cavalry

Afghans

Afghans

Afghans

From Mushaki

Dn. Hd. Qr.

flanked by a spur of the Gul Kuh Mountain, and the low pass he needed
to cross was suddenly teeming with tribesmen. To the beating of "tom-
toms" and the incitement of *mullas*, some 3,000 *ghazis* (largely
Ghilzais) swept down sword in hand heedless of the steady fire of the
British; some companies did not have time to fix their bayonets, and the
British forces were forced to fall back. Some wounded tribesmen "or
shamming dead, cut desperately up at the troops as they passed."
Eventually, the British line steadied and their superior firepower of
Martini-Henry and Snider rifles and artillery carried the day. Steward
reported Afghan losses at 800 compared to his losses of 17 dead and
120 wounded. (British estimates of the number of Afghan forces and
statistics of casualties are, at best, approximations upon which authors
disagree. According to Forbes (1892), one thousand dead bodies were
counted, and the MR lists 3,000 Afghans killed and wounded. Most of
the British wounded were injured by sword slashes and knife stabs
during hand-to-hand combat.) One British officer wrote, "Anyone with
the semblance of a heart under his khaki-jacket could not help feeling
something akin to pity to see them advancing with their miserable
weapons in the face of our guns and rifles, but their courage and their
numbers made them formidable." (Heathcote, 1980)   *See also*
INTRODUCTION.

AHMAD SHAH, ABDALI DURRANI. King of Afghanistan, 1747–73,
and founder of the Sadozai dynasty of the Abdali (Durrani) tribe. Born
in 1722 in Herat, the son of Muhammad Zaman Khan, who was
governor of Herat. After capturing Kandahar, Nadir Shah of Iran
(1736–47, q.v.) exiled Ahmad Khan to Mazandaran in northern Iran
and subsequently appointed him governor of that province. When
Nadir Shah died, Ahmad Khan was commander of an Afghan contingent
of the Persian army at Kandahar. He was able to capture a caravan with
booty from India, which assured his election as king (shah) of
Afghanistan in October 1747 by an assembly of Pashtun chiefs. The
Pashtun tribesmen rallied to his banner, and Ahmad Shah led them on
eight campaigns into India in search of booty and territorial conquest.
He added Kashmir, Sind, and the Western Panjab to his domain and
founded an empire that extended from eastern Persia to northern India
and from the Amu Daria (q.v.) to the Indian Ocean. Ahmad Shah
appointed his son Timur (*see* TIMUR SHAH) as his successor and died
a natural death two months later on April 14, 1772. He was buried in
Kandahar, which became the capital of Afghanistan until Timur Shah

(1773–93) established his capital at Kabul. Sir Percy Sykes in his *History of Afghanistan* called Ahmad Shah "a monarch whose high descent and warlike qualities made him peculiarly acceptable to his aristocratic and virile Chiefs, as well as to his warlike subjects in general. In short, he possessed all the qualities that enabled him successfully to found the kingdom of Afghanistan." (I, 367)

AHMAD SHAH, MILITARY ADMINISTRATION. Ahmad Shah founded the first regular Afghan army. He appointed a deputy (the *sipah salar*), or commander in chief, who performed all the functions of minister of war, subject to the approval of the king. A quartermaster general (*suyursatchi bashi*) was in charge of the purchase and collection of supplies, and a director of arsenals (*qurchi bashi*) was in charge of munitions.

The army was divided into the regular army (*askar-i munazzam*) and irregular tribal levies (*askar-i ghair munazzam*); the regular army comprised one-third and the irregular forces two-thirds. The regular army was voluntary and a lifetime profession and consisted of cavalry, infantry, and artillery branches, most of them stationed at the capital. A regular soldier had to provide for his food and his horse out of his pay during his nine-months of active service, after which time he was on home leave for three months. Similar to the Ottoman system, the king depended on a bodyguard (*ghulam khana*) of foreigners for his protection, many of them *qizilbashes* (q.v.) who did not have any local ties.

Three-fourths of the army consisted of cavalry, armed with matchlocks and swords and some with carbines and spears. They also carried shields, daggers, and axes. The infantry carried primarily matchlocks and swords. Light artillery (*zamburak*) was used, carried on camels provided with swivels, which permitted firing without the need for unloading. Heavy artillery was carried primarily by elephants.

The formation of the army was as follows:

One *dalgi* (section)	10 men
One *tawalli* (platoon)	10 *dalgi-ha* = 100 men
One *kundak* (regiment)	10 *tawalli* = 1,000
One *qita'* (brigade)	2 or more *kundaks*

Officers — cavalry and infantry

Dah bashi or *dalgi-mishar*	section commander
Yuz bashi or *tawalli-mishar*	platoon commander

Yuz bashi or *tawalli-mishar*	platoon commander
Mang bashi, beg bashi, or	
Kundak-mishar	regiment commander
Amir-i lashkar	brigade commander
Sipah salar or *sardar-i sardaran*	commander in chief
Officers — artillery	
Zamburakchi, shahanchi or	
Shanhangchi	artillery man or gunner
Shahanchi bashi	
or *jazailchi bashi*	artillery officer
Topchi bashi or *Mir-i Atesh*	chief artillery commander
(Singh, 361)	

The irregular army consisted of three-fourths cavalry and one-forth infantry who were tribal levies. It included the feudal units who provided service during war in lieu of payment of land revenue; tribal levies provided by chiefs who were paid or held tax-free land in exchange for supplying a commensurate number of fighters; or tribal cavalry who were employed for the protection of the borders, collection of revenues, police duties, and similar tasks.

At the call of the king, the chiefs and notables holding land rallied with the number of troops required of each. Weapons were issued to them for the duration of war

AIR FORCE, AFGHAN. The Afghan government took the first steps at creating an air force during the reign of King Amanullah. The importance of aerial warfare became apparent during the third Anglo-Afghan war when British planes bombed Jalalabad, the king's palace, and the ammunition factory at Kabul. Therefore, in 1921 Amanullah acquired a British fighter plane (which made a forced landing in Katawaz — the Afghans returned the pilot and kept the plane) and subsequently purchased a number of additional planes from Britain and the Soviet Union. By the end of the 1920s, Afghanistan's air force consisted of 22 machines (Bristol Fighters, D.H. 9s, Caprioni Scouts, and a Junkers Monoplane) that were operated by 25 officers, three of whom were Afghans, four Germans, and the rest Russians. The Soviet Union had donated a number of aircraft on condition that they be operated by Soviet nationals. Young Afghans were sent for training to the Soviet Union, Italy, India, and other countries to create a small cadre of pilots and aircraft mechanics. Amanullah used his aircrafts with considerable effect during the Khost Rebellion (q.v., 1924–25) and subsequent tribal revolts. But the conditions for maintaining an effective air force did not yet exist: Afghanistan depended on foreign supplies of spare parts and most of the king's aircraft were not in proper operating condition when he was deposed in the 1929 civil war.

During the reign of Nadir Shah (1929–1933), the Russian personnel was gradually eliminated, and in the mid-1930s, Zahir Shah's prime minister negotiated with Britain for the purchase of 24 aircraft and the training of 10 pilots, six officers, and 30 mechanics. When the British government wanted assurance that the Afghans would build up their air force from primarily British sources, negotiations came to a halt.

In the mid-1930s, landing strips existed in Herat, Kandahar, Kabul, and Jalalabad, but only Kabul had a ground organization and hangar accommodations for 16 aircraft. Aviation fuel had to be imported from India, and supplies never exceeded 10,000 gallons. To carry 15,000 gallons required more than 500 camels. Winds, excessive heat, and snow made flying conditions good only in October and November. (HBAA, 1933) Because of the war in Europe, development of the air force was limited until the Soviet Union became the major factor in the creation of modern armed forces.

In the mid-1950s, Ariana Afghan Airlines was established with technical support provided by Pan American Airways, and the airports of Kabul and Kandahar were modernized for international flights. The Kandahar airport, built with American aid, became one of the military's regional headquarters after the Soviet intervention. By 1960 the country's air force included four helicopters and about 100 Soviet combat aircraft, and in 1979 some 140–170 fighters and 45–60 helicopters were organized into a tactical force of seven air regiments, including a strength of 7,000–8,000 men, which remained relatively intact throughout the 1980s.

In the present civil war, the air force, like the army, broke into a number of sections, with General Abdul Rashid Dostum (q.v.) and the forces of President Rabbani gaining a major part. But, again, a problem of servicing and the provision of spare parts prevented any of the warring parties from gaining aerial superiority.

AK-47 (AVTOMAT KALASHNIKOV). Full or semiautomatic assault rifles of Soviet, Chinese, or Egyptian make became the weapons of choice of the *mujahedin*. Initially, they were captured, bartered, or surrendered by deserters from the Afghan army, but the need for these weapons was great. To ensure "plausible deniability" of outside support, Soviet weapons from Egyptian stores were channeled to the *mujahedin*, and when foreign assistance had become an open secret, kalashnikovs of Chinese and other origins were brought in. The kalashnikov proved to be an effective weapon in ambushes of highway convoys and fortified posts. In 1994 the enormous numbers of assault weapons in Afghan hands reduced the price of an AK-47 to $100 in Kabul. (*See* ARMS BAZAAR, AFGHAN.)

AKBAR, SARDAR MUHAMMAD (Called GHAZI). The ambitious son of Amir Dost Muhammad (1826–38 and 1842–63) and "Hero of Jamrud," who defeated the Sikh army of Hari Singh in April 1837. He was a major figure in the defeat of the British in the first Anglo-Afghan war. Akbar was the premier of the Afghan chiefs with whom the British force of occupation sought to negotiate safe passage from Kabul to India (*see* CAPITULATION, TREATY OF). During negotiations with Sir William Macnaghten (q.v.), he killed the British envoy "in a fit of passion." He saved the lives of British women and children as well as a number of officers whom he had taken into "protective" custody during the arduous retreat. Few others survived the massacre of the British expeditionary force of some 16,000 troops and camp followers (*see* DEATH MARCH). Akbar wanted to regain territory lost in the Panjab, but his father, Amir Dost Muhammad, who had been restored to the throne in 1842, favored a policy of accommodation with Britain. In 1845 Akbar rebelled, but he died at the age of 29 of poisoning before he could pose a serious challenge to his father. He is revered by Afghans and called *Ghazi* (Victor against Infidels). A residential area of Kabul and a major hospital have been named after him, Wazir Akbar Khan.

AKHTAR KHAN, LT. GEN. ABDUL RAHMAN. Director general of the Pakistani military's Inter-Services Intelligence (ISI) organization from 1980–1987, who was said to have coordinated with William Casey, director of the CIA, the operations and supply network for the Afghan *mujahedin*. Brigadier Mohammad Yousaf (q.v.), Akhtar's deputy and head of the Afghan Bureau, controlled the flow of thousands of tons of arms into the hands of the *mujahedin* and directed every aspect of military activities from training of Afghan guerrillas and logistics support to the planning of ambushes, assassinations, raids, and rocket attacks against the Soviet/Kabul forces. Akhtar was promoted to chairman of the Joint Chiefs of Staff Committee and replaced by General Hamid Gul when *mujahedin* started carrying attacks into Soviet Central Asia. Akhtar perished in a plane crash on August 17, 1988, together with Pakistani President Zia-ul-Haq, American Ambassador Arnold Raphel, Brigadier General Herbert Wassom, the U.S. defense attaché in Islamabad, and eight Pakistani generals. American sources attributed the crash to engine failure, but most Pakistanis believe it was a result of sabotage, variously blaming the KGB, WAD, or the CIA.

ALIJARIS (ELJARIS). An unpaid reserve of the Afghan army, recruited from the population. All Afghans are potential soldiers, and in case of emergency maliks and chiefs throughout the country are required to levy a specific number of troops from their communities.

ALIM. *See* **ULAMA.**

ALI MASJID. Scene of a battle during the first Anglo-Afghan war, when Lieutenant Colonel Wade proceeded from Jamrud through the Khaibar Pass and captured the town on July 27, 1839. He encountered determined resistance from Afridi forces. With 12 British officers in his force of levies, he set up fortified perimeter camps and successfully picketed the heights to ensure success. His losses were 180 killed and wounded. A small British post remained at the village. In October 1839 Khaibar tribesmen who invested Ali Masjid were bought off with the promise of an annual subsidy. In April 1842 Ali Masjid was again in the hands of the Zakka Khel Afridis and had to be recaptured by General Pollock at the cost of 135 killed and wounded. On November 21 (the second Afghan war), British forces under Sir Sam J. Browne (q.v.) failed in an attack on Ali Masjid with a force of 7,800 troops with 26 guns. The town was held by 3,500 Afghan regulars and 600 khasadars with 24 guns. A failure of coordination prevented a concerted frontal attack with a turning movement from the northeast. A battery had to be withdrawn when its ammunition was exhausted. This had a bad effect on the infantry. One portion of the force attacked prematurely without the support of other units. British casualties were 22 killed and 34 wounded. At daybreak on November 22, the main force prepared for attack only to discover that the Afghan position had been evacuated during the night.

AMANULLAH, KING (AMAN ALLAH, called GHAZI). King of
Afghanistan, 1919–29. Born in 1892, the son of Amir Habibullah and
Sarwar Sultanah, the *Ulya Hazrat* (queen). When Amir Habibullah was
assassinated in Jalalabad in February 1919, Amanullah Khan was
governor of Kabul and in possession of the arsenal and the treasury. He
was crowned in Kabul over the prior claims of his uncle Nasrullah,
whom he denounced as a usurper and an accomplice in the murder of
his father. King Amanullah (he assumed the title of king in 1926) was
an ardent reformer and contemporary of like-minded rulers, Muhammad
Reza in Iran and Kemal Ataturk in Turkey. He demanded a revision of
the Anglo-Afghan agreements concluded by Amir Abdur Rahman,
which left Britain in charge of Afghanistan's foreign relations in
exchange for protection from unprovoked Russian aggression and a
subsidy in money and military materiel (*see* AFGHAN FOREIGN
RELATIONS). British reluctance to accept a change in the status quo
led to Afghan armed attacks, culminating in the start of the third
Anglo-Afghan war on May 3, 1919. Britain was war-weary and in no
condition to wage war on the Indian frontier, and, after lengthy
negotiations in Rawalpindi, Mussoorie, and Kabul, peace was restored,
leaving Afghanistan free and independent from British control. (*See*
THIRD ANGLO-AFGHAN WAR; ANGLO-AFGHAN TREATY,
1919; 1921; and AFGHAN FOREIGN RELATIONS.) King Amanullah
became a national hero and turned his attention to reforming and
modernizing his country. He established diplomatic and commercial
relations with major European and Asian states, founded schools in
which French, German, and English were the major languages of
education, and promulgated a constitution that was to guarantee the
personal freedom and equal rights of all Afghans.

He built a new capital, named Darulaman (*Dar al-Aman* — Abode of
Peace), which included a monumental parliament and other government
buildings as well as villas of prominent Afghans. Social reforms
included a new dress code, which permitted women in Kabul to go unveiled and encouraged officials to wear Western dress. Modernization
proved costly for Afghanistan and was resented by the traditional
elements of Afghan society. The Khost Rebellion (q.v.), a tribal revolt
in 1924, was suppressed and Amanullah felt secure enough to travel to
Europe in December 1927. Upon his return he faced increasing
opposition, and, in 1928, an uprising of Shinwari tribesmen, followed
by attacks of the Kohdamani and Kuhistani forces of Habibullah Kalakani (q.v.), forced the reformer king into exile. After an unsuccessful

attempt at regaining the throne, he crossed the Indian border on May 23, 1929 and settled in Italy and Switzerland until his death on April 26, 1960. He was buried in Jalalabad at the side of the tomb of Amir Habibullah.

AMBALA CONFERENCE. A meeting in March 1869 between Amir Shir Ali and Lord Mayo, the viceroy of India, in which the amir sought an alliance with Britain. Shir Ali had recaptured the Kabul throne and had consolidated his power to the extent that he felt secure to accept an invitation by Lord Mayo's predecessor to visit the viceroy at Ambala, a town about 200 miles north of Delhi. Shir Ali was alarmed by the fact that Russian influence had reached Afghanistan's northern boundaries when the Amirate of Buchara became a tsarist protectorate. The Afghan ruler wanted a promise of British help in case of Russian aggression, support against domestic rivals, and British recognition of his dynasty and of his son, Abdullah Jan, as his immediate successor. Mayo assured the Afghan ruler of his government's sympathies, but refused to give any specific promises. As a sign of its friendship, the Indian government presented the amir with 600,000 rupees, 6,500 muskets, four 18-pounder siege guns, two 8-inch howitzers, and a mountain battery of six 3-pounder guns. But when an uninvited Russian mission under Major General Stolietoff managed to reached Kabul in the summer of 1878, a British army invaded Afghanistan on November 21, 1878. *See* SECOND ANGLO-AFGHAN WAR.

AMBUSH. A surprise attack used by Afghan forces with great success in their wars against foreign invaders. The Afghans knew the terrain, passes, valleys, and routes an invader or his supplies had to traverse. During the wars with British forces, isolated posts and convoys bringing supplies from India were the choice targets of ambushes. British and Soviet forces also resorted to this method but with relatively little success, because the Afghans usually were well informed of the enemy's movements by local villagers. McMichael (1991) quotes the *mujahedin* commander, Abdul Haq:

> In order to discourage the enemy, we simply ambush the ambushers. With reliable advance information about the time and place of the ambush we took position before the arrival of the enemy. We carried out five operations of this kind, and each time we killed 10 to 15 Russians, all the elite commandos whom the Russians were not very eager to lose, and our action produced its expected results.

AMIN, HAFIZULLAH. Born 1929 in Paghman, Kabul Province. President of the Democratic Republic of Afghanistan from September 1979 until his assassination on December 27, 1979. He was a member of the Kharoti (Ghilzai Pashtun) tribe, whose family came to Paghman in the nineteenth century. Educated in Afghanistan and the United States, where he was known as a Pashtun nationalist, he became a teacher and later principal of Ibn Sina and Teachers Training schools in Kabul. His conversion to Marxism is said to have occurred in 1964. He was elected to the thirteenth session of Parliament (1969) as a representative of Paghman. During the republican period (1973–78), he successfully recruited followers in the army in competition with Parchami efforts. After the Saur Revolt he was appointed vice premier and minister of foreign affairs. In April 1979 he became prime minister and, after he ousted Nur Muhammad Taraki, he became president on September 16, 1979. He was at odds with Alexandr Puzanov (q.v.), the Soviet ambassador at Kabul, and successfully demanded his recall. Some observers called him the Afghan "Tito" because of his independence and nationalistic inclinations. He was accused of responsibility for the assassination of thousands. Soviet special forces attacked him and his bodyguard in Darulaman, assassinating him on December 27, 1979.

AMIR. Commander, also nobleman, prince, ruler, chief (from A. *amara*, to command). Caliph Omar (634–44) first assumed the title *Amir al-Mu'minin* (Commander of the Believers). In Afghanistan the Sadozai rulers carried the title "king" (*shah*), but the Muhammadzai rulers from 1826 assumed the title "amir" until Amanullah Khan adopted the title of king in 1926. Among some *mujahedin* groups, an amir is a commander with civil and military powers.

AMU DARIA (34-40' N, 59-1' E, DARYA). A river, called Oxus by the ancient Greeks, which forms for about 280 miles the boundary between the former Soviet Union and Afghanistan. Its easternmost sources are the Ab-e Wakhan and the Ab-i Pamir, which rise in the Little Pamir Mountains and run into the Ab-e Panj near the village of Qal'a-ye Panjeh. It is fed by the Kukcha, and further west, the Kunduz Rivers, at which point it is called the Amu Daria. It then flows in a northwesterly direction to run into the Aral Sea. It is navigable only in parts, although its length from the farthest source to the mouth of the Aral Sea extends some 1,500 miles. A bridge near Hairatan, completed in 1982, links the Afghan highway from Mazar-i Sharif with the Soviet rail terminal at Termez. Another bridge was constructed at Sherkhan/Qala Kutarma in Kunduz Province. The bridges became vital links for the supply of Soviet and Afghan forces in Afghanistan.

ANGLO-AFGHAN TREATY OF 1809. *See* **ELPHINSTONE, MOUNTSTUART.**

ANGLO-AFGHAN TREATY OF 1905. Renewal in form of a treaty of agreements signed between Amir Abdur Rahman and Sir Lepel Griffin, chief political officer in Afghanistan, in June and July 1880. At the death of Amir Abdur Rahman on October 3, 1901, the British Indian government insisted that the agreements with the amir were personal and therefore subject to renegotiation with his successor. The government of India sought modifications and concessions, including a more "liberal commercial policy" on the part of Afghanistan, delimitation of the Mohmand border (between Afghanistan and India), and noninterference by Afghanistan in the politics of the transborder (Indian) tribes. Britain exerted great pressure, stopping subsidy payments and prohibiting Afghan imports of arms, but Amir Habibullah did not yield. He invited Louis W. Dane of the Indian Foreign Department to Kabul, and, after three months of negotiations, the "Independent King of Afghanistan and its Dependencies" and Louis W. Dane, "Foreign Secretary of the Mighty Government of India," signed the treaty at Kabul on March 21, 1905. For Amir Habibullah this was a great victory: none of the British objectives was won, the arrears in subsidy were paid, and Britain affirmed that it would not interfere in the internal affairs of Afghanistan. This treaty remained in force until it was repudiated by Amir Amanullah in 1919.

ANGLO-AFGHAN TREATY OF 1919. Peace treaty between the British and the Afghan governments after the third Anglo-Afghan war. It was negotiated at Rawalpindi and signed on August 8, 1919 by A. H. Grant, foreign secretary of the government of India, and Ali Ahmad Khan, Afghan commissary for home affairs. The treaty made a return to the "old friendship" between the two states contingent on negotiations started after a six-month waiting period. In the meantime Britain would not permit Afghanistan to import arms and ammunition through India, the payment of a subsidy would be ended, and the arrears in payments would be confiscated. Finally, a British commission was to demarcate undefined portions of the Khaibar, and Afghanistan was to accept the Indo-Afghan frontier as marked. An annexure stated that "the said Treaty and this letter leave Afghanistan officially free and independent in its internal and external affairs." British hopes that a contrite amir would again conclude an exclusive alliance were soon seen to be unrealistic. Amir Amanullah sent a mission to the Soviet Union, Europe, and the United States and acted on his right to establish diplomatic relations with foreign powers. The Pashtun tribes on the Indian side of the frontier were made to believe that the treaty represented only a cease-fire, after which war was to be resumed if Britain did not agree to various Afghan demands. Indeed, it was only after a fruitless, three-month conference at Mussoorie (q.v.) (April 17–July 18, 1920) and the Kabul Conference (*see* treaty below) that normal neighborly relations between Britain and Afghanistan were established.

ANGLO-AFGHAN TREATY OF 1921. Also called "Treaty of Kabul" because Henry R. C. Dobbs, the British envoy, and Mahmud Tarzi, chief of the Afghan delegation, negotiated and signed it after arduous, 11-month negotiations. The treaty restored "friendly and commercial relations" between the two governments after the third Anglo-Afghan war as well as negotiations at the Mussoorie Conference (q.v.) and Rawalpindi. The negotiations proceeded in four phases: During the first session, January 20 to April 9, 1921, the Afghan amir unsuccessfully demanded territorial concessions, while Britain wanted the exclusion of Russian consular offices from southeastern Afghanistan. In the second phase, from April 9 to mid-July 1921, Britain asked Afghanistan to break the newly established diplomatic relations with Russia in exchange for a subsidy of 4 million rupees and weapons, as well as guarantees from unprovoked Russian aggression. During the third stage, from mid-July to September 18, when the British foreign office informed the Italian government that it was about to conclude an agreement that would "admit the superior and predominant political influence of Britain" in Afghanistan, the Afghans refused to accept an "alliance." An exclusive treaty was impossible after Afghanistan announced ratification of the Russo-Afghan Treaty of 1921 (*see* SOVIET AFGHAN RELATIONS). In the fourth and final stage of negotiations, from September 18 to December 8, 1921, the British mission twice made preparations to return to India, when finally an agreement was signed at Kabul on November 22, 1921. Ratifications were exchanged on February 6, 1922.

The treaty stipulated that both governments "mutually certify and respect each with regard to the other all rights of internal and external independence." Afghanistan reaffirmed its acceptance of the boundary west of the Khaibar, subject to minor "realignment." Legations were to be opened in London and Kabul, consulates established in various Indian and Afghan towns, and Afghanistan was permitted to import arms and munitions through India. No customs duties were to be charged for goods in transit to Afghanistan, and each party agreed to inform the other of major military operations in the frontier belt. Representatives of both states were to meet in the near future to discuss the conclusion of a trade convention, which was signed in June 1923.

ANGLO-AFGHAN WARS. *See* **FIRST, SECOND, AND THIRD ANGLO-AFGHAN WAR.**

ANGLO-RUSSIAN CONVENTION OF 1907. An agreement between Great Britain and Russia concluded on August 31, 1907, which was to "ensure perfect security on their respective frontiers in Central Asia and to maintain in these regions a solid and lasting peace." It divided Iran into spheres of influence between the two powers, permitted Russia to have direct relations of a nonpolitical nature with local Afghan officials in northern Afghanistan, and provided for equal access to "commercial opportunity." Tibet was to be under Chinese sovereignty, but the British were free to deal with Tibetans in commercial matters while Russian Buddhists could deal with the Dalai Lama on religious matters. Although Britain was to continue its treaty obligation of 1905 to protect Afghanistan from unprovoked Russian aggression, and Russia declared Afghanistan outside her sphere of influence, Amir Habibullah saw this agreement as an attempt to solve the "Afghanistan Question" over his head. Amir Habibullah was on a state visit to India in January 1907 when Britain and Russia negotiated the treaty, but he was not informed of the convention until September 10, 1907. He was shocked and felt betrayed by the British, and when he was requested to agree to the convention, he took a year with his reply, refusing to ratify the agreement. Russia never obtained the expected commercial and political benefits, and the Bolshevik government repudiated the convention in 1918 in an attempt to win the goodwill of its Asian neighbors. As far as Afghanistan was concerned, the convention was a "dead letter" from the beginning.

ARG Or **ARK**. A citadel within a walled city, traditionally the residence of a ruler. After the Bala Hisar (q.v.) was destroyed by British forces in 1879, Amir Abdur Rahman built the new Arg, located in the center of Kabul. It took five years to build and housed in addition to the amir and his court the major government buildings. It was surrounded by a moat and a 50-foot wall. Later additions and modifications radically changed the original plan when modern buildings replaced the early residences. In the *Salam Khana* (Audience Hall) the affairs of government were conducted. The *Del Kusha* (Heart's Delight) Palace was added by Amir Habibullah, and the Gul Khana Palace was built to be the royal office of King Amanullah. After the coup by Muhammad Daud in July 1973, the president's office was established in the Arg. During the *Khalqi* period (1978–79), Nur Muhammad Taraki (q.v.) moved in and the Arg was renamed the "House of the People" (*Khana-yi Khalq*). In December 1979 Hafizullah Amin left the Arg and established himself in the Tapa Taj Beg Palace in Darulaman, where he was assassinated purportedly by Soviet troops. After the capture of Kabul in April 1992, the Arg became the residence of the president of the Afghan Interim Government, but in the subsequent battle for supremacy, the contending powers destroyed much of the Arg.

ARMS BAZAARS, AFGHAN. As a landlocked country, Afghanistan depended for its weapons' supply on foreign imports, smuggled and captured arms, and, to a limited extent, on local manufacture. Since most supplies had to enter Afghanistan by way of India, Britain had a monopoly on the sale of weapons and tried to control the supply and quality. Amir Abdur Rahman founded the *mashin-khana* factory, where guns and ammunition were produced. In addition, numerous workshops existed on the Afghan frontier, where guns of all types were manufactured. Because of a lack of electricity, machinery was operated by human or animal power. The tradition of arms manufacture and sales in specialized communities exists to this day. One major weapons bazaar exists in Darra on the Pakistani side of the border and is probably the largest open arms market in the world. In about one hundred shops, one can buy anything from rifles to mortars, and the price of an AK-47 in 1980 was $1500 which in 1987 was reduced to $750 (Yousaf 1992, 135) and in 1994, to $100 in Kabul. The influx of captured Soviet weapons and arms supplied by the supporters of the *mujahedin* produced quite a glut on the market. Even stinger missiles (q.v.), supplied by the United States to the *mujahedin*, were sold to the highest bidder.

ARMY, AFGHAN. Afghanistan's army evolved from its traditional beginnings under Ahmad Shah (*see* AHMAD SHAH, MILITARY ADMINISTRATION) to a process of gradual modernization throughout the nineteenth and first half of the twentieth century. First efforts at modernization began during the reigns of Amir Dost Muhammad (1826–38 and 1842–63), who mustered a standing army of 15,000 and 45 guns that was gradually increased. Shir Ali Khan (1863–79), after visiting India in 1869, adopted Indian titles: *briget* (brigadier), *karnel* (colonel), *kaptan* (captain), *subedar, havildar,* and so forth. Both lacked the type of modern weapons being employed by Afghanistan's neighbors and the nucleus of a modern officers' corps. Officers were appointed on the basis of loyalty rather than skill, and any Afghan who could ride a horse or carry a gun was considered fit regardless of age. Military skills were passed on from father to son, one cannoneer of advanced age had to be carried along on a stretcher to perform his functions. Western military technology came to Afghanistan by means of prisoners of war or foreign mercenaries. One such person, William Campbell (q.v.), alias Shir Muhammad Khan, became commander in chief of the Turkestan army. In the 1830s the composition of the Afghan army was described as "Pathan, Hindus, Kuzzelbashes, and a few deserters from the Sikh army." Muslims from neighboring countries joined the Afghan forces, including Indian officers of the "Great Sepoy Mutiny" of 1857–58. The reorganized army included a cavalry force of about 15,000 men, divided into two divisions headed by Amir Dost Muhammad's sons. A specially trained infantry force of about 2,000 men was armed with large muskets, and an artillery branch disposed of 50 to 60 serviceable guns. European-type uniforms were first used (Gregorian, 76). Military pay was partially in cash and in kind, but usually in arrears. Recruitment was often by seizure of able-bodied men, a practice not exclusive to Afghanistan at the time. There also existed a militia of *jezailchis* (riflemen) and feudal irregular forces. A British military mission headed by Major H. B. Lumsden is said to have contributed advice about the modernization of the Afghan army. Amir Shir Ali continued the modernization process. He obtained a number of artillery pieces and some 5,000 Snider rifles in 1875, but the ensuing civil war in Afghanistan postponed major military reforms to the time of Amir Abdur Rahman.

The "Iron Amir" spent most of his subsidy from the British-Indian government on the purchase of arms, and he expanded the local production of weapons. (*See also* INTRODUCTION, 12)

The first attempt to create a modern officers' corps was made in 1904 when Amir Habibullah (1901–19) founded the Royal Military College. By 1910 it enrolled 80 cadets, mostly the sons of Durrani chiefs, who studied, in addition to Islamic topics, arithmetic, geometry, and military logistics and underwent rigorous physical training and drills. In 1907 a Turkish officer, Mahmud Sami, was put in charge of the college, marking the beginning of Turkish influence in the Afghan army.

King Amanullah (1919–1929) neglected the army at the cost of his throne. He saw his as an "era of the pen — not of the sword" and devoted his resources to the modernization of his country. Turkish advisers were still prominent in the army, including Jemal Pasha, one of the triumvirate rulers of the Ottoman War government. Germans, the teachers of the Turks, were also employed as were members of various other nationalities. The nucleus of an Afghan air force was created in the 1920s, in which experts from the Soviet Union participated. *See* AIR FORCE, AFGHAN.

King Amanullah's army was about 50,000 strong, comprising an infantry of about 38,000 men divided into 78 battalions armed with Martini-Henri and Snider rifles; a cavalry of about 8,000 sabres divided into 21 units, and about 4,000 artillerymen employing some 260 breach-loading guns, mainly German Krupp 75mm and 7-pounders. (O'Ballance, 55) An arsenal at Kabul held 15,000 small-bore rifles, 400,000 Martinis, and a few old machine guns. Heliography had still not replaced telegraph communications.

Nadir Khan, as commander in chief, established six army corps headquartered at Kabul (2), Jalalabad, Matun, Herat, and Mazar-i Sharif. Kandahar was added and all were headquarters of principal formation. In practice, many corps were severely undermanned.

Nadir Shah took power with tribesmen and reconstituted the army in 1930. He faced many insurrections: 1) the Koh Daman revolt (Nov. 29–June 30); 2) the Shinwari Rebellion (Feb. 1930); 3) the Operations against Ibrahim Bey (Nov. 1930–Apr. 1931); 4) the Ghilzai threat (1931); 5) the Darre Khel revolt (Nov. 1932); 6) the Khost disturbances.

Schools for cavalry, artillery, and infantry were established. German, Italian, and Turkish officers were employed. Pay was increased, and there were improvements in clothing and accommodation by 1933.

Under Zahir Shah, a striking improvement occurred. In 1936 the army was about 60,000 strong. It played an important role in internal security, and although regularly paid and housed in better barracks, it was still inferior to British-Indian standards.

Organization in peace: Two corps Kabul; Southern Province three divisions. One division Household troops (Guards Div); one artillery division; and two independent mixed divisions. Total – 13 divisions and one artillery division. (MR)

King Muhammad Zaher (1933–1973) realized that for domestic stability and defense against foreign aggression he needed a strong, modern army. His uncle, Shah Mahmud, minister of war and commander in chief of the army until 1946, embarked on a project of military reorganization. He purchased weapons from Germany, Britain, Italy, and Czechoslovakia as well as airplanes and tanks. He also created the first mechanized forces. Additional officers' schools were established in Maimana, Mazar-i Sharif, and those in Kabul and Herat were expanded. Afghan officers were sent abroad for additional training, and Turkish officers replaced European advisers at the advent of World War II. A combination of compulsory and voluntary enlistment increased the Afghan army from 70,000 men in 1934 to 80,000 in 1936. About 50 percent of Afghanistan's revenue of 150 million afghanis was devoted to military expenditures. (Gregorian, 371)

After World War II, the Afghan army had reached its traditional size of about 90,000 men, but its weapons and equipment were largely obsolete. The Afghan prime minister, Shah Mahmud, envisaged a "small but well-trained internal security force," reducing the size of the army by half and expanding a central police force to 20,000 men. (Bradsher 1983, 18) Formal requests for arms purchases from the United States were repeatedly rebuffed; therefore in early 1955 Prime Minister Muhammad Daud turned to the Soviet Union for help. The Pashtunistan dispute with Pakistan, a member of the Baghdad Pact and unofficial ally of the United States, was one of the reasons for the growing influence of the Soviet Union in Afghanistan's army. In July 1956 the Soviet Union granted a loan of $32.4 million in military assistance, which greatly helped to modernize the Afghan army. But Afghanistan became dependent on Soviet expertise and supplies, and some 3,725 Afghan military personnel went to the Soviet Union for training. On the eve of the Marxist coup in 1978, the Afghan army included all branches of infantry divisions, mechanized, paratroop, commando, and artillery brigades. Equipment included a sizable tank force and an air force of some 140–170 fighter planes and 45 to 60 helicopters. (*See* INTRODUCTION, 19, and AIR FORCE, AFGHAN.) Following the Soviet intervention, a Status of Armed Forces Agreement was signed in April 1980, which legalized the presence of the Limited Contingent of Soviet Forces in Afghanistan (q.v.).

ARMY OF THE INDUS. The British-Indian army and Shah Shuja's forces that invaded Afghanistan during the first Anglo-Afghan war totaled some 39,000 men. It was composed of three sources, the Bengal army, the Bombay army, and the army of Shah Shuja, most of whose men were transfers from the East India Company's troops. The Bengal army consisted of the British 16th Dragoons (Lancers), the 13th Foot (Light Infantry), one regiment of Bengal European infantry, two of Light Cavalry, two of Local Horse, and seven of Native Infantry. They were complemented with one troop of all-European horse artillery and two all-Indian companies of sappers and miners. From the Bombay army came the 4th Light Dragoons and the 4th and 17th Regiments of Foot (all from British service), one regiment of Light Cavalry and one of Local Horse, two troops of horse artillery, two companies of foot artillery (all European), four regiments of Native Infantry and one company of sappers and miners.

The British infantry, engineers, and heavy cavalry wore red coats; the Light Cavalry and artillery wore blue coats. The Indian sepoys in the infantry wore red uniforms, and the cavalry gray, whereas the irregular troops did not wear uniforms. Most were equipped with flintlock muskets. (O'Ballance, 10)

Shah Shuja's forces included two regiments of cavalry, four regiments of infantry, and a troop of horse artillery. Two additional infantry regiments were recruited later. Altogether his forces comprised 6,000 men. Shah Shuja's son Timur commanded a force of 6,000 Sikhs and 4,000 of Shah Shuja's men who invaded Afghanistan from Peshawar.

Because of the lack of roads fit for wheeled traffic, the Army of the Indus depended on animal transport. Some 60,000 Indian and several thousand Afghan camels were employed, as well as hundreds of bullock carts and a number of baggage elephants. The invasion proceeded without great difficulty. The British forces reached the Kandahar area on April 14, 1839, and on April 25, Shah Shuja entered the city to popular acclaim. Sir John Keane (q.v.), the commander in chief, departed from Kandahar on June 27, 1839 and moved against Ghazni, and on July 23, he succeeded in capturing the city after blowing in the Kabul Gate (*see* GHAZNI, CAPTURE OF). The British army took Kabul in the face of little opposition, and on August 7, Shah Shuja formally entered the city. In September the Bombay Division returned to India, and a month later parts of the Bengal Division left. Most of the remaining troops and camp followers did not survive the invasion. *See* DEATH MARCH; and ANGLO-AFGHAN WARS.

ARMY RANKS. In the late 1920s, army ranks were as follows:

Wazir-i Harbiya	Minister of War
Arkan:	General Officers:
Sipah Salar	Commander in Chief
Na'eb Salar	General
Firqa Mishar	Divisional Commander
Amiran:	
Ghund Mishar	Regimental Commander
Kandak Mishar	Divisional Commander
Zabitan:	Junior Commissioned Officers
Katib-i Ghund	Regimental Head Clerk
Toli Mishar	Company or Squadron Commander
Katib-i Kandak	Battalion Head Clerk
Boluk Mishar	Platoon or Troop Commander
Khurd Zabetan:	
Sarparak Mishar	Sergeant Major
Katib-i Toli	Company Clerk
Parak Mishar	Sergeant
Salahandar:	Riflemen
Dalgai Mishar	Corporal
Sepoy	Private (HBAA, 1927)

AUCKLAND, LORD. Governor General of India (1837–42), who in defiance of the Court of Directors of the East India Company, started the disastrous first Anglo-Afghan war to replace Amir Dost Muhammad with Shah Shuja.

He subsequently wrote to the court of directors that "the increase of Russian and Persian influence in Affghanistan, and the impression of the certain fall of Herat to the Persian army, have induced the Ameer Dost

Mahomed Khan tro avow and to insist upon pretensions for the cession to him, by Maharajah Runjeet Sing, of the Peshwur territory, and to take other steps which are tantamount to the rejection of the friendship and good offices of the British Government; and have in consequence led to the retirement of Captain Burnes from the territories of Cabool."

"The emergency of affairs may compel me to act without awaiting any intimation of your views upon the events which have recently occurred in Persia and Affghanistan." (Auckland to Secret Committe of the decraration of war.

Initially, it was decided to give a major role in the task of restoring Shah Shuja to the Kabul throne to Ranjit Singh and his army, but the Sikh ruler was not eager and Auckland subsequently felt that he could not be trusted to carry it out successfully. Therefore, the British "Army of the Indus" (q.v.) was to do the job. Early successes in the war led to his being created Earl of Auckland in 1839. Following the debacle, Auckland was denounced and recalled. *See* FIRST ANGLO-AF-GHAN WAR.

AYUB KHAN, MUHAMMAD (AYYUB). Son of Amir Shir Ali and full brother of Yaqub Khan (q.v.). At the death of his father, Yaqub Khan was crowned King at Kabul, and Ayub took over the governorship of Herat. When he learned of the British occupation of Kabul, he incited the Afghan *sardars* to rise and expel the invaders. In June 1880 the *ulama* at Herat proclaimed him amir and he had coins struck in his name as a sign of his sovereignty. He then marched his army against Kandahar and on July 27, 1880, he met General Burrows at Maiwand and virtually wiped out his forces. (*See* MAIWAND, BATTLE OF.) Ayub then proceeded to Kandahar and laid siege to the city, but General Roberts came to the rescue and he was forced to retreat to his base at Herat. He again moved on Kandahar in June 1881, at a time when Britain had recognized Abdur Rahman as amir of Kabul. The Iron Amir easily defeated Ayub's forces at Kandahar in September 1881 and at the same time dispatched his general, Abdul Quddus Khan (q.v.), to capture the lightly garrisoned city of Herat. Being deprived of his base, Ayub was forced to flee to Iran, and after a number of years accepted asylum in India for himself and his retinue of 814 individuals.

- B -

BABA WALI KOTAL, BATTLE OF (31-40' N, 65-40' E). A village and pass, named after a holy man whose tomb is located about 3 1/2 miles northwest of Kandahar. It had been the scene of battles during the first and second Anglo-Afghan wars. On March 25, 1842, a portion of the Kandahar force under Colonel Wymer (q.v.) met an Afghan contingent headed by Shahzada Saftar Jang and defeated the Afghans with only three killed and 39 wounded. Two months later, on May 29, 1842, Akhtar Khan's forces were attacked by General Nott (q.v.) and driven with great loss through the pass and over the Arghandab River. In August 1880, after defeating General Burrows at the Battle of Maiwand (q.v.), Sardar Ayub Khan stationed his forces at the pass and opened artillery fire on Kandahar. And on September 1 General Roberts dispatched his Bombay Division and the 72nd Highlanders to capture the village of Pir Paimal and, after turning the right flank of the Afghans, threatened the Afghan position in the rear. The *ghazis* made a determined stand, but a charge of the 92nd Highlanders with support of the 2nd Gurkhas and 23rd Pioneers carried the position. The 3rd Sikhs carried the Afghan position by storm, and the British forces captured Ayub Khan's camp and artillery. British cavalry put 350 *jehadis* (holy warriors) to the sword and buried 600 Afghans and estimated another 600 dead carried off by the Afghans. According to General Roberts, British losses amounted to 40 killed and 228 wounded. (Heathcote, 162)

BACHA-I SAQQAU. *See* **HABIBULLAH KALAKANI**.

BAGH, BATTLE OF. A village on the British side of the Durand Line and the scene of two battles during the third Anglo-Afghan war. It was occupied by Afghan troops on May 4, 1919, as a move to cut off the water supply to Landi Kotal. On May 8, British forces, including five battalions of infantry, two batteries of guns, a machine-gun company, a company of sappers, and two troops of lancers moved on Landi Kotal. Brigadier General G. D. Crocker (q.v.) ordered an attack to drive the Afghan forces from Bagh. The Afghans easily held their ground, and the British forces (the 1/15th Sikhs and the 1/11 Gurka Rifles) had to dig in to establish a defensive position. In the words of one historian, "The First Battle of Bagh, did little to convince the wavering tribes of the overwhelming might of the British." (Heathcote, 180) British airmen (and later, Soviet pilots elsewhere) suffered the unusual experience of being shot at by rifle fire from the crests of the flanking mountains. With considerable reinforcements the 1st Division, commanded by Major General Fowler, again attacked Bagh on May 11 with six battalions, covered by the fire of 18 pieces of artillery and 22 machine guns. He had another battalion covering his flank and three in reserve. Under the cover of darkness and after careful preparation, assault units moved up the steep foothills and, backed by covering fire, reached the Afghan *sangars* (stone barriers) and engaged the Afghans in hand-to-hand combat. Having protected their flanks, the British forces could advance and capture the village of Bagh. The British lost eight killed and 32 wounded and buried 65 Afghan soldiers. British estimates of Afghan casualties amounted to 100 killed and 300 wounded.

BAGH-I BALA. A garden in Kabul, near the present Intercontinental Hotel, where Amir Abdur Rahman's palace is located. After his death, the garden and building were closed and fell into neglect. Because of its strategic location on top of a hill overlooking the city, it has become an important command post during wars. Habibullah Kalakani (q.v.) made it his base in the 1929 civil war, it was a government post during the Soviet occupation, and has become a valued outpost during the present civil war of the *mujahedin* groups.

BAGRAM (BEGRAM) (34-58' N, 69-17' E). Site of an ancient city with an abundance of Buddhist, Graeco-Roman, and Phoenician artifacts. According to some sources, it is the site of *Alexandria ad Caucasum* (Alexandria by the Caucasus, built by Alexander the Great in 330–329 B.C.), which flourished for centuries until it was destroyed by the hordes of Genghis Khan in the thirteenth century. The town is north of Kabul near the confluence of the Panjshir and Ghorband Rivers, about five miles west of Charikar. Bagram is now a small town, the center of the district of the same name in Parwan Province. It is the location of an air base built with Soviet assistance in the 1950s. On July 7, 1979 the first Soviet paratroop battalion deployed there, apparently in preparation for its occupation in December 1979, when one regiment of the 105th Guards Airborne Division landed. Bagram became a primary regional center for independent air regiments as a base for the protection of Kabul and the Salang Pass. Although well fortified, Bagram air base was frequently attacked. On June 3, 1985 *mujahedin* forces under Commander Abdul Karim led an attack in which he allegedly destroyed 60 to 70 aircraft and killed scores of Soviet soldiers. After the *mujahedin* capture of Kabul, Bagram became an important base of Rabbani's government.

BALA HISAR. A citadel within a walled town usually on the crest of a mountain or hill, serving as the residence of an Afghan ruler or governor. The Bala Hisar of Kabul is a huge complex built southwest of the ancient wall on Sher Darwaza Mountain. Until the nineteenth century its high stone walls surrounded a strong citadel that was the residence of the Kabul ruler and his court. Babur Shah and Timur-i Lang are said to have resided in it. High military and civilian officials were quartered within the outer walls. In the first Anglo-Afghan war, the British forces built their defenses around a rectangular cantonment in the valley below, instead of seeking the security of the Bala Hisar. This turned out to be a fatal mistake. The six-century-old fortress was destroyed on order of the British general Roberts after an explosion on October 16, 1879 in the arsenal killed a British officer and a number of soldiers of his Gurka unit. The fortress lay in ruins until Nadir Shah in the early 1930s started the process of reconstruction. It has served as a military college and garrison since 1939. On August 5, 1979 an army regiment at the Bala Hisar revolted against the *Khalqi* regime, and it took a four-hour battle in which MI-24 gunships and considerable heavy artillery were employed before the revolt was suppressed. Subsequently, the fortress was able to withstand *mujahedin* attacks and fell into their hands only with the capture of Kabul. In the present civil war the Bala Hisar of Kabul was occupied by the Uzbek forces of Dostum (q.v.), who was in turn expelled by the forces of Rabbani (q.v.). Aeriel warfare and modern weapons technology have made fortresses of this type obsolete.

BARRETT, GEN. SIR ARTHUR. 1857–1926. Commanded North-West Frontier Force in the third Anglo-Afghan war. Previously served in the second Afghan war and participated at the Battle of Kandahar.

BASMACHIS. An irregular force, called *basmachis* (T. bandits) by the Soviet government, that fought the Red Army in the mountains of Tajikistan and Ferghana in Central Asia from 1919 until the 1930s. Their leaders included Muhammad Amin Beg, Ibrahim Beg (q.v.), and Enver Pasha (q.v.), the Ottoman minister of war during the First World War. King Amanullah supported their efforts for some time in the hope of ruling over a confederation of Central Asian states, but when it threatened relations with the Soviet Union, he abandoned that hope. During the Soviet occupation of Afghanistan, the Soviets called the *mujahedin basmachi* or *dushman* (D. enemy). *See also* IBRAHIM BEG.

BEHESHTI, SAYYID ALI. President of the Revolutionary Council of the Islamic Union of Afghanistan (Shura-yi Inqelabi-yi Ittifaq-i Islami-yi Hazarajat), which until 1982 controlled large portions of the Hazarajat. He is a native of Bamian and was educated in Saudi Arabia and Iraq, where he was a contemporary of Ayatollah Khomeini. He opened a *madrasa* in Waras to spread his revivalist ideas among Hazaras and was speaker in the Takkia Khana at Kabul until the Marxist coup. In September 1979 he was elected president of the *shura* by a council of elders and *Mirs*. Formed a traditional Islamic resistance group, commanded by Sayyid Muhammad Hasan "Jagran" (Major), with headquarters in Waras in Ghor Province and became a major force in the Hazarajat until the Shura lost ground to the Islamist forces of *Nasr*. The Shura recruited its fighters from the Hazara peasantry, led by sayyids (*Sadat*), and had commanders in Bamian, Ghor, Nimruz, Uruzgan, and Wardak provinces.

BIDDULPH, LT. GEN. SIR M.A.S. Commanded the Quetta Division, Kandahar Field Force and the Thal-Chotiali Field Force from formation to their breakup during the second Anglo-Afghan war. Took part in the original advance on and occupation of Kandahar and Girishk.

BIN-I HISAR (BENI HISSAR). A village, at the foot of a spur of the same name, running down from the Takht-i Shah, which is of great strategic importance, because it lies on the road to Kabul and commands a view of part of the city. Sir Frederick Roberts camped in this area on October 7, 1879 after the battle at Charasia (qq.v.). It was from the Bin-i Hisar spur that the 92nd Highlanders advanced on December 18, 1879, when the Takht-i Shah (q.v.) was carried. In the present civil war for Kabul, the *Taleban* (q.v.) have advanced to Bin-i Hisar, where they are able to bombard the Kabul airport.

BLOCKING TACTICS. An operation aimed at securing the advance of the main force by enveloping or encircling the enemy and threatening his rear and flanks. Called *killaband* by the Afghans, the method was perfected by Ayub Khan and was employed to pin down the British firing line, while the tribal contingents and cavalry moved around the British flanks and threatened the baggage train and logistic elements in the enemy's rear. (Heathcote, 149) Soviet counterinsurgency tactics included the *blokirovka* enveloping formation, achieved by landing heliborne detachments in the rear and flanks of *mujahedin* forces to cut escape routes, and access to supply lines as well as to protect the advancement of heavy infantry or motorized convoys on the ground axis.

BLOWPIPE MISSILE. The *mujahedin* received British Blowpipe missiles in August, 1986. The Blowpipe is an operator-guided missile, rather than heat-seeking, and therefore cannot be diverted by flares from the target. Brigadier Muhammad Yussaf, head of the Afghan Bureau of Pakistan's Inter-Services Intelligence (ISI), which supported the *mujahedin* effort, had a low opinion of the Blowpipe. He called it obsolescent and unable to take targets moving across the firer's front. The firer had to remain standing to aim, fire, and then guide the missile optically on to the target. Half of the missiles would not accept the command signal and would go astray. Yousaf claimed, "I do not recall a single confirmed kill by a Blowpipe." (1992, 88–89) It was the American-made stinger (q.v.) which marked the turning point in the war of the *mujahedin*. Soviet aerial superiority was threatened with this escalation in weaponry.

BOMBERS. The Soviet forces employed the TU-16 Badger medium and SU-24 Fencer all-weather light bombers as well as the modern intermediate-range bomber in its counterinsurgency operations. High-altitude bombing was used in preparation for offensives against *mujahedin*-held bases or for shielding ground troops during engagements. This type of air war became especially important when *mujahedin* missiles made air transport and helicopter support difficult.

BRITISH EAST INDIA COMPANY. *See* **EAST INDIA COMPANY, BRITISH.**

BROWNE, SIR SAMUEL J. (1824-1901). Commanded 1st Division of the Peshawar Valley Field Force from its formation during the second Anglo-Afghan war. In charge of all troops in northern Afghanistan.

Participated in the attack on Ali Masjid, forcing the Khaibar, and on the advance to Dakka, Jalalabad, and Gandomak.

BRYDON, DR. WILLIAM (1811–73). Assistant surgeon with Shah Shuja's contingent of Hindustani Infantry who was the sole survivor to reach Jalalabad on January 13, 1842, after the disastrous retreat that routed the British "Army of the Indus" and camp followers. Later, hostages and other survivors of the British expeditionary force of some 16,000 reached the safety of India. A painting by Elisabeth, Lady Butler, forcefully depicted the wounded physician on a dying pony at the gates of Jalalabad. A powerful reminder of the extraordinary loss to British prestige and fulfillment of a supposed prediction of Akbar Khan (q.v.) that he would annihilate the British army and leave only one man to tell. *See also* DEATH MARCH.

BURNES, ALEXANDER (1805–41). A captain in the Indian army who was sent by Lord Auckland, governor general of the East India Company, to the court of Amir Dost Muhammad in September 1837 for the purpose of concluding an alliance with Britain and establishing peace between the Afghan ruler and Ranjit Singh (q.v.), who had captured Kashmir and occupied Peshawar. Burnes was well received at Kabul, and it appeared that an agreement with the amir was possible; but in spite of Burnes's recommendations Lord Auckland was not willing to make any promises. He recommended that Dost Muhammad waive his claims on Peshawar and make peace with the Sikh ruler. The Afghan amir's correspondence with Russia and the presence of a purported Russian emissary at Kabul, named Vitkevich (q.v.), were India's reasons for starting the first Anglo-Afghan war (q.v.). Burnes returned to Kabul with the invading forces to serve as deputy and presumed successor to Sir William Macnaghten (q.v.), the envoy and minister of the British government at Kabul. A revolt in Kabul resulted in the assassination of Sir Alexander (he had been knighted shortly before) on November 2, 1841 and the British debacle in the war (*see* ANGLO-AFGHAN WARS; and SIR WILLIAM MACNAGHTEN).

BURROWS, BRIG. GEN. G. R. S. Sent to oppose Ayub Khan's army, General Burrows met the Afghan forces on July 27, 1880 near the village of Maiwand and was totally defeated. (*See* MAIWAND, BATTLE OF.)

- C -

CAMELS. The shaggy Bactrian breed of camel was the most important pack animal in Afghanistan. It is shorter and has stronger legs than the Indian camel. During the second Anglo-Afghan war, Indian camels starved, whereas the Afghan hill camel thrived. According to British military reports of 33,632 Sind and 55,979 Panjab camels, 66,000 were lost during the first phase of the war. Later, 39,000 out of 45,853 Panjabi camels were lost, making a total loss of 99,000 camels. (MR, 1925) *See also* TRANSPORT, MILITARY.

CAMPBELL, WILLIAM. A Scotsman, officer in the East India Company service, who fought in the army of Ranjit Singh (q.v.) and during the second Anglo-Afghan war in the service of Shah Shuja. He was wounded and captured by forces of Dost Muhammad and became a military adviser and an artillery instructor in the Afghan army. He eventually converted to Islam, assuming the name Shir Muhammad Khan, and rose to the rank of general and commander in chief of the Turkestan army at Balkh. As a youth, Amir Abdur Rahman learned his military sciences from Campbell and succeeded him at his death in 1866 as commander in chief of the Turkestan army.

CAMP FOLLOWERS. Because of the caste system and the large number of servants English officers kept in India, the Indian army depended on a large number of camp followers "comprising the servants, suttlers, cantiniers, hostlers, water-carriers, snake-charmers, dancers, conjurers, and women." In February 1839, when a Bengal army of 15,000 men left Shikapoor for Afghanistan, it was accompanied by no fewer than 85,000 camp followers. The commander took with him six weeks' food for the entire 100,000, which quickly proved to be inadequate.
As for the perceived needs of British officers, a German visitor to India in the 1850s commented: "I saw a Captain of the Bengal army, on his way to the army of reserve at Ferozepore, with two large wagons drawn by oxen full of geese, fowls, pigeons, wine, sugar, coffee, tea, and numberless tin cases of delicacies, to say nothing of the goats, sheep, and the camels which carried his tents." (Cohen, 1971)

CAPITULATION, TREATY OF. On December 11, 1841 the British forces negotiated a surrender with Afghan chiefs, after it was clear that they were unable to defend themselves from increasing Afghan attacks.

The treaty was signed by Eldred Pottinger, the political agent at Kabul, Major General William Elphinstone, commander of the British forces in Afghanistan, and by Afghan notables, including Muhammad Akbar Khan (qq.v.). It demanded that the British troops speedily quit the territories of Afghanistan and march to India, and not return. Two *sardars* were to accompany the army to Afghanistan's border "so that no one should offer molestation on the road." Six English gentlemen were to remain "as our guests [and] shall be treated with courtesy." They would be permitted to leave when Amir Dost Muhammad returned. The British force at Jalalabad was to proceed to Peshawar before the Kabul army arrived, and the troops at Kandahar and other parts of Afghanistan were to depart. All property belonging to Sardar Dost Muhammad Khan was to be returned. If the Afghans needed assistance against foreign invasion, the British government should help, and all detained Englishmen, including the sick and wounded at Kabul, would be permitted to leave. "All muskets and ordnance stores in the magazine shall, as a token of friendship, be made over to our agents." Affixed to the treaty were the seals of 18 chiefs, including Muhammad Akbar Khan, son of Amir Dost Muhammad. (The text of the treaty differs to some extent from the version given by Lady Sales in her *Journal of the Disaster in Afghanistan*. This may be due to the fact that the treaty was amended several times before the final version was signed.) The treaty was never implemented because none of the parties trusted the other. Sir William Macnaghten was killed by Sardar Akbar Khan after he tried to make a deal with the *sardar's* enemies, and the British refused to surrender all their weapons. The British army started its evacuation of Kabul on January 6, 1842 and was routed on its way to the border. (*See* FIRST ANGLO-AFGHAN WAR; and DEATH MARCH. For the complete text of the treaty, see Sykes, 344–51.)

CAVAGNARI, SIR PIERRE LOUIS (1841-1879). A man of mixed British and French ancestry described variously as having "great charm and ability" and being a man "of overbearing temper, consumed by the thirst for personal distinction." He was signatory for the British government of the Treaty of Gandomak (1879) with Amir Yaqub Khan (qq.v.). As commissioner of Peshawar, he crossed the Afghan border on September 21, 1878 with a small party to prepare the way for a British mission led by Sir Neville Chamberlain (q.v.) to Kabul. The party was stopped at Ali Masjid by the Afghan general, Faiz Muhammad, and the British government made this a *casus belli*. On November 21 an Indian army invaded Afghanistan. Cavagnari was appointed British envoy to the amir's court at Kabul after the conclusion of the second Anglo-Afghan war. He arrived in Kabul in July 1879, but on September 3, mutinous soldiers, joined by Kabuli citizens, attacked the British residence and killed Cavagnari and his staff. The British government feared a debacle similar to the first Anglo-Afghan war and extricated its forces from Afghanistan by recognizing Abdur Rahman Khan (q.v.) as the new amir. It was not until 1922 that a British envoy was again appointed to Kabul. *See also* ANGLO-AFGHAN WARS; and ALI MASJID.

CAVAGNARI, SIR LOUIS, RECEPTION OF. A Kabul telegram of July 26, 1879 reported that the "Embassy entered city this morning, and received a most brilliant reception. Four miles from city Sirdars Abdullah Khan, Herati, and Mullah Shah Mahomed, the foreign minister, with some cavalry and two elephants, met us. We proceeded on the elephants with a large escort of cavalry. . . . Large crowd assembled, and was most orderly and respectful." Cavagnari had an audience with the amir, and a news writer reported "that the general opinion in Kabul is that now that the British Envoy has arrived, the arrears of pay due to the troops will be paid; that compulsory enlistment will be discontinued; and that oppressive taxes on the peasantry and on the trading classes will be considerably reduced." But on August 3 it was reported that the amir contemplated a reduction of the allowance hitherto paid to the Muhammadzai *sardars*. Three days later it was reported that the "Herati troops move around town in a most disorderly manner, and creating some excitement amongst the rabble of the place." To appease them, two Herati regiments were paid, and two regiments were deprived of their ammunition. Eventually, all were paid and their ammunition was taken, but on September 4 the embassy was attacked and all members killed.

In a letter dated September 6, Amir Yaqub lamented to the British government: "Troops, city, and surrounding country have thrown off yoke of allegiance. . . . Workshop and magazines totally gutted: in fact, my kingdom is ruined. After God I look to the Government for aid and advice..." (PP, Col.)

CHAMBERLAIN, SIR NEVILLE BOWLES (1820–1902). Commander in chief of the Madras army, selected by Lord Lytton for "his striking presence and address," to lead a mission to Kabul in September 1878. He was refused passage at Ali Masjid by the Afghan general, Faiz

Muhammad. This "insult" was taken as the *casus belli* for the British invasion of Afghanistan. Chamberlain served with General Nott's force during the first Anglo-Afghan war at Kandahar, Ghazni, Kabul and Istalif, and was wounded many times.

CHARASIA (CHARASIAB) (34-24' N, 69-9' E). A village about 10 miles south of Kabul that was the scene of a battle between Sir Frederick Roberts's "Avenging Army" and Afghan forces under Nek Muhammad, son of Amir Dost Muhammad Khan. Roberts was marching on Kabul on October 6, 1879, when he found the range separating him from the Kabul valley occupied by Afghan troops. Parties of Ghilzais appeared on hills along both flanks of his camp. One historian reported with some exaggeration that General Roberts's army was

> a mere detachment marching against a nation of fighting men plentifully supplied with artillery, no longer shooting laboriously with jezails but carrying arms of precision equal or little inferior to those in the hands of our own soldiery. But the men, Europeans and Easterns, hillmen of Scotland and hillmen from Nepaul, strode along buoyant with confidence and with health, believing their leader in their discipline, in themselves. (Forbes, 192–93)

According to British estimates, no fewer than 13 regiments of the Afghan army, supported with large contingents of irregular fighting men, awaited the Britishers at the Sang-i Nawishta Pass. Roberts sent General Baker with 2,000 infantry and four guns to attack the Afghan right flank, and, following along the crest of the mountain, they were able to open the pass. Roberts was able to capture most of the Afghan artillery. British losses were 27 killed and 60 wounded, compared to Afghan losses estimated at about 300 killed. Roberts's forces then moved on to Kabul to take vengeance for the massacre of the British mission a month before.

CHARIKAR (35-1' N, 69-11' E). A town located at the mouth of the Ghorband about 40 miles north of Kabul in Parwan Province. The position of Charikar is of great importance because the roads over the Hindu Kush unite in its neighborhood. Charikar was a major British military outpost, manned by the 4th (Gurkha) Infantry. On November

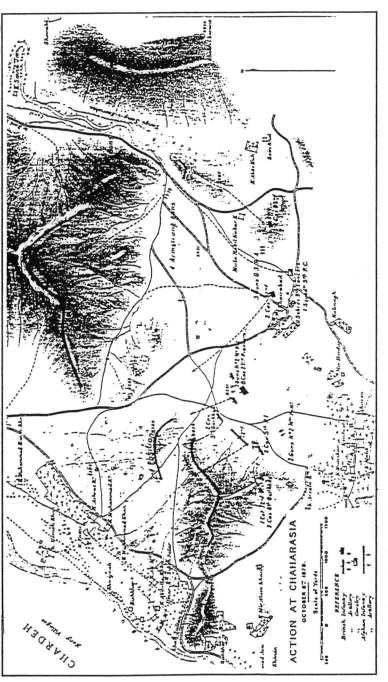

Plan 2. Action at Chaharasia. Source: OA2

13, 1841 with their water supply cut, some 200 men, still able to fight, tried to break through the besieging Kuhistani forces, but were wiped out. Only two British officers, including Eldred Pottinger (q.v.), and a native managed to survive.

CHEMICAL WARFARE. According to one writer, the Soviet forces in Afghanistan employed "non-persistent agents," including harassing, incapacitating, blister, blood, and nerve agents, as well as napalm. The weapons were used sparingly in tactical operations, except during 1983 and 1986, when the primary motive seemed to be to use the battlefield as a testing ground (McMichael, 109). All the evidence is circumstantial and no confirmation has been obtained from Russian sources since the breakup of the Soviet Union.

CHRISTIE, JOHN (1805–1869). Raised for Shah Shuja's army the First Irregular Cavalry, which became later known as Christie's Horse. Commanded his force during the occupation of Kabul, 1839–42. Participated in the occupation of Kandahar and fought at Ghazni and Kabul. Joined Captain James Outram in the pursuit across the Hindu Kush of Amir Dost Muhammad. Received the "Order of the Durrani" for his services in Afghanistan. Later became aide de camp (A.D.C.) to Queen Victoria.

CLARENDON-GORTCHAKOFF AGREEMENT. An agreement concluded in 1872–73 between Britain and Russia defining part of Afghanistan's northern frontier. The czar accepted the river Oxus (Amu Daria) down to Khwaja Salar as the northern boundary of Afghanistan, and pledged Russia to consider Afghanistan outside her sphere of influence. The Afghan amir was not consulted. *See* GRANVILLE-GORTCHAKOFF AGREEMENT.

CLIMATE AND WAR. Foreign invaders of Afghanistan encountered extremes in temperature, both seasonal and diurnal, hot wind storms and blizzards, and lack of precipitation during much of the year. During the march from Kabul to Kandahar in August 1880, British troops faced temperatures of 39 degrees at dawn and 110 degrees in the shade at noon. Temperatures in tents rose to 115 degrees. *Pakka wa Pustin* weather, as the Afghans call it. The *bad-i sad-o-bist ruza* (wind of 120 days) in the southwest of Afghanistan reaches a velocity of 110 miles per hour, and the *shamal* (northerly) raises clouds of dust and sand. Precipitation amounts to only about 11 inches of rain, and most of the irrigation of fields derives from the melting snow. The lack of water was often a serious problem for invaders. The passes of the Hindu Kush are snowbound in winter, and until completion of the Salang Pass in 1964, communications north from Kabul were not possible during the winter. For climatic reasons, invaders would choose spring or fall to stage their campaigns. Overtaken by the winter, as during the first Anglo-Afghan war, the weather contributed to the disastrous defeat of the British "Army of the Indus." *See* also LOGISTICS.

CLIMO, MAJOR GENERAL S. H. Commanded the Waziristan Force, consisting of the Bannu and Derajat areas, in the third Anglo-Afghan war.

CLOSE-BORDER POLICY. After the third Anglo-Afghan war, Waziristan on the North-West Frontier of India was in rebellion, and the Indian government vacillated between a "forward policy" and a "close-border policy." The secretary of state to India described the forward policy "in these days of acutest financial stringency" a mere councel of perfection, and a close-border policy nothing more than leaving the tribesmen "free in their devils kitchen of mischief to brew incalculable trouble for us." But Sir Denys Bray, foreign secretary to the government of India, held, "In the domain of India's foreign politics I know of one fixed and immutable rule only. What India has, let India hold." Therefore, the Indian government decided against containment of the tribes and began to built roads into tribal territory to better pacify them. (Maconachie, 1928) However, the frontier tribes have been able to maintain their autonomy to this day.

CONSTITUTIONAL DEVELOPMENT. Until the late-nineteenth century Afghanistan was governed by a tribal aristocracy, first under the Sadozai and later under the Barakzai branch of the Durranis. Power was decentralized, and members of the royal clan ruled autonomously in the provinces, accepting the suzerainty of the king, or amir, in the capital. Although various administrative departments had already existed since the time of Ahmad Shah (q.v.), the king headed all departments and made the influential officers share in the responsibilities of decisions. As his sign of sovereignty, his name was mentioned in the Friday sermon (*khutba*) and coins (silver and copper) were struck in his name.

The courts were in the hands of the clergy (*ulama*), but the death penalty had to be approved by the king or a governor. Ahmad Shah forbade the mutilation of limbs, and he drafted a code that was, however, never enacted. Little was changed until the time of Amir Shir Ali, who was the first Afghan ruler to establish an advisory council to serve as a consultative body. Amir Abdur Rahman, who increasingly centralized all powers in his hands, took the first steps to institutionalize a consultative body. He relied on advice from a council that was composed of three forces: the *sardars*, members of the royal clan; loyal tribal chiefs; and the *ulama*. The "Iron Amir" claimed all temporal and spiritual powers (*imarat* and *imamate*), and there existed no restraint on his arbitrary rule, except the obligation to conform his actions to the rules of Islamic law. Amir Habibullah, Abdur Rahman's son, continued the tradition of his father.

The first written document detailing the prerogatives of the ruler and the rights of the ruled was the Afghan constitution (*nizam-nama- yi tashkilat-i asasiya-yi Afghanistan*), promulgated by King Amanullah in October 1923. It consisted of 73 articles that enumerated the rights and prerogatives of the king, presented a "bill of rights" of Afghan citizens, and outlined the duties of ministers and government officials. It authorized the establishment of an advisory committee and provincial councils, half of whose members were to be elected by the people, and established a supreme court (*divan-e ali*). Financial affairs and the activities of provincial departments were defined.

King Amanullah was the chief executive, commander in chief, and last court of appeals. He appointed the ministers and presided over cabinet meetings, unless he delegated this task to the prime minister. He was the "defender of the faith," had the sole right to issue currency and have his name invoked in the Friday sermons (*khutba*) during noon prayers. His power was absolute, but he established institutions that could have evolved into representative government and a constitutional monarchy. The constitution promised civil rights to all, abolished slavery, granted non-Muslims religious freedom (but missionary activity was forbidden), and declared the homes of citizens immune from forcible entry. A number of later statutory enactments (*nizam-nama*) further defined the powers and composition of Parliament, which was housed in a new building just completed in Darulaman. Social reforms, such as the emancipation of women and free compulsory education, were decreed. King Amanullah's constitution was never completely implemented, and his reforms were abandoned in a wave of reaction by a coalition of forces led by Habibullah Kalakani (q.v.). Amir Habibullah (Kalakani) abrogated all constitutional reforms and attempted to rule in the tradition of Amir Abdur Rahman.

A new attempt at constitutional government was made in October 1931 by Nadir Shah (1929–33). His fundamental law (*usul-i asasi-yi daulat-i Afghanistan*) was similar to Amanullah's constitution. It included 16 sections with 110 articles, which outlined general principles and enumerated the rights of the king, the rights of the people, and the duties of a national council (*shura-yi milli*) and provincial advisory committees. Like his predecessor, Nadir Shah enjoyed emergency and veto powers. Non-Muslims had equal rights and were not required to pay a poll tax or be obligated to wear a distinctive type of dress. No legislation was to be contrary to Islamic law, but a distinction was made between civil and religious courts. Torture and confiscation of property were prohibited; publications, including newspapers, and free commercial activity were permitted. As a concession to the religious establishment, two members of the Mujaddidi family held the position of minister of justice until 1935. Members of the royal family held the important position of prime minister until 1963.

A new, liberal era began with the promulgation of the 1964 constitution (October 1, 1964, *qanun-i asasi-yi Afghanistan*), which limited the participation of members of the royal family in government. Members of the royal family could serve in the foreign service, be advisers (*mushawer*), and hold low-level positions in government departments, but they could not hold the positions of prime minister, supreme court justice, and membership in Parliament. This was directed against Sardar Muhammad Daud (q.v.), the king's cousin, a strong prime minister (1953–63) whose Pashtunistan policy (q.v.) had been a disaster in foreign relations. While Zahir Shah (q.v., 1933–73) continued to hold supreme powers, he permitted an unprecedented degree of democratic government. His constitution, the result of a constitutional drafting committee, included a preamble and 11 titles, comprising 128 articles. Primogeniture was introduced with a provision that "the Throne shall pass to his [Zahir's] eldest son." Freedom of thought, possession of property, unarmed assembly, and education were guaranteed. Afghan citizens were given the right to a free press and to form political parties, subject to the provisions of certain ordinances, provided that no actions would be in violation of traditional norms and Islamic law. The king never ratified the provision on formation of political parties.

From the time of King Amanullah, constitutional development represents a process of modernization and the gradual introduction of concepts of the division of power and individual rights. It also brought into being a process whereby the symbols of democratic government were beginning to gain concrete reality. But socioeconomic factors prevented the rapid implementation of political reforms. Universal education, envisioned by the constitution, remained an aim rather than a reality, and Afghanistan has remained largely illiterate. The introduction of secular schools, in addition to the traditional mosque/*madrasa* system, produced two essentially hostile elites. Afghanistan is still predominantly agricultural, and a great division exists between the urban and rural populations. Sectarian and ethnic differences have prevented the forging of a heterogeneous population into a nation. When Sardar Muhammad Daud staged his coup in 1973, the experiment with democracy came to a halt.

Daud wanted a one-party government and "democracy based on social justice." His constitution (*qanun-i asasi-yi daulat-i jumhuri-yi Afghanistan*), promulgated on February 14, 1977, aimed at the "exercise of power" by the majority, the "farmers, workers, and enlightened people and the youth." In 13 chapters and 136 articles, the republican government presented its aspirations. It called for the "elimination of exploitation in all its forms," nationalized the mineral resources of the state, large industries, communications, banks, and "important food procurement establishments." Land reforms were to be carried out and cooperatives were to be encouraged. Women were to enjoy equal rights and obligations, and every Afghan 18 years or older was to have the right to vote. President Daud enjoyed absolute power: he could convene and dismiss the national assembly (*milli jirgah*), whose members were nominated by his party, and could veto any law. He felt he had to be strong to fight the evils of "hunger, ignorance, and disease," but his one-man rule proved to be fatal. His leftist supporters in the army did not permit Daud's shift to the right, and before he could eliminate them from positions of power, they staged the Saur Revolt of April 27, 1978 (q.v.).

The new regime wanted to establish a government of workers and peasants, with the PDPA as a vanguard to implement its revolutionary objectives. Decrees demanded the emancipation of women, land reforms, and the introduction of far-reaching social changes. But the provisions of the "Fundamental Principles of the Democratic Republic of Afghanistan" could never be implemented. Armed resistance rose within a few months, which turned into a war of liberation after the Soviet intervention (q.v.).

The government of Dr. Najibullah virtually eliminated the trappings of Marxist government in its Constitution of 1987, and the Afghan Interim Government of the seven *mujahedin* groups in Peshawar published the outlines of a constitution that favored the establishment of an Islamic state. The traditional groups, represented by Sayyid Ahmad Gailani, Sebghatullah Mujaddidi, and Muhammad Nabi Muhammadi, favor the establishment of a democratic Islamic government, not excluding the possibility of a constitutional monarchy. The Islamist groups, headed by Gulbudin Hekmatyar, Abdul Rasul Sayyaf, Yunus Khales, and Burhanuddin Rabbani, as well as the newly formed *Taleban* movement, tend with some variations to favor an "Islamic state" on a more authoritarian model. They would limit the sphere of activity of women in public life and tend to limit manifestations of Westernization. The Shi'a groups appear to favor a federated state in which the interests of the minorities are protected. The Shi'a community claims to constitute a fifth of the Afghan population and wants this to be reflected in parliamentary representation. As long as their claimed popular strength was not reflected in an Afghan Interim Government (AIG), they refused their participation. The war in Afghanistan has politicized a large part of the hitherto quiescent population, and the prospects are for greater grassroots participation in the political life of Afghanistan. The future form of the Afghan government will depend on the outcome of the present civil war.

CONVENTION OF 1907. *See* **ANGLO-RUSSIAN CONVENTION.**

CONVOY OPERATIONS. Modern invaders of Afghanistan depended on supplies from beyond the borders of the country, and their lines of communication were always vulnerable to attack. Afghan guerrilla activities centered on harassing the enemies' lines of logistics. Until the third Anglo-Afghan war, British armies depended on pack animals to transport war materiel and supplies that could not be obtained locally. The caravans, or convoys, were slow and the animals subject to disease and the inhospitable climate. Almost 100,000 camels were lost during the second Anglo-Afghan war.

Russian and Kabul government convoys, much more mobile and protected by aerial support, proved to be equally vulnerable. The *muhajedin* would block the movement of a highway-bound convoy by immobilizing some vehicles in a suitable location and destroying the trapped convoy before relief could arrive. The Salang Pass, located at an altitude of 13,350 feet, and the Soviet-built tunnel were frequent targets of attack. The vulnerability of the Salang Tunnel was clearly demonstrated in October 1982, when an explosion (or *mujahedin* action) in the tunnel was said to have caused the death of 1,000 people, including 700 Soviet troops. *See also* TRANSPORT, MILITARY.

CORRELATION OF FORCES. A doctrine with political, social, and ideological aspects that referred to the relative strength of socialism and capitalism as evaluated in Moscow. Its political aspect was seen in the "number of Communist countries in the world, their dynamism in international affairs, their prestige and self-confidence, as well as the strength and influence of Communists in other countries." The social aspect was manifested in "the Soviet view of class struggle and the influence that Marxist ideas have upon peoples throughout the world." The ideological aspect related to "the extent of revolutionary forces. . . leading to a Marxist system with a Leninist control imposed on it" (Bradsher, 1983, 128). The Soviet leadership felt that the correlation of forces had changed to the advantage of the socialist camp, and, although it downplayed its military aspect, it induced it to embark on such actions as the intervention in Afghanistan.

COTTON, SIR WILLOUGHBY (1783–1860). Described as a roly-poly old general who had served far too long in India and was slow and not very bright (Macrory, 98). Commanded the Bengal Division of the Army of the Indus, 1838–39. On his way to Afghanistan, he was prevented from heading in the opposite direction to plunder the rumored wealth of Haiderabad. When he handed over command to General Elphinstone (q.v.), he told him, "You will have nothing to do here, all is peace" (*ibid.*, 165). He served at Ghazni and left Afghanistan via Kabul in 1839.

COUNTERINSURGENCY. Conventional forces never quite succeeded in solving the problem of containing the Afghan tribes. The British leveled villages, destroyed crops, uprooted fruit trees, and, in 1916, constructed a 17-mile electric fence, which electrocuted 400 Mohmand tribesmen, but could not prevent them from penetrating the administered territories (Nichols, 22).

The Soviet Union lacked a counterinsurgency doctrine to guide and organize its activities. Soviet forces were prepared for a conventional war with offensive operations for territorial gain, conducted by heavy armor that was supported by aerial and missile operations, as well as special units for defensive chemical warfare. Their force structure and tactical doctrine were not suited to military operations in Afghanistan. Eventually, adjustments were made permitting greater decentralization of command, the creation of small independent units to fight the *mujahedin* in inaccessible areas, night operations, and the employment of airborne, air assault/airmobile, designated reconnaissance flights, and special operations units, *spetsnaz*. The latter were involved in much of the fighting and took the brunt of casualties. The Soviets were forced to fight a light infantry war in which the advantage of numbers and light weapons favored the *mujahedin*. (McMichael)

CROCKER, BRIG. GEN. G. D. Described as "a gallant, but impetuous man," he commanded the 1st (Peshawar) Infantry Brigade during the third Anglo-Afghan war. He was unsuccessful in the first battle of Bagh on May 9, 1919 (q.v.), when he underestimated the strength of the Afghan forces and employed an unduly large force for protective duties. He succeeded in the second battle with aerial support and fire from Horse and Mountain Artillery and an ample amount of machine guns which enabled him to capture Dakka on May 17. However, because of Nadir Khan's (q.v.) success on the Waziristan front, the attempt at advancing on Jalalabad had to be aborted.

- D -

DANE, SIR LOUIS W. Foreign secretary to the government of India and head of a British mission to Kabul (Jan. 1 to Dec. 2, 1904–05) that negotiated the Treaty of 1905. *See* ANGLO-AFGHAN TREATY OF 1905; AFGHAN FOREIGN RELATIONS.

DAR AL-HARB. In Muslim constitutional law the world is divided into the *Dar al-Islam* (Abode of Islam), land under Muslim rule, and the *Dar al Harb* (Abode of War), potentially a land of war, *jehad* (holy war), which was to be brought under the domain of Islam. Some schools also recognize the *Dar al-Sulh* (Abode of Agreement), land not under Muslim rule, but in a tributary relationship with Islam. In 1920 the *hijrat* (emigration) movement arose in India, denouncing India, the *Dar* *al-Harb*, and making it incumbent on Muslims to migrate to Afghanistan, the country of Islamic rule. The movement became known as the *khilafat* movement, and the emigrants were known as the *muhajerin*. King Amanullah encouraged the movement, hoping to gain skilled immigrants who might contribute to the development of Afghanistan, but his hopes were disappointed when most of the several thousand immigrants turned out to be poor and unskilled and depended on support from the Afghan government. After enthusiastic beginnings, the movement quickly dissolved.

DAUD MUHAMMAD. *See* **MUHAMMAD DAUD.**

DEATH MARCH. After signing a treaty of virtual capitulation to Afghan chiefs in December 1841 (*see* CAPITULATION, TREATY OF), the British forces of occupation and camp followers, amounting to about 16,500 persons (690 British fighting men, 2,840 Indian infantry, 970 cavalry, and over 12,000 camp followers — servants and merchants in charge of nonweapons logistics and a large number of women and children) embarked on a march toward the Indian border in which few survived. The retreat began on January 6, 1842, and only six miles were covered on the first day. The march quickly turned into a rout as traffic jams impeded crossing the Logar River and much of the baggage was abandoned. On the second day only five miles were covered to the well-fortified Khurd Khaibar Pass. A number of people froze to death, and Amir Shah Shuja's (q.v.) cavalry escort deserted. On the next day the British rearguard was attacked. British officers tried unsuccessfully to separate their troops from the camp followers. Ghilzai *ghazis* attacked the retreating forces, killing some 500 troops and 2,500 camp followers. British women and children, as well as their husbands and a number of officers, were surrendered as hostages to Sardar Akbar Khan and managed to survive. Eldred Pottinger claims that Akbar Khan treacherously shouted, "Spare them" in Persian and "Kill them" in Pashtu. (George Pottinger, 1993, 163) On the fifth day a last stand was made at Jagdalak, by which time about 12,000 members of the retreating force had perished. Sardar Akbar Khan offered to pay 200,000 rupees to the Ghilzai chiefs if they would stop their attacks, but the Ghilzai were out for revenge. By the eighth day two British officers and seven or eight wounded men were taken prisoners, and only one man, Dr. Brydon (q.v.), managed to reach safety at Jalalabad. (Dupree,

1967) This gave rise to the legend that Akbar Khan had predicted he would wipe out the British army and leave only one man to tell the tale.

DEFECTIONS, DESERTIONS, AND MUTINIES. Defections were common in the wars of the Afghan princes, as well as in wars of Afghan *ghazis* with British-supported Afghan troops. To avoid bloodshed and destruction, forces facing defeat deserted to the superior enemy. When Sardar Ayub Khan moved with his army against Kandahar in July 1880, the troops of the Wali, governor of Kandahar, deserted in a body to Ayub, taking with them their guns and ammunition. In the third Anglo-Afghan war, a large number of the Khaibar Rifles, a tribal militia of Pashtuns from the British side of the Durand Line, deserted, and the entire force had to be disbanded.

One year after the Soviet intervention in Afghanistan in December 1978, the size of the DRA (q.v.) army had dwindled from 100,000 men to about 50,000. Most of the loss was due to desertion. According to one source, the rate of defection from the DRA army was more than 10,000 per year. (Amstutz) The defecting soldiers and officers frequently took with them their arms, including tanks and armored vehicles, trucks, assault rifles, and heavy artillery pieces. A large number of deserters with specialized military skills enrolled in the forces of the *mujahedin*. One of the largest defections occurred on February 16, 1989, when three regiments amounting to nearly 10,000 men defected in Takhar and Badakhshan provinces. Most of their weapons became part of Commander Ahmad Shah Mas'ud's (q.v.) arsenal.

The summary execution by Yunus Khalis's forces of some 37 deserters from the Kabul army in September 1982 may have been a reason for a reduced number of desertions in subsequent years. In the civil war for supremacy of the former *mujahedin*, commanders and leaders of parties frequently changed sides, regardless of ideological orientation.

DENNIE, WILLIAM HENRY (1785–1842). Commanded a brigade in 1838–39 and led the storming party at Ghazni on July 23, 1839. Encountered an Uzbek force with Amir Dost Muhammad at Bamian on September 18, 1840 and dispersed it, but the amir managed to escape. Accompanied General Sale's forces from Kabul to Jalalabad in 1841. At the siege of Jalalabad he led a sortie and was fatally wounded on April 6, 1842.

DIN MUHAMMAD, MUSHK-I ALAM (1790–1886). Considered a national hero by Afghans because of his implacable hostility to the British. A frontier mulla whose grandfather came from India and settled among the Andar Ghilzai near Ghazni. He studied with various *ulama* and was given the name *Mushk-i Alam* (Scent [or Musk] of the World), by one of his teachers because of his excellent mind. He was a militant mulla who opened a *madrasa* (school of higher Islamic studies) for the training of mullas and gained considerable influence among the Ghilzais (q.v.). He received an allowance from Amir Shir Ali and preached *jehad* against the British during the second Anglo-Afghan war. When Amir Abdur Rahman tried to restrict his activity, he incited the Mangals and Ghilzais to rebellion. After his death in 1886, his son, Mulla Abdul Karim, led a Ghilzai uprising against Amir Abdur Rahman, which was suppressed only with great difficulty.

DOBBS, SIR HENRY. British envoy and chief of the British mission to Kabul that negotiated the Anglo-Afghan Treaty of 1921 and established "neighborly" relations after the end of the third Anglo-Afghan war. Before that, he also headed the British contingent at the Mussoorie Conference (April 17–July 18, 1920), which failed to normalize Anglo-Afghan relations. He first came to Afghanistan in 1903, when as a political officer he directed a small British contingent whose task was to restore or repair boundary pillars at the Russo-Afghan border. *See* ANGLO-AFGHAN WARS; and AFGHAN FOREIGN RELATIONS.

DOST MUHAMMAD, AMIR (1826–38 and 1842–63). Afghan ruler, known as the "Great Amir," *Amir-i Kabir*, who was ousted by the British in the first Anglo-Afghan war but was able to regain the Afghan throne after four years in Indian exile. He was born in 1792 in Kandahar, the son of Painda Khan, who was killed by Shah Zaman (q.v.) when Dost Muhammad was only eight years old. He became acting governor of Ghazni and, after the death of Muhammad Azam in 1824, established himself as ruler of Kabul. He next defeated his rival, Shah Shuja (q.v.), at Kandahar and gradually extended his control over the rest of Afghanistan. He defeated the Sikhs at the Battle of Jamrud (1837) and assumed the title *Amir-ul-Mu'minin* (Commander of the Faithful). The British-Indian government turned against him when Dost Muhammad made overtures to Russia and Persia and permitted a Russian agent to come to Kabul. Dost Muhammad wanted to regain territory captured by Ranjit Singh (q.v.) and was willing to ally himself with the British, but the British government decided to support the Sikh ruler and restore Shah Shuja to the Afghan throne. A British army invaded Afghanistan and destroyed Kabul on July 23, 1839. On November 2, 1940, after a few skirmishes, Dost Muhammad gave up; he surrendered to the British, who took him as a hostage to India. However, the British occupation of Afghanistan became increasingly tenuous as their lines of communication were disrupted and tribal forces slowly expelled garrisons from outlying areas. Eventually, the army in Kabul was forced to negotiate an ignominious retreat in which most of the British army was destroyed (*see* ANGLO-AFGHAN WARS; and CAPITULATION, TREATY OF). Facing a situation of chaos in Afghanistan, the Indian government permitted Dost Muhammad to return and regain his throne. But it took him a number of years to consolidate his power: he took Kandahar in 1855 and Herat in 1863. Dost Muhammad died a few days after he entered Herat. Of his 27 sons, Muhammad Afzal and Muhammad Azim ruled for short periods, followed by Shir Ali (*see* individual entries).

DOSTUM, GEN. ABDUL RASHID. During the 1980s, commander of the Jozjani "Dostum Militia," comprising some 20,000 regular and militia soldiers, most of them Uzbek, and entrusted with guarding Jozjan, Fariab, and Sar-i-Pol provinces for the Kabul government. He was awarded the distinction "Hero of the Republic of Afghanistan" and was a member of the central council of the Watan (formerly PDPA) party. Born in 1954 in Khwaja Dokoh, Jozjan Province, of an Uzbek family, he worked for the Oil and Gas Exploration Enterprise of Shiberghan and in 1980 went to the USSR for training. He then joined the ministry of state security and became commander of Unit 374 in Jozjan Province. His forces served in various parts of the country, and it is said that one thousand of his soldiers were captured in the *mujahedin* conquest of Khost. At the breakup of the Marxist regime, Dostum gained control of the north-central provinces of Afghanistan. He and a number of generals turned against President Najibullah and assisted the *mujahedin* in the conquest of Kabul. Dostum's followers are united in a party, called *Junbish-i Milli-yi Islami*, which, at the time of this writing, controls most of Balkh, Fariab, Jozjan, and Samangan provinces. When President Rabbani was unwilling to legitimize Dostum's position by giving him a cabinet post, the latter joined forces with other opposition groups. *See also* MAZAR-I SHARIF, FALL OF.

DRA. Acronym for the Democratic Republic of Afghanistan, which was changed under President Najibullah to Republic of Afghanistan (ROA). After the conquest of Kabul by the *mujahedin*, the designation Islamic Republic of Afghanistan (IRA) was adopted. *See also* PEOPLE'S DEMOCRATIC PARTY OF AFGHANISTAN.

DURAND AGREEMENT. An agreement that Sir Henry Mortimer Durand and Amir Abdur Rahman signed on November 12, 1893 at Kabul and that defined the boundary between Afghanistan and British India, subsequently called "Durand Line." This boundary was drawn without regard to the ethnic composition of the population and severed a large portion of Pashtu-speaking Afghans from their brothers in Afghanistan. Amir Abdur Rahman accepted "under duress" a line running from "Chitral and Baroghil Pass up to Peshawar, and thence up to Koh-e Malik Siyah in this way that Wakhan, Kafiristan, Asmar, Mohmand of Lalpura, and one portion of Waziristan" came under his rule. He renounced his claims for "the railway station of New Chaman, Chagai, the rest of Waziri, Biland Khel, Kurram, Afridi, Bajaur, Swat, Buner, Dir, Chilas and Chitral." The Durand Line was never completely demarcated because of the hostility of the tribes and the fact that the tribes on the Indian side of the border never came under the direct administration of the Indian, or subsequently Pakistani, government. Abdur Rahman obtained an increase in subsidy of 6,000,000 rupees and a letter with the assurance that Britain would continue to protect Afghanistan from unprovoked Russian aggression, provided that the amir "followed unreservedly the advice of the British Government" in regard to his external relations. The Afghan government subsequently claimed that the agreement was forced on Afghanistan in the form of an ultimatum. After the death of Amir Abdur Rahman, Britain insisted that the treaties with the late ruler were personal, rather than dynastic, and therefore subject to renegotiation, but it excluded the Durand Agreement as not subject to this provision.

Article 5 of the treaty of peace, concluded at Rawalpindi (q.v.) on August 8, 1919, stated that "the Afghan Government accept the Indo-Afghan frontier accepted by the late Amir [Habibullah]," and the Treaty of Kabul (q.v.) carried a similar provision. When the State of Pakistan was created in 1947, the Afghan government demanded the right of the Pashtuns to decide whether they wanted an independent Pashtunistan, union with Afghanistan, or union with Pakistan. The Kabul government did not accept a plebiscite that allowed only a choice for union with

Pakistan or India, and in 1979 the Afghan Parliament repudiated the Durand Agreement. The "Pashtunistan question" (q.v.) has since remained an issue between Afghanistan and Pakistan and has prevented the establishment of cordial relations between the two Muslim countries. *See also* AFGHAN FOREIGN RELATIONS and PASHTUNISTAN.

DURAND, SIR HENRY MORTIMER (1850–1924). Foreign secretary to the government of India, sent to Kabul in September 1893 for the purpose of negotiating an agreement defining the Indo-Afghan boundary, subsequently called the Durand Line. (*See* DURAND AGREEMENT.) Served in the north-west provinces during 1829–38. Political secretary to Sir Roberts in Kabul in the campaign in 1879. Also served at Charasia and in the defense of Sherpur (qq.v.). Foreign secretary from 1884 to 1894.

DURRANI DYNASTY (1747–1973). The Durrani dynasty was founded in 1747 by Ahmad Shah "Durr-i Durran" (q.v.), who ruled Afghanistan until 1978. Ahmad Shah was a direct descendant of Sado, an Abdali chief at the court of the Savafid ruler Shah Abbas the Great (1588–1629). The Durrani are divided into the Sadozai branch (a section of the Popalzai tribe) and the Muhammadzai (a section of the Barakzai tribe). The succession from Ahmad Shah to Muhammad Daud, who established a republican government, is as follows:

Sadozai Dynasty 1747–1817

Ahmad Shah	1747–1773
Timur Shah (s.o. Ahmad)	1773–1793
Zaman Shah (s.o. Timur, deposed)	1793–1800
Mahmud Shah (br.o. Zaman, deposed)	1800–1803
Shah Shuja-ul-Mulk (br.o. Zaman, deposed)	1803–1809
Mahmud Shah (br.o. Zaman)	1809–1817
(loses Kabul and Kandahar)	

Ruling in Herat 1817–1863

Mahmud Shah (Sadozai, assassinated?)	1817–1829
Kamran (s.o. Mahmud, assassinated?)	1829–1841
Yar Muhammad	1841–1851
Said Muhammad Khan (s.o. Yar Muhd.)	1851–1855
Muhammad Yusuf Khan (Sadozai, deposed)	1855

Sirtap Isa Khan (Herati)	1855
Herat conquered by Persians, 1856	
Sultan Ahmad Khan (Jan)	1855–1863
(Nephew of Dost Muhammad)	
Dost Muhammad Khan	1863

Ruling in Kabul 1817–1863

Muhammad Azim Khan	1817–1822
Habibullah Khan (s.o. Muhammad Azim)	1822–1826
(deposed)	
Dost Muhammad Khan (deposed)	1826–1839
(Uncle of Habibullah Khan)	
Shah Shuja-ul-Mulk (Sadozai)	1839–1841
Zaman Khan (Barakzai)	1841–1842
Fath Jang (Sadozai Contender)	1842?
Dost Muhammad	1842–1863

Ruling in Kandahar 1817–1863

Pur Dil Khan	1817–1839
Shah Shuja-ul-Mulk (deposed)	1839–1841
Kohan Dil Khan (br.o. Pur Dil)	1842–1855
Dost Muhammad Khan	1855–1863

Ruling Afghanistan 1863–1973

Civil war and anarchy	1863–1868
Shir Ali Khan (br.o. Dost, deposed)	1863–1866
Muhammad Afzal Khan	1866–1867
Muhammad Azim Khan (br.o. M. Afzal)	1867–1868
(deposed)	
Shir Ali Khan	1868–1879
Yaqub Khan (s.o. Shir Ali, abdicated)	1879
Second Anglo-Afghan War 1879–1880	
Abdur Rahman Khan (s.o. Muhd. Afzal)	1880–1901
Habibullah Khan (s.o. Abdur Rahman)	1901–1919
(assassinated)	
Amanullah Khan (s.o. Habibullah, deposed)	1919–1929
Inayatullah Khan (three days, abdic.)	1929
(Habibullah Kalakani, Tajik (Jan. to Oct.)	1929
(Son of a Water Carrier)	
Nadir Shah (Musahiban Family)	1929–1933

(assassinated)
Zahir Shah (deposed)   1933–1973
Muhammad Daud (President)   1973–1978
  (assassinated)

DURRANI, LAND TENURE. Nadir Shah Afshar gave the Durranis the
land of Kandahar as a military fief. The land had previously been held
by a mixed peasantry population that paid taxes to the suzerain ruler
since Safavid times. The land of Kandahar had been traditionally
divided into *qulba* (plows), which designated the portion of irrigated
land cultivated by one person, operating one ox and one plow, and
which gave double space for sowing two *kharwar* of grain (one
kharwar, literally a donkey load, amounted to 100 *man* [*maund*], the
exact weight varied in different localities), one-half of which was
cultivated each year while the other half remained fallow. Nadir Shah's
agents ascertained the productivity of the land in various areas as a
return of 25 *kharwar* for one *kharwar* of seed. Each *qulba* was assessed
a land tax (*kharaj*) of 10 percent. As an innovation, every garden, tree,
and vine was assessed one copper *pice*.

About 3,000 double *qulba* were distributed to Durrani tribes in *tiyul*
(fiefs), in exchange for providing 6,000 horsemen, one for each *qulba*.
The following table shows the allotment of land under Ahmad Shah:

Durrani Tribes	No. of *Qulbas*	Quota of Horses
Popalzai	965¼	806
Alikozai	1,050	851
Barakzai*	1,018½	907
Alizai	661¾	819
Nurzai	868½	1,169
Ishaqzai	357½	635
Khugiani**	163	423
Maku	121½	100
Total	5,206	5,710

*These numbers probably include the Achakzai (LWA).
** Spelled *Khakwani* in some older sources.
The Durranis were estimated at 100,000 families at the time. Six non-
Durrani tribes held 110 *qulbas* but had to provide a much larger
contingent of 2,890 horsemen.

Ahmad Shah Durrani greatly increased the land in control of Durrani chiefs, who were paid from 100 to 1,000 *tomans* (one tuman was 20 Kandahar rupees) annually. During military service a horseman was paid 25 *tomans* either in money from the royal treasury or in *barat* (written assignment).

DYER, GENERAL REGINALD EDWARD H. (1864-1927). In command of the "Thal Relief Force," during the third Anglo-Afghan war, to end General Nadir Khan's siege of the strategically important town. His own 45th Infantry Brigade was strengthened with part of the 16th Division, which formed part of the Central Reserve. On May 30, 1919, he moved via Togh and Darmsamand and reached Thal on June 1. In the north-west he faced a few Afghan regulars with four guns and some 2,000 tribesmen. To the north and east, the tribes were waiting in the hills, not yet determined whether they should attack. On the hills south of the Kurram River was the Afghan main force. Dyer was able to disperse the tribes, and while making preparations for an attack on the main force, he was informed that King Amanullah had ordered a suspension of hostilities. When, on June 3, Dyer moved against the Afghan camp, he found it abandoned (Molesworth, 120). Dyer had won notoriety as commander at Amritsar, when he dispersed a political meeting, opening fire without warning, and in 10 minutes killed some 379 men and boys and wounded 1,500 in the "Amritsar Massacre." General Charles C. Munro, the commander in chief of the Indian Army, relieved him of his command.

- E -

EAST INDIA COMPANY, THE BRITISH. The British East India Company was started in 1600 with a capital of £30,000 and a charter from Queen Elizabeth for 15 years to have a monopoly of trade "together with limited authority to make laws and punish interlopers." The charter was periodically renewed, and by the middle of the eighteenth century the company was the de facto ruler of Bengal. Its Board of Control appointed a governor general as executive who governed the company until 1858, when the Crown ended the charter and appointed a viceroy, subject to the control of the London government. The company concluded treaties with local potentates and waged wars in its attempt to become the paramount power in India, and it bore the responsibility for the debacle of the first Anglo-Afghan war. Three presidencies in Bengal, Bombay, and Madras furnished the company's armies, which included both British and Indian branches of cavalry, artillery, and infantry. Vassals and mercenaries were also employed.

ECONOMIC WARFARE. Economic warfare, such as blockades, the destruction of villages, their fields, orchards, water resources, and livestock has been practiced by invaders since time immemorial. British forces resorted to it in fighting rebellious tribes, and Soviet forces employed it against areas supportive of the *mujahedin*. The orchards around towns and villages were excellent bases for ambush — they were often walled and surrounded by irrigation ditches, which made it difficult to bring in wheeled transport and necessitated hand-to-hand combat. Villages and trees were leveled to deprive the *ghazis* or *mujahedin* of shelter. *See also* COUNTERINSURGENCY.

ELPHINSTONE, MOUNTSTUART (1779–1859). British envoy to the court of Shah Shuja in 1808–9 who negotiated an alliance of "eternal friendship" with the Afghan ruler and called for joint action in case of Franco-Persian aggression. He left Delhi on October 13, 1808 with an escort of 400 Anglo-Indian troops and reached Peshawar on February 25, 1809, where he presented Britain's proposals to the Afghan ruler. This was the first contact between a British official and an Afghan ruler. Elphinstone used the opportunity to learn as much as he could about the "Forbidden Kingdom" and later published a book on Afghanistan, *An Account of the Kingdom of Caubul* (1815), which is one of the first comprehensive accounts on Afghan society. He was rewarded for his services with the appointment governor of Bombay. Elphinstone College in Bombay bears his name. Remarking on the proposed war, Elphinstone said:

> If you send 27,000 men up the Bolan Pass to Candahar (as we hear is intended), and can feed them, I have no doubt you will take Candahar and Caubul and set up Soojah [Shuja]; but for maintaining him in a poor, cold , strong, and remote country, among a turbulent people like the Afghans, I own it seems to me hopeless. (Macrory, 94–95)

See AFGHAN FOREIGN RELATIONS; ANGLO-AFGHAN WARS; and SHAH SHUJA-UL-MULK.

ELPHINSTONE, MAJ. GEN. WILLIAM (1782–1842). Commander of
the British army in Afghanistan in 1841 and the person held responsible
by British historians for the debacle in the first Anglo-Afghan war.
General Elphinstone was 60 years old and infirm when he accepted the
army command. (In the nineteenth century, old soldiers did not fade
away.) Forbes (64) describes Elphinstone as

> wrecked in body and impaired in mind by physical ailments
> and infirmities, he had lost all faculty of energy, and such mind
> as remained to him was swayed by the opinion of the person
> with whom he had last spoken.

Elphinstone did not take "decisive" action when Alexander Burnes
(q.v.), the assistant to the British envoy at Kabul, was assassinated with
members of his mission. He quartered his troops in the vulnerable
cantonment, which was commanded from the nearby hills, instead of
moving them to the protection of the Bala Hisar (q.v.) fortress.
Surrounded by Afghan tribal armies, the British had to negotiate a
retreat that turned into a rout in which most of the 16,000 troops and
camp followers were massacred or died of the freezing cold weather.
Elphinstone did not survive the disaster; on April 23, 1842 he died in
captivity of exhaustion and various maladies. *See* ANGLO-AFGHAN
WARS; AFGHAN FOREIGN RELATIONS; AKBAR, SARDAR
MUHAMMAD; and CAPITULATION, TREATY OF.

ENGLAND, SIR RICHARD (1793–1883). Commanded the Bombay
Division in 1841. Was repulsed at Haikalzai on March 28, 1942, losing
a quarter of his forces, who were killed or wounded, and was forced to
withdraw to Quetta. Ordered to proceed to Kandahar, he joined General
Nott in Kandahar and in the victory over Akbar Khan at the Khojak
Pass.

ENVELOPING TACTICS. A method of encirclement employed in ancient
times as well as in more recent engagements. Soviet forces employed it
in the rugged terrain of Afghanistan. McMichael describes it as follows:

> A special tactical formation split off from the main body and sent by
> a separate route to the rear or flank of the enemy in order to support
> the advance of the main body, or, to execute a separate mission
> which is complementary to the mission of the main body.

The method was used mainly as a blocking action to prevent the withdrawal of the *mujahedin* when faced with a direct assault. It was normally assigned to an airborne, air assault, or reconnaissance company. (McMichael, p 68) *See also* BLOCKING TACTICS.

ENVER (ANWAR) PASHA. Minister of war and, with Jamal Pasha (q.v.) and Talat Pasha, member of the ruling triumvirate in the Ottoman war government (1913–18). Sentenced to death in 1919, he fled in a German submarine to Germany after the war and then to the Soviet Union. He failed to gain Soviet support in replacing Kemal Ataturk as the head of the Turkish government and moved to Central Asia. He apparently intended to seek a safe haven in Afghanistan, where Jamal Pasha had already preceded him and was active as an adviser to King Amanullah. Basmachi (q.v.) counterrevolutionaries captured him, but he convinced them of his sympathies and became one of their leaders. He fought on their side against the Red Army until he was killed in a skirmish on August 4, 1922.

ETHNIC GROUPS. The Afghan population is made up of numerous ethnic groups, speaking various dialects or mutually unintelligible languages. The largest ethnic groups are the Pashtuns, followed by the Tajiks, Uzbeks, and Hazaras. Orywal (1986) lists the following ethnic groups in Afghanistan:

Pashtun	Tajik	Uzbek
Hazara	Turkoman	Aimaq
Taimani	Tahiri	Baluch
Mauri	Brahui	Arab
Qirghiz	Moghol	Gujar
Qipchaq	Eshkashimi	Munjani
Rushani	Sanglichi	Shighnani
Vakhi	Farsi/Farsiwan	Qarliq
Nuristani	Pashai	Firuzkuhi
Jamshidi	Timuri	Zuri
Maliki	Mishmast	Jat
Jalali	Ghorbat	Pikragh
Shadibaz	Vangavala	Qazaq
Qizilbash	Tatar	Parachi
Tirahi	Gavarbati	Ormuri
Shaikh Muhd.	Jogi	Kutana

Jews (Yahudi)   Sikh   Hindu

Estimated population figures (Groetzbach, 1990) are:

Pashtun	6 million
Tajik & Farsiwan	4 million
Uzbek	1.3 million
Hazara	1.1 million*
Aimaq	.5 million
Turkmen	.4 million
Baluch & Brahui	.16 million
Arab	.1 million
Nuristani	.1 million
Pashai	.1 million
Tatar	.06 million
Qizilbash	.04 million
Hindu & Sikh	.03 million
Qirghiz & Moghol	.11 million

* According to Hazara claims, they number as many as two million in Afghanistan and another two million in Iran and Pakistan.

Virtually all Jews left Afghanistan in the 1970s (of some 600 families, only six individuals remained in Kabul in the 1980s).

The introduction of state-sponsored education dictated the use of Dari as the language of instruction. Dari has been the language of royal courts since Ghaznavid times and was widely used by the Turkic rulers of Central Asia and the Moghuls of India.

Since the early twentieth century, Afghan governments have promoted Pashtu as the national language, but any attempts to replace Dari in education have failed. One of the first decrees (No. 4) issued by the Marxist government was to recognize and permit the use of Turkmani, Uzbeki, Baluchi, and Nuristani as "national languages" to ensure the "essential conditions for evolution of the literature, education, and publication in mother tongues of the tribes and nationalities resident in Afghanistan." It ordered the respective ministries to start broadcasting on radio and television and in the publication of newspapers in these languages. This was an adoption of the Soviet nationalities policy and was seen by some as an attempt to divide and rule.

- F -

FAIZ MUHAMMAD. Governor of the Eastern Province who stopped the British mission under Neville Chamberlain (q.v.) from entering Afghanistan on the eve of the first Anglo-Afghan war. Louis Cavagnari (q.v.) crossed the border on September 21, 1878 and met Faiz Muhammad at Ali Masjid. He asked whether the Afghan governor would permit Chamberlain to pass. He said no, and added, "You may take it as kindness, and because I remember friendship, that I do not fire upon you for what you have already done" [crossing the border without permission]. The British chose this "insult" as the *casus belli* for the first Anglo-Afghan war.

Faiz Muhammad headed an army of 3,000 regular infantry, 600 levies, 200 cavalry, and 24 cannons and met General Sam Browne (q.v.) at the battle of Ali Masjid. Faiz Muhammad was forced to retreat and the British invaders marched on Kabul. (Heathcote, 101)

FAQIR OF IPI, HAJI MIRZA ALI KHAN. A frontier mulla residing with the Waziri tribe on the Indian side of the Durand Line. He was an implacable foe of the British who incited the tribes to wage *jehad* against India. He collaborated with the Axis Powers during World War II and was in touch with their legations in Kabul. The Germans gave him the code name *Feuerfresser* (fire-eater) and supported his efforts by paying him a regular subsidy. The faqir's activities compelled Britain to keep large forces on the Frontier that could have been deployed elsewhere. At one time an army of 40,000 troops was searching for him; he always found shelter among the Waziris. After the creation of Pakistan, the faqir demanded independence for Pashtunistan (q.v.); he was elected "president" of Pashtunistan by a tribal council and continued his fight against the new state. He received financial support from the Afghan government until his death in 1960.

FATEH KHAN (FATH). Oldest son of Painda Khan (head of the Muhammadzai branch of the Barakzai tribe), born in 1777 in Kandahar. He was a skillful politician and soldier and helped Shah Mahmud (1799–1803 and 1810–18) gain the Afghan throne, capturing Farah and Kandahar, from the forces of Zaman Shah. He was given the position of grand wazir, established law and order, and conducted the government for Mahmud with great skill. When Shah Shuja (1803–10 and 1839) (qq.v.) succeeded to the Kabul throne, Fateh Khan was again appointed grand wazir, but Fateh Khan remained loyal to Mahmud and helped to restore him to power. Fateh Khan consolidated Afghan control over Kashmir and established order in Herat. Kamran, son of Shah Mahmud, was jealous of Fateh Khan's increasing power and had him blinded and, in 1818, killed. The Barakzai chiefs revolted, and the ensuing conflict led to the overthrow of the Sadozai dynasty and the assumption of power by the Barakzai/Muhammadzai branch of the Durranis.

FIRST ANGLO-AFGHAN WAR (1838–42). In the nineteenth century, European rivalry for commerce and empire quickly extended to the Middle East. In 1798 the Napoleonic invasion of Egypt temporarily established a French foothold in this strategic area, which Britain feared as an important step in a move against India. Russia moved into Central Asia and by the end of the nineteenth century the czar's influence extended to the Amu Daria. Britain was moving into the Panjab in search of a "scientific" frontier to make sure that her possessions in India were safe.

In Kabul, internecine warfare led to the ouster of Shah Shuja, the last of the Sadozai rulers, and Dost Muhammad, first of the Muhammadzai rulers, ascended the throne in 1826 (q.v.). He wanted an alliance with India and hoped to regain Peshawar, which had been lost in 1818 to the emerging Sikh nation under Ranjit Singh (q.v.). Lord Auckland, the British governor general of India, chose an alliance with the Sikh ruler instead and decided to restore Shah Shuja to the Afghan throne. The presence of a purported Russian agent at Kabul (*see* VITKEVICH, CAPT IVAN) and Dost Muhammad's hostility to the Sikh ruler were the reasons given for the declaration of war (*see* SIMLA MANIFESTO). In July 1838 a tripartite treaty was signed between Shah Shuja, Ranjit Singh, and Lord Auckland, and the "Army of the Indus" (q.v.) invaded Afghanistan. The invaders met with little resistance, Ghazni was captured on July 23 (*see* GHAZNI, CAPTURE OF), and Kabul was occupied on August 7. Shah Shuja was put on the Kabul throne, and Dost Muhammad was forced into Indian exile. The major part of the British army left Kabul on September 18.

But it was soon apparent that the Sadozai ruler needed British protection to maintain himself in power, and the army became a force of occupation. The families of British officers came to Kabul, and thousands of Indian camp followers engaged in the lucrative business of importing from India the necessities of colonial life. But all was not well. On November 2, 1841 a Kabuli crowd stormed the British mission

First Afghan War

A. Cantonment
B. Mission Residence
C. Mission Offices
D. Magazine Fort
E. Commissariat Fort
F. Muhammad Sharif's Fort
G. Rikabashi Fort
H. Muhammad Khan's Fort
I. Sulfikar's Fort
J. Camp as Siah Sang
K. King's Garden
L. Masjid
M. Bimaru Village
N. Private Garden
O. Bazar
P. Kulistan Gate of City
Q. Empty Fort near Bridge
R. Brig. Anquetil's Fort
S. Magazine in Orchard
T. Yabu Khana
V. Capt. Trevor's Tower
W. Sir A. Burnes House
X. Lahore Gate of City
Y. Ruins of Serg. Dean's House
Z. Capt. Johnson's Treasury
* Spot where Envoy was killed

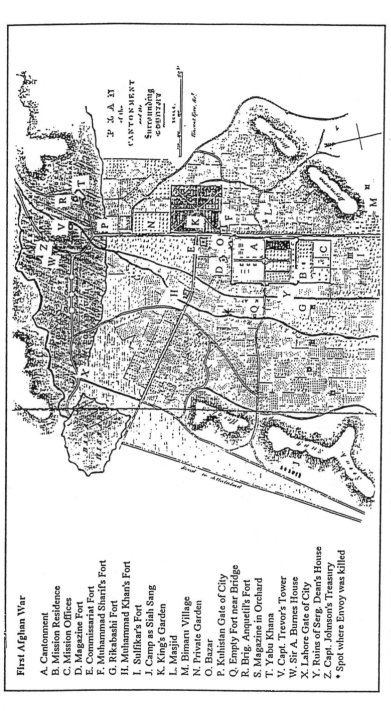

Plan 3. Plan of the Cantonment. Source: IOL, Eyre

and killed its members, including Alexander Burnes (q.v.), its head. The Afghans captured some £17,000 from the treasury in an adjacent house and plundered the commissariat stores located in a number of forts outside the cantonment. Muhammad Akbar (q.v.), a son of Dost Muhammad, together with a number of chiefs, now rallied his forces and increasingly threatened the occupiers. Major General William Elphinstone (q.v.) ordered the army to withdraw to the cantonment, which was commanded from nearby hills. He commanded seven regiments of horse and foot, with guns and sappers, English and Indian, and decided to recall General Sale from Gandomak and Nott (qq.v.) from Kandahar. But the roads were blocked by the onset of winter and by strong contingents of tribal *lashkars*, preventing a strengthening of the Kabul garrison. A raiding party sent out to silence Afghan guns was badly decimated and had to return, leaving their wounded behind. On December 11, 1841, the British were forced to negotiate a retreat that only few of the 16,000 troops and camp followers survived. (*See* CAPITULATION, TREATY OF; and DEATH MARCH.) Britain felt it necessary to have its martial reputation restored, and in September 1842 General George Pollock (q.v.), wreaked vengeance on Kabul, laying torch to the covered bazaar and permitting plunder, which destroyed much of the rest of the city. The British forces left, and Amir Dost Muhammad returned in December 1842 to rule Afghanistan until he died a natural death 20 years later. The war cost Britain £20 million and some 15,000 lives of all ranks as well as camp followers.

Forces Employed. Army of the Indus - for action in Sind and Afghanistan:

A Bengal column, with 2,430 cavalry, 5,570 infantry, and 31 guns.

A Bombay column, with 1,200 cavalry, 4,280 infantry, and 24 guns.

Shah Shuja's contingent of Indian troops with British officers, with 950 cavalry, 5,000 infantry, and 12 guns.

The Shahzadah's (Prince Timur) contingent.

An army of observation furnished by Ranjit Singh.

In reserve at Ferozpur: A mixed Bengal division, 3,000 strong.

On the lines of communications: Karachi, 5,000 men. Base supply depot was at bridge of boats near Sukkur.

Concentration. The Bengal column, including 250 sappers and miners and 240 pioneers concentrated at Karnal at the end of October 1838; marched thence to Ferozpur, the point of assembly for the shah's con-

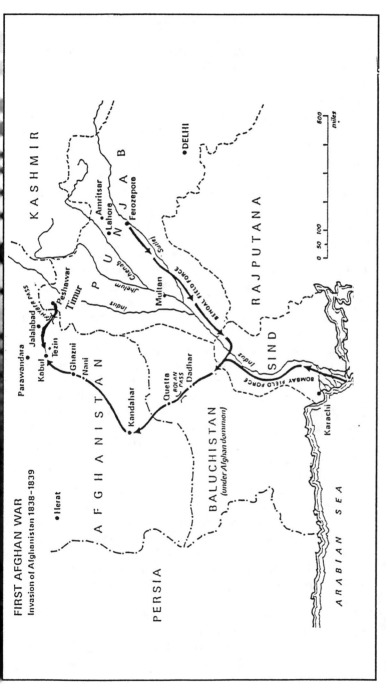

Plan 4. First Afghan War. Adapted from Anglesey

tingent and Ranjit Singh's forces; left Ferozpur in early December and traversed the 38 marches to Rohri via Bahawalpur, by January 24, 1839.

The Bombay column, including 100 sappers and miners, landed near Karachi in December 1838, and marched up the right bank of the Indus. Shah Shuja's contingent marched ahead of the Bengal column and arrived at Shikarpur in January 1839.

All assembled at Shikarpur between February 16 and 20, 1839, and formed what was named the "Army of the Indus," under the command of Lieutenant General Sir John Keane, commander in chief in Bombay (q.v.). The regulars were armed with smootbore percussion muskets, the irregulars with flintlocks, both inferior in range to the matchlocks of the Afghans.

The transport consisted of about 60,000 Indian, and several thousand Afghan, camels, as well as a number of baggage elephants. Servants and camp followers raised the number of mouths to feed to about 100,000. Beyond Shikapur, no supply depots had been established; water was scarce and bad. Only the Bombay troops carried water bottles. The 150 miles of desert between Shikapur and the Bolan Pass caused severe losses among the followers, camels, and horses. Followers were put on half rations. The Bengal column reached Quetta by the end of March 1839, but supplies promised by the Khan of Kalat were not forthcoming. The distance from Quetta to Kandahar, 147 miles, took 20 days. Three days were needed to cross the Khojak Pass — guns and wagons had to be dragged up by hand and lowered by ropes down a precipitous western side. Afghan raiders harassed and looted the ammunition, baggage, and supply columns.

The British paid the chief of the Kakar tribe 1,000 pounds to win his support, which led to the flight of the Barakzai brothers and the governor of Kandahar. On April 25, 1839 Shah Shuja entered Kandahar, one day ahead of the leading portion of the Bengal column. Within the next two weeks the total British force at Kandahar numbered 8,800 men and 30,046 camp followers. The British forces had only three days of supplies. The Bengal column lost 20,000 camels and 350 horses. The excessive heat and low rations caused considerable sickness.

When on June 27 Sir John Keane left Kandahar for Ghazni, some 230 miles away, his troops were again on half rations.

Advance from Peshawar. During the invasion of southern Afghanistan the Shahzada's contingent was raised from Pathan tribesmen under Sikh domination. It included 1,000 cavalry, 3,500 infantry, and four guns. To this was added Ranjit Singh's contingent of Muslim Panjabi mercenaries, comprising 1,050 cavalry, 4,800 infantry, and 12 guns. They were strengthened by the addition of two Bengali infantry battalions and four *ghund* of the regular army. The forces reached Peshawar on March 20 and were placed under the command of Lieutenant Colonel Wade. He started from Jamrud on July 22, moved into the Khaibar Pass, and captured Ali Masjid (q.v.) on the 27th. By this time some of Amir Dost Muhammad's supporters began to desert him, and most of the *Qizilbash* deserted. The Army of the Indus entered Kabul on August 7, and Colonel Wade's forces reached the capital on September 3. Ranjit Singh's troops did not proceed beyond the Khaibar Pass. (MR, 1924 and OASW)

FIRST ANGLO-AFGHAN WAR: CAUSES. During the siege of Herat in 1838, Lord Auckland determined to restore Shah Shuja to the throne of Kabul, in the hope of establishing a friendly power in Afghanistan, which was to form the first line of defense against the threatened advance of Russia on India. A tripartite treaty was concluded through English pressure, but neither Ranjit Singh nor Shah Shuja was happy. The former did not want to send his troops into Afghanistan, and the latter did not want to resign his claim on the Panjab and Sind. Lord Auckland (q.v.) informed the directors of the East India Company that

> the increase of Russian and Persian influence in Afghanistan, and the impression of the certain fall of Herat to the Persian army, have induced the Ameer Dost Mahomed Khan to avow and to insist upon pretensions for the cession to him, by Maharaja Runjeet Sing, of the Peshawur territory, and to take other steps which are tantamount to the rejection of the friendship and good offices of the British Government; and have in consequence led to the retirement of Captain Burnes from the territories of Cabool.

The Persian siege of Herat was ended, but Auckland was determined to make war. The resulting disaster was subsequently termed "Auckland's Folly."

FIRST ANGLO-AFGHAN WAR: COSTS. The cost of the war amounted to £17 million, ten thousand fighting men were killed, or died of wounds and sickness, and tens of thousands of camp followers perished. (MR, 28)

FLARES. Flare-emitting devices air dropped or fitted to aircraft to confuse the heat-seeking head of a missile. When the *mujahedin* acquired SA-7 missiles in 1983, the aerial superiority of Soviet forces was threatened and they began using various types of flares. To overcome these defensive measures, the *mujahedin* began to use British Blowpipe missiles (q.v.), which had command-guided, rather than heat-seeking, systems. They did not prove to be very efficient, but stingers, though heat-seeking, threatened Soviet control of the skies. (q.v.)

FORAGING. British military manuals suggested that foraging, to collect supplies for men and animals, by cavalry alone, possible in other countries, was not advisable in Afghanistan. The generally difficult terrain gave the Afghans numerous opportunities for cutting off horsemen. They were not only handicapped by the livestock and supplies they tried to carry off, but also by their own horses. (Kandahar, 1933, secret document) *See also* SUPPLIES; and LOGISTICS.

FOREIGN RELATIONS. *See* **AFGHAN FOREIGN RELATIONS.**

FORWARD POLICY. *See* **AFGHAN FOREIGN RELATIONS.**

FOWLER, MAJ. GEN. C. A. General officer commanding the 1st (Peshawar) Division during the third Anglo-Afghan war. Directed the second, and successful, attack on Bagh on May 11, 1919. *See* BAGH, BATTLE OF.

- G -

GAILANI, SAYYID AHMAD (AFANDI SAHIB, GILANI). Descendant of the Muslim Pir Baba Abdul Qadir Gailani (1077–1166) and hereditary head of the Qaderia sufi fraternity. He succeeded to his position upon the death of his older brother, Sayyid Ali, in 1964. Born in 1932 in Kabul, the son of Sayyid Hasan Gailani, he was educated at Abu Hanifa College and the Faculty of Theology at Kabul University. He left Afghanistan after the Saur Revolt (q.v.) and founded the National Islamic Front (NIFA – *Mahaz-i Milli-yi Islami-yi Afghanistan*) in Peshawar. His movement was part of the seven-member alliance which in 1989 formed the "Afghan Interim Government." It is a liberal, nationalist, Islamic party and, according to its manifesto, advocates the protection of the national sovereignty and territorial integrity of Afghanistan as well as the establishment of an interim government that would draft a national and Islamic constitution with the separation of executive, legislative, and judicial powers. It demands an elected and free government, would guarantee such fundamental rights as free speech, freedom of movement, the protection of private property, and social justice, including medical care and education for all Afghans. At the time of this writing, NIFA denies the legitimacy of Professor Rabbani's tenure and calls for the convening of a *loya jirga* to prepare for elections of a broad-based democratic government.

GANDOMAK (34-18' N, 70-2' E). A village on the Gandomak stream, a tributary of the Surkhab, about 29 miles southwest of Jalalabad. The area was the scene of a number of battles between British and Afghan forces, including the massacre of the last remnants of the British army in 1842. It was also the scene of a treaty that Major Louis Cavagnari and Amir Yaqub Khan (qq.v.) concluded and signed on May 26, 1879. *See* GANDOMAK, TREATY OF.

GANDOMAK, TREATY OF. A treaty concluded between the British government and Amir Yaqub Khan, signed by the amir and Major Louis Cavagnari on May 26, 1879 (qq.v.), and ratified by Lord Lytton, viceroy of India on May 30, 1879.

The treaty was to establish "eternal peace and friendship" between the two countries upon conclusion of the second Anglo-Afghan war (Article 1). It provided amnesty for Afghan collaborators with the British occupation forces (Article 2) and obligated the amir to "conduct his relations with Foreign States, in accordance with the advice and wishes of the British Government." In exchange, Britain would support the amir "against any foreign aggression with money, arms, or troops" (Article 3). A British representative was to be stationed at Kabul "with a suitable escort in a place of residence appropriate to his rank and dignity," and an Afghan agent was to be at the court of the viceroy of India (Article 4). A separate commercial agreement was to be signed (Article 7), and a telegraph line from Kurram to Kabul was to be constructed (Article 8). The Khaibar and Michni Passes were to be controlled by Britain (Article 9), Kandahar and Jalalabad were to be "restored" to the amir with the exception of Kurram, Pishin, and Sibi which were to be under British control but were not "considered as permanently severed from the limits of the Afghan kingdom." Afghan

Plate 1. Amir Yaqub Signs Treaty of Gandomak

historians consider the treaty a sellout to Britain and a treasonable act by Amir Yaqub Khan.

GENEVA ACCORDS. The result of "proximity" talks between Afghanistan and Pakistan in Geneva, initiated on June 16, 1982 by Diego Cordovez under the auspices of the United Nations and concluded on April 14, 1988. The accords consisted of four documents and an annex: three between the Republic of Afghanistan and the Islamic Republic of Pakistan; one between the Soviet Union and the United States, promising to "refrain from any form of interference and intervention"; and an annex with a memorandum of understanding, assisting the United Nations in the implementation of the agreements. The United States and the Soviet Union were to be the guarantors of the accords. The talks aimed at ending the "external interference" in the war in Afghanistan with a view toward establishing peace. The accords resulted in the withdrawal of Soviet troops in mid-February 1989, but failed to end foreign interference or to bring the warring parties closer to peace. One reason for the failure was that the *mujahedin* were not a party to the accords, another was that Washington, and virtually everyone else, expected the Marxist government to disintegrate promptly. When the Soviets departed, they left a considerable amount of war materiel and promised to supply more under the Treaty of Friendship of December 1978. The United States was obligated to cease military support of the *mujahedin*. The result was a haggling over "symmetry" and "negative symmetry" of arms supplies, not part of the formal agreements. Eventually, the Soviets and the United States informally agreed on "positive symmetry," that is to say, they reserved themselves the right to send arms in response to shipments by the other. The result was that both powers continued to support their "clients," and Pakistan continued to permit the passage of weapons through its territory. The war continued, and the superpower guarantees of noninterference in the internal affairs of Afghanistan were ignored.

GHAUSUDDIN KHAN, GEN. Commander of Afghan forces during the Panjdeh Incident (q.v.) in March 1885. He confronted Colonel Alikhanov, commander of the Russian forces, but was defeated by the superior power of the Russians. A British officer called him "a very superior Afghan. . . . He selected his position at Ak Teppe with a great deal of judgements. He. . . has shown much tact in his dealings with the Sarikhs [a Turkoman tribe], among whom he is as popular as an Afghan

[Pashtun] can be." He is buried in Caliph Ali's Mausoleum in Mazar-i Sharif. *See* PANJDEH INCIDENT.

GHAZI. Originally the designation for Arab beduin raiders who would strike from their desert refuge, carrying raids (*ghazw*) for booty into enemy territory. (The European term *razzia* for a predatory raid or police raid is a corruption of *ghazw*). After the advent of Islam, a *ghazi* was a holy warrior fighting against a non-Muslim enemy, synonymous with the term *mujahed* (pl. *mujahedin*) used by the Afghan resistance in the 1980s. During the Anglo-Afghan wars, *ghazis* were irregular fighters who took vows to die in battle against the unbelievers and staged suicidal attacks against superior forces, for Paradise was assured to the martyr. They were often poorly armed, but their reckless bravery made them a dangerous enemy. A British military historian said:

> A true ghazi counts no odds too great to face, no danger too menacing to be braved; the certainty of death only adds to his exaltation . . . . If every Afghan were a ghazi . . . our defenses would have been carried, and enormous slaughter would have followed on both sides. (Hensman, 333–34)

The term became a title given to a victorious commander. Mahmud of Ghazni, King Amanullah, Habibullah Kalakani, Nadir Shah (qq.v.), and others claimed this title.

GHAZNI (33-33' N, 68-26' E). The name of a province and town in eastern Afghanistan. The town had about 30,000 inhabitants in 1978 and is located at an elevation of some 7,000 feet on the road from Kabul to Kandahar, about 80 miles southeast of Kabul. The old town on the left bank of the river is walled and guarded by a citadel that was garrisoned by Afghan army units until it was taken by the *mujahedin*. Ghazni derives its fame from the fact that it was the capital of the Ghaznavid dynasty (977–1186). It is strategically located and was the scene of severe fighting between Afghan and British forces during the first two Afghan wars. A British garrison stationed in the town during the first Anglo-Afghan war was wiped out in December 1841. (*See* GHAZNI, CAPTURE OF.) The population of the town is largely Tajik, with some Ghilzais, Durranis, Hazaras, and a few Hindu shopkeepers.

GHAZNI, CAPTURE OF. In July 1839, during the first British invasion of Afghanistan, Sir John Keane (q.v.) marched his army from Kandahar

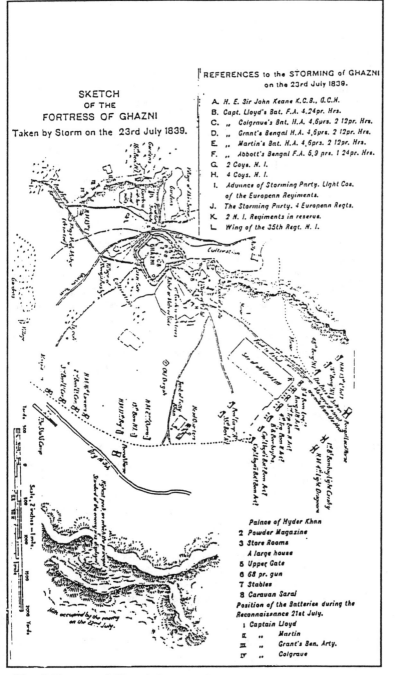

Plan 5. Fortress of Ghazni. Source: IOL

against Ghazni, which he thought to be only weakly fortified. Having left his siege guns at Kandahar, he decided to take the town in a *coup-de-main* by blowing up the Kabul Gate. A renegade Afghan had furnished the information that all gates had been bricked up, except for the Kabul Gate, which had been kept open in the expectation of reinforcements from Kabul. In the early hours of July 23, an explosion party, headed by three British officers, three sergeants, and 18 sappers, succeeded in carrying 300 pounds of gunpowder in 12 sandbags and, having positioned their artillery on both sides of the road leading to the Kabul Gate, successfully demolished it. An assault column of four European regiments commanded by General Sale made good their entry into the city. The British found the citadel deserted by the Afghan commander Afzal Khan and took possession of it. Afghan losses were estimated at 600 killed, and the British forces counted 18 dead and 173 wounded. (Heathcote, 41–42) On July 30 the British army moved against Kabul, leaving a garrison in command of the citadel. But Afghan forces returned and with the help of the inhabitants gained access to the town. The 27th Bengal Native Infantry was forced to retire to the citadel, where they held out until March 6, 1842, when lack of snow deprived them of their water supply. They then quartered themselves in town, where they were eventually forced to surrender. Most were killed or sold into slavery, but in September 1842 Major General Nott (q.v.) advanced and reoccupied the town, liberating 327 *sepoys* (Indian soldiers) who had survived. General Nott gave orders to destroy the citadel to deprive Afghans of the stronghold.

GHAZNIGAK, BATTLE OF. A town near Tashkurghan where a battle was fought on September 27, 1888 between the forces of Amir Abdur Rahman, headed by General Ghulam Haidar and Sardar Abdullah, against Ishaq Khan, a cousin of the amir and his governor of Afghan Turkestan. It was a bloody battle, lasting from early morning to late at night. Some of the amir's forces defected and

> galloped toward the hill where Mahomed Ishak was seated, to submit themselves to him. He, thinking . . . [they were] to take him prisoner, and that his army was defeated, fled away. Ishaq Khan fled to Russian Turkestan where he died shortly thereafter. (AR, 269)

GHILZAI. A major Pashtu-speaking tribe inhabiting an area roughly bounded by Kalat-i-Ghilzai in the south, the Gul Kuh range in the west, the Sulaiman range in the east, and the Kabul River on the north. The Ghilzai call themselves Ghaljai (pl. Ghalji) and count themselves the descendants of Ghalzoe, son of Shah Husain, said to have been a Tajik or Turk, and of Bibi Mato, who descended from Shaikh Baitan (the second son of Qais — progenitor of the Afghan nationality). The origin of the name Ghilzai comes from either *Ghal Zoe* (thief's son), *Khilji*, the Turkic word for swordsman, or the name of Khilji Turks who came into the area in the tenth century. From Ghalzoe the tribe divided into the Turan and Burhan Ibrahim branches.

The Sulaiman Khel are the most important of all, and the Ali Khel are the most important of the Burhan. In the nineteenth century they were said to number about 100,000 families, with 30,000 to 50,000 fighters. They were largely nomadic and called *Powindas* in India where they often travelled, making a living as merchant nomads.

The Hotaki Ghilzais achieved their fame in Afghan history as the liberators of Kandahar from Safavid control and as the leading tribe in the invasion of Iran and the destruction of the Persian Empire in 1722. Mir Wais (q.v.), a descendant of Malakhi, a leading chief at Kandahar, was taken by the Safavid governor to Isfahan, but was later permitted to return. He raised a revolt against the Kandahar governor and ruled over the province for some years (1709–15). His son Mahmud raised an army and invaded Persia, defeating the Safavid armies at the battle of Gulnabad in 1722 (q.v.). However, Mahmud was unable to hold on to his conquest. Nadir Khan (q.v.), founder of the short-lived Afsharite dynasty, reunited the Persian Empire and in turn invaded Afghan lands. After the death of Nadir Shah, the Ghilzai were weakened to such an extent that they could not prevent the emergence of the Durrani dynasty (q.v.). The Ghilzai fought the British when they invaded Afghanistan and subsequently became the major rivals of the Durranis. They revolted repeatedly against Muhammadzai rule and were suppressed only with difficulty in 1801, 1883, 1886, and 1937. Urban Ghilzai have since intermarried with Muhammadzai. The Ghilzai were well represented in the Marxist leadership (Taraki, Najibullah, Hafizullah Amin, Watanjar, Layeq, Rafi'i, and many others) but also among the resistance (Hekmatyar and Sayyaf), which prompted one expert to remark that for the first time power has passed from the Durrani to the Ghilzai. *See also* ABDUL KARIM.

GILANI. *See* **GAILANI.**

GORTCHAKOFF. *See* **GRANVILLE-GORTCHAKOFF AGREE-MENT.**

GRANVILLE-GORTCHAKOFF AGREEMENT. An Anglo-Russian agreement based on assurances given in 1868–69 and confirmed several times later in an exchange of letters between the foreign ministers, Lord Granville and Prince Gortchakoff, which stipulated that "Badakhshan with its dependent district of Wakhan from Sar-i-Kul on the east to the junction of the Kokcha River with the Oxus (or Panja) forming the northern boundary of this Afghan Province throughout its entire length." Further west, however, the border was not clearly defined, which eventually enabled Russia to annex Panjdeh (q.v.). Russia agreed that Afghanistan was outside its sphere of influence and, except for the territorial changes of Shignan and Roshan and the Panjdeh oasis, the Afghan border has remained as it is today. The agreement is also known as the Clarendon–Gortchakoff Agreement (q.v.).

GREAT GAME. A term attributed to Rudyard Kipling describing the competition between Russia and Great Britain in the conquest of the territories lying between their colonial possessions. Russia was aiming at gaining access to the warm-water ports of the Persian Gulf if not to the riches of India, and Britain wanted to prevent it. Afghanistan was a major player in this, desired by both as an ally. Afghan rulers realized that Russia needed to take Afghanistan to realize its objectives and therefore concluded a cautious alliance with Britain. Twice, during the nineteenth century, British armies invaded Afghanistan for the purpose of finding a "scientific frontier" on the crests of the Hindu Kush or the Amu Daria (Oxus) River. When direct control failed, Britain resigned itself to concluding an alliance with the Afghan ruler and to support him against the eventuality of Russian aggression. When Britain left India in 1947, the "Great Game" seemed to be over, because the United States was unwilling to guarantee Afghanistan's territorial integrity from Soviet aggression. Therefore, the Soviet Union seemed to have won the game when, in 1978, it intervened militarily in support of the Marxist government of Afghanistan. As during previous invasions, the Afghan people eventually prevailed.

GRENADIER. Originally a soldier employed to throw hand-grenades and subsequently the tallest and finest member of the elite company of every infantry battalion. The Grenadier Guards were the first regiment of foot guards in the British Household Brigade of Guards and were considered the finest corps in the army. It comprised 2,697 officers and men, was divided into three battalions, and was commanded by men of nobility or distinguished landed gentry. Grenadiers, auxiliaries were employed during sieges for special tasks. British grenadiers served in the Anglo-Afghan wars, including the fateful battle of Maiwand.

GRIFFIN, SIR LEPEL (1840-?). Chief political officer at Kabul during the second Anglo-Afghan war whose negotiations with Sardar Abdur Rahman led to the recognition of the latter as Amir of Afghanistan. At the death of Amir Shir Ali and the abdication of Yaqub Khan, Abdur Rahman entered Afghanistan with the intention of driving the British from his country. Realizing their untenable position, the British government recognized Abdur Rahman to ensure an orderly withdrawal of its army to India.

GROMOV, LT. GEN. BORIS V. Commander of the 40th Army, comprising the "Limited Contingent of Soviet Forces in Afghanistan," who spent three tours in Afghanistan. The 45-year-old general led a combined Soviet/Afghan force of some 10,000 troops from Gardez against Khost, temporarily lifting the siege of this strategic town in January 1988. It was the last major Soviet operation facing considerable *mujahedin* opposition and the type of action not originally considered his task. Gromov stated that Soviet forces were intended to establish garrisons, stabilize the situation, and refrain from significant combat operations, leaving counterinsurgency to the DRA forces. (McMichael, 10) Eventually, only about 30 percent to 35 percent of Soviet forces were devoted to security and defense of fixed sites, and it was inevitable that defense also required counterinsurgency operations. McMichael quotes Gromov as saying, "The war in Afghanistan demonstrated a large rupture between theory and practice." But he felt it was unavoidable. Gromov was assigned the task of evacuating the last contingent of 450 armored vehicles and about 1,400 Soviet troops from Afghanistan. On February 14, 1989 he was the last Soviet soldier to cross the "Friendship Bridge" into Soviet territory. He announced to the assembled reporters, "We have fulfilled our international duty to the end." (O'Ballance, 196) He became minister of the interior in 1990 and commander of all Russian ground troops in 1992.

GUERRILLA WARFARE. Military operations conducted by informal forces during foreign invasion or civil war, mainly of the hit-and-run type, against a superior enemy. It was the typical warfare of the *ghazis* and *mujahedin* against British and Soviet forces. A temporary concentration of forces go on the offensive and quickly disperse before countermeasures can be taken. Counterinsurgency measures, therefore, include the destruction of entire villages, crops, fruit trees, livestock, channels of irrigation (*karez)*, and other sources to deprive the guerrillas of their suppport. Although the Afghan *ghazis,* or *mujahedin,* fought under the banner of Islam, tribalism and nationalism, as well as sectarian allegiance may in fact have been the dominant ideology. Unlike resistance movements in other parts of the world, the Afghans generally lacked a unified command. This was seen as a weakness by some, but turned out to be a factor of strength during the war; only when the war was won did the fragmentation of power contribute to the ongoing civil war for political control of the country. *See also* AFGHANS, METHODS OF FIGHTING.

GULNABAD, BATTLE OF. An important victory of Afghan forces under Mahmud, son of the Ghilzai chief Mir Wais, which marked the end of the Safavid Empire of Iran. On March 8, 1722, Mahmud met and decisively defeated a superior Iranian army and then besieged Isfahan for six months before taking the capital of the empire. The Ghilzais proved to be better soldiers than empire-builders; they were forced to yield power to Nadir Shah Afshar and withdrew to their Afghan homeland, where they were superseded by the Durranis as the dominant tribe. *See also* NADIR SHAH, AFSHAR; MIR WAIS; and GHILZAI.

- H -

HABIBULLAH, AMIR (HABIB ALLAH 1901–1919). Amir of Afghanistan who kept his state neutral in World War I, but wanted to end Britain's quasi protectorate over his country. He was born in Samarkand on April 21, 1871, the son of Amir Abdur Rahman and an Uzbek lady from Badakhshan. He succeeded to the throne on October 3, 1901 and assumed the title *Seraj al-Millat wa'd-Din* (Torch of the Nation and Religion). He increased the pay of the army, permitted exiles to return, including many *sardars* (nobles) and their families, released prisoners, and promised reforms.

The British government was not satisfied with some of the provisions of the agreements concluded with Amir Abdur Rahman, and therefore wanted to force certain changes before it recognized the new amir. London maintained that the agreements were with the *person* of the amir, not the State of Afghanistan, and therefore had to be renegotiated with his successor. In spite of severe pressures, Habibullah did not yield. In December 1904, he finally agreed to meet in Kabul with Louis W. Dane, foreign secretary of the government of India. The result was a complete victory for Habibullah. Britain was forced to renew the agreements concluded with Amir Abdur Rahman in the form of a treaty. *See* ANGLO-AFGHAN TREATY OF 1905.

Amir Habibullah showed great interest in Western technology and embarked on a process of modernization. He imported automobiles and built roads, founded Habibia School in 1904, the first modern school in Afghanistan, and brought electricity to Kabul. In January 1907 Amir Habibullah traveled to India and was cordially received by the viceroy, Lord Minto. A crisis in relations with British India occurred when Habibullah learned that Afghanistan's neighbors had concluded the Anglo-Russian Convention of 1907 (q.v.). This agreement divided Afghanistan (and Iran) into spheres of influence, with provisions for "equality of commercial opportunity" in Afghanistan for Russian and British traders and the appointment of commercial agents in Kabul. The amir was invited to ratify the agreement, but he refused and the convention was never implemented.

The outbreak of World War I posed another crisis in foreign relations: in spite of warnings not to do so from the viceroy of India, Amir Habibullah received a German mission at Kabul. He met with members of the Hentig-Niedermayer expedition (q.v.) and initialed the draft of a secret treaty of friendship and military assistance with Germany to provide for the eventuality of an Allied defeat. Germany could not deliver, and Britain promised a handsome reward for Afghan neutrality; therefore, a realistic appraisal of the situation prompted the Afghan ruler to stay out of the war.

Britain showed itself miserly and, once the crisis was over, wanted to reestablish its exclusive control over Afghanistan. The "war party" at his court felt that the amir had failed to take advantage of a unique opportunity of winning independence from Britain and conspired to depose him. He was assassinated on February 20, 1919, while he was on a hunting trip at Kala Gosh in Laghman.

HABIBULLAH KALAKANI, AMIR. A Tajik of humble origins who was a leader of the antireformist reaction that swept King Amanullah from power and placed him on the throne. He was known as *Bacha-i-Saqqao* (son of a water carrier), the occupation of his father, Aminullah, a Tajik from the village of Kalakan in the Kohdaman district (north of Kabul). With the support of a loose coalition of Kohistani forces, he took advantage of a tribal revolt to capture Kabul and have himself proclaimed amir. Following the custom of Afghan rulers, Habibullah adopted the title "Servant of the Religion of the Messenger of God" (Khadem-i Din-i Rasulullah) and set about to consolidate his power.   Two factors militated against his royal aspirations: he was of Tajik, rather than the dominant, Pashtun ethnic background, and he was known as a brigand, albeit of a Robin Hood nature, as seen from the perspective of his Kohistani brothers.

Habibullah was a natural leader and had a charismatic personality, but his assumption of the throne was challenged from the beginning. A British officer reported from Peshawar that "Bacha-i-Saqqao's accession has come as a profound shock to the tribes on both sides of the Durand Line." Even the Shinwaris whose revolt had started the civil war were not willing to submit to the new king. The fact that Habibullah had found some £750,000 at the conquest of the Arg (royal palace) permitted him to pay his troops and win some tribal support.

Forces loyal to King Amanullah were unable to recapture the throne, but Muhammad Nadir (q.v.) and his brothers succeeded. Shah Wali Khan, brother of Nadir and brother-in-law of King Amanullah, captured the Arg in October 1929, and Habibullah was forced to surrender. On November 1 Habibullah, his brother Hamidullah, and Sayyid Husain together, with nine leaders of their turbulent regime, were executed.

HARAKAT-I INQILAB-I ISLAMI. *See* **MUHAMMADI, MAULAWI MUHAMMAD NABI.**

HARAKAT-I ISLAMI. *See* **MUHSINI, AYATOLLAH MUHAMMAD ASEF.**

HASHT-NAFARI. A system of recruitment imposed on the frontier tribes by which they were to provide one able-bodied man out of eight (D. *hasht,* eight, nafar, persons). Amir Abdur Rahman introduced this system in 1896; similar to previous feudal levies, the notables and chiefs of tribes had to make the selection and provide the enlistee with all his needs. The tribes were willing to perform military service, but wanted to do so only during emergencies; therefore, there were occasional revolts, protesting the hasht-nafari recruitment during peacetime. Discontinued and, reintroduced in 1922, upon the advice of Jamal Pasha (q.v.), the *hasht-nafari* system contributed to the growing opposition to King Amanullah.

HAZARAS and **HAZARAJAT**. The Hazarajat, heartland of the Hazara people, comprises Ghor, Oruzgan, Bamian, and portions of adjoining provinces. Hazara communities also exist in virtually all the major towns of Afghanistan. At the turn of the century the Hazara were estimated at about 500,000 people, or some 120,000 families but their number has since increased to about 1.5 million. They are not tribally organized, but have been loosely identified under some seven or eight sections.

The Hazaras derive their name from the Persian *hazar,* meaning one thousand, which indicates that they may be the descendants of units of one thousand of the thirteenth century Turco-Mongolian invaders who assimilated with local Tajiks. They speak a Persian dialect called *Hazaragi*, which also includes a number of eastern Turkic words and a few of Mongol origin. They are largely Shi'as of the Twelver (*ithna 'ashariya*), or *imami*, school, which is dominant in Iran, and may have been sunnis until the Safavids converted them to shi'ism in the sixteenth century.

Since the founding of Afghanistan in 1747, the Sadozai kings carried expeditions into the Hazarajat. The Besud, Foladi, and Bamian sections of the Hazarajat as well as the Turkman and Shaikh Ali Hazaras of the Hindu Kush, were taxpaying subjects of Zaman Shah (1773–93). In 1842 Yar Muhammad, the de facto ruler of Herat, carried a campaign into Afghan Turkestan and transported a large number of Hazara families to the lower valley of the Hari Rud. During the reign of Dost Muhammad (1826–48) much of the Hazarajat was under Kabul control, and Amir Shir Ali (1863–79) brought additional sections under Afghan rule. (qq.v.) In their struggle against Kabul the Jaghori Hazaras collaborated with Britain during the second Anglo-Afghan war, and in 1886 Hazaras supported the rebellious Ghilzais against the government of Amir Abdur Rahman. The Iron Amir finally subdued them in 1893, after a series of bloody wars (*see* HAZARA WARS).

The Hazarajat rose against the *Khalqi* regime in 1979 and, under the *shura* (Revolutionary Council of the Islamic Union of Afghanistan) of

Sayyid Ali Beheshti (q.v.), ruled the Hazara heartland until challenged by newly emerging Islamist movements. In the "battle for Kabul" the *Hizb-i Wahdat*, a coalition of largely Hazara groups, headed by Abdul Ali Mazari (killed in March 1995 while in *Taleban* custody), was one of the principal contenders for power. Ayatollah Muhammad Asef Muhsini (q.v.), a Pashtu-speaking Hazara from Kandahar Province, heads a small independent group called *Harakat-i Islami*.

HAZARA WARS. When in July 1880 Britain recognized Amir Abdur Rahman as "Amir of Kabul and its Dependencies," it was not certain what the "dependencies" would be. Britain had toyed with the idea of severing Herat and Kandahar from Kabul control, and Russia coveted Turkestan territory, finally annexing a section of northwestern Afghanistan in 1885 in the "Panjdeh Incident" (q.v.). Afghanistan's boundaries were not clearly defined, and the "Iron Amir" found it necessary to extend his authority to every corner of his realm lest his powerful neighbors continue their forward policies. In a series of wars he eliminated rivals to his power and gained control of Kandahar, Herat, Afghan Turkestan, the Hazarajat, and Kafiristan (now Nuristan).

This extraordinary achievement of nation-building proved to be a calamity for the Hazara community. Amir Abdur Rahman stated his reasons for the war:

> The Hazara people had been for centuries past the terror of the rulers of Kabul, even the great Nadir who conquered Afghanistan, India, and Persia being unable to subdue the turbulent Hazaras; the Hazaras were always molesting travelers in the south, north, and western provinces of Afghanistan; they were always ready to join the first foreign aggressor who attacked Afghanistan. . . . (AR, I, 276)

And, indeed, the Hazaras shared the inclination to raiding with other ethnic communities. As a religious minority, they were willing to collaborate with the enemies of the Kabul regime.

Initially, Amir Abdur Rahman embarked on a gradual process of reconquest. After three campaigns in 1881, 1882, and 1883, as well as attempts at peaceful penetration, the Shaikh Ali Hazaras northwest of Bamian were the first to be pacified in 1886. Shortly thereafter all Hazara tribes with the exception of those of Pas-i-Koh in Oruzgan Province were forced to pay taxes on land and livestock. In 1890 Abdur

Rahman appointed Sardar 'Abd al Quddus governor of Bamian and ordered him to win the submission of the Oruzgan Hazaras. The latter accepted a deal in which they were to retain their internal autonomy and pay no taxes for a number of years.

When Abd al-Quddus again entered Hazara territory a year later with a 10,000-man force, he claimed to have met armed resistance and began to disarm Hazara communities and collected taxes from them. Thereupon the Sultan Muhammad Hazaras, headed by Mir Husain Beg, rose in rebellion and defeated the forces of Abd al-Quddus as well as a relief force sent by the amir under Faiz Muhammad. Their success encouraged other Hazara sections to join the general revolt, and the amir realized that the situation required a large-scale campaign to suppress the rebellion.

Amir Abdur Rahman felt that an all-out effort, including psychological warfare, was needed. The amir claimed that Iranian publications in the possession of Afghan Shi'as had insulted the sunni caliphs as usurpers and urged the Shi'a community to rise against sunni control. The amir's chief *mufti* (canon lawyer) issued a legal opinion, *fatwa*, declaring Shi'as infidels and proclaiming holy war on the Hazara. A council of Hazaras countered that instead of obeying a temporal ruler, they relied on their spiritual ruler, "the Master of the sword of Zulfikar" (Hazrat Ali, the Shi'a *imam* and fourth of the sunni caliphs).

In addition to regular forces, tribal levies were called up with great success as there was considerable promise of booty. Mullas accompanied the troops to keep passions high and incite them to heroic feats. Pashtuns flocked to the colors in considerable numbers, and, according to a British observer, "the Ghilzays . . . showed more zeal than the Durranis." In spite of the holy-war *fatwa*, levies of Hazaras of the Dai Kundi, Behsud, and Jaghori sections were enlisted, but most of those who survived defected during the war.

In spring 1891 Amir Abdur Rahman ordered a concerted attack by Sardar Abd al-Quddus from Bamian, Shir Muhammad from Kabul, and Brigadier Zabardast from Herat that led to the occupation of Oruzgan. Hazara chiefs were brought to Kabul in an attempt to win their submission. But in spring 1892 the Hazara chiefs Muhammad Azim and Muhammad Husain, supported by their chief *mujtahid* (legal expert) Kazi Asghar, turned against Amir Abdur Rahman. Rebellion rose with new fury, and it was only when a concerted attack from Turkestan, Kabul, Ghazni, Herat, and Kandahar was renewed that the Hazara uprising was quelled. It was not until September 1893 that all Hazara sections were subdued. The amir had given the permission that "everybody would be allowed to go and help in the punishment of the rebels," and punishment was indeed severe. Forts were demolished and governors, judges and *muftis* were appointed in every district. About 16,000 Durrani and Ahmadzai Ghilzai tribesmen were ordered to settle in Oruzgan Province, and large numbers of Hazaras emigrated to Mashhad (Iran), and Quetta (India, now Pakistan) where they are still living today. In accordance with an old tradition, conquest by force (*'anwatan*) permitted the enslavement of prisoners, and thousands of Hazaras were taken to Kabul.

HEKMATYAR, GULBUDDIN. Amir (chief) of the *Hizb-i Islami-yi Afghanistan* (q.v., Islamic Party of Afghanistan), one of the seven *mujahedin* groups formed in Peshawar. His party is radical Islamist and fights for the establishment of an Islamic republic, to be governed according to its interpretation of Islamic law. Born in 1947 in Imam Sahib, Kunduz, a Ghilzai Pashtun, Hekmatyar studied engineering at Kabul University for two years and became involved in campus politics. He became a member of the "Muslim Youth" movement in 1970 and - was elected to its executive council (*shura*). He was imprisoned in Dehmazang jail in Kabul, from 1972 to 1973, and, after the Daud coup of 1973, fled to Pakistan. In 1975 he became leader of the *Hizb-i Islami* and began armed attacks from bases in Pakistan with clandestine support from the Bhutto government. Isolated raids developed into modern guerrilla warfare after the Saur Revolt of April 1978. The party adopted from the Muslim Brotherhood such features as centralized command structure, secrecy of membership, organization in cells, infiltration of government and social institutions, and the concept of the party as an Islamist "vanguard" in Afghan society.

Being Islamist rather than nationalist, the party enjoyed considerable support from like-minded groups in Pakistan and the Gulf. His party received most of the armed support from the West and Gulf sources, and apparently was able to hoard a considerable amount of weapons, which served him well in the subsequent battle for Kabul. He surprised friends and foes alike when he allied himself with Lieutenent General Shahnawaz Tanai (q.v.), a radical *Khalqi*, in a coup against the Kabul government of Dr. Najibullah. After the downfall of the Marxist regime, many of the *khalqi* military officers joined Hekmatyar's forces, as did General Dostum, a former Parchami, who controls large portions of northern Afghanistan. The *Hizb-i Islami* of Gulbuddin Hekmatyar and the *Jam'iat-i Islami* of Burhanuddin Rabbani were the major protagonists in the war for the conquest of Kabul until a new force, the *Taleban* (q.v.), expelled Hekmatyar from his headquarters in Charasia and portions of Kabul. Hekmatyar fled to Sarobi, where his party has another base. In summer 1996, Hekmatyat made peace (or a temporary alliance?) with Rabbani and became his prime minister in Kabul. *See also* ISLAMIST MOVEMENT.

HELICOPTERS. Helicopters were first used in warfare during the Soviet intervention in Afghanistan. In 1980 the Afghan air force included about seven squadrons of 45–60 Soviet Mi-4s, Mi-8s, Mi-17s, and Mi-24s. This number rose within a year to almost 300, to which must be added the considerable aerial capacity of the Soviet forces. Helicopters were employed primarily for logistical support, reconnaissance, convoy security, evacuation, tactical lift, and fire support. They were utilized for such tasks as mine dispersal and counterinsurgency operations, where they proved to be extraordinarily effective and greatly feared by the *mujahedin*. The Mi-24 Hind and the Mi-8 Hip were the "workhorses" of the rotary-wing force. Helicopters were less effective in ground-support operations in narrow valleys, where their mobility was greatly limited and were they where subject to fire from above for which they were not sufficiently protected. The rotary blades of the Mi-24s, with a span of almost 60 feet, were highly vulnerable to damage. When the *mujahedin* acquired surface-to-air missiles, their efficiency in providing tactical support was further reduced.

HELIOGRAPHY. A method of signaling invented by the American Indians, called looking-glass signaling, and adopted by the British military in India prior to the introduction of telegraphic communication. A concave mirror is used to reflect the sunlight, or an artificial light, to signal in a prearranged code information to troops, covering as many as 40 mile distances in a direct line of sight. Heliography was to a certain extent the equivalent of Afghan drums (*dhol*), except that the latter were limited to simple signals. The Afghan term for the heliograph is *a'ina-i barqi*. Visual signaling, whether by flags, discs, lamps, or heliography, had the disadvantage that it could be used only within the line of vision and could be seen by the enemy, exposing the signaler to attack.

HENTIG-NIEDERMAYER EXPEDITION. An expedition conceived in August 1914 by the German general staff for the purpose of "revolutionizing India, inducing Afghanistan to attack India, and securing Iran as a bridge from the Ottoman empire to Afghanistan." The leading members were Werner Otto von Hentig, a young German diplomat who had served in Iran, and Oskar von Niedermayer, a captain in the German army. They were accompanied by Kazim Bey, a Turkish officer, Maulawi Barakatullah and Mahendra Pratap, two Indian revolutionaries, and a number of Afridi Pashtuns who had been recruited from a prisoner of war camp. Hentig carried an unsigned letter purported to be from the German kaiser and a message from von Bethmann-Hollweg, the chancellor, for Amir Habibullah. He was to establish diplomatic relations and conclude a treaty of friendship or, if possible, an alliance, with Afghanistan. Niedermayer was to discuss matters of a military nature and the Indians were to appeal to Amir Habibullah for support in the fight against the British in India. Kazim Bey was to convey special messages from the sultan-caliph and the leaders of the Ottoman war government. Members of the expedition crossed Iran and entered Afghanistan in August 1915 and five weeks later reached Kabul.

Amir Habibullah was well aware of the power of Britain and, even though his heart and ultimate loyalty were with the Ottoman sultan-caliph, he was not willing to rush into a risky adventure. He initialed the draft of a treaty that was so extravagant in its demands that only a victorious Germany could have provided the financial and military support requested. The expedition disbanded in May 1916, and Hentig returned by way of the Wakhan Corridor to China and from there to the United States and Germany. Niedermayer went through Russian Central Asia to Iran and the Ottoman Empire. The expedition was the first diplomatic contact with Germany and marked the beginning of the end of Britain's monopoly over the conduct of Afghan foreign relations. *See also* AFGHAN FOREIGN RELATIONS.

HERAT (34-20' N, 62-12' E). Herat is a province in northwestern Afghanistan with an area of 16,107 square miles and a population of about 685,000 in 1979. The capital of the province is the city of Herat with about 140,000 inhabitants, and it is the third largest city in Afghanistan. Located at an altitude of 2,600 feet, the city is the major commercial center of western Afghanistan. The old town was surrounded by a wall built in 1885 and mostly destroyed in the 1950s. Herat is of great strategic importance and therefore has been the site of fortified towns since antiquity. It is an ancient city, first mentioned in the

Avesta (the holy book of Zoroastrianism) as *Hairava*, which Afghan historians conjecture to be derived from Aria, or Ariana, the first "Afghan" kingdom flourishing around 1,500 B.C. The town was on the route of the Achaemenid armies of Cyrus and Darius and two centuries later of Alexander the Great, who in 330 B.C. built *Alexandria Ariorum* on the site of Herat. In the eleventh century Herat became a famous urban center in Islamic Khorasan (q.v.) where scholars like Khwaja Abdullah Ansari and others flourished. In the twelfth century , Turkomans had destroyed the city numerous times, and a century later the hordes of Genghis Khan destroyed it, with only a handful of the population surviving a general massacre. In the fourteenth century Timur-i-Lang's forces devastated the city. Rebuilt by Timur's son Shah Rukh, the city experienced a period of glory. Again in the early sixteenth century, Sultan Husain Mirza Baiqara made Herat "the most renowned center of literature, culture, and art in all Central and Western Asia."

In 1509 the city came under Safavid rule until, in about 1715, the Abdalis took control. In 1730 it was captured by Nadir Shah Afshar and in 1750 by Ahmad Shah Durrani (qq.v.). Next, Herat was ruled by various princes whose internecine fighting invited Persian attack. In 1834 and 1837 the Qajar ruler, Muhammad Shah, besieged the city, but the endurance of the Heratis and British intervention in the Persian Gulf forced him to give up after a nine-month-long effort. Nasiruddin Shah captured the city in 1856, but was forced to pull out when British troops attacked Bushire in 1857. Amir Abdur Rahman (q.v.) ended Herat's semi-independence. The present war in Afghanistan has lead to considerable destruction. It began in March 1979 with a popular revolt against the Kabul government that was severely repressed. (*See* HERAT UPRISING.) Herat was regained for the Kabul government, but the *mujahedin* were able to control much of the countryside in spite of divisional offensive sweeps by Soviet/Kabul forces. In April 1988, some 3,000 government forces defected to the *mujahedin* when they were offered amnesty. After the fall of the Najibullah government, Ismail Khan became the paramount chief of Herat Province until he was dislodged in September 1995 by the newly emerging forces of the *Taleban* (qq.v.).

HERAT, SIEGE OF. Persia, encouraged by Russia, laid siege to Herat (1837–38), but was unable to capture the city. A British officer, Major Eldred Pottinger (q.v.), claimed an important role in the defense of the

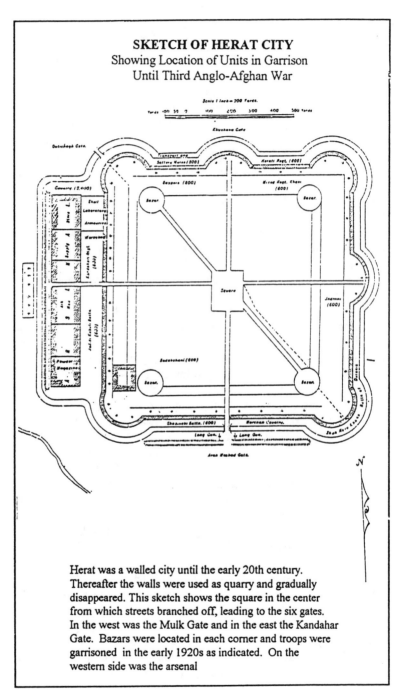

SKETCH OF HERAT CITY
Showing Location of Units in Garrison
Until Third Anglo-Afghan War

Herat was a walled city until the early 20th century.
Thereafter the walls were used as quarry and gradually
disappeared. This sketch shows the square in the center
from which streets branched off, leading to the six gates.
In the west was the Mulk Gate and in the east the Kandahar
Gate. Bazars were located in each corner and troops were
garrisoned in the early 1920s as indicated. On the
western side was the arsenal

Plan 6. Sketch of Herat City. Source: MR, 1925

city. When Britain could not induce the shah to desist, Indian troops landed, on June 19, 1838, on the island of Kharak in the Persian Gulf. It was only then that Persia lifted the siege and withdrew in September 1838.

HERAT UPRISING. On March 21, 1979 demonstrators against the Kabul regime seized control of the city and liberated political prisoners. They proceeded to attack government officials and killed many of the Soviet advisers and their families, carrying the heads of some on pikes through the city. When the Marxist government sent troops to quell the uprising, the entire Afghan 17th Division mutinied and a powerful resistance organization was born, headed by Captain Ismail Khan. The Kabul government brought in air strikes, which eventually broke the resistance at the cost of some 5,000 deaths.

HIZB-I ISLAMI *See* **HEKMATYAR, GULBUD-DIN.**

HIZB-I ISLAMI (KHALES). *See* **KHALES, MUHAMMAD YUNUS.**

HIZB-I WAHDAT. A coalition of eight Hazara Shi'a parties led by Abdul Ali Mazari centered in the area of Bamian and Wardak. It forged an alliance with Hekmatyar's *Hizb-i Islami* in August 1993 and controlled parts of Kabul west of the Darulaman road and south of Sarak-i Say-i Aqrab, as well as parts of Kabul University and all of Kabul Polytechnic compound. Mazari prevailed in a power struggle with Muhammad Akbari, who was head of the *Wahdat*'s political committee (Akbari was forced to flee and joined the forces of Rabbani). In January 1995 *Hizb-i Wahdat* was fighting for turf with the Shi'a *Harakat-i Islami* of Ayatollah Muhsini (q.v.). When Hekmatyar's forces were driven from Kabul in February 1995, *Jam'iat* captured the territory of the weakened *Wahdat* and Mazari joined, or surrendered to, the *Taleban* and was killed while in captivity on March 13, 1995. He is succeeded by Muhammad Karim Khalili.

- I -

IBRAHIM BEG. A Uzbek Basmachi (q.v.) leader who fought the Bolshevik government in Central Asia, at times using Afghan territory as a safe haven. He visited Kabul in 1926 and was entertained as a state guest by King Amanullah, who was not averse to the idea of becoming ruler of a Central Asian confederation of Muslim states. In May 1929, Ibrahim Beg supported Habibullah Kalakani (q.v.) and fought King Amanullah's general, Ghulam Nabi Charkhi, taking a prominent part in the capture of Mazar-i Sharif. In 1930, after repeated representations by the Soviet Union, the government of Nadir Shah took steps to prevent Ibrahim Beg from raiding across the border, with the consequence that he started raiding in Afghanistan as well. Therefore, he was finally driven from Afghan territory and captured by Soviet troops. Afghans call the battle between Afghan troops and Ibrahim Beg's supporters *Jang-i Laqay* (War of the Laqai, name of Ibrahim's Uzbek tribe). He was executed in April 1931.

INTER-SERVICES INTELLIGENCE (ISI). A Pakistani military intelligence organization, headed by General A. R. Akhtar from 1979 to 1987 and subsequently by General Hamid Gul, which was heavily involved in the war against Soviet/Kabul government forces in Afghanistan. Brigadier Muhammad Yousaf, head of the Afghan Bureau of the ISI, claims credit for coordinating the logistics, recruitment, training, and assignment of missions, including raids into the Soviet Union. The ISI distributed the weapons and funds provided by friendly countries while the government of Pakistan maintained an increasingly "implausible deniability" of involvement in the war. Muhammad Yousaf detailed ISI activities in a book entitled *The Bear Trap: Afghanistan's Untold Story*, edited by the military historian Mark Adkin.

ISLAMIC ALLIANCE FOR THE LIBERATION OF AFGHAN-ISTAN. A loose coalition founded on January 27, 1980 by five *mujahedin* groups with headquarters in Pakistan. The sixth group, Hekmatyar's Hezb, did not participate because it was not given preeminent status. The alliance was formed for the purpose of gaining recognition as a government in exile and to secure support from the Islamic Foreign Ministers Conference, held in Islamabad in May 1980. The alliance disintegrated in December of the same year. In early 1981 the Pakistan government announced that it would henceforth recognize only six groups (later seven) and that all refugees in the country must register as members of one of these groups. Refugee aid as well as *mujahedin* support would be channeled through these groups. Thus in 1985 the Alliance reconstituted itself under the label *Islamic Unity of Afghan Mujahedin*, with the moderates in the "Unity of Three" (Gailani, Mujaddidi, and Muhammadi) and the radicals organized in the "Unity of Seven," of whom only four (Rabbani, Hekmatyar, Sayyaf, and Khales) represented viable groups (qq.v.). While the moderates were reasonably united, the radicals were constantly at odds, especially the groups headed by Rabbani and Hekmatyar. In May 1983 the alliance elected Sayyaf chairman for a term of two years, but when, in 1985, he attempted to remain in this position, the members of the alliance objected.

Subsequently, a chairman of the alliance served on a rotational basis for three months. There was otherwise little coordination between the groups. Upon becoming spokesman in February 1988, Pir Sayyid Ahmad Gailani announced the formation of an Afghan Interim Government (AIG) with Eng. Ahmad Shah as prime minister. Unity however, was not to be achieved. After the fall of the Marxist regime and the capture of Kabul in April 1992, an interim government was headed for two months by President Mujaddidi, who was followed by Burhanuddin Rabbani. Rabbani remains president of the Islamic Republic of Afghanistan (IRA) in defiance of other major *mujahedin* groups and has been embroiled in a struggle for control of the Afghan capital, which has led to considerable destruction of the city without the conflict being resolved.

ISLAMIST MOVEMENT. The movement was born in reaction to the process of Westernization in Afghanistan and the growth of secular, liberal ideologies among Afghan youth. The movement owes much of its organization and ideology to the influence of the Muslim Brotherhood of Egypt (*Al-Ikhwan Al-Muslimun*), and its adherents were therefore dubbed *Ikhwanis* by their opponents. The party originated in religious, intellectual circles in the late 1950s and had as its chief ideologues and mentors Dr. Ghulam Muhammad Niazi, Burhanuddin Rabbani, Dr. Sayyid Musa Tawana, and others who had studied at al-Azhar University in Egypt and taught at the Faculty of Theology of Kabul University. They recruited a circle of like-minded students, who organized themselves in 1970 into the Islamic Youth (*Jawanan-i Muslimin*) Movement. At first they went through a process of ideological development, studying the works of Islamic thinkers such as Hasan al-Banna' (1906–49), the "Supreme Guide" of the Ikhwanis; Sayyid Qutb, executed in Cairo in 1966; and Abu'l Ala Maududi (died 1979), founder of the Pakistani *Jama'at-i Islami* (q.v.) and author of religiopolitical treatises. The movement took a political turn during the premiership of Sardar Daud (1953–63) and the subsequent liberal period. Islamist students staged demonstrations, protesting government policies and such international issues as Zionism and the war in Vietnam. By 1970 Islamists won a majority in student elections, a fact that alarmed the Marxists and their supporters. In 1971 the movement began to formally organize at a meeting in Kabul at the house of Professor Rabbani. A leadership council was formed of which Rabbani was the chairman, Abdul Rasul Sayyaf, his deputy (q.v.), and Engineer Habibur Rahman, the secretary. Council members were assigned responsibility for financial, cultural, and political tasks. Some leaders, like Niazi, refrained from open participation; others, like Hekmatyar, were jailed. The organization selected the name *Jam'iat-i Islami* (Islamic Society), but the student faction, operating quite openly, was known as the Jawanan Musulman (Muslim Youth) and popularly called *Ikhwanis*. Other Islamist individuals and circles, not affiliated with the Jam'iat were Minhajuddin Gahiz, who in 1968 published his newspaper *Jarida Gahiz*, (Dawn); Khuddam al-Quran (Servants of the Koran), founded by the Mujaddidi family; and the *Jam'iat-i Ulama-i Muhammadi* (Society of Muslim Ulama), founded by Sebghatullah Mujaddidi (q.v.).

After the coup of Muhammad Daud (July 17, 1973), the movement was forced to go underground. Rabbani raised the question of armed struggle, and weapons were collected; but before any action could begin, the government police arrested many of the members, including Ghulam Muhammad Niazi. Rabbani and Hekmatyar fled to Pakistan, where they sought help from the Pakistan government and the Islamist *Jama'at-i Islami*. In 1975, Hekmatyar staged sporadic raids into Afghanistan, and when the attacks failed, the differences between Rabbani and Hekmatyar became public.

After the Saur Revolt of April 1978, an attempt at reconciliation was made. Each party nominated seven members to a 21-member reconciliation committee, including the mediators. The *Jam'iat* members voted for Rabbani to be president of the party, and Hekmatyar's party voted for Qazi Muhammad Amin as deputy president. The mediators voted for Maulawi Fayez, who became the compromise president. But the Islamists were also divided on ethnic and tactical lines. The largely Tajik supporters of Rabbani favored preparation rather than precipitous armed activity. Hekmatyar aspired to leadership of the Islamist Movement and advocated immediate armed struggle. In April 1978 Maulawi Nabi Muhammadi was chosen as a compromise leader, but the movement broke up over the distribution of funds provided by foreign donors. Hekmatyar organized the *Hizb-i Islami*, and the traditionalist Muhammadi founded his own *Harakat-i Inqilab-i Islami* party. Rabbani worked with Mujaddidi and his *Jabha-yi Najat-i Milli-yi Afghanistan* (National Liberation Front) and continued to lead his own Jam'iat. Yunus Khales formed his own Hizb in 1979.

The Islamists were puritanical moralists who perceived moral laxity, lack of respect for traditional values, and an infatuation with Western secular culture among the Afghan youth and were determined to impose the laws of Islam on the social and political life of the state. They were not fundamentalists, but reformist, and supported a political activism first seen in the great Pan-Islamist, Jamaluddin Afghani. They were critical of the fundamentalist views of the *ulama* and were themselves the objects of criticism of the clergy. They went underground and organized into cells, and were accused of resorting to political assassinations and were themselves the objects of assassination. They rejected aspects of both communism and democracy although they copied from both. The present civil war between the Islamist forces has shown that ideological purity is readily abandoned as Islamist parties ally themselves with factions of the former Marxist regime to win political supremacy. For additional information, see individual party entries and ISLAMIC ALLIANCE FOR THE LIBERATION OF AFGHANISTAN.

ISMAIL KHAN. *See* **MUHAMMAD ISMAIL.**

ITTIHAD-I ISLAMI BARAYI AZADI-YI AFGHANISTAN. *See* **SAYYAF, ABDUL RASUL.**

- J -

JABHA-YI MILLI NAJAT-I AFGHANISTAN. *See* **MUJADDIDI, SEBGHATULLAH.**

JAGIR. A feudal, military fiefdom, such as granted by Ahmad Shah Durrani to chiefs of his tribe. It was an allotment of land that was tax-free but required its holder to provide a number of troops and arms corresponding to the size of the *jagir* (also called *tiyul* and A. *iqta'*). Land was divided into divisions called *qulba* (plow), which designated the portion of irrigated land cultivated by one person, employing one ox and one plow. The area was divided into two sections for sowing two *kharwar* of grain (one *kharwar*, literally a donkey load, amounted to 100 *man*, up to 160 pounds). One section was cultivated each year while the other half remained fallow. About 3,000 double *qulba* were distributed to Durrani tribes in Kandahar for which they had to provide 6,000 horsemen for the amir's army.

JALALABAD (36-46' N, 65-52' E). The capital of Nangarhar Province which had an estimated 54,000 inhabitants in the 1970s, reportedly increased in 1995, as a result of the influx of internal refugees, to about 200,000. The population is largely Pashtun of Khugiani, Shinwari, Tirahi (Tira'i), Mohmand, and Ghilzai tribal background, in addition to Sikhs, Hindus, and some Tajiks and Sayyids. It had the largest community of Sikh and Hindu merchants (about 4,000) of any Afghan city. Situated at an altitude of 1950 feet in a fertile valley watered by the Kabul and Kunar Rivers some 90 miles east of Kabul, Jalalabad lies on the trade route to the Indo-Pakistani subcontinent. Invaders passed through the Jalalabad valley, including Alexander the Great (330 B.C.), Babur Shah (1504), and the British who occupied the town in two Anglo-Afghan wars.

Babur Shah, the founder of the Moghul Empire of India, first planted beautiful gardens in the area, and in A.D. 1560 his grandson Jalaluddin Akbar founded the town, hence its name Jalalabad. In the nineteenth century it was a walled town with about 2,000 inhabitants, whose numbers increased during the winter to some 20,000. In March 1989 *mujahedin* forces attacked the city but were unable to take it. The city was occupied by *mujahedin* groups after the fall of the Kabul government and has since been ruled by a council of several parties. *See* JALALABAD, ATTACK ON.

JALALABAD, ATTACK ON. Soviet forces had left in February 1989 and Kunar was taken by the *mujahedin*, and the time seemed ripe for the insurgents to progress from the stage of guerrilla to conventional warfare. Jalalabad seemed a suitable target for the first capture of a major Afghan city. It was located only about 37 miles from the Pakistani border and within easy access to reinforcement of men and munitions. If taken, the city could have served as the capital of the Afghan Interim Government (AIG) to be recognized and openly assisted by its foreign supporters. Hamid Gul, director of Pakistani military intelligence (ISI), was heavily involved in various stages of the campaign. In March the *mujahedin* had gathered some 7,000 men in the area amid great publicity about their intended target. The men came primarily for Hekmatyar, Khales, Sayyaf and Gailani's forces (qq.v.), although other groups also participated. The garrison was estimated at about 4,500, and the defenses were under the command of General Delawar, the Afghan chief of staff. Mine fields provided a secure perimeter and munitions had been collected in anticipation of the attack. The *mujahedin* seemed to be well supplied with heavy artillery and surface-to-air missiles (SAM), including the dreaded stinger, and began their attack on March 6, 1989, proclaiming an amnesty for enemy soldiers in the hope of achieving massive defections. They quickly captured Samarkhel, an important post in the defense of the city, and rocketed the airport to prevent supplies from being brought in. But the fighting quickly bogged down. The *mujahedin* fought only during the daylight hours and returned to rear bases for the night. Commanders did not always coordinate their actions, Hekmatyar being the major culprit, and they failed to maintain the blockade of the road from Kabul, which permitted convoys to supply the city. High-altitude bombing and close air support by MIG-21s, as well as SCUD missiles with 1,700 pounds of warheads, exacted a heavy toll of the *mujahedin*. In April the defenders were able to recapture the airport, and, after a 10-week-long siege, the Kabul government prevailed. On May 10 foreign journalists were permitted to visit Jalalabad to see that the *mujahedin* had been defeated with heavy losses. One source claims that some 5,000 casualties resulted on all sides and most of the *mujahedin* casualties were caused by bombing and mines. On July 4 the Kabul government launched a surprise attack and consolidated its control of Samarkhel and the surrounding area, achieving a badly needed boost in morale for the Afghan army and permitting the Kabul regime to continue in power for another three years. It was only after the fall of Kabul in April 1992 that Jalalabad was taken by a council of *mujahedin* commanders.

JALALABAD, SIEGE OF. During the siege of the Kabul cantonment in the first Anglo-Afghan war, Jalalabad became an important base for British-Indian troops. Sir Robert Sale, the commanding general, was unable to come to the rescue of the Kabul forces; therefore, he decided to remain and took possession of the town on November 13, 1841. He worked on reinforcing the walls and fortifications, having only some 1,600 troops and six guns to defend a perimeter of about 2,200 yards. On November 15 an Afghan force, estimated by British officers at about

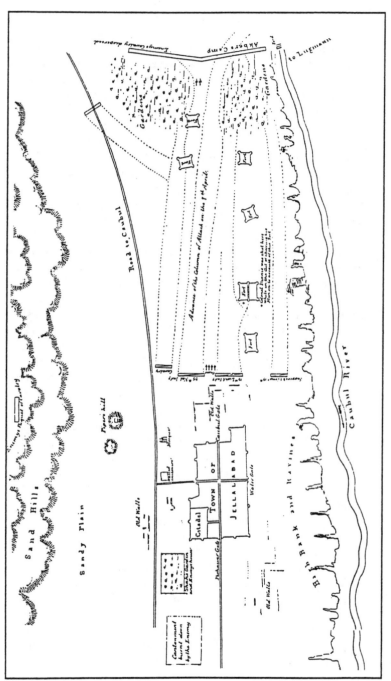

Plan 7. Gen. Sale Defeats Akbar Khan's Forces, April 7, 1842. Adapted from Stocqueler

5,000 tribesmen, surrounded the town but was initially dispersed; however, the Afghans eventually captured the town, forcing the British brigade to withdraw into the citadel. On January 6, 1842 the Afghan commander demanded the British brigade to depart with honor to India in fulfillment of the Kabul Treaty of Capitulation (q.v.), but General Sale refused, not trusting the promise of safe conduct. On February 19, 1842 an earthquake destroyed the parapets, making a considerable breach in the ramparts, which had to be restored. Two days later, Sardar Akbar Khan attacked British foraging parties and established a rigorous blockade that lasted until April 7. Various sallies succeeded in capturing livestock for provisions, but the native troops were put on half rations and the camp followers on quarter rations. Starvation was averted when the British were able to capture a flock of 500 sheep and goats that had been grazing a little too close to the wall of the town. On April 7 General Sale sallied out with virtually all his forces and defeated Muhammad Akbar's army of some 6,000 men. According to British accounts, only 31 officers and men were killed and 131 wounded. On April 16 General Pollock reached the city practically unmolested. Before the British departed, they destroyed the defenses of Jalalabad.

JAMAL PASHA (JEMAL). Member of the Ottoman ruling triumvirate, serving as minister of the navy and governor of Syria during World War I. On October 27, 1920 he came with a small staff to Afghanistan to escape extradition for "war crimes." He took charge of the reorganization of the Afghan army and founded the "Qita Namuna," an elite force, comprising a battalion of infantry and a regiment of cavalry. He was responsible for reinstituting and expanding the hated *hasht nafari* (q.v.) recruitment system and other unpopular reforms. He left Afghanistan with some members of his staff in September 1921 and was assassinated by an Armenian near Tiflis on July 21, 1922.

JAM'IAT-I ISLAMI-YI AFGHANISTAN. *See* **RABBANI, BURHAN-UDDIN.**

JAMILURRAHMAN, MAULAWI HUSAIN (JAMIL AL-RAHMAN). Amir of the *Jama'at-i Da'wa*, an Islamic revivalist movement whose members call themselves *Salafis* and are popularly called "Wahhabis." He captured most of Kunar Province and proclaimed an "Islamic Amirate," which he ruled for a time to the exclusion of other *mujahedin* groups. Born in 1933 in the Pech district of Kunar Province of a Safi tribal family, he received a traditional education. In the early 1970s he became a member of *Jam'iat-i Islami* (q.v.) and took part in armed attacks against the government of President Daud. After the Saur Revolt he joined the *Hizb-i Islami* of Hekmatyar (q.v.) and until 1982 was his amir in Kunar Province. Eventually, he broke with Hekmatyar and ousted other *mujahedin* groups from his area. He issued decrees allowing only bearded men to enter his territory and prohibited the consumption of tobacco in all its forms.

On April 20, 1991 an explosion at his Asadabad headquarters so decimated the ranks of his followers (including numerous Pakistanis and Arabs) that Hekmatyar's forces, supported by commanders of other groups, were able to capture Asadabad and expel most of the "Wahhabis" from Kunar Province. Muhammad Husain, alias Jamilur-rahman, was assassinated by an Egyptian in Pakistan. One Maulawi Sami'ullah succeeded him as leader of the party.

JEZAIL. A long-barreled musket with a thin, curved butt that was the major Afghan firearm during the nineteenth century and can still be seen in the bazaars of the country. It was muzzle loaded and therefore required several minutes to prepare, but it is said to have had greater accuracy and could outrange the British muskets (Sir Charles Napier claimed the musket was, on balance, the better weapon, Macrory, 170). A *jezailchi* (rifleman) would carry several *jezail* on his horse and fire them in rapid succession, after which he would retire or join the enemy in hand-to-hand combat. It was the major Afghan firearm during the Anglo-Afghan wars and was eventually replaced by the breech loading Martini-Henry and other rifles of foreign and domestic manufacture.

JEHAD. *Jehad*, holy war (A. literally "great effort," but generally "holy war"), is the obligation to fight against "unbelievers" until they accept Islam or submit to Islamic rule. Monotheists with a sacred book, like Christians and Jews, are not forced to convert and enjoy the status of protected subjects (*dhimmis*, q.v.). A Muslim who dies in *jehad* is a martyr, *shahid*, and is assured of Paradise. Technically, Muslims constitute one community, *umma*, and war between them is forbidden; therefore, an enemy is proclaimed sinful or apostate before he can be legally fought. During *jehad*, all tribal hostilities must temporarily stop. Muslim modernists quote a Koranic passage: "Fight in the Way of God against those who fight against you, but do not commit aggression. . . ," maintaining that the obligation of *jehad* was binding only for the early

Islamic period and that *jehad* also means fighting political and social wars and inwardly waging war against the carnal soul – a kind of moral imperative.

Since the downfall of the Marxist government in April 1992, the *jehad* has ended and civil war for political power between the *mujahedin* has begun.

JIRGA. A tribal council, which has legislative and juridical authority in the name of the tribal community. Although the Afghan government claims exclusive jurisdiction, it permits Pashtun tribes in the border areas to resolve internal disputes in their traditional manner. *Jirgas* can be composed of chiefs and notables or of adult male members of a tribe. A chief, or respected graybeard, leads the discussion, and votes are weighed according to the importance of the individual rather than being counted. The decision of a *jirga* is binding on all members of the tribe. *Jirgas* also resolve intratribal disputes, often with the mediation of a respected member of the *ulama* (clergy) or *pirs* (leaders of mystical orders).

In times of national emergency Afghan rulers have convened a *Loya Jirga* (q.v., Great Council), which includes representatives from all parts of the country. Its decisions thus become an expression of the "national will."

JOZJANIS. A militia composed largely of Uzbeks from Jozjan Province, numbering about 3,000 – 4,000 men in the 1980s, who served the Kabul government as a reliable and effective force in southern and western Afghanistan. It replaced the Soviet troops in Kandahar, where it protected the airport. After the fall of Kabul to the *mujahedin*, the Jozjanis seemed to have merged with the Uzbek forces of General Dostum and become one of the contenders for control of portions of Kabul. They first helped Jam'iat to capture Kabul and subsequently pulled out of the city at the insistence of Hekmatyar in a deal with Rabbani (qq.v.). Later, they joined Hekmatyar when Rabbani was unwilling to include Dostum in his government. The Jozjanis were feared as a fierce and unruly mercenary army and appear to be the defenders of Uzbek ethnic interests in present Afghanistan. They are now part of General Dostum's army in north-central Afghanistan.

JUNBESH-I MILLI-YI ISLAMI. *See* **DOSTUM, GEN. ABDUL RASHID.**

- K -

KABUL (34-31' N, 69-12' E). The capital and largest city in Afghanistan, situated at an altitude of almost 6,000 feet, and a province with an area of 1,822 square miles and a population of 1,372,000. In 1978 the city had some 500,000 inhabitants, but this number has, according to UN estimates, increased to about 1,500,000 as a result of the influx of refugees from war-ravaged areas. Kabul is strategically located in a valley surrounded by high mountains and at the crossroads of north-south and east-west trade routes. Therefore, it has been the site of towns since antiquity, called Kubha in the Rigveda (about 1500 B.C.) and Kabura by Ptolemy (second century A.D.). Muslim Arabs under Abdur Rahman Samurah captured Kabul in the middle of the seventh century A.D., but it took the Islamic invaders another 200 years before the Hindu rulers of Kabul were finally ousted. Kabul continued to be disputed, resulting in much destruction until Islam was definitely established under the Saffarids (ninth century A.D.). The city was part of the Ghaznavid Empire to suffer again from Genghis Khan's hordes (thirteenth century A.D.). Kabul became the capital of a province of the Moghul Empire, whose founder, Babur Shah, is buried on the eastern slope of the Sher Darwaza Mountain. In 1775–76 Timur Shah made Kabul his capital, and Afghan amirs ruled henceforth from that city. In the nineteenth century Kabul endured British occupation during the two Anglo-Afghan wars and suffered considerable destruction.

The city includes the old town, between the northern slope of the Sher Darwaza Mountain and Kabul River, and a new town (*Shahr-i nau*) begun in 1935. A large wall, 20 feet high and 12 feet thick, parts of which archaeologists believe to date from the fifth century A.D., still stands. It extends to the Bala Hisar (q.v.), the citadel, an imposing fortress that was destroyed by the British in 1878 and rebuilt to serve as a garrison and military college in 1939. Afghan amirs resided in the Bala Hisar until, in 1888, Amir Abdur Rahman constructed the Arg (q.v.), a walled palace, in the center of town. At the beginning of this century Amir Habibullah further modernized the town, providing electricity for the Arg and eventually for other parts of the town. In the 1920s the city had 60,000 inhabitants. King Amanullah constructed his own capital in Darulaman, about six miles from the center of town, with several government buildings and an imposing Parliament building. Members of the royal court and high government officials built their

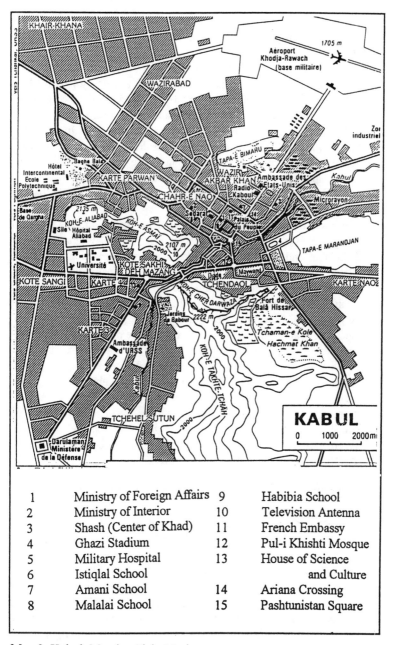

1	Ministry of Foreign Affairs	9	Habibia School
2	Ministry of Interior	10	Television Antenna
3	Shash (Center of Khad)	11	French Embassy
4	Ghazi Stadium	12	Pul-i Khishti Mosque
5	Military Hospital	13	House of Science
6	Istiqlal School		and Culture
7	Amani School	14	Ariana Crossing
8	Malalai School	15	Pashtunistan Square

Map 3. Kabul. Map by Alain Marigo

villas in the new capital, but after his fall from power, the center of government moved back into town.

The city grew rapidly after World War II with the addition of new quarters. *Karta-yi Chahar* (the Fourth District) was developed in 1942, followed by Khairkhana in the northwest, Nur Muhammad Shah Mina east of the old town, Nadir Shah Mina to the northeast, Wazir Akbar Khan east of Shahr-i Nau, and Khushhal Khan Mina. In 1953 the *Jada-yi Maiwand* (Maiwand Street) was drawn through the old city, followed by paved avenues, villas, high-rise buildings, and prefabricated apartment complexes that replaced much of the old town. With Soviet assistance, the streets were paved and a grain silo and bakery were constructed.

A network of paved roads connects Kabul via the Salang Pass tunnel to the north, via the *Tang-i Gharu* (Gharu Gorge) to Pakistan, via Kandahar and Herat to Iran. Hydroelectric power stations in Sarobi (1957), Mahipar, and Naghlu (1966) provided electricity for the city. Soviet-style city planning and the construction of prefabricated apartment complexes have given parts of the town the appearance of a Soviet Central Asian town. Since the late-eighteenth century, Kabul has been the seat of political power and is still the preeminent city in Afghanistan. Its population increased temporarily to almost two million as large numbers of the rural population fled to Kabul to escape the hardships of war. After the *mujahedin* conquest of Kabul in April 1992, large areas of the city were destroyed as a result of fighting between contending powers. At the time of this writing, the major contenders for control of Kabul are the forces of *Jam'iat-i Islami* and the newly emerged power of the *Taleban* (q.v.). For military action at Kabul, *see* ANGLO-AFGHAN WARS; and SHERPUR, SIEGE OF.

KABUL, TREATY OF. *See* **ANGLO-AFGHAN TREATY OF 1921.**

KAFIRISTAN (35-30' N, 70-45' E). "The Land of the Infidels" was an area in eastern Afghanistan that since 1906 had been called Nuristan (q.v.), the "Land of Light," meaning the light of the Islamic religion that was brought into the area by conquest in 1896. The Kafirs, estimated at about 60,000 in the 1880s, had still preserved their traditional culture and religion, but spoke a number of related but mutually unintelligible languages. Only at the fringes of their territory had some converted to Islam when Abdur Rahman decided to integrate them into Afghanistan. They had a reputation as excellent fighters, and their mountainous, forested country had given them a refuge from their Islamic neighbors. When the Durand Agreement of 1893 (q.v.) included the larger part of Kafiristan within Afghan territory, Amir Abdur Rahman lost little time in taking control. *See* KAFIR WAR. Today, all Nuristanis are Muslims.

KAFIR WAR. In his biography (AR 238–92) the amir gave the reasons for his action as necessitated by Russian penetration of the Pamir region and British control of eastern Kafiristan. If Kafiristan remained independent, the Russians (or British) might want to annex it, and, since Panjshir, Laghman, and Jalalabad once belonged to the Kafirs, the Russians "might persuade them to reclaim their old possessions." Furthermore, the warlike Kafirs would always pose a threat when the amir was engaged in fighting an enemy elsewhere. The Kafirs had continuously raided into Afghan provinces and had to be stopped once and for all.

The amir decided to start his campaign in the winter, when snow cover would prevent the Kafirs from seeking the safety of their mountain retreats. If the passes were open, the Kafirs could retreat into Russian territory and seek the support of that power. The war had to be short, before the neighboring powers could react and the Christian missionaries could make "unnecessary trouble."

In fall 1895, Abdur Rahman organized an army under Captain Muhammad Ali Khan, whose main force proceeded through Panjshir to Kulam; another force under General Ghulam Haidar Charkhi approached Kafiristan from the direction of Asmar and Chitral; and a third force under General Katal Khan approached the area from Badakhshan. A smaller, fourth force proceeded from Laghman under its governor, Faiz Muhammad Charkhi. Since all four bases were near the Afghan border, the movement of troops did not raise any suspicions of what was to come; suddenly in winter of 1895 the four armies, supplemented by tribal levies, attacked simultaneously and conquered Kafiristan within 40 days. The Kafirs did not have a chance. Their weapons consisted primarily of spears, bows and arrows, and a few rifles, and their numbers, about 60,000, were no match against the amir's army which was divided into well-equipped artillery, cavalry, and infantry branches. Some Kafir prisoners were settled in Paghman, and after conversion to Islam a large number of their youth was trained for military service. Within a few years, all Kafirs were converted to Islam, and in 1906 Amir Habibullah changed the name of the country to Nuristan, the "Country Enlightened by the Light of Islam." This

conquest greatly increased the reputation of the amir as the Islamic king
of a unified and solidly Muslim state.

In commemoration of this victory, Abdur Rahman's general left behind
the following inscription: "In the reign of Amir Abdur Rahman Ghazi,
in 1896, the whole of Kafiristan, including Kullum, was conquered by
him, and the inhabitants embraced the true and holy religion of Islam.
[A Koranic inscription added:] Righteousness and virtue have come,
and untruth has disappeared."

KANDAHAR (QANDAHAR) (31-35' N, 64-45' E). A province in
south-central Afghanistan with an area of 19,062 square miles and a
population of 699,000, the second largest town in Afghanistan lying at
an elevation of 3,050 feet and comprising an area of 15 square miles. In
the late 1970s the city counted about 178,000 inhabitants. Its strategic
location has made it a desirable spot for settlements since ancient times.
It was the capital of Afghanistan from 1747 until 1775, when Timur
Shah (q.v.) established his capital at Kabul. It is one of the major
Pashtun cities and is inhabited mostly by Durranis, but also has a
Hazara population and Afghans of other ethnic groups. The old, walled
town, of which only traces remain, was built by Timur Shah. The
mausoleum of Ahmad Shah (q.v.), founder of modern Afghanistan, is
one of the major architectural features, as is the mosque of the *Khirqa
Sharif*, where the cloak of the Prophet Muhammad is believed to be
kept under lock and key.

The city was part of the Achaemenid Empire of Darius I (521–485
B.C.). It was rebuilt by Alexander the Great in 329 B.C., hence the
name Kandahar, a corruption of *Iskander*, the Eastern name for
Alexander. Muslim Arabs conquered Kandahar in the seventh century.
Thereafter, Kandahar formed part of various Islamic kingdoms.

In the sixteenth century the city was disputed between the rulers of the
Safavid and Moghul empires until Mir Wais (q.v.), a Ghilzai chief of
Kandahar, revolted against Safavid control and began the process that
led to the establishment of Afghanistan in 1747.

British forces occupied the city in two Anglo-Afghan wars and suffered
one of their severest defeats nearby at the Battle of Maiwand (July 27,
1880), when Sardar Muhammad Ayub wiped out a British brigade
under General Burrows (qq.v.).

When Russian troops evacuated the city in spring 1989, the Kabul
government installed Nur-ul-Haq Ulumi, a Durrani, as governor.
Subsequently, Kandahar was controlled by a council of various parties,

and since November 1994 it has become the headquarters of the *Taleban* forces.

KANDAHAR, BATTLES OF. In the **Battles of Princes**, ex-king Shah Shuja marched in May 1834 from Shikarpur on the Indus River in present Pakistan and advanced on Kandahar. He defeated Kohandil Khan at the Khojak Pass and laid siege to Kandahar. It was a murderous engagement that seriously weakened both the defenders of the city and Shah Shuja's forces. The walled city was surrounded by large gardens, each enclosed in a wall and intersected by numerous irrigation channels, which greatly impeded the mobility of the cavalry, of which both forces were composed. Soldiers trapped in enclosures fought to the end, resulting in enormous casualties. On June 29 Shah Shuja led a sustained attack, but was eventually forced to retire when Amir Dost Muhammad came to the rescue of the besieged city. The butchery lasted for 54 days and is said to have cost the lives of about 16,000 men. William Campbell (q.v.), alias Shir Muhammad Khan, was captured by Dost Muhammad's forces and entered the services of the amir.

During the **First Anglo-Afghan War,** the "Army of the Indus" took possession of the city on April 20, 1839 without any resistance. All was quiet, but in September 1841 Afghan *ghazis* cut the city's link with Ghazni, and by March 1842 tribal forces closed in on the city. General Nott (q.v.) conducted an aggressive defense, sending out raiding parties and defeating a force under Safdar Jang, a Sadozai chief, while the city was preparing its defenses. The gates were secured by piling grain sacks against them, and on March 10, the Afghan attack on the Herat Gate began. A British report said, "So reckless and daring were the assailants, that, notwithstanding the fearful havoc among them, eight or ten men actually forced their way by tearing down the burning fragments of the gate, and scrambling over the bags of grain. These were instantly shot. . . ." The British were able to bring in supplies and caused some disorder in the ranks of the Afghans. Another assault took place at the Shikarpur Gate, which also failed, and the Afghan forces suddenly retired in the early morning of March 10. On August 8, 1843 General Nott evacuated the city and marched on Kabul prior to the British withdrawal from Afghanistan.

In the **Second Anglo-Afghan War**, an advance force 6,000 strong under Sir Michael Biddulph moved from Quetta north and occupied Kandahar on January 8, 1879, without any opposition. The city was held by General Steward and subsequently by General J. M. Primrose with

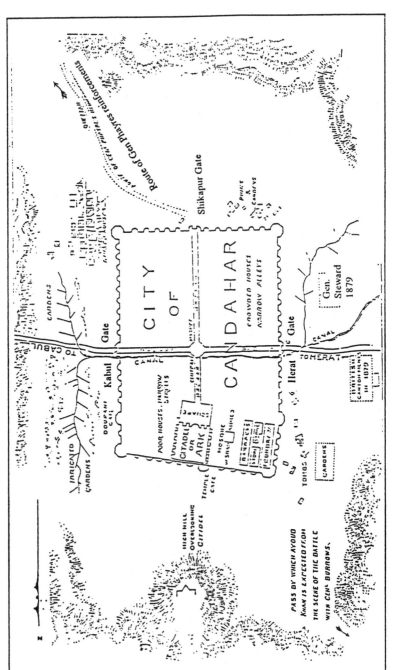

Plan 8. Kandahar. Source: ILN, August 7, 1880

a garrison of about 5,000 men. When after his victory at Maiwand, Ayub Khan advanced toward Kandahar, Primrose panicked. He gave orders to abandon the cantonment, where the troops had been stationed, and ordered a retreat into the city. All gates, except one were, closed and troops posted to defend some 6,000 yards of the city wall. Supplies coming from Quetta and the remnants of General Burrows' brigade had difficulty entering the city through the one open gate. The British made feverish preparations for the defense: buildings outside the walls were razed, trees felled to provide a clear field of vision, and the Pashtun population of some 15,000 was expelled from the city. On August 8 the garrison had only two months' rations and 15 days of forage for their horses. On August 5 Ayub Khan reached the outskirts of the city and two days later the siege began. A sortie by Brigadier General Brooks, with a force of 300 cavalry, four companies of Royal Fusiliers, and eight companies of Bombay Infantry ended in heavy losses; 106 were killed, including Brooks, and 118 wounded. Having learned of the disaster at Maiwand, Sir Frederick Roberts left Kabul on August 8 and came to the relief of Kandahar by the end of the month. He met the forces of Ayub Khan at the Baba Wali Pass, and with an army of 3,800 British and 11,000 Indian troops as well as 36 guns, he was able to defeat Ayub Khan (*see* BABA WALI KOTAL, BATTLE OF). Abdur Rahman Khan occupied Kandahar, and on April 21, 1881 the British flag was hauled down, and six days later all British forces had left Afghan soil. Ayub Khan tried his fortune once more: he captured Kandahar in August 1881, but was decisively defeated on September 22 by Amir Abdur Rahman.

KARMAL, BABRAK. President and secretary-general of the PDPA from January 1980 until May 1986, when Dr. Najibullah took over control of the Afghan government. Born in 1929 in Kabul, the son of Major General Muhammad Husain (one-time governor of Paktia Province and purported to be a Ghilzai Pashtun). He adopted the pen name *Karmal* (friend of labor) in about 1954. A founding member of the PDPA, he was a student activist at Kabul University and known as a Communist. Jailed from 1953 to 1956, he then worked for the ministries of education and of planning. In 1965 and 1969 he was elected to Parliament as representative of Kabul. He was a member of the central committee and subsequently secretary of the central committee of the PDPA. As a result of a dispute with Nur Muhammad Taraki over leadership of the party in 1965, the party divided and he led the

Parcham faction until it reunited with the *Khalqis* in 1977. In 1978 he was imprisoned after the funeral of Mir Muhammad Akbar Khaibar, but liberated as a result of the Saur Revolt. He was then elected vice-chairman of the revolutionary council and deputy prime minister of Afghanistan. In July 1978 the *Khalqi* regime purged the Parchami leadership, appointing Karmal Afghan ambassador to Czechoslovakia. In August 1978 he was accused of plotting against the *Khalqi* government and stripped of party membership and all his positions. Restored to power with Soviet support, he succeeded Hafizullah Amin on December 27, 1979. Karmal was described as an idealist, rather than a revolutionary. He was an eloquent orator in Dari, an expert propagandist, and the best known member of the Marxist leadership. He was unable to consolidate his position, and in 1986 he was replaced by Dr. Najibullah. He left Afghanistan for Moscow, but returned to Kabul in June 1991. After the fall of the Marxist regime in April 1992, many Parchamis joined *Jam'iat*. Babrak continued to reside in Microrayon, but eventually moved to Mazar-i Sharif, where his former comrade, Abd al-Rashid Dostum, is the dominant political leader, and from there to Moscow.

KAUFMAN, GEN. CONSTANTIN P. Conqueror of Samarkand in 1868 and Khiva in 1873, he became the first governor general of Russian Turkestan and subsequently aide de camp to the czar. He corresponded with Amir Shir Ali and his foreign minister and sent General Stolietoff (q.v.) to Kabul to conclude an alliance with Russia.
A treaty signed by the amir offered Russian support "either by means of advice or by such other means as it may consider proper." When Britain made war, Russia did not send any assistance, but advised Amir Shir Ali to make his peace with Britain. *See* SHIR ALI, AMIR; STOLIETOFF; and FIRST ANGLO-AFGHAN WAR.

KEANE, LT. GEN. SIR JOHN (1781–1844). In 1838 commanded the Bombay Division of the Army of the Indus during the first Anglo-Afghan war. Was given command of both the Bengal and Bombay columns advancing into Afghanistan via Quetta and Kandahar. Took Ghazni on July 23, 1839 and occupied Kandahar on August 7. Returned to India in October 1839.

KHAD Later **WAD.** *See* **AFGHAN SECURITY SERVICE.**

KHAIBAR PASS. (KHYBER) (34-1' N, 71-10' E). A historic pass leading through a gorge and barren hills from the Afghan border to Peshawar, Pakistan. It starts at Ali Masjid, about 10 miles from Peshawar, narrows to about 200 yards, and reaches its highest point at 3,518 feet. The population controlling the pass is largely Afridi (q.v.). Britain gained control of the pass in the Treaty of Gandomak (q.v.), and this "Gateway to India" is now on the Pakistani side of the Durand Line. It was long considered impregnable, and many an invader of India preferred to pay for passage rather than try to enter by force. Akbar the Great, 1587, was said to have lost 40,000 men in attempting to force the pass.

KHALES, MUHAMMAD YUNUS. Leader (Amir) of the *Hizb-i Islami,* one of two groups with the same name headquartered in Jalalabad. He was born in 1919 in Gandomak, Khugiani, and educated in Islamic law and theology. He is a radical Islamist and fervent anti-Communist and in the 1960s contributed articles to the conservative *Gahis* newspaper. After the Daud coup in 1973 he was forced to flee to Pakistan, because he had made many enemies among Daud's supporters. A member with Hekmatyar (q.v.) of *Hizb-i-Islami,* he seceded and formed his own group with the same name, which fought the Kabul government in the Khugiani area. It is represented primarily in Pashtun regions, especially in Nangarhar and Paktia provinces. His group enjoys some tribal support, especially among Khales's own Khugiani and the Jadran tribes. Ideologically, the party of Khales differs little from the other Islamist groups (*see* HIZB-I ISLAMI [Hekmatyar]), but, unlike Hekmatyar's group, favors cooperation with all sunni *mujahedin* parties. Khales is opposed to universal suffrage, the emancipation of women, and has opposed Shi'a participation in the Afghan Interim Government (AIG). In May 1991 he resigned from his position as interior minister of the AIG. His base presently is in Jalalabad, where he had offered his services as Afghan president to succeed Burhanuddin Rabbani (q.v.). *See* ISLAMIST MOVEMENT.

KHALQ. *See* **PEOPLE'S DEMOCRATIC PARTY OF AFGHANISTAN.**

KHASADAR. A tribal militia supplementing the regular Afghan army, usually under the direct command of provincial governors or district chiefs. They were employed in various duties, including collecting fines and as border guards. They were stationed throughout the country and only during campaigns did they come under the direct command of the army commanders. Many were recruited from Wazir and Mahsud tribes from the British side of the border, in spite of British protests.

KHATAK, KHUSHHAL KHAN (1613–89). A celebrated warrior-poet and tribal chief of the Khatak tribe who called on the Afghans to fight the Moghuls then occupying their land. He admonished Afghans to forsake their anarchistic tendencies and unite to regain the strength and glory they once possessed. But he was pessimistic, saying, "The day the Pashtuns unite, old Khushhal will arise from the grave." Khushhal Khan was born near Peshawar, the son of Shahbaz Khan, a chief of the Khatak tribe. By appointment of the Moghul emperor, Shah Jehan, Khushhal succeeded his father in 1641; but Aurangzeb, Shah Jehan's successor, kept him a prisoner in the Gwaliar fortress in Delhi. After Khushhal was permitted to return to Peshawar, he incited the Pashtuns to revolt. His grave carries the inscription "I have taken up the sword to defend the pride of the Afghan, I am Khushhal Khattak, the honorable man of the age."

KHORASAN. "Land of the Rising Sun," the historical name of an area that included eastern Iran and Afghanistan and was the heartland of Ahmad Shah's kingdom. A province in northeastern Iran still carries the name Khorasan.

KHOST, FALL OF (33-22' N, 69-52' E). A town and district in Paktia Province, which had seen severe fighting because it was a major government base for cutting the line of *mujahedin* forces. The town was commonly called "Little Moscow" because many of the Marxist leaders were native to this area and therefore enjoyed the support of the population. Located only about 18 miles from the Pakistan border, the town was under siege since 1986 and had to be supplied mostly by air. The town was protected by a 3,000-man garrison, supported by militia units, and fortified with a mined perimeter that could not be easily breached. In March 1991 a unified *mujahedin* force, headed by a 23-member council in which Jalaluddin Haqani had a prominent role, began to close in on the town. The Kabul government may have had information of *mujahedin* plans and had reinforcements airlifted into the besieged town. High-ranking officers had arrived, among them Colonel General Muhammad Zahir Solamal, a deputy minister of defense. On

March 13, a few days before the beginning of *Ramadhan* (the month of fasting), the *mujahedin* started with a three-day rocket barrage, followed by ground attacks from all sides, but it was not until March 30 that the airport was captured and a day later the garrison surrendered. Bad weather and surface-to-air missiles (SAM), including stingers, did not permit close aerial support, but some 40 SCUD missiles were fired. It appears that the surrender was achieved largely as a result of negotiations, and the militia units are said to have changed sides in time to permit their escape. About 2,200 Kabul soldiers were taken, and 500 wounded were transported to receive medical assistance. About 300 were killed. Among the prisoners were Colonel General Solamal; Major General Ghulam Mustafa, chief of political affairs of the armed forces; Major General Muhammad Qasim, commander of artillery; Major Muhammad Azam, an air force commander; and Lieutenant General Shirin, commander of the Khost militia units. For the *mujahedin,* this was a major morale booster; the Kabul government announced a "day of mourning" and accused the *mujahedin* of violating the "sanctity of Ramadhan." It blamed the defeat on *Khalqi* betrayal and claimed that Pakistani forces had participated in the assault. The relatively lenient treatment of the prisoners — some 2,000 (1,200 according to AFGHANews) families of Kabul supporters were permitted to find shelter in Pakistan — may be explained by the surrender and the fact that the battle was primarily between Pashtuns who did not want to incite tribal feuds. The town suffered from reprisal bombing and *mujahedin* plunder. The *mujahedin* obtained large quantities of arms and ammunition, including tanks, armored cars, helicopters, light and heavy guns. Hekmatyar's forces were blamed for having snatched more than their "allotment." The number of *mujahedin* casualties was not given.

KHOST REBELLION. A rebellion led by the Mangal tribe that seriously threatened the rule of King Amanullah. The revolt started in March 1924 in response to the king's reforms. The Mangals under Abdullah Khan and *Mulla-i-Lang* (the Lame Mulla) were able to establish a base in Khost and were about to advance on Kabul. At the same time, Abdul Karim, son by a slave girl of ex-Amir Yaqub Khan (q.v.), escaped from British-Indian exile and joined the rebels. In April 1924 the rebels were beaten but not yet defeated. Sulaiman Khel and Ali Khel tribes joined the revolt. In August King Amanullah dramatically proclaimed holy war against them. But it was not until January 1925 that the rebels were defeated. Abdullah Khan and Mulla- i-Lang were captured and executed together with 53 prisoners. The citizens of Kabul were treated to a victory parade, which carried the booty, followed by almost 2,000 prisoners, including women and children, organized according to tribal affiliation. The prisoners were, in the words of the German representative in Kabul, "wild men with sullen, taciturn faces who did not take the least notice of the amir." The revolt slowed down the amir's process of reform until 1928, when King Amanullah again forced the process of Westernization.

KHURD KABUL PASS (34-23' N, 69-23' E). A pass about 20 miles east of Kabul, extending for a length of about six miles and only about 100 to 200 yards wide through which passes a road, crossing the Kabul River 23 times. On the third day of their Death March (q.v.) during the British retreat on January 8, 1842, Ghilzai forces blocked the pass and opened fire on the British troops and camp followers, causing panic of the "frightened mass, abandoning baggage, arms, ammunition, women and children, regardless of all but their lives." (GAZ 5) Some 3,000 soldiers and camp followers perished.

- L -

LASHKAR. Afghan tribal armies, recruited during emergencies in support of the regular army. They fought under their own chiefs, often in competition with other *lashkars*, and therefore not always cooperating in joint operations. The Sulaiman Khel Ghilzais were able to muster some 20,000 fighters and, the Afghan nomads, traveling yearly to India, could muster as many as 100,000 fighters. For a long time they were superior to the regular army, considered so brave as to be reckless, but out for plunder and of limited staying power. They would be reluctant to operate far from their tribal areas. Feuds, temporarily ended to face a foreign invader, were quickly resumed. During the war of the 1980s, both the Kabul government and the *mujahedin* engaged tribal forces to protect their lines of supply. With the growth and modernization of the Afghan army, the *lashkars* lost much of their importance.

LAWRENCE, COL. T. E. The Britisher of "Lawrence-of-Arabia" fame is suspected by many Afghans to have been a link in a conspiracy to topple King Amanullah from his throne. The Afghan government learned from reports in the London *Sunday Express* of September 13, 1928 that Lawrence was on the Afghan border on a "secret" mission. He was indeed there under the alias "Shaw." The Afghan paper *Aman-i Afghan* of December 12, 1928 commented that it was certain that the man who had "gathered the miserable Arabs in a revolt against the Turks" was up to mischief in Afghanistan. But the paper debunked his effectiveness on the Afghan Frontier, for, after all, "he is only an Englishman." The London *Daily News* of December 5, 1929 reported that Lawrence was in India, busily learning Pashtu and "inferred he intends to move into Afghanistan." Much of the non-British press was convinced that this was a conspiracy in support of Habibullah Kalakani (q.v.). No sources have been found in British archives to support this conspiracy theory, and the British government denied all charges. After the British minister to Kabul, Sir Francis Humphrys, frantically appealed to London, Lawrence was finally sent back to Britain.

LIMITED CONTINGENT OF SOVIET FORCES IN AFGHANISTAN (LCSFA). Soviet term for its forces in Afghanistan, which included, according to McMichael (14), 85,000 ground troops, 25,000 support troops, and 10,000 air force troops. To this should be added some 30,000 soldiers and airmen who operated from Soviet territory. The ground units constituted the 40th Army Headquarters, five motorized rifle divisions, four to five separate motorized rifle brigades or regiments, three to four air assault or airmobile brigades, one to three brigades or special operations troops (*spetsnaz*), one engineer rgiment/brigade, and one army artillery brigade. About one-third of the force was concentrated in the Kabul area, and the rest was deployed in Jalalabad, Kunduz/Mazar-i Sharif, Herat/Farah, Shindand, and Kandahar. Smaller garrisons were stationed in other towns. *See also* ORDER OF BATTLE; LOGISTICS; and GROMOV, LT. GEN. BORIS V.

LOGISTICS. The activities and methods connected with supplying an army with all its provisions, including facilities for storage, transport, and distribution, have always been a serious problem for an invader of Afghanistan. British forces included baggage trains, which limited the mobility of the army and were vulnerable to plunder during combat. Rations (q.v.), officially designated, were seldom fully provided. Local resources were often inadequate and withheld and could be collected only by coercive measures.

The lack of water was always a serious problem, and many areas of Afghanistan would not support operations by large forces. The *Dasht-i Margo* and *Registan* "The Country of Sand," in eastern and southern Afghanistan were waterless deserts that long formed a natural barrier to an invader. In many operations water had to be carried along.

The amount of existing accommodation, usable for military purposes, was negligible, and troops had to be sheltered in tents at extremes in temperature. There were not enough facilities for the repair of equipment required by European armies. The Soviet forces had to undertake a building program to construct depots and storage facilities, repair or build roads, and expand or design new airfields. Fuel was scarce and had to be collected by foraging units or, during the 1980, imported from the Soviet Union.

Diseases took a toll of an invader's forces. Casualties from smallpox, malaria, dysentery, cholera, heatstroke, frostbite, pulmonary, and other diseases often exceeded those from combat. In the second Anglo-Afghan war five per thousand Europeans died of cholera. Medical facilities were inadequate, even during the Soviet intervention. About half of all Soviet conscripts were treated for dysentery, and about 20 percent were treated for skin infection. *See also* TRANSPORT, MILITARY; and CLIMATE AND WAR.

LOYA JIRGA. Great (or national) Council, it is the highest organ of state power that Afghan rulers convened to decide matters of national importance. Ahmad Shah's assumption of the Afghan throne was legitimized by a *loya jirga* of tribal chiefs, as were the constitutions of King Amanullah (1923) and Zahir Shah (1964). When in October 1941 the Allies forced the Afghan government to expel all Axis nationals, the *loya jirga* reluctantly gave its approval, but insisted that they be given free passage through Allied territory. When Prime Minister Daud in the 1950s decided to accept weapons from the Soviet Union, he also sought the approval of a *loya jirga*. The Marxist regime tried to legitimize its power with *jirga* approval, as did various *mujahedin* groups, with little success. One problem is that the *loya jirga* very often proved to be a rubber stamp for decisions decided by government; another, that it can be easily packed by supporters of one or another faction. President Rabbani convened a *shura* (council) of "the people with power to loose and bind" (*ahl al-hall wa-al-'aqd*), trying to legitimize his position, but it is not clear whether he intended to Islamize or replace the institution of the *loya jirga*.

- M -

MACGREGOR, SIR CHARLES M. Quartermaster general, commanded the First Division of the Peshawar Valley Field Force. During the second campaign in the second Anglo-Afghan war, he was chief of staff to Sir Frederick Roberts (q.v.). He served with the Kabul Field Force and later commanded the Third Brigade of the Kabul-Kandahar Field Force. Participated in the advance and occupation of Kabul, the relief of Kandahar, and the defense of Sherpur.

MACNAGHTEN, SIR WILLIAM (1793–1841). British chief secretary to the Indian government, appointed envoy and minister to the court of Shah Shuja, after the occupation of Kabul on August 7, 1839, in the first Anglo-Afghan war (qq.v.). With the benefit of hindsight, historians gave him a good measure of the blame for the British debacle, which also cost Sir William his life. Soon after the invasion it became apparent that Shah Shuja would not be able to maintain himself on the throne without the protection of a British garrison. Therefore, Macnaghten was prepared for an indefinite occupation of Afghanistan. He became the power behind an insecure throne, paying subsidies to tribal chiefs and directing the affairs of the country to safeguard British imperial interests. Deceived by the apparent quiescence of the Afghan chiefs, he permitted the families of British officers to come to Kabul to join a colony of some 4,500 soldiers and 11,500 camp followers. All seemed well, and, as a reward for his services, Macnaghten was to receive the much coveted governorship of Bombay; Alexander Burnes (q.v.) was to succeed him in Kabul. But Afghan forces began to harass the British lines of communications and eventually a mob in Kabul attacked Burnes's residence and killed the members of the mission. Realizing the danger of his situation, Macnaghten concluded a treaty with the dominant tribal chiefs that provided for the withdrawal of the British army to India. But he had still not given up hope. Trying a divide-and-rule tactic, the envoy bribed some of the *sardars* after contracting with Sardar Muhammad Akbar, the ambitious son of Amir Dost Muhammad (qq.v.). When the latter discovered the duplicity, he killed Macnaghten in a "fit of rage." Only a few survived the retreat of the "Army of the Indus." (*See* ANGLO-AFGHAN WARS; SIMLA MANIFESTO; and AFGHAN FOREIGN RELATIONS.)

MAHAZ-I MILLI-YI AFGHANISTAN. *See* **GAILANI, SAYYID AHMAD.**

MAHMUD OF GHAZNI (998–1030). Son of Sebuktigin and creator of the Ghaznavid Empire that had its capital at Ghazni (q.v.), southwest of Kabul, and controlled an empire extending from eastern Iran to the Indus River and from the Amu Daria to the Persian Gulf. Muslims see him as the epitome of the *ghazi* warrior, the "Breaker of Idols," as he called himself, and Hindus remember him as the plunderer of Hindustan. He lavished the treasures he had amassed in India on a court that was famous for its wealth and splendor and for being a center of intellectual life. The British historian Sir Percy Sykes called Mahmud "a great general who carefully thought out the plan of each campaign that he engaged in," who was not a fanatic, and "whose encouragement of literature and science and art was as remarkable as his genius for war and for government." Mahmud's tomb was spared Ghorid destruction and can still be seen in the outskirts of Ghazni.

MAIWAND, BATTLE OF. A battle on July 27, 1880, in which a force of 2,600 men under Brigadier General G. R. S. Burrows was totally defeated. At the end of the second Anglo-Afghan war, Britain had decided to dismember Afghanistan, severing Kandahar Province under Wali Shir Ali Khan, who was to be a vassal of Britain. Sardar Abdur Rahman was recognized as "Amir of Kabul and its Dependencies," but his cousin Ayub also had aspiration to the throne and had himself proclaimed amir at Herat. Kandahar was held by a garrison of some 4,700 British troops of all ranks to which were added the Afghan forces of the newly appointed "hereditary" ruler, Shir Ali Khan, when it was learned that Ayub Khan's army was moving south. Shir Ali felt he could not rely on his forces against Ayub and requested the assistance of a British brigade. General Primrose, the commander of Kandahar, dispatched Brigadier General Burrows with a brigade, about 2,300 strong, consisting of a troop of Horse Artillery, six companies of the 66th, two Bombay Native Infantry, and 500 Native Troopers. At the approach of Ayub Khan, Shir Ali Khan's forces deserted en masse, taking most of their weapons with them. According to British estimates, Ayub Khan's regular forces numbered about 4,000 cavalry and between 4,000 and 5,000 infantry, as well as about 2,000 deserters and an unknown number of irregular *ghazis*. Burrows forces fell back to the vicinity of Kushk-i Nakhud, about 30 miles from Girishk and 40 miles

Plate 2. British Defeat at Maiwand. Source: ILN

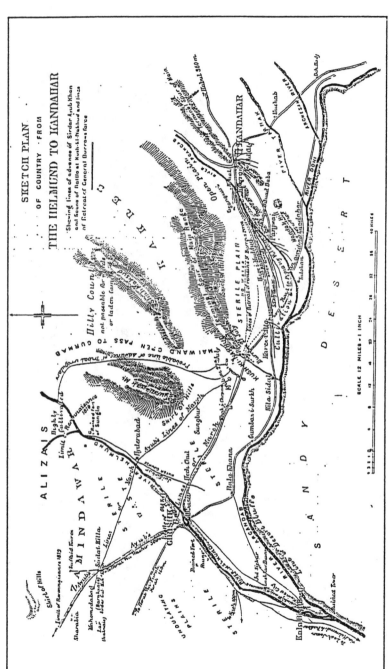

Plan 9. Sketch Plan of Helmand. Source: ILN

from Kandahar, to block Ayub's approaches to these towns, but Ayub succeeded in moving his army around Burrows's forces, interposing himself between the British forces and Kandahar. The British brigade thereupon moved toward Maiwand in anticipation of Ayub's advance and to secure the provisions available at that village. On July 27, 1880, at about 10:00 a.m., the British brigade, replenished to 2,600 men, made contact with the Afghan forces, which had moved toward Maiwand on their left flank. At a ravine, the 66th Foot was on the right, its flank thrown back to prevent it from being turned. On the left were four companies of Jacob's Rifles (30th Native Infantry) and a company of sappers, while the center was held by the Horse Artillery and smooth-bore guns. The cavalry was in the rear to prevent the Afghans from encircling the British forces. The baggage was about 1,000 yards in the rear only lightly guarded. In an artillery duel, lasting about two hours, the Afghans with 30 guns proved to be superior against the brigade's 12. By 2:00 p.m., the British cavalry had lost about 14 percent of its men and 149 horses (out of 460), and the Afghan horsemen had succeeded in surrounding the brigade. Now swarms of *ghazis* went on the attack, quickly demoralizing the British troops. The 66th regiment was overwhelmed: "The slaughter of the sepoys was appalling — so utterly cowed were they that they scarcely attempted to defend themselves."(Forbes, 301) Afghan sharpshooters began to pick off British officers, who could be recognized by their helmets. A call for counterattack was ignored, and the British forces were in full flight, except for several attempts at a last stand, which no British eyewitness survived. The British lost seven guns, 2,424 baggage animals and their loads, about 1,000 dead, and only 168 wounded survived. The rest fled to Kandahar, where many were ambushed on the way by Afghan villagers. British estimates of Afghan casualties were 1,250 regular troops and some 600 tribesmen (1,500 regulars and 3,000 tribesmen, according to Heathcote, 151). General Primrose, the commander of Kandahar, panicked and called for a British retreat inside the walls of the city, where they soon came under siege. *See* KANDAHAR, BATTLES OF. Legend has it that Malalai, a tribal maiden, used her veil as a banner to incite the Afghan forces to heroic deeds. The defeat at Maiwand was a factor in convincing the British occupation forces that Afghanistan could not be held at a tolerable cost.

MAIWAND, TELEGRAM FROM COL. ST. JOHN. Kandahar, to Foreign Department Simla, August 2, 1880. "Burrows marched from

Kushk-i Nakhud on morning, 27th, having heard from me that Ayub's advanced guard had occupied Maiwand, about three miles from the latter place. Enemy's cavalry appeared advancing from direction of Haidrabad, their camp on Helmund ten miles above Girishk. Artillery and cavalry engaged them at 9 A.M., so shortly afterwards whole force of enemy appeared and formed line of battle — seven regiments, regulars in centre, three others in reserve; about 2,000 cavalry on right; 400 mounted men and 2,000 Ghazis and irregular infantry on left; other cavalry and irregulars in reserve; five or six batteries of guns, including one of breechloaders, distributed at intervals. Estimated total force 12,000. Ground slightly undulating, enemy being best posted. Till one P.M., action confined to artillery fire, which so well sustained and directed by enemy that out superior quality armament failed to compensate for inferior number of guns. Formation being lost, infantry retreated slowly; and, in spite of gallant efforts of General Burrows to rally them, were cut off from cavalry and artillery. This was at 3 P.M., and followers and baggage were streaming away towards Kandahar. After severe fighting in enclosed ground, General Burrows succeeded in extricating infantry and brought them into line of retreat. Unfortunately no efforts would turn fugitives from main road, waterless at this season. Thus majority casualties appear to have occurred from thirst and exhaustion. Enemy's pursuit continued to ten miles from Kandahar, but was not vigorous. Cavalry, artillery, and a few infantry reached banks of Arghandab, 40 miles from scene of action, at 7 A.M.; many not having tasted water since previous morning.

Nearly all ammunition lost, with 400 Martini, 700 Sniders, and 2 nine-pounder guns. Estimated loss, killed and missing, — 66th, 400; Grenadiers, 350; Jacob's Rifles, 350; Artillery, 40; Sappers, 21; Cavalry, 60. Officers killed, or missing, — Majors Blackwood, Osborne, Maclaine, Artillery; Hennn, Engineers, Galbright, McMath, Garratt, Cullen, Roberts, Rayner, Honeywood, Barr, Chute, 66th; Owen, 3rd Cavalry; Hinde, Whitby, Grenadiers; Smith, Justice, Cole, Jacob's Rifles. Wounded, — Fowell, Artillery; Lynch, Preston 66th; Anderson, Grant, Grenadiers; Iredell, Jacob's Rifles.

Preparations being now made for siege. Durani inhabitants expelled. Provisions and ammunition plentiful. Wali was present during action, and is now with us, assisting actively. Of course, whole country will rise." (PP. L/P&S/20/MEMO/2)

MALLESON, MAJ. GEN. W. Headed the East Persian Cordon with headquarters in Meshed for the purpose of preventing Turkestan Bolsheviks from sending armed assistance to Afghanistan during the third Anglo-Afghan war.

MANPOWER, AFGHAN ARMY 1936. According to an assessment of the Afghan army by the British-Indian general staff, Afghan manpower resources were as follows: Of a total population of 10 million, the maximum manpower was estimated at 1 million. There existed no arrangement for mobilizing the full manpower of the country, nor was there a reserve system or sufficient reserves of arms and clothing. Tribal levies can be raised only depending on a number of factors: whether the war was popular; in what area it was to be fought; tribal attachment to the existing regime; the amount of government power over tribe; funds available to buy their loyalty; the season of the year; and prospects of booty. Therefore, maximum regulars numbered 100,000 and tribal levies 300,000. Unless they can be fed, tribal forces will not remain more than a few days.

Recruitment. The best fighters are the tribes, but they won't furnish their quota. Therefore, the easiest supply comes from Hazaras, Wardaks, Shinwaris, Tajiks, Ahmadzais, and Durranis, as well as some Afridis from the British side of the border.

There were two systems of recruitment: *Hasht-nafari*, chosen by lot; and *Qaumi*, where a tribe has to provide a definite quota. Each village had to contribute fixed sums for the recruits' expenses. Service was for two years — recruits were often compelled to serve longer. Some extend their service. Soldiers were badly paid (in 1936 Rs. 24 1/2 = Rs. 7 Indian) and had to pay for their rations. There were no pensions and discipline was only fair.

Officers. Were recruited from cadet college (Maktab-i Harbiya) and from the ranks. Courses lasted for three years, and separate classes existed for each arm.

Ranks of Officers:

Sipah Salar	Field Marshal
Naib Salar	General
Firqa Mishar (awwal)	Lt. General
Firqa Mishar (dowwum)	Major General
Ghund Mishar (awwal)	Brigadier
(dowwum)	" "
Kandak Mishar	Lt. Colonel

Toli Mishar	Captain
Baluk Mishar (awwal)	Lieutenant
(dowwum)	2nd Lieutenant

Promotion to Lieutenant	3 years
to Captain	9 years
to Lt. Colonel	15 years

Thereafter by selection. Promotion up to *toli mishar* was made by the ministry of defense on recommendation of the divisional commander; higher ranks by the king on recommendation of the ministry of defense. Pay was bad and training neglected. No terms of service were laid down for officers; they were permitted to resign or be placed on a reserve list at their own request.

NCO Ranks:

Dalgai Mishar	Section commander
Parak Mishar	Sergeant
Sar Parak Mishar	Sergeant Major

Promotion was slow, those with some education or from good families occasionally got commissions. Good and loyal service was sometimes rewarded by grant of a commission.

Administration. The nominal head was the king, but in fact, the minister of national defense, then   Shah Mahmud, who was also commander in chief. The deputy (*muawin*) refers important matters to the minister.

Principal staff officers:

Rais-i Arkan	Chief of Gen. Staff
Rais-i Urdu	Adjutant General
Rais-i Harb	Master General of Ordnance
Rais-i Lowazim	Quartermaster General

The Committee of Improvements and Reforms (*anjuman-i islah wa taraqqi*) made suggestions for improvements.

Areas of command corresponded with provincial boundaries. There was no staff college or permanent general staff.

Organization of a Corps Staff:

Chief of Staff
G.S.O. Operations
G.S.O. Training
G.S.O. Intelligence
One 'Q' Staff Officer
One Medical Officer

One Veterinary Officer

Organization of Divisional Staff:

    Commander

    A.D.C.

    Chief of Staff

    G.S.O. Operations and Training

    G.S.O. Intelligence

    G.S.O. Appointments

    One 'Q' Staff Officer

    A Courts-Martial Officer

    A Medical Officer.

Auxiliary Units and Semimilitary Forces:

    Militia — Urgun Militia, of Wazirs, Mahsuds, and Kharots. Mostly from British side of border.

    Armed Police (*Kotwali*), a gendarmerie. Under control of the ministry of interior. Units existed in every province. Used to maintain public security. Mostly in big towns, posts along roads, and some at frontier.

    Unarmed Police Ranks: Komandan, a Ghund Mishar; Sar Mamur, Chief Superintendent, a Kandak Mishar; Mamur, Superintendent, usually a Toli Mishar.

    Khasadars, chiefly for road protection, wear Khaki uniform.

    Tribal Levies. Response depended on: 1. degree of popularity of war, 2. whether *jehad* was called, 3. amount of money tribes can make for passage of army.

Tribal patriotism is local. A tribal *lashkar* will never stay for long in the field at full strength, as tribesmen will always be coming and going, particularly after a success when loot has to be taken home.

Special Bodyguard Troops: In Kabul, the Hazirbash — 300 men, recruited mostly from the southern province. Bodyguards of the royal family — resemble in dress the militias on the British side of border. They were under the command of the Guards Division.

Education. Cadet Colleges: 1. Maktab-i Ihzarieh, Preparatory School, 600 students, five-year course; 2. Maktab-i Rushdiyeh, Middle School, 280 students, three-year course, specialization begins; 3. Maktab-i Harbiya, 240 students, three-year course. All controlled by ministry of war. At 1. and 2. instructors are both civilian and military, education is general. Drill and physical training were taught and cadets wore military uniform. Kurs-i Ali, Advanced Course for Senior Officers, opened in 1935. It had 45 students and took three years. Chief instructor was a retired major of the German army. (Notes on the Afghan Army, 1936, General Staff, India L/MIL/17/14/18)

MANUPUR, BATTLE OF. A battle on March 11, 1748 between an Afghan army of some 30,000 under Ahmad Shah Durrani and a Moghul army of some 60,000 and 140,000 camp followers under the command of Prince Ahmad, the heir apparent of the great Moghul emperor, Muhammad Shah. Ahmad Shah arrived near Lahore on January 8, before the Moghul army could reach the city. In a quick move Ahmad Shah crossed the Sutlij River and took possession of Sirhind Fort, where the Moghul baggage train was sheltered. The Moghul army camped at Sirhind and desultory fighting started on March 3. The Afghan army disposed of only one heavy gun, placed on a hill that overlooked the camp of the Indians, who had a greater arsenal of heavy artillery. By a lucky chance a cannon shot from the Afghan side killed Qammaruddin, the Moghul commander in chief. The Moghul army was hard pressed and its Rajput contingent deserted, when reinforcements saved the Moghul army from defeat. An explosion of ammunition stores caused heavy losses in the Afghan camp, and Ahmad Shah retreated, carrying his Sirhind treasure with him to Afghanistan. Prince Ahmad's father was in poor health; therefore the Moghul prince decided to return to Delhi rather than give pursuit.

MARATHAS (MAHRATTAS). *See* **PANIPAT, BATTLE OF.**

MARATHA WEAPONS. The Marathas used old and new weapons. Stones were hurled from fortresses. At Panipat, bows and arrows were still used. Bows were of bamboo and steel. Crossbows were also employed. Cavalry used swords — mostly straight — daggers, spears, lances, and mace. Soldiers wore turbans, the officers, helmets and chain armor. Shields were fashioned of rhinoceros skin and steel, which "would easily turn a pistol ball." Cannons, pistols, revolvers as well as matchlocks — long barrel usually attached to the stock by leather strips. Guns were drawn by buffaloes.

MASHK-I ALAM. *See* **DIN MUHAMMAD.**

MAS'UD, AHMAD SHAH (MASSOUD). One of the most publicized *mujahedin* leaders from the Panjshir valley of Parwan Province, north of Kabul. He withstood numerous Russian invasions into his territory, but in 1983 he concluded a temporary truce with Soviet forces, which was described as a tactical measure since it did not prevent him from carrying out attacks elsewhere. He organized a supervisory council and is one of few commanders who sought to set up a civil administration, instill discipline in his troops, and use modern military principles of tactical warfare. He is a member of the *Jam'iat-i Islami-yi Afghanistan*, headed by Professor Burhanuddin Rabbani (qq.v.), which is largely of non-Pashtun background. After the withdrawal of the Soviet troops from Afghanistan, he was able to extend his territorial control, establishing his headquarters at Taluqan. His group was involved in bloody clashes with Gulbuddin Hekmatyar's *Hizb-i Islami* (q.v.), which resulted in considerable casualties to both sides. Because of his successes, Mas'ud is called "The Lion of Panjshir" by his admirers. Born in 1956, he was educated at Istiqlal High School and the Military Academy, where he graduated in 1973. He was a member of the radical Islamist Movement. Mas'ud captured Kabul with the help of the Uzbeki forces of General Dostum, but other groups, including the Shi'a Wahdat, carved out areas under their control and fighting has continued over control of the city. Mas'ud was elected minister of defense, a post he relinquished in an attempt at compromise with the *Hizb-i Islami* of Gulbuddin Hekmatyar. Nevertheless, Mas'ud continued to control the armed wing of the *Jam'iat-i Islami*, and he gained control of the entire city of Kabul after defeating the other *mujahedin* groups. He is now engaged in a struggle for survival against the *Taleban*, who have captured most of western and southern Afghanistan.

MAUDE, LT.-GEN. SIR F. F. Commanded the 2nd Division Peshawar Valley Field Force of some 5,000 troops in the second Anglo-Afghan war from its formation until it was broken up on the conclusion of the first campaign. In December 1878, he commanded the first and second punitive expeditions against the Afridis in the Bazar Valley, causing great damage to the land, but little to the tribesmen who had withdrawn into the mountains.

MAZARI, ABDUL ALI. Chief of the radical *Nasr* (Victory) party, which succeeded in capturing most of the Hazarajat from traditional groups. In 1989 he joined the *Hizb-i Wahdat*, a coalition of seven Shi'a parties, and subsequently became its head. He collaborated with Rabbani, but eventually allied himself with Hekmatyar. A hardliner, he was accused of having liquidated some of his opponents. He was himself killed in *Taleban* captivity, after he surrendered to this new force. He was buried in Mazar-i Sharif. *See also* HIZB-I WAHDAT.

MAZAR-I SHARIF, FALL OF. The fall of Mazar-i Sharif precipitated the fall of President Najibullah and his Kabul government. It occurred in March 1992, not as a result of military conquest, but rather as the consequence of a power struggle within the Marxist leadership. Najibullah wanted to replace the Tajik general, Mumin, commander of the Hairatan garrison and guardian of the major weapons depot in the northern province, with the Pashtun general, Rasul. Mumin refused to go and allied himself with General Dostum (q.v.), commander of the Jozjani militia, and Sayyid Mansur Nadiri, head of the Ismaili forces that control the area north of the Salang Pass. They cooperated with Mas'ud and assisted the latter in the capture of Kabul on April 25. Dostum then founded the National Islamic Movement, *junbesh-i milli-yi Islami*, with Nadiri and others and has since controlled the entire north-central area of Afghanistan. *See also* DOSTUM.

MCMAHON, A. H. Political agent at Zhob, 1891 and 1893. Accompanied Durand Mission to Kabul in 1893. Was British commissioner for the demarcation of the boundary between Baluchistan and Afghanistan, 1894–96, and commissioner to settle the Perso-Afghan boundary in 1903.

MILITIA. *See* **ARMY, AFGHAN.**

MINES. Mines, detonated by contact, magnetic, proximity, or electric command, were first used during the Soviet intervention in Afghanistan, where they were used by all parties as a weapon of passive defense to protect bases and offensively to block lines of logistics. Villages suspected of harboring rebels were made uninhabitable by widespread sowing of mines. Antipersonnel mines, especially the PFM-1 "butterfly" mine, were most commonly dispensed by helicopters and scattered at random. The *mujahedin* eventually obtained various types of mines from foreign supporters, including plastic ones, which made detection difficult. The *mujahedin* mined roads in ambush operations, choosing places where an entire convoy could be blocked. According to McMichael, the Soviet forces planted literally millions, and the *mujahedin* thousands, of mines, which still pose a severe threat to life in Afghanistan three years after the end of the war.

MIR WAIS KHAN HOTAKI (1709–15). A Ghilzai Pashtun and founder of the short-lived Hotaki dynasty (1709–38). Leader of the Afghan tribal revolt against Persian domination that led to the foundation of modern Afghanistan. He was a Ghilzai chief who lived as a hostage at the court of the Safavid ruler in Isfahan while Kandahar was ruled by Gorgin Khan, a Georgian governor. Mir Wais got permission to go on a pilgrimage to Mecca, where he obtained a *fatwa* (legal decision) authorizing revolt against the Shi'a domination of western Afghanistan (which is largely sunni). Upon his return to Kandahar he used the *fatwa* to win the support of tribal chieftains and, in 1709, staged a successful revolt against Gorgin Khan's troops. Mir Wais and his Afghan forces defeated all attempts by the Safavid armies to recapture Kandahar and laid the basis for the Afghan invasion of Persia and the defeat of the Safavids at Gulnabad in 1722. *See also* HOTAKI; and GHILZAI.

MUHAMMAD DAUD, SARDAR (1909–1978). President of the Republic of Afghanistan from July 1973 until his assassination in April 1978 as a result of the Saur Revolt (q.v.). Born in 1909 in Kabul, the son of Sardar Muhammad Aziz, and educated in Kabul and France. He embarked on a military career and was governor and general officer commanding the Eastern Province (1934), Kandahar (1935), and the Central Forces (1939–47). He was stationed in Kabul and served as minister of defense 1946. He was minister of the interior (1949–50) and the prime minister (1953–63). He encouraged social reforms and in 1959 permitted women to abandon the veil, thus contributing to their emancipation and participation in the public life of Afghanistan.

He initiated two five-year plans (1956–61 and 1962–67) and a seven-year plan in 1976, and relied for military and developmental aid on the Soviet Union. He demanded the independence of Pashtunistan (q.v.), the North-West Frontier Province of Pakistan, which led to repeated crises with Pakistan and ended with his forced resignation in 1963. Ten years later Muhammad Daud staged a coup against his cousin, King Zahir, and in July 1973 proclaimed Afghanistan a republic. Whether he just wanted power, or felt that the political liberalization during the democratic decade (1963–73) had failed to remedy the social and economic problems of Afghanistan, is not clear. He relied on the support of leftists to consolidate his power, crushed the emerging Islamist movement, and in 1975 established his own "National Revolutionary Party" as an umbrella organization for all political movements. Thus he wanted to limit the power of the Left and create a Left-of-Center movement loyal to him.

Toward the end of his rule he attempted to purge his leftist supporters from positions of power and sought to reduce Soviet influence in Afghanistan. Financial support from Iran and the Arab Gulf states would enable him to repay Soviet loans and improve his relations with the West. He and members of his family were assassinated on April 27, 1978, as a result of the Saur Revolt, which brought Marxist parties to power in Kabul.

MUHAMMADI, MAULAWI MUHAMMAD NABI. Leader of the *harakat-i inqilab-i Islami* (Islamic Revolutionary Movement), a traditional Islamic *mujahedin* group headquartered in Pakistan. He was born in 1921 in Logar, the son of Haji Abdul Wahhab, and educated in *madrasas* (religious colleges) in Logar Province. In the 1950s he was one of the first members of the religious establishment who agitated against "Communist influence" in the Afghan educational system and was elected to Parliament in 1964 as a representative of Logar Province. After the Marxist coup, he fled to Pakistan and utilized a network of *maulawis* (graduates of *madrasas*) to organize armed resistance against Kabul. In the early 1980s his Harakat was the largest of *mujahedin* groups, but it lost members to the more radical Islamist parties of Sayyaf (q.v.) and Rabbani. He has since joined Hekmatyar against Rabbani. His party has primarily Pashtun support.

MUHAMMAD ISHAQ. Son of Amir Muhammad Azim Khan and cousin of Amir Abdur Rahman (q.v.) who in June 1888 had himself proclaimed amir and unsuccessfully fought Abdur Rahman for the throne. Born about 1851 of an Armenian mother, he was at age 18 in command of Abdur Rahman Khan's forces in Afghan Turkestan. He was defeated by Amir Shir Ali (q.v.) and lived with Abdur Rahman in exile at Samarkand. In 1879 he returned with Abdur Rahman Khan to Afghanistan. When the latter assumed the Kabul throne, he appointed Muhammad Ishaq governor of Turkestan, as the northern provinces were then called. Ishaq Khan was ambitious; he demanded autonomy amounting to virtual independence, subject to token allegiance to the Kabul throne. He next extended his control over Herat Province, and when Amir Abdur Rahman was ill in 1888, he proclaimed himself amir. The Iron Amir finally defeated him on September 29, 1888 at the Battle of Gaznigak.

MUHAMMAD ISMA'IL. *Mujahedin* commander affiliated with the *Jam'iat-i Islami* headquartered in Herat. He was the "Amir" of Herat, Badghis, Ghor, and Farah provinces and is said to have built a good military organization and was a good administrator. He was born in 1946 in Shindand, and after completing his elementary education in Shindand, he continued his education at Kabul Military School and the Military Academy. He was a second lieutenant in the 17th Division stationed in Herat when he defected and participated in the uprising of March 1979. When the uprising was suppressed, he fled to Iran and made his way to Pakistan, where he joined the forces of the *mujahedin* leader Burhanuddin Rabbani (q.v.). In 1987 he was said to have received stinger missiles, which helped him to secure control of much of Herat Province. He called himself "Amir" and seemed to have ambitions for autonomous rule, but was defeated by *Taleban* forces and forced to flee the country on September 5, 1995.

MUHAMMAD JAN, GEN. One of the ablest Afghan generals who outmaneuvered Generals Baker and Macpherson in December 1879 and defeated a force under General Massey. He captured Takht-i Shah (q.v.) and forced the British to retire to Sherpur. Muhammad Jan led the attack on Sherpur (q.v.), but was unable to overcome the British defenses.

MUHAMMAD NADIR SHAH. King of Afghanistan, 1929–33. Born in 1883, the son of Sardar Muhammad Yusuf Khan, he embarked on a military career. Appointed a brigadier in 1906, he was promoted to lieutenant general, *naib salar*, for his services in suppressing the Mangal Revolt in December 1912. He was appointed general, *sipah salar*, in 1914. He and other members of the Afghan court had accompanied Amir Habibullah to Jalalabad, the winter capital, and when the amir was assassinated in his sleep, Nadir was arrested. Amir Amanullah exonerated him of any involvement and sent him to command the troops in Khost Province. During the third Anglo-Afghan war, Nadir Khan led an army across the Afghan border into Waziristan and invested the British base at Thal. This threatened to cause a general uprising among the "British" Afghans and was one of the factors forcing

Britain to accept Afghan independence (*see* THIRD ANGLO-AFGHAN WAR). Amir Amanullah appointed him minister of war in 1919, in which post he served until 1924, when he was appointed Afghan minister in Paris. After the abdication of King Amanullah in January 1929, Nadir left France for India and established himself at the Afghan frontier. He collected tribal support, including Waziri tribal forces from the Indian side of the border, and, after initial setbacks, defeated Habibullah Kalakani (q.v.) and captured Kabul on October 13, 1929. Nadir Khan was proclaimed king two days later. He was assassinated in 1933 and succeeded by his son Muhammad Zahir (q.v.)

MUHAMMAD YUSUF (MOHAMMAD YOUSAF). Brigadier Muhammad Yusuf, head of the Afghan Bureau of the Inter-Services Intelligence of the Pakistan military from 1983 to 1987. He claims to have held a pivotal position in the war of the Afghan *mujahedin* against the Soviet and Kabul forces. In his book, *The Bear Trap: Afghanistan's Untold Story* (coauthored with Mark Adkin), this "commander in chief" of the *mujahedin* forces controlled the distribution of weapons bought with CIA and Saudi Arabian funds from the United States, Britain, China, and Egypt. He organized the training of rebels and planned missions of sabotage, ambushes, and assassinations inside Afghanistan and the Soviet Union. He was succeeded in 1978 by General Hamid Gul, at a time when the Soviet government had decided to end its involvement in Afghanistan.

MUHSINI, AYATOLLAH MUHAMMAD ASEF. A Hazara, born in 1935 in Kandahar Province and educated at the Shi'a universities in Iraq. He is called Ayatollah by his supporters. Upon his return to Afghanistan he founded a cultural organization called "Dawn of Knowledge" (*sobh-i danesh*), which became the nucleus of the rural-based *mujahedin* group, *harakat-i Islami-yi Afghanistan* (Islamic Movement of Afghanistan). In 1980 he was elected chairman of the "Afghan Shi'a Alliance," a *mujahedin* umbrella group headquartered in Iran, but he subsequently left the alliance and moved to Quetta. His group once rivaled *Nasr* in importance and collaborated with *Nasr* in expelling the Shura of Ayatollah Beheshti (qq.v.) from most of the Hazarajat. In June 1990 the Shi'a groups announced formation of a new organization, "The Unity Party" (*hizb-i wahdat*), but Muhsini presented a number of conditions for his joining the coalition. Some of his commanders joined the *hizb-i wahdat*. Muhsini is known as a moderate who did not receive any support from Iran. Since the fall of the Marxist regime, his party has supported the government of President Rabbani.

MUJADDIDI, SEBGHATULLAH. Elected president in February 1989 of an "Afghan Interim Government" (AIG) made up of members of the seven-party alliance of *mujahedin* headquartered in Pakistan (*see* MUJAHEDIN). He founded and still leads the National Liberation Front of Afghanistan (*jabha-yi najat-i milli-yi Afghanistan,* q.v.), which conducted armed attacks on Soviet and Afghan government forces since about 1980. Born in 1925 in Kabul, the son of Muhammad Masum, he was educated in Kabul and at al-Azhar University in Egypt, and subsequently taught Islamic studies at high schools and colleges in Kabul. He publicly denounced "unbelievers" and Communists and was imprisoned (1959–64) for involvement in a purported plot to assassinate the Soviet premier, Nikita Khrushchev. When he was freed, he traveled abroad for two years, and upon his return he founded the *jam'iat-i ulama-yi Muhammadi* (1972, Organization of Muslim Clergy). He was again politically active and participated in antireformist demonstrations in Kabul in the 1970s and was forced to flee abroad in order to escape arrest. He was head of the Islamic Center in Copenhagen, Denmark (1974–78) and after the Saur Revolt, he went to Pakistan, where he led the armed resistance of the National Liberation Front. His supporters are primarily Pashtun members of the Naqshbandi sufi order in Paktia and Kandahar provinces. In spite of his radical background, he is counted among the moderate groups who do not rule out the establishment of a constitutional monarchy. After the fall of the Marxist government in April 1992, Mujaddidi served as interim president for two months, in which capacity he amnestied his Communist opponents and promoted Abd al-Rashid Dostum to the rank of general. In the present power struggle in Kabul, Mujaddidi supported Hekmatyar against Rabbani, when the latter refused to step down at the end of his two-year appointment.

MUJAHEDIN (MUJAHEDUN). Fighters in a holy war (*jehad*). Afghan resistance fighters adopted this designation to indicate that they were waging a lawful war against an "infidel" government (according to Islamic law, a *jehad* can be fought only against non-Muslims and apostates). *See also* JEHAD.

MUNRO, GEN. SIR CHARLES. Commander in chief in India, directed
operations in the Third Anglo-Afghan war.

MUSHK-I ALAM. *See* **DIN MUHAMMAD.**

MUSSOORIE CONFERENCE. A conference held between April 17 and
July 18, 1920, at Mussoorie, north of Delhi in India, which was to
restore "friendly" relations between the governments of Afghanistan and
British India after the third Anglo-Afghan war. It was a sequel to the
peace treaty of Rawalpindi and pitted the Afghan foreign minister,
Mahmud Tarzi, against the foreign secretary of the government of India,
Sir Henry Dobbs, in a fruitless attempt to conclude a treaty of friendship
between the two states. Lacking any agreement acceptable to the
Afghans, a British *aide-mémoire* provided for some economic
assistance but postponed the establishment of normal, "neighborly
relations" for another conference at Kabul. *See also* ANGLO-AFGHAN
TREATY OF 1919; and 1921.

- N -

NADIR SHAH, AFSHAR. Ruler of Iran (1736–47) and founder of the
short-lived Afsharid dynasty (1736–95). Born in 1688 as Nadir Quli in
northern Khurasan (q.v.), the son of Imam Quli, a member of a clan
affiliated with the Afshar tribe, he started life as a raider for booty and
became one of the last great nomadic conquerors of Asia. He ended the
Ghilzai dream of ruling an empire after Mahmud, son of Mir Wais
(q.v.), captured Isfahan in 1722. Nadir defeated the Afghans and drove
them out of Iran. He attacked Herat and invaded India, where he
defeated the Moghul army at Karnal, near Delhi, in 1739. Rather than
fighting the Afghan tribes he enlisted them into his army, making
Ahmad Khan Abdali (the subsequent Ahmad Shah, q.v.) one of his
military commanders. He moved the Abdali tribe from Herat to their
original home in the Kandahar area and settled them on Ghilzai land.
This led to the ascendancy of the Abdalis (Durrani) over the Ghilzais
and contributed to the longstanding rivalry between these two Pashtun
tribes. (Nadir Shah also settled Jewish and Armenian traders from Iran
in Afghan towns to encourage trade with India.) Ruling over a
heterogeneous population, he wanted to unite his subjects by
proclaiming Shi'ism the fifth (Jafarite) orthodox school of sunni Islam.
The Shi'a clergy objected to this. Nadir became increasingly tyrannical

and was eventually killed by his own tribesmen. Some of Nadir's Qizilbash (q.v.) soldiers settled in Afghanistan, where their descendants had successful careers in the army, government, the trades, and crafts. At the time of Nadir Shah's death, Ahmad Khan Abdali was able to fill the political vacuum and become the first Durrani ruler of Afghanistan.

NAJIBULLAH (NAJIB ALLAH). President of the Republic of Afghanistan and general secretary of the PDPA from May 1986 to April 1992. Born in 1947 in Kabul of an Ahmadzai (Ghilzai Pashtun) family, he was educated at Habibia High School and Kabul University, graduating from the College of Medicine in 1975. He became a member of the *Parcham* faction of the PDPA in 1965 and was repeatedly arrested for his political activities. After the Saur Revolt he was appointed Afghan ambassador to Tehran (July–October 1978), in a move to get leading *Parchamis* out of the country, but was quickly dismissed with other *Parchamis* by the Taraki government, when they were accused of plotting a coup. He remained abroad and returned to Kabul with Babrak Karmal after the ouster of Hafizullah Amin (qq.v.) in the final days of December 1979. He next held the position of general president of KHAD (1980–86, q.v.) and in 1986 replaced Babrak Karmal as secretary general of the PDPA. He purged the central committee, brought in new members, and reorganized the government in 1988 and 1990. In March 1990 he successfully withstood a *Khalqi* coup, headed by Shahnawaz Tanai (q.v.), his defense minister. He downplayed Marxist ideology and annulled most of the early "reforms." When he agreed to step down in April 1992, members of his party deserted him and the *mujahedin* were able to capture Kabul. He has since remained in a building of the United Nations in Kabul and has not been permitted to go into exile. He is married to a Muhammadzai. *See also* PEOPLE'S DEMOCRATIC PARTY OF AFGHANISTAN.

NASR. A radical Islamist organization which is now part of the Shi'a *Hizb-i Wahdat* (q.v.).

NATIONAL ISLAMIC FRONT OF AFGHANISTAN. *See* **MAHAZ-I MILLI-YI AFGHANISTAN.**

NATIONAL LIBERATION FRONT OF AFGHANISTAN. *See* **JABHA-YI MILLI NAJAT-I AFGHANISTAN.**

NIGHT LETTERS. Clandestine leaflets attacking Afghan rulers and government officials, which became a potent propaganda tool in the war of the *mujahedin* with the Soviet/Kabul forces. Night letters, protesting the secular policies of Afghan government, were handwritten and copied and distributed by Islamist groups since the 1960s. President Daud was the target of such leaflets, as were the Marxist and Soviet governments after 1978. Letters, written in Dari and Pashtu, called for resistance against government policies, urging Afghans not to "accept the orders of the infidels, wage *jihad* against them." (Bradsher,1983, 208) Soviet soldiers were addressed in Russian and told to resist the policies of their dictatorial regime. On February 21, 1980 one successful campaign summoned the citizens of Kabul to shout, "Allahu Akbar" (God is Great) from their rooftops. This was followed by rioting and a general strike, which was severely repressed. The letters were distributed at night, hence the name *shab-nama* (D. *shab,* night, *nama,* letter).

NOTT, GEN. SIR WILLIAM (1782–1845). British general attached to the Bombay Force of General Keane during the first Anglo-Afghan war. Defeated Afghan forces at Kandahar in 1839, but failed to come to the assistance of the Kabul garrison. He conducted an expedition against the Ghilzai in the spring of 1841 and successfully defended Kandahar from a Durrani attack. He left Kandahar in August 1842, evacuating Afghanistan by way of Ghazni, where he liberated some 327 British survivors captured when the city fell into Afghan hands. Returned to India via Kabul and Jalalabad. Described as short-tempered but competent. *See* GHAZNI, CAPTURE OF.

NURISTAN. *See* **KAFIRISTAN.**

- O -

OERLIKON AA GUN. The Oerlikon 20mm antiaircraft gun was one of the first antiaircraft weapons supplied to the *mujahedin*. It was used at the Battle of Zhawar (q.v.), close to the Pakistani border, where it could be deployed without the need for long-distance transport. Mohammad Yousaf described it as a "prestige weapon" that was not particularly effective. In fact, Yousaf claims that the Pakistani Inter-Services Intelligence (ISI) rejected the CIA gift as not suitable for Afghanistan. The gun was too heavy (1,200 pounds) and had a long, cumbersome barrel, which could not easily be transported on mules in the difficult terrain. The weapon was deployed in three sections that required 20 mules for transport. Its high rate of fire, 1,000 rounds a minute at the cost of $50 a bullet, required a considerable supply of ammunition. It was a weapon more suited for the defense of strong points than offensive operations because it impeded the mobility of the *mujahedin*. ISI objections were overruled and 40–50 guns were supplied. (Yousaf, 87)

OJHIRI CAMP EXPLOSION. Ojhiri Camp was the ISI command post for the war in Afghanistan. It comprised an area of 70–80 acres, located on the northern outskirts of Rawalpindi, about 8 miles from Islamabad. The camp included a training area, a psychological warfare unit, a stinger training school, and mess halls for some 500 men. Most important, it contained the warehouses where 70 percent to 80 percent of all arms and ammunition for the *mujahedin* were held. On April 10, 1988 the entire stock was lost in a giant explosion. According to Yousaf (220), "Some 30,000 rockets, thousands of mortar bombs, millions of rounds of small–arms ammunition, countless anti–tank mines, recoilless rifle ammunition and stinger missiles were sucked into the most devastating and spectacular firework display that Pakistan is ever likely to see." About 100 persons died, and over 1,000 were wounded as people as far away as eight miles were hit by falling rockets. The depot was stocked to capacity with four months' supplies needed by the *mujahedin* for their spring offensive. The cause of the explosion was never examined in a public inquiry, and Zia–ul–Haq dismissed the government, which wanted to blame the ISI and the Pakistani army for this disaster. Conspiracy theorists saw it as a result of KGB or CIA sabotage, while others called it an accident. Fire was supposed to have started in a box of Egyptian rockets, which had not been diffused before shipping. A box was dropped, wounding several people, and the fire was permitted to burn for several minutes while the wounded were carried away. Ten minutes later, the entire depot went up and secondary explosion occurred for the following two days.

ORDER OF BATTLE – AFGHAN GOVERNMENT.

Distribution of Troops – Third Afghan War, 1919

Badakhshan	3 Bns. Infantry

	1 Regt. Cavalry 12 Guns
Herat & Farah	12 Bns. Infantry 3 Regts. Cavalry 26 Guns 85 Obsolete Guns
Kabul (Reserve)	11 Bns. Infantry 5 1/2 Regts. Cavalry 40 Guns 6 Obs. Guns
Kandahar	13 Bns. Infantry 3 Regts. Cavalry 60 Guns 62 Obsolete Guns
Khost & Ghazni	16 Bns. Infantry 2 Bns. Pioneers 60 Guns 6 Obs. Guns 4 Regts. Cavalry
Kunar	6 Bns. Infantry 8 Guns 12 Obs. Guns
Nangarhar	14 Bns. Infantry 1 Bn. Pioneers 1 1/2 Regts. Cavalry 44 Guns 4 Obs. Guns (OA3)

For distribution of troops under Amir Shir Ali, *see* SECOND ANGLO–AFGHAN WAR.

Distribution of Troops, 1979 & 1988

Unit	Location, Dec. 1979	Location, Feb. 1988
Army GHQ	Kabul	Kabul

I Corps HQ	Kabul	Kabul
II Corps HQ	Kandahar	Kandahar
III Corps HQ	Gardez	Gardez
4th Armored Bde.	Pul–i Charkhi	Pul–i Charkhi
7th Armored Bde.	Kandahar	Kandahar
15th Armored Bde.	Pul–i Charkhi	Pul–i Charkhi
2nd Div. (1)	Not in OB	Panjshir
7th Div. (2)	Kabul	Moqor
8th Div. (3)	Qargha, Kabul	Qargha, Kabul
9th Div. (4)	Asadabad, Kunar	Asadabad, Kunar
11th Div. (5)	Jalalabad	Jalalabad,Samarkhel
12th Div. (6)	Gardez	Gardez
14th Div. (7)	Ghazni	Ghazni
15th Div. (8)	Kandahar	Kandahar
18th Div. (9)	Mazar–i Sharif	Mazar–i Sharif
17th Div. (10)	Herat	Herat
20th Div. (11)	Nahrin, Baghlan	Nahrin, Baghlan
25th Div. (12)	Khost, Paktia	Khost, Paktia
37th Commando Bde.	?	Kabul
38th Commando Bde.	?	Kabul
444th Commando Bde.	Kabul area	Panjshir?
666th Commando Bde.	?	Paktia?
252nd Recon Bn.	Kabul	Kabul
212th Recon Bn.	Gardez	Gardez
203rd Recon Bn.	Kandahar	Kandahar
GHQ Artillery Brig.	Kabul area	Kabul?
880th MRL Brig.	Kabul	Kabul
26th Airborne Bn. (13)	Kabul	Bagram
88th SAM Regt. (13)	Bagram/Shindand	Bagram/Shindand
99th SAM Regt. (13)	Kabul	Kabul
77th ADA Regt. (13)	Kabul	Kabul
1st Frontier Bde. (14)	not in OB	Jalalabad
2nd Frontier Bde. (14)	not in OB	Khost
3rd Frontier Bde. (14)	not in OB	Badakhshan
4th Frontier Bde. (14)	not in OB	Nimruz
5th Frontier Bde. (14)	not in OB	Herat area
6th Frontier Bde. (14)	not in OB	Paktika
7th Frontier Bde. (14)	not in OB	Kandahar
8th Frontier Bde. (14)	not in OB	Paktika
9th Frontier Bde. (14)	not in OB	Kabul

10th Frontier Bde. (14)   not in OB   Kunar
24th Sarandoy Regt. (15)not in OB   Badakhshan
(Isby, 1989, 90)

BRITISH–INDIA FORCES

Distribution of Troops – Third Afghan War, 1919

Rawalpindi, Peshawar & Khaibar	Striking Force	Internal Security
	22 Bns. Infantry	4 Bns. Infantry
	Khaibar Rifles	Mohmand Militia
	1 Bn. Pioneers	14 Guns
	6 Regts. Cavalry	12 Machine Guns
	104 Machine Guns	9 Armored Cars
	2 Fd. Tr. S & M	
	66 Guns	
	4 Fd. Coy S & M	

Kohat – Kurram   4 Bns. Infantry
                                  Kurram Militia
                                  1 Regt. Cavalry
                                  6 Pack Guns
                                  1 Fd. Coy S & M
                                  3 Armored Cars

Waziristan   7 Bns. Infantry
                                  N. Wazir Militia
                                  S. Wazir Militia
                                  2 Regts. Cavalry
                                  12 Guns 2 Fd. Coy S & M
                                  9 Armored Cars

Quetta – Zhob   12 Bns. Infantry
                                  4 1/2 Regts. Cavalry
                                  24 Guns
                                  34 Machine Guns
                                  1 Fd. Tr. S & M
                                  2 Fd. Coy S & M

At the time Britain also had the following troops in Iran:

Mashhad	1 Bn. Infantry
	1 Regt. Cavalry
Southeastern Iran	2 Bns. Infantry
	1/2 Regt. Cavalry
	1 Bn. Pioneers
	2 Fd. Coy S & M

(OA, 3)

SOVIET FORCES

Distribution of Troops in 1985

40th Army/Turkestan Military District	Kabul, Tajbeg Camp
103rd Guards Air Assault Division	Kabul, Darulaman Camp
Guards Motor Rifle Division	Shindand, Farah
108th Motor Rifle Division	Kabul, Khair Khana
201st Motor Rifle Division	Kunduz Province
66th Motor Rifle Brigade	Jalalabad
70th Motor Rifle Brigade	Kandahar
56th (?) Motor Rifle Brigade	Kandahar
345th Independent Guards Air Assault Regiment	Bagram, Parwan
191st Indep. Motor Rifle Regiment	Ghazni
866th Indep. Motor Rifle Regiment	Faizabad, Badakhshan
181st Motor Rifle Regiment	Bagram, Parwan
187th Motor Rifle Regiment	Mazar-i Sharif
Spetsnaz Brigade	Kandahar
Spetsnaz Brigade	Kabul
Spetsnaz Brigade	Shindand
Artillery Brigade (?)	Kabul
40th (?) Airfield Defense Battalion	Begram, Parwan
Guards (military police) Battalion	Pul-i Khumri
Motor Transport Regiment	Khair Khana, Kabul
Construction Regiment	Shindand, Farah
40th (?) Signal Regiment	Bala Hisar, Kabul
Pipelaying Battalion	Pul-i Khumri

Engineer Battalion   Jalalabad
Urban, 1991, 229)

For Army of the Indus, *see* FIRST ANGLO-AFGHAN WAR. For British forces during the second Anglo-Afghan war, *see* SECOND ANGLO-AFGHAN WAR, OPERATIONS. The regular Afghan army was usually only the nucleus, which was augmented by irregular tribal forces whose numbers fluctuated with circumstances. *See also* SOVIET INTERVENTION/INVASION; and MANPOWER, AFGHAN.

OXUS. *See* **AMU DARIA**

- P -

PAIWAR KOTAL, BATTLE OF. A battle for capture of a pass lying at an altitude of 8,531 feet astride one of the great lines of communication between India and Afghanistan. It was on one of the routes of invasion during the second Anglo–Afghan war on December 2, 1878. General Frederick Roberts commanded a force of 5,500 men and 24 guns, which pushed forward in two columns. Lacking proper intelligence, Roberts ordered the left column to turn right of the supposed Afghan position to cut off the Afghan's access to the pass. But the Afghans were already in possession of the pass, forcing the left column to withdraw. The Afghan force, estimated by British officers at 3,500 regulars and a large number of tribal irregulars, was met by Brigadier Cobbe, who commanded the 8th (Queen's) and the 5th Panjab Infantry regiments, a cavalry regiment, and six guns. General Roberts directed the rest, consisting of the 29th Native Infantry, the 5th Gurkas, and a mountain battery — all under the command of Colonel Gordon; followed by a wing of the 72nd Highlanders, 2nd Panjab Infantry, and 23rd Pioneers with four guns on elephants under Brigadier Thelwall. The Gurkas and 72nd carried the first stockade, and the Afghan flank was turned and driven back. But the Afghans made a resolute resistance and General Roberts decided to desist and make another turning movement, which brought the British forces to the rear of the Afghans. In a frontal attack Cobbe's infantry was able to move from ridge to ridge within 800 yards of the Afghans, placing the Afghans in a cross fire, which eventually forced them to abandon the pass. The British lost 21 killed and 72 wounded. The British estimated Afghan losses at about 500 killed and wounded.

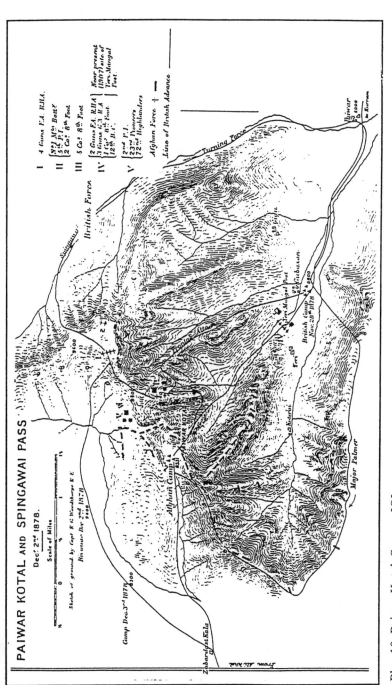

Plan 10. Paiwar Kotal. Source: IOL

PANIPAT, BATTLE OF. A battle on January 14, 1761, in which Ahmad Shah Durrani decisively defeated the Maratha tribal confederation near the town of Panipat some 50 miles north of Delhi. The Maratha Empire, founded in 1680 by Shivaji in the present Maharashtra Province, gradually grew in size and in a successful guerrilla war supplanted the Moghuls in a wide area of India. They were warriors and champions of Hinduism and became a serious threat to the Afghans when they occupied the Panjab. Ahmad Shah was able to cross the Jumna River unopposed and took up a position near the Maratha army, commanded by Sadashiv Bhau. For two months the two armies engaged in skirmishes with varying success, but eventually the Afghan forces were able to block the Indian's supply routes. Both armies were organized in the traditional left and right wings with large center divisions; the Afghans had the advantage in numbers, about 60,000 against 45,000 Indian troops. The Marathas were handicapped with most of their camp followers, families, and supplies located in Panipat, which made it impossible for the Marathas to retreat quickly. Sadashiv Bhau therefore tried to negotiate, but when the Afghans refused to deal, he was forced into combat. The Afghans' pieces of artillery were lighter and more mobile than the heavy guns of the Marathas; nevertheless, in a desperate move, the Marathas seemed to be able to penetrate the Afghan center. But the Afghans were able to bring in reinforcements and envelop the Marathas from three sides. One squadron after another discharged their muskets, leaving the Indians little opportunity to compose themselves. Wishwas Rao, the nominal head of the Marathas, and Sadashiv were killed and the Marathas were routed. The battle ended the dreams of both the Marathas and the Afghans to becoming the rulers of India. Ahmad Shah's troops hated the heat of the Indian plains and wanted to return home with their plunder, forcing the Afghan ruler to return.

PANJAB. An area watered by five rivers (D. *panj*, five, *ab*, water), the Indus, Jhelum, Chenab, Rawi, and Sutlej in northern India. It is now divided into the western Panjab of Pakistan and the eastern Panjab of India. It is a rich and fertile area and has been the scene of numerous battles.

PANJDEH INCIDENT. A military encounter in 1885 in which a Russian force under General Alikhanov annexed the Panjdeh district north of Herat Province (now part of Turkmenistan). The military action pitted superior Russian troops against about 500 defending Afghan soldiers headed by the Afghan general, Ghausuddin (q.v.). Afghan rulers claimed the area by virtue of the fact that the Turkomans of Panjdeh had been their occasional tributaries, but the Russians insisted that they were part of the Turkoman nation of Khiva and Merv, which Russia had annexed in 1881 and 1884.

An Anglo-Russian commission was to meet and resolve the dispute, but military action began on March 30, 1885 before Sir Peter Lumsden, a British Indian general, and his Russian counterpart arrived on the scene. Amir Abdur Rahman learned of the incident while he was on a state visit in Rawalpindi, India, and accepted the fait accompli at the urging of Lord Dufferin, the viceroy of India. The fact that Britain did not come to Afghanistan's defense, as she was obligated to do in case of unprovoked Russian aggression, confirmed the Afghan ruler in his belief that he could not rely on British promises of support.

PANJDEH, PRELIMINARIES TO WAR. When Russia extended its influence to Turkestan in 1884, the question arose whether the area of Panjdeh was part of Turkoman territory or part of the domain of the Afghan ruler. The Afghans had had governors there since 1860, and subsequently the area was under Herat control. Therefore, the governor of Herat appointed a governor over Panjdeh in April 1884 and sent Afghan troops to occupy the area. On June 16, 1884 Aminullah Khan, the new governor, accompanied General Ghaus Khan with 1,000 levies, horse and foot, and 200 irregulars, with two guns. He had orders to construct a fort at Hauz-i Abdullah Khan, the northernmost point of Panjdeh. British reports stated, "The Sarik Turkomans were at this time hesitating as to 'which side they would incline,' and Russian emissaries, accompanied by Yulatan Sariks, were 'busily engaged in collecting information and tampering with the tribes.'"

Amir Abdur Rahman wanted British and Russian officers to meet with the Afghan agent on the spot to define the border. The British appointed Sir Peter Lumsden to find the "true limits of Afghan territory to which the agreement of 1872–73 applied." In a note of December 23, 1884, Lord Granville informed the Russian government that Britain did not agree with them "that Pul–i–Khatun and Panjdeh were outside the limits of Afghanistan."

After the Afghans occupied Ak Tapa and Sari Yazi in October 1884, the viceroy assured the amir that the British mission would do all in its power to "secure his just rights, and to lay down a frontier which might prevent future discussion."

The total forces at Panjdeh on March 11, 1885 were: four 9–pounder guns, four mountain 9–pounder guns. Artillery, 140 men; cavalry, 400 regular, 500 irregular; infantry, 1,000 regular, 400 irregular. Total eight guns and 2,040 men.

General Komarof with 100 horsemen and a large quantity of provisions had come to Hazrat Imam. Colonel Alikhanof advanced with 100 Cossacks and Turkoman horsemen, with the intention of entering Panjdeh on November 22. Aminullah sent him a letter, saying that he would fight him if he proceeded further. The generals now hurled insults at each other.

Ali Khanoff sent a letter to General Ghaus–ud–Din, saying:

> Be it known to Ghaus–ud–din. I thought you were a wise man and were a General of an army, and I therefore wanted to come and see you. As you are such a bad man I do not want to see you, and I consider it a disgrace to meet you. But you must know that the order of our General is that, so long as the frontier dispute is not settled, your sowars should not come to this side of Arsh Doshan, nor will our sowars go beyond that place towards Panjdeh.

The reply:

> From General Ghaus–ud–din Khan, Ghazi. Be it known to Ali Circasion [sic]. You write that, until the surveyors of the two Governments come, Arsh Doshan should be the frontier. You are mistaken. If God please, through the blessings of the Prophet, I will turn you out of Kara Bolan. All the servants who are in Panjdeh were glad to think that to–morrow they would be called Ghazis.

Russian forces: A regiment of infantry (4,000 men) and two regiments of Cossacks (800 men) left for Baku and the Afghan border. From Tiflis 20,000 troops had already left for same area. (IOR: L/P&S/18/A58.d on March 27, 1885.)

Captain Yate, a British officer at Panjdeh, reported on March 26, 1885 that Russian troops were "encamped in front of Ak–Tepe; a troop of about 100 Turkoman sowars came in to Kizil–Tepe and advanced toward Pul–i–Khisti; the Afghan picket there warned them not to advance, and they at once retired. . . ."

PANJDEH, THE BATTLE. In another wire of March 29, Captain Yate stated: "Notwithstanding Russian assurances therein contained [between British and Russians], Russians are now drawn up in force almost within range of Afghan position, notwithstanding that Afghans have neither attacked nor advanced, and Panjdeh is perfectly quiet. . . .

On Friday Colonel Alikhanoff with 300 horses, in spite of remonstrances, pushed through Afghan pickets with the intention of proceeding to Panjdeh around left flank of position, but was forced to return by superior Afghan force sent in pursuit. Simultaneously three companies of Russian infantry crossed the river and advanced around the right flank towards Panjdeh, but were anticipated, and retired before the Afghan force. Fighting is now imminent. Afghans cannot resist successfully. If defeated, road will be open to Herat."

In a telegram of April 1, it was reported that Captain Yate and all British officers at Panjdeh had left and "Russians attacked and defeated Afghans, and occupied Panjdeh on the 30th [March]. Afghans are said to have fought gallantly, and have lost heavily, two companies being killed to a man in entrenchments. Survivors retreated along Maruchak road. British officers, who were neutral, left, as Colonel Alikhanoff was reported to have urged Sariks to attack them, and have offered 1,000 krans a head."

On May 4, the Panjdeh question was solved. The secretary of state reported: "We propose to accept in principle this arrangement, which would leave to the Amir the three points, viz., Zulfikar, Gulran, and Meruchak. . . . The whole agreement to be ultimately embodied in a Convention between us and Russia." (L/P&S/18/A. 48–53/A.)

PANJSHIR (34-38' N, 69-42' E). An administrative district in northern Parwan (now Kapisa) Province with an area of about 273 square miles and an agricultural population of about 30,000. The district is traversed by the Panjshir River, which rises on the southern slopes of the Hindu Kush in the vicinity of the Khawak Pass.

The population is largely Tajik, which has been converted to sunni Islam since the sixteenth century. The area was often independent or autonomous, and, although the Panjshiris acknowledged the Afghan amir as their ruler, they rarely paid taxes to the Kabul government. It was only since the time of Amir Abdur Rahman that the Kabul government asserted its sovereignty over the area.

The Panjshir valley is quite inaccessible; therefore, the Soviet and Kabul forces have never succeeded in bringing it under full government control. Its location, impinging on the strategic Salang road, which connects Kabul with the northern provinces, made the Panjshir valley an ideal base for *mujahedin* activity. Ahmad Shah Mas'ud (q.v.) called "The Lion of Panjshir" by his admirers, was able to withstand numerous Soviet incursions and was not evicted from the valley, making him one of the most successful *mujahedin* commanders.

PANJSHIR, SOVIET OFFENSIVE. Of about nine offensives, the seventh Soviet Panjshir offensive of April–May 1984 has been cited by military historians as the typical example of Soviet frustration in fighting a counterinsurgency war in this area. It began in response to Ahmad Shah Mas'ud's refusal to renew his 1983 cease fire with Soviet forces and involved some 10,000 Soviet and 5,000 Afghan troops (20,000 Soviet and 6,000 Afghans according to Isby, 1989, 32). According to Brigadier Yousaf (1992, 71–73), Mas'ud had learned of the planned offensive and organized the evacuation of hundreds of villages in the lower portion of the Panjshir valley. He laid mines along the road up the valley, and in one successful ambush, was able to destroy 70 fuel tankers and two important bridges. He then pulled back his forces before the start of aerial bombardment. Mountain ridges, rising to 19,000 feet, border the narrow valley and hindered proper approaches of the TU–16 (Badgers) and SU-24 (Fencer) bombers. The high–altitude bombing was often way off the mark, permitting the *mujahedin* to make spoiling attacks from the flanks. Heliborne units, landing in side valleys, executed blocking actions, but several landed too far from aerial support and were decimated by *mujahedin* forces. In eight days, the Soviets advanced about 40 miles up to the village of Khenj, and by May 7 Dasht-i Ravat was occupied. Afghan garrisons were established in the valley, and the Soviet/Kabul troops withdrew, permitting the *mujahedin* to move back into the valley by the end of June. Total Soviet casualties were said to have been about 500 and some 200 *mujahedin* were killed. The Afghan garrisons found themselves isolated in hostile territory and eventually developed a *modus vivendi* in which they coexisted without causing much harm to each other. Mas'ud was soon again free to attack Soviet convoys on the Salang highway, which provided much of the needs for the survival of the Kabul government. Eventually, the *mujahedin* captured isolated posts when the garrisons surrendered or defected. Since the fall of the Kabul regime in April 1992, Panjshir has formed the heartland of Mas'ud's territory.

PAPUTIN, GEN. LT. VICTOR S. First Deputy Minister of Internal Affairs, said to have been in command of the Soviet special forces' attempt to capture, or assassinate, President Hafizullah Amin. Paputin and Colonel Bayerenov, a KGB officer, were killed in the mission. According to another version, Paputin committed suicide because of the failure of his mission to capture Amin alive.

PASHTUN (PAKHTUN, PATHAN). The Pashtuns have been the politically dominant group in Afghanistan, with a population estimated at from 6 to 7 million concentrated largely in the west, south, and east, but also scattered throughout Afghanistan. Another 7 million Pashtuns live in Pakistan across the Durand Line. Except for the Turis and a few groups in Pakistan, all Pashtuns are sunni Muslims, and most were converted to Islam by the tenth century A.D. The Pashtuns are excellent soldiers, and many an invader of India chose to enlist them in his armies rather than force his way through their territory. Tribal society organized along family, clan, and sectional lines. The tribe, *qabila*, is usually named after its ancestor and carries the suffix "zai," as in *Muhammadzai*, the "sons of Muhammad." Although the tribal system has undergone changes, traditionally, chiefs have to be successful leaders and exemplify Pashtun values. They are not absolute rulers of their fellow tribesmen. Each clan decides matters of its welfare by council, the *jirga* (q.v.). *Jirgas* also arbitrate disputes between tribes.

The Pashtuns living in the inaccessible areas on both sides of the Durand Line (q.v.) adhere to their traditional code of behavior, the *Pashtunwali*, which guides the *jirgas* in resolving disputes. The principal pillars of this code are *nanawati* (mediation or protection); *badal* (retaliation); and *mailmastia* (hospitality). Urban Pashtuns still have a direct or emotional link to their tribes. The frontier Afghans are politically autonomous along the tribal belt on both sides of the Durand Line, but the rest have come increasingly under the control of the central governments.

PASHTUNISTAN. "Land of the Pashtuns" (or Afghans), the name given by Afghan nationalists to the North-West Frontier Province and parts of Baluchistan in present Pakistan. It was part of Afghanistan when the state was founded in 1747, but soon came under the control of the Sikh ruler Ranjit Singh (q.v.) and subsequently the British-Indian government.

Direct rule of the area was difficult because it is mountainous and difficult to access; therefore, the Pashtun tribes were allowed a considerable measure of autonomy. The British government cut the area from Afghanistan in 1893, drawing a border without regard to ethnic and cultural boundaries. Amir Abdur Rahman had scarcely consolidated his power and felt he had to accept "under duress" the Durand Line as his border (*see* DURAND AGREEMENT). In 1901, the British-Indian government created the North-West Frontier Province (NWFP), but left the tribal lands outside of the directly administered areas. Five Tribal Agencies (Malakand, Khaibar, Kurram, North Waziristan, and South Waziristan) were set up with autonomous *khans* (chiefs), governed by tribal councils. A British agent protected the interests of the government. Tribesmen were engaged as militia to keep order in their own areas, and if a tribe conducted raids into the lowlands, punitive campaigns were organized.

In 1947, when India was to be divided on the basis of a plebiscite, the Afghan government and Pashtun nationalists demanded that the Pashtuns be given an option to vote, if not for union with Afghanistan, then for the creation of an independent "Pashtunistan." This option was not given, and, as a result of a boycott by members of the Frontier Congress, a Muslim party allied with the Hindu Congress party, 68 percent of a low-voter turnout agreed to union with Pakistan. Afghanistan protested the procedure and cast the only vote against Pakistan's admission to the United Nations. Afghanistan's relations with Pakistan were subsequently plagued by the "Pashtunistan Question." The Afghan government supported the Pashtun nationalists, and Pakistan retaliated by closing the border at times and supporting guerrilla activities by Islamist forces against the government of President Daud. Pashtun nationalists have protested the fact that the NWFP is the only province in Pakistan not named after its inhabitants, and unsuccessfully demanded the adoption of the name *Pakhtunkhwa* (P. for Pashtunistan). *See also* AFGHAN FOREIGN RELATIONS; and DURAND AGREEMENT.

PEOPLE'S DEMOCRATIC PARTY OF AFGHANISTAN (PDPA). The Afghan Marxist party (after June 1990 called *Hizb-i Watan*, Fatherland party) was founded in 1965 and succeeded to power on April 27, 1978, in a coup, called the Saur Revolution (named after "Saur," the month of the revolt). The party was officially founded on January 1, 1965, at a meeting of 27 persons in Nur Muhammad Taraki's (q.v.)

house in Karte Char, Kabul. Taraki was chosen general secretary of the party and Babrak Karmal (q.v.) deputy secretary and secretary of a central committee, whose membership consisted of Taraki, Karmal, Ghulam Dastagir Panjshiri, Dr. Saleh Muhammad Zirai, Shahrullah(?) Shahpar, Sultan Ali Keshtmand, and Taher Badakhshi. Alternate members were Dr. Shah Wali, Karim Misaq, Dr. Muhammad Taher, and Abdul Wahhab Safi. The party drafted a manifesto, which stated that it was a workers' party. It declared Afghanistan a feudal society that should be transformed into a socialist state and announced its intention of obtaining power by democratic means.

From the beginning there was rivalry between the two leading personalities, Karmal being urbane and known from his activities on the campus of Kabul University and as a member of Parliament. He attracted followers among the Kabul intelligentsia, students, and government officials, and some military officers of various ethnic backgrounds. Taraki, on the other hand, was more successful among the Pashtuns, military officers, and students and teachers at schools in which tribal Pashtuns predominated. The PDPA published a newspaper, *Khalq* (Masses), which first appeared on April 11, 1966. Only six issues appeared until it was banned on the recommendation of Parliament for being "anti-Islamic" and opposed to the new constitution. By 1967 the party split into two entities, subsequently called *Khalq* and *Parcham*, after their respective newspapers. *Parcham* (Banner) was founded in 1968, published by Sulaiman Layeq and edited by him and Mir Akbar Khaibar. Having been successful in winning a parliamentary seat, Babrak Karmal was willing to cooperate with Afghan governments, while the *Khalqis* remained aloof. In 1977 the two factions reunited in a tenuous coalition with the help of Soviet and Indian Communist party mediation.

The Saur Revolt was precipitated when the *Parcham* ideologue, Mir Akbar Khaibar, was assassinated, according to some sources, by *Khalqis* who resented his recruiting efforts in the army. The Marxists, however, accused the government of the deed, and the party followed up with a funeral procession that turned into a public demonstration of a crowd of about 15,000 against the Daud government. The government reacted with arrests of the leadership, but three days later, on April 27, 1978, Marxist officers in the armed forces staged their successful coup. The Democratic Republic of Afghanistan (DRA) was proclaimed, and in early May the formation of a government was announced with Nur Muhammad Taraki as president and premier and Babrak Karmal as deputy premier. The majority of cabinet members were *Khalqis*. By July the *Khalqis* had purged members of the *Parcham* faction, including Babrak Karmal.

A number of decrees issued by the *Khalq* revolutionary council established Taraki as the "great leader" (No. 1), set up a government with Taraki as president of the revolutionary council and Karmal as vice president (No. 2), and abrogated the Daud constitution (No. 3). Subsequent decrees elevated the Uzbeki, Turkmani, Baluchi, and Nuristani languages to the status of "national languages," to be promoted in the Afghan media (No. 4), deprived members of the royal family of their citizenship (No. 5), canceled mortgages (No. 6), gave equal rights to women (No. 7), and ordered land reforms (No. 8). Former government officials and political opponents were arrested, and thousands were assassinated.

Khalqi supremacy did, however, not end strife in the PDPA. Hafizullah Amin (q.v.) had become vice premier and minister of foreign affairs, and on July 8, 1978 he was elected secretary of the secretariat of the central committee. By that time it became apparent that he was the dominant personality in the party. He became prime minister and minister of foreign affairs in April 1979, and president on September 16, 1979. Barely a month later, on October 9, Taraki was assassinated. A split occurred in the *Khalqi* faction between the "Red *Khalqis*" of Taraki and the "Black *Khalqis*" of Amin. A third faction, the followers of a Dr. Zarghun, already existed. They were called the "Paktia *Khalqis*." Increasing guerrilla activity of *mujahedin* forces prevented further strife in the *Khalqi* camp. Amin was said to have shown a tendency to develop into an "Afghan Tito" and demanded the recall of the Soviet ambassador, Alexandr M. Puzanov (q.v.), who expected Amin to follow his bidding. Puzanov was reported to have been implicated in a plot to assassinate Amin.

Mass arrests and executions, blamed on the Taraki era, were not ended, as was apparent from a list published with about 12,000 names of killed or missing persons. Hafizullah Amin's intelligence service, KAM, replaced Taraki's AGSA, and new government and party positions were announced. About 5,000 Soviet advisers resided in Afghanistan when, on December 25, 1979, an airlift of Soviet troops began that eventually brought in some 115,000 troops. On December 27, a *Parchami* coup, with Soviet armed support, replaced Hafizullah Amin with Babrak Karmal.

Karmal announced a government that included the dreaded head of AGSA, Asadullah Sarwari, as deputy premier and two other *Khalqis*, Sayyid Muhammad Gulabzoi as minister of interior, and Sherjan Mazduryar as minister of transport. KAM was purged and renamed KHAD, and the *Parchami* regime promised a new deal and an end to the excesses of the previous governments. Additional Soviet troops arrived in Afghanistan and established bases in various strategic locations. The government proclaimed a general amnesty and opened the doors of the feared Pul-i-Charkhi prison. Early *Khalqi* decrees of land reform (Nos. 6 and 8) and the emancipation of women (No. 7) were rescinded, and the tricolor replaced the red flag. But it was too late to overcome the "sins" of the past. The presence of Soviet forces in Afghanistan quickly transformed a civil war into a war of national liberation, and many of those freed from jail augmented the growing forces of the *mujahedin*. Karmal's lack of success in destroying the *mujahedin* was the likely reason for his resignation (or ouster) on May 4, 1986 and his replacement by Dr. Najibullah, the one-time head of KHAD.

Ideological evolution continued under Najibullah when the Kabul government initiated a policy of "national reconciliation" and changed the name of the PDPA to *hizb-i watan* (Fatherland Party). The early orthodoxy of adherence to Marxist-Leninism was gradually replaced by a general, socialist orientation and political liberalization, as the *Parchamis* attempted to survive in a national front coalition of "progressive" parties. Soviet troops withdrew from Afghanistan on February 15, 1989, but the party continued in power until President Najibullah announced his resignation in April 1992.   After the *mujahedin* conquest of Kabul, the party ceased to exist, and many of its members joined opposing groups. In fall 1994, it was reported that members of the Communist party met in the Microrayon quarter of Kabul and elected Mahmud Baryalai, half brother of Babrak Karmal, as its head. At the time of this writing, most of the Marxist leaders have found political exile abroad.

PESHAWAR, TREATY OF 1855–56. Opened diplomatic relations between Britain and Afghanistan. The treaty stipulated that "perpetual peace and friendship should be established between the two governments; that the British Government should respect the territories in possession of the Amir; that the Amir on his part should respect the territories of the British Government, and be the friend of its friends and the enemy of its enemies; and that the British should assist the Amir against his enemies, if they thought fit to do so" (MR, 28). Amir Dost Muhammad never knew whether the British "thought fit" to assist him against his enemies.

POLLOCK, GEN. GEORGE (1786–1872). Commander of the "Army of Retribution" after the British debacle in the first Anglo-Afghan war. Pollock gathered an army of about 8,000 men composed of eight infantry regiments, three cavalry corps, a troop and two batteries of artillery, and a mountain train. He entered the Khaibar Pass on April 5, 1842, where he overcame an Afridi attack, and after additional encounters on the way, rescued Jalalabad, whose British garrison had nearly been starved so that it would surrender. Marching on the route of the British retreat, Pollock's army saw the remnants of the "Army of the Indus," the wheels of the gun carriages crushing the bones of their comrades. He defeated Akbar Khan in the Battle of Tezin (q.v.) and entered Kabul on September 16, 1842. He destroyed the fortification of the Bala Hisar (q.v.) and Kabul's magnificent bazaar and permitted his troops to plunder the city, which resulted in nearly total destruction. Many hundreds of Afghans were killed or executed (O'Ballance). In September he got the British hostages released, after offering Saleh Muhammad, their guardian, a "reward" of 20,000 rupees and a pension of 12,000 rupees per year for life. Pollock's forces then moved against Istalif and Charikar and destroyed the towns, before evacuating Afghanistan on October 12, 1842.

POTTINGER, MAJ. ELDRED (1811–43). Sent to explore Central Asia and came to Kabul disguised as a horse dealer. Reached Herat in 1837, and assisted in the defense of the city. Auckland (q.v.) called him the "Hero of Herat," responsible for the successful defense of Herat during the second Persian siege of the city in 1837–38. As a reward, he was appointed political officer to Kamran, the ruler of Herat. He was one of two Englishmen to survive the destruction of a British outpost at Charikar (q.v.) in November 1841, in which the 4th (Gurka) Infantry was wiped out. As the senior surviving officer at Kabul, he negotiated the Treaty of Capitulation (q.v.) with Afghan *sardars* in December 1841. And as a hostage of Sardar Muhammad Akbar, he was instrumental in negotiating a deal for the release of the hostages in exchange for a monetary reward to their guardian, Saleh Muhammad Khan. The seemingly indestructible Pottinger returned to India, where a court of inquiry in 1842–43 accused him of drawing bills for 19 lakhs in favor of the Afghans and for signing a treaty without authorization. He was exonerated but did not get his back pay and was refused the award of a medal for his services. He died in Hong Kong of typhus.

PRIMROSE, LT.-GEN. J. M. Commanded the Reserve Division, Kandahar Field Force in December 1878, and in January 1879, proceeded to Kandahar to take command of the 1st Division. During the second campaign, commanded the Kandahar Field Force from March 1880 and the Kandahar force throughout the siege, and at the Battle of Kandahar. *See* KANDAHAR, BATTLES OF.

PUZANOV, ALEXANDR. Soviet ambassador assigned to Kabul in 1972, the final year of Zahir Shah, and an important figure during the republican and early Marxist periods. He was an active politician in Kabul and was therefore dubbed the "little czar." He was credited with helping to reunite the two factions of the PDPA in 1977, and was quoted as saying that the Saur Revolt "came as a complete surprise to me." One expert describes him as "an alcoholic seventy-two-year-old castoff from Kremlin political struggles. . . [who] was trout fishing in the Hindu Kush" (Bradsher, 1983, 83) when the Saur Revolt occurred. He supported Nur Muhammad Taraki against Hafizullah Amin and was said to have lured Hafizullah Amin into an ambush. The "palace shoot-out" of September 14, 1979 misfired and Amin demanded the recall of Puzanov; he left Kabul on November 19, 1979.

- Q -

QIZILBASH. Meaning "Red Heads," who are named after the red pleads in their turbans. They were one of seven Turkic tribes who revered the Safavid ruler Ismail (1499–1524) as both a spiritual and temporal ruler. The Persian ruler, Nadir Shah Afshar, stationed a rearguard (*chandawol*) of *Qizilbash* troops at Kabul during a campaign into India. They are Shi'ites, and some 30,000 live in Herat, Kandahar, and Kabul. They performed a military function as a royal bodyguard until the 1860s, after which time they were employed in various functions in the administration of Afghanistan.

- R -

RABBANI, BURHANUDDIN (BURHAN AL-DIN). Leader of the *Jam'iat-i Islami-yi Afghanistan* (Islamic Society of Afghanistan), the largely non-Pashtun group, and president of the Islamic Republic of Afghanistan. Born in 1940 in Faizabad, Badakhshan Province, and educated in Islamic studies at Kabul University and Al-Azhar University, Cairo, where he received an M.A. degree in 1968. After returning to Afghanistan, he taught at the Faculty of Theology at Kabul University. He became editor of *Majallat-i Shari'at* (Journal of Islamic Law) in 1970 and was a leading member of the Islamist Movement (q.v.) since the late 1950s. He organized university students to oppose the secular trend in Afghanistan and to counteract the activities of leftist students on campus. The 15-member high council of the *Jam'iat-i Islami* selected him as its leader in 1971, and in 1974 he fled to Pakistan, where he sought the support of the Pakistan government and the *Jama'at-i Islami*, a radical Islamist party. In 1975, the *Jam'iat* carried out raids into Afghanistan, and failure of the armed attacks revealed policy disagreements between Rabbani and Hekmatyar (q.v.). Thereupon Hekmatyar founded his *Hizb-i Islami* in 1976. Rabbani continued to lead the *Jam'iat* after the Saur Revolt. At the fall of the Najibullah regime, Rabbani's forces, under Commander Ahmad Shah Mas'ud, entered Kabul on April 25 and quickly expelled members of Gulbuddin Hekmatyar's forces from the presidential palace and the interior ministry. The Uzbek forces of General Dostum also cooperated with *Jam'iat* and other groups, including the Shi'ite *Hizb-i Wahdat*, who occupied portions of Kabul and began the struggle for power between the *mujahedin*. In March 1993, Rabbani succeeded Sebghatullah Mujaddidi as president of the Islamic Republic of Afghanistan, but he did not effectively control Kabul or the rest of Afghanistan. His refusal to step down after a two-year term resulted in considerable fighting and bombardment of Kabul, primarily by the forces of Hekmatyar. The rise of the *Taleban* (q.v.) posed a serious threat to Rabbani, but an attack on Kabul in February 1995 was repulsed and the *Taleban* and *Hizb-i Wahdat* were driven from the greater Kabul area, leaving Rabbani in control of the capital.

RAIDS. Tribal raids for booty have been refined over the centuries and carried out in a distinct manner. The tribesmen are divided into three groups: the actual raiders, fit men who are well armed, active young men, and younger boys and old men. Ridgeway (26) describes the enterprise as follows:

> The first party proceed to the scene of operations, and there conceal themselves, waiting patiently for their opportunity for hours and even for days; the second and third parties meanwhile halt at certain prearranged places on the homeward route. Directly the raid has been committed, the raiders hurry off the cattle with all speed to the second party in reserve, and then disperse to find their way home by unfrequented routes; meanwhile the second party, taking over the cattle and other spoil, hurry off to the third party, and so, by relays, the loot is rapidly borne away, far from the scene of the raid, in an incredibly short span of time.

Closer to home, the raiders protect the retreating parties. The raided party, if it guesses the origin of the raiders, will try to intercept them to recover their property. Since cattle cannot be moved very rapidly, they may have a chance at success. In warfare with Indian forces, the British have at times been able to snatch victory from defeat by intercepting the convoys with plunder.

RANJIT SINGH. King (1780–1839) of the newly founded Sikh nation, a religiopolitical entity, who in 1820 controlled most of the northern Panjab, Kashmir, and Peshawar. He captured Lahore from its Afghan garrison in 1798, compelling Shah Zaman (q.v.) to appoint the Sikh chief as governor of the Panjab. Ranjit Singh was described as of small stature and blind in his right eye, but quite fearless and a brilliant soldier. Lord Auckland, governor general of India, sided with the Sikh ruler and concluded an alliance with Ranjit Singh and Shah Shuja for the purpose of restoring the latter to the Afghan throne (*see* SIMLA MANIFESTO; SIKH; and ANGLO-AFGHAN WARS). Ranjit Singh, at that time "an old man in an advanced state of decrepitude" was wise enough not to send his army into Afghanistan and therefore did not share the British disaster. Ranjit Singh died in 1839, and his empire was soon annexed by his former British allies.

RATIONS OF BRITISH ARMY. SECOND AFGHAN WAR.
Daily Rations of British Forces:

Europeans	Meat	1 1/4 lb.
	Bread	1 1/4 lb.
	Vegetables	1 1/4 lb.
	Rice	4 oz.

	Salt	2/3 oz.
	Tea	3/4 oz.
	Sugar	3 oz.

Natives	Atta	12 Chittacks
	Dhal	2 Chittacks
	Ghi	1 Chittacks
	Salt	1/3 Chittacks
	Meat	1 lb. biweekly
	Rum	1 dram on Payment!

Gen. Roberts's despatch, April 17, 1880. (OA 2, 674–677)

THIRD AFGHAN WAR, 1919.

Europeans
 Daily Issues:

	Bread	1 lb.
	Meat	1 lb.
	Bacon	3 oz.
	Potatoes	10 oz.
	Onions	6 oz.
Other fresh vegetables		8 oz.
	Tea	3/4 oz.
	Sugar	3 oz.
	Jam	3 oz.
	Condensed milk	2 oz.
Tinned or dried fruit		2 oz.
	Salt	1/2 oz.
Vegetable oil for cooking		1 oz.
	Fuel, wood	3 lbs.

Weekly Issues:

	Pepper	1/7 oz.
	Mustard	1/7 oz.
	Cigarettes or	20
	Tobacco or	2 oz.
	Sweets	4 oz.
	Matches	2 boxes

Thrice Weekly:

	Oatmeal with	3 oz.

Condensed milk	1 oz.
Rice	1/3 oz.
Curry powder	7/8 oz.
Fresh lime juice	1/2 fluid oz.

Indian Troops
Daily Issues:

Atta	1 1/2lbs.
Fresh meat	8 oz.
Dhal	3 oz.
Ghi	2 oz.
Sugar	2 1/2 oz.
Potatoes	2 oz.
Onions	2 oz.
Other fresh vegetables	1 oz.
Tea	1/2 oz.
Fresh lime juice	1/2 fluid oz.
Mixed condiments	3/4 oz.
Fuel, wood	2 lbs.

Weekly Issues:

Tobacco or	2 oz.
Cigarettes or	40
Sweets	4 oz.
Matches	2 boxes

Thrice Weekly:

Ground nuts	2 oz.

Climatic conditions necessitated a more generous scale of rations than was customary. But owing to congestion at railheads and the shortage of transport, it was seldom that full rations were issued to troops in forward areas.

Heatstroke stations had to be set up; ice and mineral water, mosquito nets, goggles, and spine pads were provided (they covered the entire back and were thought to be necessary in the Afghan climate). Men and animals had to be provided with water, which was difficult at times. *See also* SUPPLIES, COLLECTION OF.

RAWALPINDI CONFERENCE. *See* **ANGLO-AFGHAN TREATY OF 1919.**

RAWLINSON, SIR HENRY C. (1810–1895). Political assistant to Sir W. Macnaghten (q.v.) at Kabul and Kandahar. Participated in the Battle of Kandahar on May 29, 1842. Retired with General Nott to India via Kabul. Deciphered the fifth century B.C. Behistun inscriptions of Darius at Behistun in 1846. Subsequently was a member of the viceroy's council of India, from 1858 to 1859 and 1868 to 1895.

ROBERTS, GEN. SIR ABRAHAM (1784–1873). Commander of Shah Shuja's "Army of the Indus" in the first Anglo-Afghan war (1838–42). He escaped the British debacle when he was recalled by Lord Auckland (q.v.), governor general of India, who disliked Roberts's criticism of his policy. His son (below) was a British general in the second Anglo-Afghan war. *See also* ANGLO-AFGHAN WARS.

ROBERTS, GEN. SIR FREDERICK S. (1832-1914). British general, the son of Sir Abraham (above), who commanded the Kurram Field Force in the second Anglo-Afghan war (1878–80). He invaded Afghanistan through the Kurram valley and reached Kabul on October 12, 1879, where he was the de facto ruler after the abdication of Yaqub Khan (q.v.). Fought at Paiwar Kotal (q.v.) on December 2, 1878. After Cavagnari's assassination at Kabul, September 3, 1879, commanded the Kabul Field Force. Fought at Charasia, October 6. Received Amir Yaqub Khan's abdication and sent him to Indian exile. Engaged in operations around Sherpur, December 1879. After Maiwand, marched from Kabul to Kandahar and defeated Ayub Khan at Kandahar, September 1. He was a legendary figure, called "Bobs" by his fellow generals and famous, or infamous, for ordering indiscriminate executions of Afghans. He arrested Yahya Khan, a nephew of Amir Dost Muhammad, for the purpose of looting his house. General MacGregor (q.v.) said of him: "Bobs is a cruel blood-thirsty little brute, he has shot some 6 men already in cold blood. I have saved three men from his clutches already" (Trousdale, 1985). Although Sir Frederick was able to defeat Ayub Khan (q.v.), the Indian government agreed to withdraw from Afghanistan in April 1881 to avoid a repetition of the disaster of the first Anglo-Afghan war. Sir Frederick died in 1914. *See* ANGLO- AFGHAN WARS.

Plate 3. Execution of the Kotwal, Intelligence Officer of Kabul. Source: ILN

Plate 4. Execution of a Ghazi. Source: PIN

ROBERTS AND "RETRIBUTION." The London *Times* (February 18, 1879) reported that General F. S. Roberts had caused numerous villages to be looted and burned; that he ordered the cavalry to take no prisoners; that some 90 prisoners, tied together, were slaughtered. In response the general admitted that nine villages were looted and burned in retaliation for Mangal attacks after they were warned not to do it. He called it an "act of retributive justice." He ordered Major J. C. Steward, who, with 40 sabres, charged some 400 men running out of a village, to take no prisoners — but he said he merely meant to disperse them. Only 30 to 40 were killed, but "a nought got added during its [official telegram] transmission" and the number appeared to be 300 to 400 killed. His force was too small; therefore, he felt justified in giving the order to kill. Admits that native officers tried to prevent the escape of prisoners and shot nine and wounded 13 mostly by bayonets. But he claimed that "every possible care was given to the wounded." Dated Camp Peiwar, April 1, 1879.

Roberts tried a number of Afghans before a military commission for participation in the attack on the British mission in Kabul. Four were executed "for dishonoring the bodies of the officers" in the embassy; four for possession of property belonging to the mission; six for being armed within five miles of the camp; four for attempting to free Afghan prisoners; and 69 for "murdering camp followers, participating in the attack on the Residency, inciting people to rise, carrying arms, traitorously firing and killing wounded soldiers."

ROKETI, MULLA SALAM. A colorful individual of Sayyaf's (q.v.) *Ittihad-i Islami* party who was robbed by Pakistanis of three stinger missiles he wanted to sell. In retaliation, he took 10 Pakistani hostages, including the deputy commissioner of Ziarat and two Chinese engineers. He demanded his brother to be freed from a Pakistani prison and the return of his stingers, but he was eventually forced to give up his hostages when the Pakistan government threatened to close Sayyaf's offices in Pakistan.

RULERS OF AFGHANISTAN. *See* **DURRANI DYNASTY.**

RUTSKOI, ALEXANDR. One of the Russian Afgantsy (q.v.) who became vice president of Russia and head of the parliamentary opposition to President Yeltsin in October 1993. He spent five months in Leforto prison in Moscow as a result of his challenge to Yeltsin. Rutskoi is leader of the conservative Great Power party. He served in Afghanistan in 1985–86 and again in 1988 and was a "Hero of the Soviet Union," having flown 428 combat missions and been shot down twice, once over Pakistan (Galeotti, 128). He became deputy commander of the 40th Army's air forces, and with other Afgantsy is an important actor on the political scene in Russia.

- S -

SALANG PASS/TUNNEL (35–12' N, 69–13' E). A village and district in Parwan Province located near the Salang Pass at an altitude of 13,350 feet. It is a choke point to north-south traffic on the 300-mile-long Termez-Salang-Kabul Highway. The highway, and a 1.7-mile-long tunnel, located at an altitude of 11,000 feet, was built by Soviet experts and opened to general traffic in 1964. It was one of the routes of Soviet occupation in December 1978 and soon proved to be vulnerable to mujahedin attacks. In October 1984 an explosion in the tunnel was said to have led to the deaths of 1,000 people, including 700 Soviet troops. Commander Mas'ud, whose center of operations included the Panjshir valley, staged numerous ambushes against the road, including one in March 1984, when he was reported to have destroyed 70 fuel tankers destined for Kabul. Repeated Soviet Panjshir campaigns could not secure safe passage through this vital link to Kabul.

SALE, LADY FLORENTIA (1790–1853). Wife of Brigadier Sir Robert Sale, commander of the garrison at Jalalabad during the first Anglo-Afghan war (q.v., 1838–42). Lady Sale was a hostage with other British women and some of their officer husbands and thus escaped the general massacre of the British forces. She recorded her experience in a book *A Journal of the Disasters in Afghanistan, 1841-2*, which is an important source on the British misadventure. *See* ANGLO-AFGHAN WARS.

SALE, GEN. SIR ROBERT HENRY (1782–1845). Controversial general, called "Fighting Bob" for his exploits in the Burmese War in 1823. When the "Army of the Indus" invaded Afghanistan during the first Anglo-Afghan war, Sale was in command of the First Brigade of the Infantry Division of the Bengal Column. Commanded advanced brigade to Kandahar, April 1839; he was at Girishk, Ghazni, and Kabul and wintered in Jalalabad. Defeated Amir Dost Muhammad at Parwan

Darra, November 2, 1840. He forced the Khurd Kabul and reached Jalalabad on November 12, 1841. Unable to return as ordered by General Elphinstone, he remained besieged in Jalalabad until April 7, 1842, when he sallied out of the city with almost his entire force of 1,430 men and six guns and defeated Akbar Khan. Was relieved by General Pollock's "Army of Retribution" and went to Kabul, September 1842. A severe disciplinarian, he ordered hundreds of lashings for the least infringement by his soldiers. Returned to India in September 1842. Made a Knight Commander of the Bath for the capture of Ghazni in spite of the fact that he "nearly muffed the whole operation" when he ordered the bugler to sound the retreat at the time a storming column had already effected a breach. He pursued Dost Muhammad into Bamian, but was repulsed by his forces and failed to come to Elphinstone's aid at Kabul. "He would have surrendered Jalalabad without firing a shot if Havelock and Broadfoot [two of his officers] had not intervened. His victory over Akbar outside Jalalabad was only achieved because his officers forced him to attack against his own judgement" (Pottinger/Macrory, 153). Many times wounded, Sale was killed in a battle with the Sikhs in 1845.

SARAI. A resting place for travelers and their animals, surrounded by high walls for protection from marauding bandits or tribes. Before the advent of aerial warfare, fortified sarais existed to garrison troops and ammunition. They were built at intervals of 12 miles along main roads and in major towns, accommodating as many as 300 men. The average sarai covered an area of 80 to 100 yards square with sun-dried brick walls 15 to 20 feet high and two to three feet thick. A covered gateway ten feet wide led to loopholed corner bastions, and firing platforms existed on top of the wall. Quarters for troops were located along the interior of the walls, and a well, often in the center of the yard, provided potable water of varying quality. Governors and high military officials would reside in sarais provided with a citadel for defense, and all officials of rank and distinguished visitors would be offered hospitality there. The use of heavy artillery has rendered the sarai obsolete as a fortification in modern military warfare, and it serves now primarily as a shelter for passing caravans where motor transport is not possible. In the frontier area tribal chiefs maintain sarais with watchtowers and fortifications, which provide adequate protection in local skirmishes.

SARANDOY (TSARANDOY). The name of the Afghan Boy Scouts organization begun in 1932 and headed by the Afghan crown prince Muhammad Zahir (the subsequent king) and later by his son Ahmad Shah.

President Daud organized a gendarmerie force called *Sarandoy* of some 20,000 men, which the *Khalqi* government continued and Babrak Karmal in 1981 reorganized into a defense force of six brigades, 20 battalions of 6,000 men, and various support units. The Sarandoy forces were stationed in major urban areas held by the Kabul government. The Sarandoy was under the direction of the ministry of interior and was a *Khalqi* stronghold under Colonel General Gulabzoy and his successors. It used to rival the power of *Parcham*-dominated KHAD (q.v.) until the Tanai (q.v.) coup of March 1990. After the fall of the Marxist regime the organization disintegrated, its members joining competing *mujahedin* groups.

SARDAR. Title of the heads of Durrani clans, meaning leader, general, or prince. The title was also awarded by the king to commoners but subsequently only referred to members of the Afghan royal family.

SAUR REVOLT (REVOLUTION). Marxist coup of April 27, 1978, named after the Afghan month (7 of Saur 1357), which initiated 11 years of rule by the PDPA. *See* PEOPLE'S DEMOCRATIC PARTY OF AFGHANISTAN.

SAYYAF, ABDUL RASUL (ABD AL-RABB AL-RASUL). Leader of the *Ittihad-i Islami Barayi Azadi-yi Afghanistan* (q.v., Islamic Alliance for the Liberation of Afghanistan), a radical Islamist movement that aims at the establishment of an Islamic state in Afghanistan (*See* ISLAMIST MOVEMENT). He was born in 1946 in Paghman and was educated in Paghman, at Abu Hanifa Theological School, and at the Faculty of Theology at Kabul University. He went to Egypt and obtained an M.A. degree at Al-Azhar University. He was a member of the Islamist Movement and in 1971 deputy of Burhanuddin Rabbani. In 1974, when he was about to leave for the United States for legal training, he was arrested at Kabul International Airport by intelligence officers and spent more than 5 years in prison. Freed by the Parcham regime in 1980, he went to Peshawar and joined the *mujahedin* as spokesman for the alliance. Elected for a period of two years (1980 to 1981), he wanted to continue in this position but was forced to step down. He then formed his own group, the Islami Union for the Liberation of Afghanistan, *Ittihad-i Islami Barayi Azadi-yi Afghanistan*. He is an eloquent speaker in Arabic and has been able to receive financial support from Arabic Gulf states. He is ideologically close to the groups headed by Hekmatyar and Khales, and had allied himself with Arab "Wahhabi" *mujahedin* groups. During the present civil war he had frequent clashes with the *Hizb-i Wahdat* (q.v.) and has allied himself with the *Jam'iat* of Rabbani. Driven from his base in Paghman, he fled with his forces to Jalalabad. *See also* ISLAMIST MOVEMENT; and ISLAMIC AL-LIANCE FOR THE LIBERATION OF AFGHANISTAN.

SAYYID-I KAYAN. Sayyid Shah Nasser Nadiri, commonly called Sayyid-i Kayan, is head of the Ismaili community in Afghanistan and leader of a force that has attempted to protect its community from Soviet/Kabul attacks and *mujahedin* penetration of their territory. In a series of tactical alliances, the Sayyid-i Kayan's forces were cooperating with General Dostum against *jam'iat* forces.
Sayyid Nadiri was born in 1933 in Darra-yi Kayan in Baghlan Province. He was elected to Parliament in 1965, and in 1968 he became vice president of the *wolesi jirga*. Six months after the republican coup of 1973, Sayyid Nadiri and his four brothers were imprisoned. Freed after two years, Sayyid Nadiri and his brothers were again jailed after the Saur Revolt. He was in Pol-i Charkhi prison until Babrak Karmal proclaimed an amnesty in 1980. Sayyid Shah Nasser Nadiri left Afghanistan in 1981 and now lives in England. His brother Sayyid Mansur is acting head of the community.

SCUD MISSILE. The SCUD-B is a tactical, guided, battlefield missile with a range of about 200 miles and a warhead of 2,000 pounds, which was introduced into Afghanistan in 1988 by the Soviet Union and employed for the protection of major cities. Although not very accurate and useful in fighting insurgency forces, the missiles were successfully employed in the siege of Jalalabad in February–November 1989. Several hundred are said to be still in possession of Afghan commanders, including one launching area in Darulaman, which was the prize possession of *harakat-i Islami* of Muhsini, but was captured by Hekmatyar's forces in September 1994, and by the *Taleban* in 1995. With the departure of Soviet advisers, it is not clear whether any of the *mujahedin* groups are able to operate them.

SECOND ANGLO-AFGHAN WAR (1878–79 [–81]). The "Signal Catastrophe" of the previous war inclined the British to pursue a policy of "masterly inactivity," which was to leave Afghanistan to the Afghans. But a generation later the advocates of a "forward policy" to counter Russian moves in Central Asia succeeded in being heard. Technology had considerably advanced since the first Anglo-Afghan war and British conquests had extended across the Indus River and approached the passes leading into Afghanistan. British-Indian telegraph lines and rail terminals had reached the borders of Afghanistan. The Indian forces, now wearing khaki uniforms, were equipped with breech-loading Martini-Henry and Snider rifles, which were faster to operate. The Afghan army still depended largely on the *jezail* (q.v.) and muzzle-loading rifles.

Amir Shir Ali (q.v., 1863–79), a son of Amir Dost Muhammad, had ascended the Afghan throne after eliminating a number of rivals. He gained British recognition in 1869 and was invited to meet Lord Mayo in Ambala, India. Shir Ali was worried about Russian advances in Central Asia and wanted British guarantees from Russian aggression and recognition of his son, Abdullah Jan, as crown prince and his successor; but the viceroy was not willing to make any such commitment and merely gave the Afghan king 600,000 rupees and a few pieces of artillery. Disappointed, Shir Ali was receptive when General Kaufman, the Russian governor general at Tashkent, made overtures, promising what Britain was not willing to give. General Stolietoff (q.v.) arrived uninvited in Kabul on July 22, 1878, with the charge to draft a treaty of alliance with the Afghan ruler. Lord Lytton was now alarmed and sent General Neville Chamberlain (q.v.) to lead a British military mission to Kabul. Arrangements had been made with the independent tribes on the frontier for the mission's escort of one thousand troops, but when the British reached the border, they were prevented from entering Afghan territory. In response to this "insult," the Indian government issued an ultimatum and dispatched an army under General F. Roberts (q.v.) That entered Kabul on July 24, 1879. Shir Ali fled north in the hope of receiving Russian support. No help was forthcoming, and the amir died of natural causes in Mazar-i Sharif on February 21, 1879.

Britain recognized his son Yaqub Khan (q.v.) as the Afghan ruler (Abdullah Jan had preceded his father in death) at the cost of his signing the Treaty of Gandomak (q.v.) on May 26, 1879. Louis Cavagnari was established as British envoy at Kabul, and history repeated itself when

Plate 5. Bala Hisar. Source: Burke

GENERAL ROSS'S DIVISION CROSSING THE LOGHUR RIVER ON ITS WAY TO MEET SIR DONALD STEWART.

Plate 6. Source: ILN

Plate 7. Evacuation of Wounded. Source: ILN

Plate 14. Kabul Tank Force. Source: *Afghanistan Today*

Plate 9. Guns over the Khojak Pass. Source: ILN

Plate 10. Ghazis Fire from Sangar. Source: PIN

on September 3, 1879, mutinous troops, whose pay was in arrears, stormed the British mission and assassinated the envoy and his staff. The incident encouraged attacks on British positions elsewhere, which grew, in spite of British attempts at pacification, culminating in the rout of General Burrows at the Battle of Maiwand (q.v.) July 27, 1880. Fearing a repetition of the "Signal Catastrophe," the British-Indian government recognized Abdur Rahman (q. v.) as "amir of Kabul and its dependencies" and thus facilitated an orderly exit from Afghanistan. *See also* SHIR ALI; ABDUL RAHMAN; and YAQUB KHAN.

For India, the war was an economic disaster, instead of the original estimate of £5 million it cost £19.5 million exclusive of 395,000 rupees paid to the amir, and an additional sum of 50,000 rupees per month for six months. The exchequer bore the share of £5,000,000, the Indian revenues paid the rest. (OA 2, 723)

The greatest number of troops employed in Afghanistan at any one date was about 20,000, with 72 guns in the main theater and 50,000 men with 74 guns on the lines of communication. (MR, 65)

According to one source (Hanna, 1910), the British suffered 40,000 casualties, which, if correct, must include thousands of camp followers. Almost 99,000 camels perished, a loss that was long felt in the areas from which they had been requisitioned.

O'Ballance says, "The real winners of this war were the breech-loading Martini and Snider rifles, and the disciplined direction under which they were employed." (49)

SECOND ANGLO-AFGHAN WAR, OPERATIONS. The plan of campaign was an advance by three lines as follows:

Northern line – Peshawar forces under Lieutenant General S. Browne with 10,000 combatants, 48 guns, and 10,000 followers with the objective of taking Dakka.

Central line – Kohat force under Major General F. Roberts with 6,500 combatants, 18 guns, and 6,500 followers with the objective of moving up the Kurram valley.

Southern line – Quetta force under Lieutenant General D. M. Stewart with 12,800 combatants, 78 guns, and 12,000 followers.

Reserves for the northern and central lines under Brigadier General Maude consisted of 5,000 troops; and for the southern line under Brigadier General Primrose 6,000 combatants. The entire British forces amounted to 40,300 combatants, 144 guns, and 29,300 followers.

The advance of the northern line was secured with the promise of payment of an annual allowance of 87,000 rupees to the Khaibar tribes to compensate them for the loss of a subsidy from the Afghan amir. Not all tribes accepted. The first operation began with an attack on November 21 on Ali Masjid. A force of 7,800 British troops with 26 guns faced an Afghan force of 3,500 Afghan regulars and 600 khasadars with 24 guns. After a vigorous resistance, Afghan forces abandoned the post. (*See* ALI MASJID.) The British forces moved on and occupied Jalalabad on December 20 without any resistance. A minor expedition into the Bazar valley was of limited success as the Zakka Khel and other Afridis withdrew and continued to inflict losses when the British "punitive" force withdrew. A squadron of the 10th Husars trying to ford the Kabul River were swept down the stream and one officer and 46 men drowned.

The central line crossed the Afghan frontier at Thal on November 21 and advanced to the Kurram fort. After a failed attempt on an Afghan force near the Paiwar Kotal, General Roberts was able to turn the Afghan lines, and on December 2, 1878, he defeated the Afghans, who lost about 500 killed or wounded compared to 98 British casualties. Four days later Ali Khel was occupied, where the British forces remained until April 1879.

The southern line concentrated at Quetta early in November 1878, and crossing the Khojak and Gwazha passes the troops proceeded to Takhta-i Pul and entered Kandahar on January 8. On January 16, the 2nd Division, leaving a garrison at Kandahar, started for Girishk with 20 days of supplies, for British and three days for Indian troops. Girishk was occupied from February 2 to February 22, but on the return British forces were harassed with some losses. Cholera took a heavy toll of the Kandahar force, claiming the lives of about 500 men.

On the northern line, the Peshawar Field Force established itself in Nangarhar Province. Supplies were collected locally and punitive expeditions were staged against hostile Shinwari tribes. Lacking sufficient transport to proceed to Kabul, the 1st Division established itself at Gandomak in April 1879. A month later Yaqub Khan succeeded Amir Shir Ali to the throne and signed the Treaty of Gandomak (q.v.) with Britain. This ended the first phase of the second Anglo-Afghan war, and British forces withdrew from Afghanistan, except for a force at Kandahar.

Second phase, 1879–1881. As a result of the attack on the British mission in Kabul on September 3, 1879, and the assassination of its staff, the Indian government decided to take punitive measures. The plan of operation was as follows:

1. An invading column, called the "Kabul Field Force," was set up. It was headed by General Roberts and included one cavalry brigade (one British and two Indian regiments); two infantry brigades (two British and five Indian battalions); three batteries and two gatlings, one company of sappers and miners; altogether 6,600 fighting men, 18 guns, and 6,000 followers, to march from Kurram to Kabul.

2. Two mixed infantry brigades, 4,000 strong, to keep the line between Thal and Ali Khel open.

3. A force, 6,600 strong, to secure the Khaibar-Jalalabad-Gandomak line, with a movable column to establish communications onward to Kabul.

4. A strong reserve force between Peshawar and Rawalpindi.

5. A force of 9,000 strong to hold southern Afghanistan, dominate the Kandahar Province, occupy Kalat-i Ghilzai, and threaten Ghazni, with its communications to the Indus kept open by a brigade of Bombay troops.

Transport was again a serious problem for the invaders: only 2,000 mules, 750 camels, 650 bullocks, and 100 donkeys, could be organized within a short time. Nevertheless, General Roberts was able to reach Charasia in October 1879 (*see* CHARASIA, BATTLE OF), where he was able to prevail in a battle on October 6.

The Peshawar force, consisted of one British and four Indian cavalry regiments, five British and 12 Indian battalions, seven companies of sappers and miners, three horse, one field, and two mountain batteries. The army consisted of 13,400 combatants. The forces left Landi Kotal and occupied Jalalabad on the 12th and Gandomak on the 24th of October and opened communications with General Roberts by December.

The Kandahar garrison, 4,726 strong, dispatched on September 23, a column of all arms, 1,400 strong with 1,300 followers and a month's worth of supplies to proceed via Kalat-i Ghilzai toward Ghazni. Kalat-i Ghilzai was garrisoned and the troops returned to Kandahar.

In the meantime General Roberts established himself in Kabul and set up a court of retribution, which speedily executed a number of Afghans, including 49 men of the regiments that had attacked the British mission. Yaqub Khan abdicated on October 12, 1879, and General Roberts started a number of punitive expeditions. Not all was well for the British, as large numbers of Afghan forces, estimated by the British at about 100,000, laid siege to General Roberts's forces at the Sherpur

Cantonment (*see* SHERPUR, SIEGE OF). A victory by General Steward at Ahmad Khel on April 19, 1880 was followed by the disastrous Battle of Maiwand (qq.v.) in which Ayyub Khan defeated General Burrows on July 27. To avoid the disaster of the first Afghan war, Britain recognized Abdur Rahman Khan as amir of Kabul and its Dependencies.

SECOND ANGLO-AFGHAN WAR, BRITISH OBJECTIVES. The Indian government wanted the "Complete establishment of British influence in Afghanistan, and the rectification of the frontier." It did not want too much territory, "only the passes leading into India." (OA 2, 177)

SECOND ANGLO-AFGHAN WAR, DECLARATION OF WAR. On November 21, 1878, Lord Lytton, the viceroy of India, issued a proclamation in which he recalled the British assistance given to Shir Ali to consolidate his power and help in fixing the boundary with Russia. He complained,

> For all these gracious acts the Amir Shir Ali Khan has rendered no return. On the contrary, he has requited them with active ill-will and open discourtesy. . . . He has closed against free passage to British subjects and their commerce the roads between India and Afghanistan. He has maltreated British subjects, and permitted British traders to be plundered within his jurisdiction, giving them neither protection nor redress. [Having refused to receive a British mission and not answered communication] he has, nevertheless, received formally and entertained publicly at Kabul an Embassy from Russia. . . . The Amir has forcibly repulsed, at his outposts, an English Envoy of high rank. . . .

He added ominously, "The Amir Sher Ali Khan, mistaking for weakness the long forbearance of the British Government, has thus deliberately incurred its just resentment. With the *sardars* and people of Afghanistan this Government has still no quarrel, and desires none. . . . Upon the Amir Sher Ali Khan alone rests the responsibility of having exchanged the friendship for the hostility of the Empress of India." (OA 2, 636–38)

SECOND ANGLO-AFGHAN WAR, FORCES OF AMIR SHIR ALI.

1. Distribution of troops of Amir Shir Ali in March 1878.

	Men	Men	Station
14 regiments of infantry	600	8,400	
1 squadron of cavalry	150	150	
2 elephant batteries	70	140	10,010 Kabul
6 troops of horse artillery	150	900	
6 mule mountain batteries	70	420	
3 regiments of infantry	600	1,800	
2 regiments of cavalry	600	1,200	3,200 Jalalabad
1 troop of horse artillery	150	150	
1 mule mountain battery	70	70	
5 regiments of infantry	600	3,000	
1 troop of horse artillery	150	150	3,220 Sherabad
1 mule mountain battery	70	70	
3 regiments of infantry	600	1,800	
2 regiments of cavalry	600	950	
2 troops horse of artillery	150	300	3,190 Kurram
2 mule mountain of batteries	70	140	
4 regiments of infantry	600	2,400	
6 regiments of cavalry	600	3,600	
2 troops of horse artillery	150	300	6,370 Kandahar
1 mule mountain battery	70	70	
17 regiments of infantry	600	10,200	
4 troops of horse artillery	150	600	11,220 Herat
2 mule mountain batteries	70	140	
4 bullock batteries	70	280	
4 regiments of infantry	600	2,400	
2 troops of horse artillery	150	300	2,840 Maimana
1 mule mountain battery	70	70	
1 bullock battery	70	70	
12 regiments of infantry	600	7,200	
6 regiment of cavalry	600	3,600	
4 troops of horse artillery	150	600	11,820 Balkh

| 4 mule mountain batteries | 70 | 280 |
| 2 bullock batteries | 70 | 140 |

| | | Total | 51,890 |

2. Military resources of Afghanistan at the close of March 1877.

A. Received by the amir from the English Government:

12,000
2,000
15,000

Total: 29,000 rifles, muzzle loading
5,000 rifles, breech loading (Snider)
Total 34,000 rifles

1 elephant battery – 4 guns and 2 mortars
1 mule mountain battery – 6 guns
In the arsenal were 30,000 stands of firearms, principally muzzle-loading muskets, smoothbore and rifles.

Regular forces:	Artillery	5,190
	Cavalry	9,600
	Infantry	37,200
Total		51,990

Irregulars:	foot levies	8,000
	mounted levies	16,000
Total		24,000

In time of war every headman and chief of every clan or tribe is called upon and made to furnish levies. (OA 2, 633–35.) *See also* ORDER OF BATTLE; MANPOWER; and AFGHAN ARMY, 1936.

SECOND ANGLO-AFGHAN WAR, PROCLAMATION BY SIR F. ROBERTS TO THE PEOPLE OF KABUL, October 12, 1879.

I warned against offering any resistance to the entry of the troops. . . .
That warning has been disregarded. The force under my command has

now reached Kabul, and occupied the Bala Hissar; but its advance has been pertinaciously opposed, and the inhabitants of the city have taken a conspicuous part in the opposition offered. They have therefore become rebels against His Highness the Amir, and have added to the guilt already incurred by abetting the murder of the British Envoy and of his companions . . . . It would be but a just and fitting reward for such misdeeds if the city of Kabul were now totally destroyed, and its very name blotted out. But the great British Government is ever desirous to temper justice with mercy. . . and I now announce. . . that the city will be spared. [But] such of the city buildings as now interfere with the proper military occupation of the Bala Hissar, and the safety and comfort of the British troops to be quartered in it, will be at once levelled with the ground. Further, a heavy fine, the amount of which will be notified hereafter, will be imposed on the inhabitants, to be paid according to their capabilities. . . . . All persons convicted of bearing a part in it [assassination of British mission] will be dealt with according to their deserts. [City and surroundings placed under martial law] a military governor of Kabul will be appointed to administer justice and to punish with a strong hand all evil-doers. [Carrying of weapons of all types prohibited] any person found armed within these limits will be liable to the penalty of death. Property looted from British must be returned, anyone found with any articles from the British Embassy will be subject to the severest penalties. [Weapons seized by Afghan troops will be purchased.] A reward was to be given for the surrender of anyone who participated in the attack of the British Embassy. (OA 2, 656.) The Kotwal, chief of police, of Kabul was hanged, and a good number of Afghans, who were not aware of the proclamation, were executed for carrying arms or being in possession of items belonging to the British mission.

SECOND AFGHAN WAR, REASONS FOR ENDING. An interesting source as to the reasons for ending the Second Afghan war is a Memo by T. F. Wilson, July 10, 1880. It gave the "political and financial reasons why we should withdraw from Northern Afghanistan." It stated that for 18 months the government had carried on a war for the establishment of peace. Not a petty war, but one involving 50,000 men and more. "This has denuded India to a great extent of troops, and left our garrisons weak, especially in European soldiers...." The majority of the viceroy's council had protested against the war, and he quotes Sir Henry Durand, "Peace in India is but an armed truce." Our Asiatic subjects see "that we have met with considerable difficulty and opposition, while the persistent drain on the country for transport animals, such as bullocks, asses, mules, ponies, and camels, has brought the matter home in a convincing manner to even remote parts of India by the detrimental effect which it has more or less exercised on agricultural industry. . . ." Members of the Native Army were away too long. He quotes the commander in chief, "The position is very serious; we have to face extended operations in Afghanistan, and a more or less prolonged occupation of the country. Our cavalry regiments on service, instead of being 500 strong, have only 378 effectives, and our infantry corps, instead of 800, have only 587 effectives. Constant marching and fighting, and harassing fatigues, and the vicissitudes of a climate severe and trying beyond measure for natives of India, have reduced our numbers and impaired the health of every Native regiment, while recruiting is at a standstill, the entire Bengal Army having obtained only 46 recruits during the month of January late. . . . Such is the picture of the Bengal Native Army in 1880, painted by its own chief. Even in the darkest days of the mutiny of 1857 no difficulty existed in raising new regiments. Stories of First War seem to discourage others. [We] underestimated cost of war at 14 million, add to this renewals required, pensions to Afghan collaborators - altogether no less than 20 million."

"It is now nine months since we occupied Cabool - after a resistance just sufficient to throw the Commander of the army off his guard... followed by the narrowest escape of his force from destruction; this last resulting in a scare which has never been entirely shaken off.

"In fact, the occupation of Cabool has been marked by three distinct epochs; the first that of heedless audacity and misguided unnecessary executions and severity; the second by surprise and defeat, followed by timidity, want of enterprise, and a general condonation of all offenses; and the third by aimless, costly, and weak attempts at diplomacy resulting in fruitless efforts to win over influential people to our interests.

"Since early in January last, our force at Cabool has not been less than from 8 to 9,000... yet it has never taken the initiative or ventured to do much more than hold the position of Sherpore ... fortifications continued to be piled on each other, the army being allowed to grow into a belief that it could only command the ground on which it stood behind its defenses.

"Seeing all this, and remembering how their foot soldiers captured our horse artillery guns, drove us into Sherpore, and plundered the city at their leisure under our eyes; is it to be wondered at that the Afghan nation continue elated and defiant?

"Kabul is 190 miles from Peshawar, 19 marches, but 15,000 men are barely sufficient to keep the line open.

"In short, our military position in Afghanistan is this. We have 11,500 men at Candahar, and on its line of communication with India; 20,000 at Cabool, or in its immediate vicinity; 15,000 holding the line through Jellalabad and the Khyber to Peshawar; and 8,500 locked up in the Kurram valley; or a total of 57,000 men in the field, yet we command little more than the ground on which we stand.

"The creation of `the strong and friendly Government at Cabool,' and our determination `to have an English Ambassador at the Dooranee Court,' are now but dreams of the past, from which Englishmen turn to the thought of, How can we best get our army back to India? How can we best disentangle ourselves from the false position we occupy?

"We have recently based our hopes on Abdool Raheeman as the best candidate for the vacant masnud... [but] we must not forget that he has for years past been in receipt of a liberal pension, and an honored guest in Russian dominions. This need not result in any gratitude to the Russians for whatever he may now say or promise, he will in the future act only according to his own views and belief. . . if we can come to some patched up arrangement with this man that will enable us to quit the country without absolute discredit. . . .

"Whenever we withdraw care must be taken to avoid all appearance of precipitancy. . . the enemy should be prevented from following our troops. The last withdrawal awoke in India a belief that we had at last met with a nut we could not crack; and two legacies resulted - the long and severe struggle with the Punjab and the Mutiny.

"In every Native Court it will be said 'the Feringhees could not hold Cabool.' "

He did, however, recommend to keep Kandahar and demand some border adjustments.

"In the present temper of Parliament, and the people of England... .whether we leave the 'strong and friendly Government' behind us or anarchy. . . Government or no Government, Ameer or no Ameer, *coute qu'il coute*, we shall withdraw early in the autumn."

"Abdool Raheeman is playing with us. . . . Evidently he is not such a fool as to come to Cabool and accept the throne from us. . . ." And, indeed, the amir came with an army, possibly to make war with Britain, but he concluded an agreement which permitted the British forces to withdraw with a semblance of dignity.

SHAH SHUJA-UL-MULK (1803–10 and 1839–42). Born about 1792, the seventh son of Timur Shah, he became governor of Peshawar in 1801 during the reign of his full brother Shah Zaman (q.v.). In 1803 he captured Kabul, imprisoned his brother Mahmud, and proclaimed himself king. He accepted a British mission in 1809 under Mountstuart Elphinstone (q.v.) and concluded a treaty of alliance, which states in Article 2:

> If the French and Persians in pursuance of their confederacy should advance towards the King of Cabool's country in a hostile manner, the British State, endeavoring heartily to repel them, shall hold themselves liable to afford the expenses necessary for the above-mentioned service to the extent of their ability.

This treaty was to prevent a Franco-Persian invasion of India that never occurred; but it did not protect the amir from attack by Persia alone. At that time Mountstuart Elphinstone described the Afghan ruler as "a handsome man. . . his address princely," and he marveled "how much he had of the manners of a gentleman, or how well he preserved his dignity, while he seemed only anxious to please." (Macrory, 32) Two years later Mahmud, who had managed to escape, captured Kabul and forced Shah Shuja to flee to Bukhara and later to India, where he remained as an exile for almost 30 years. En route to India he had to pass through the territory of the Sikh ruler Ranjit Singh (q.v.), who took from him the Kuh-i-Nur, a prized diamond that is now part of the British crown jewels. The internecine fighting between the Sadozai princes brought Dost Muhammad to power and marked the end of the Sadozai dynasty. In 1839 Britain invaded Afghanistan and restored Shah Shuja to the throne in a campaign that became known as the first Anglo-Afghan war (q.v.). At that time the amir was described as "elderly, stout, pompous and unheroic." (Macrory, 298) The Sadozai ruler was not able to govern without British protection; he remained ensconced in the protection of the Bala Hisar (q.v.) and was assassinated by a Barakzai *sardar* on April 25, 1842, only a few months after the British army was forced to a disastrous retreat. *See* ANGLO-AFGHAN WARS.

SHAH ZAMAN (1793–1800). Born in 1872, one of 23 sons of Timur Shah (q.v.), and his successor to the throne in 1793. During most of his reign he was engaged in intermittent warfare with his brothers Mahmud and Humayun. He wanted to win the British for a concerted war against the Maratha confederacy in India. Instead, the British concluded an alliance with Persia to keep the Afghans out of India (*see* AFGHAN FOREIGN RELATIONS). Shah Zaman appointed Ranjit Singh (q.v.) governor of Lahore, in spite of the fact that he had previously revolted. He abolished the hereditary posts established by Ahmad Shah Durrani and carried out bloody executions that antagonized many Afghans. While he was in the Panjab, Mahmud captured the Kabul throne. Shah Zaman was blinded and imprisoned but eventually escaped and lived in Indian exile until his death in 1844.

SHELTON, BRIG. JOHN (D. 1844). Commander of the 44th Regiment during the first Anglo-Afghan war and second in command to General Elphinstone (q.v.). He had lost his right arm in a previous campaign and was said to have only two qualifications for the post: "long service in India and a good measure of physical bulldog courage." (Macrory, 164) He was an angry, morose, obstinate, and cantankerous man, and his contempt for his commanding officer was only exceeded by his violent dislike of his superiors. He refused to cooperate with General Elphinstone, and his defeat in an action on the Bimaru Hills contributed to breaking Elphinstone's spirit of resistance. He became one of the prisoners of Akbar Khan (q.v.) and thus survived the general massacre. After returning to India, he was court-martialed for issuing unauthorized orders to prepare for retreat, for showing open contempt for his senior officer, and for negotiating with Akbar Khan for forage to feed his own horse, but he was only given a reprimand. (Pottinger, 1987, 205)

SHERPUR, SIEGE OF. General Frederick Roberts, who had become the de facto ruler of Kabul after the abdication of Yaqub Khan in October 1879, soon realized that his position in Kabul was in danger. He ordered the British troops to withdraw into the Sherpur cantonment from the Bala Hisar, where an explosion had resulted in British casualties, and from Kabul city, which was increasingly threatened by *ghazis* (qq.v.). The cantonment abutted on the Bemaru hills, the crests of which were strengthened with earthen breastwork. It had been originally built by Amir Shir Ali to station his newly created army, and was near the cantonment that sheltered the British army during the first

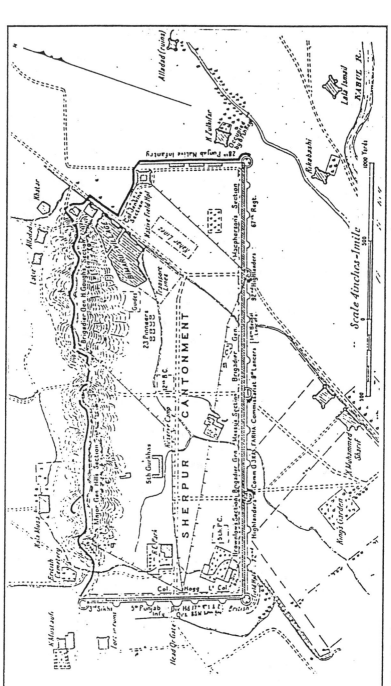

Plan11. Sherpur Cantonment. Source: MR

Anglo-Afghan war. The cantonment was large enough to shelter all European and most native soldiers, as well as their horses, and transport animals and adequate supplies. Provisions were forcefully collected from nearby villages under the maxim "Soldiers must live, although villagers starve." (Forbes) Feverish repairs were made on the walls, and the army of some 6,500 men went into defensive positions. The Afghans were not long in starting their siege. General Roberts was asked by an emissary to forthwith leave the country and threatened, "We have a lakh (100,000) of men; they are like wolves eager to rush on their prey. We cannot much longer control them" (Forbes, 257), and the Afghans were quick to attack: "From beyond Behmaroo and the eastern trenches and walls ... came a roar of voices so loud and menacing that it seemed as if an army of fifty thousand strong was charging down on our thin line of men." (Forbes, 260) But the British were able to hold. They survived the winter and with reinforcements were able to execute a peaceful evacuation, after recognizing Sardar Abdur Rahman in July 1880 as amir.

SHINDAND (SABZAWAR) AIR BASE (33–18' N, 62–8' E). A town and district in Farah Province and the location of the largest operational air base of Soviet forces in Afghanistan. It was one of the objectives in a pincer move into Afghanistan on December 27, 1978, when the 357th Motorized Rifle Division advanced from Kushka to Herat and established its control at Shindand. The airfield was considerably expanded in 1980–82 to become the largest Soviet air base in Afghanistan. It was the main base of Hind D helicopters, and the 5th Guards MRD, as well as some 45 fighter and fighter bombers, which operated from the relative safety of the base. It was located in flat territory and surrounded by a three-ringed security belt, covering an area of 40 kilometers. Although it was well protected, *mujahedin* claim to have destroyed some 22 aircraft, two helicopters, and 18 oil tankers in a spectacular case of sabotage on June 8, 1985. After the fall of the Kabul regime, Shindand became the major air base of Ismail Khan until it was captured by the *Taleban* (qq.v.) on September 2, 1995.

SHIR ALI, AMIR (1863–79). One of Amir Dost Muhammad's 27 sons who became amir of Afghanistan in 1862–3, and spent much of his tenure to meet challenges from his brothers, who governed various provinces. By 1869 he had consolidated his power and traveled to Ambala, India, in response to an invitation from the viceroy, Lord

Mayo. He was willing to form an alliance with India in exchange for British protection from Russian attacks, assistance in weapons and money, and recognition of the succession of his favorite son, Abdullah Jan. But the viceroy merely expressed his pleasure that the civil war among the princes had come to an end and, as a gesture of friendship, gave the Afghan ruler a present of 600,000 rupees and a few pieces of artillery.

Disappointed in his dealings with Britain, the amir decided to listen to Russian overtures. Russia sent General Stolietoff (q.v.) to Kabul on July 22, 1878, and the general promised what Britain was not willing to grant. Alarmed, the viceroy's government decided to send General Neville Chamberlain to Kabul, but he was not permitted to enter Afghanistan. Following an ultimatum, a British army invaded Afghanistan in a campaign known as the second Anglo-Afghan war (q.v.). Shir Ali left his son Yaqub in command at Kabul and went north to seek Russian support, but General Kaufman, the Russian governor general of Turkestan Province, merely advised Shir Ali to make peace with the British (qq.v.). Shir Ali died on February 21, 1879, in Mazar-i Sharif, and was succeeded in Kabul by his son Yaqub.

Shir Ali was the first to initiate modern reforms: he established an advisory council to assist in the administration of the state and created an army organized along European lines. He abolished the feudal system of tax-farming, set up a postal system, and published the first Afghan newspaper, *Shams al-Nahar* (Sun of the Day).

SHURA. Council, a consultative body or parliament. Islamic political theory demands that rulers seek council, *shura*. Islamic modernists base their demands for a representative government on this principle. After the downfall of the Marxist government in Kabul, local *mujahedin* groups, remnants of the Afghan army, and even some Marxist groups have united in *shuras* to maintain local control in various areas of Afghanistan.

SHURA-I INQILAB-I ITTIFAQ. *See* **BEHESHTI.**

SIKH, SIKHISM. A religiopolitical community that rose in the Panjab, India, in the fifteenth century, founding a state that reached its height under Ranjit Singh (q.v.) in the late eighteenth century. Sikhism began as a syncretist religion, combining Islamic and Hindu beliefs under Nanak, the first *guru* (sage). Subsequently, belief in 10 *gurus* and the

Granth Sahib, their sacred book, constituted the creed of the Sikhs. In constant conflict with Indian and Afghan rulers, the Sikhs became increasingly militant and under Ranjit Singh captured Multan in 1818, Kashmir in 1819, and Peshawar in 1834.

The Sikh nation supported the British invasion of Afghanistan in the first Anglo-Afghan war (q.v.), but after the death of Ranjit Singh, the British ended Sikh rule when it annexed the Panjab in the "Sikh wars" of 1845–46 and 1848–49. In the 1970s there were about 10,000 Sikhs in Afghanistan.

SIKHS, WEAPONS OF. In 1831 Ranjit Singh reorganized his army. He modernized his artillery, which was horse-driven (*aspi*); bullock-driven (*gavi*); elephant driven (*phili*); and camel-driven (*shutari*). He used European weapons: the matchlock — with a long barrel, attached to a wooden belt and wrapped with metal bands. Priming powder was loaded with muzzle-loading rods. The flintlock was introduced in India in the late sixteenth century, but replaced the matchlock only in the eighteenth, which "had self-contained ignition mechanism. A hammer striking the flint caused sparks which ignited priming powder." The *jezail* (swivel gun) eight feet long, carrying iron balls; it was fixed on a pivot or wall. And the carbine, "Blunderbuss," with a three-foot long barrel and trumpet-shaped mouth. It was a cavalry weapon. Ranjit also used cannons, howitzers for siege, mortars, field guns and siege guns. *Studies in Indian Weapons and Warfare.* (Pant, 1970)

SIMLA MANIFESTO. A document issued by the governor-general of India on October 1, 1838, which declared war on the Afghan amir, Dost Muhammad. It accused him of "a sudden and unprovoked attack" on its ally, Ranjit Singh (q.v.), and announced Britain's intention of restoring to the Afghan throne Shah Shuja (q.v.) "whose popularity throughout Afghanistan had been proven to his Lordship [the governor general] by the strong and unanimous testimony of the best authorities." (Sykes, 339) The result was the first Anglo-Afghan war (1839–42) and the British disaster in Afghanistan. *See* ANGLO-AFGHAN WARS; and AFGHAN FOREIGN RELATIONS.

SOVIET-AFGHAN RELATIONS. Formal diplomatic relations between Russia and Afghanistan began in June 1919, when the Soviet Union and Afghanistan announced their intention to establish legations in Kabul and Moscow. A cease-fire had just been declared in the third

Anglo-Afghan war, and King Amanullah wanted to demonstrate Afghanistan's independence by establishing diplomatic relations with European powers. A mission, headed by Muhammad Wali, proceeded to Tashkent and Moscow, where it was given a rousing welcome. N. N. Nariman, a spokesman of the foreign ministry, announced that "Russian imperialism, striving to enslave and degrade small nationalities, has gone, never to return." Muhammad Wali expressed the hope that "with the assistance of Soviet Russia, we shall succeed in emancipating our Afghanistan and the rest of the East." He presented V. I. Lenin a letter from King Amanullah, which was received "with great pleasure." A Bolshevik diplomat, Michael K. Bravin (who subsequently defected and was killed by an Afghan), proceeded to Kabul to arrange for the arrival of a permanent representative, Z. Suritz, in January 1920. Suritz immediately set about to negotiate the preliminaries for the Treaty of 1921, which recognized the "mutual independence" of both states and bound them not to "enter into any military or political agreement with a third State, which might prejudice one of the Contracting Parties." The Soviet Union agreed to permit free and untaxed transit of Afghan goods and recognized the independence and freedom of Khiva and Bukhara "in accordance with the wishes of the people." It provided for Soviet technical and financial aid of one million rubles in gold or silver and promised a return of the "frontier districts which belonged to the latter [Afghanistan] in the last century," a reference to the area of Panjdeh (q.v.). Britain had held a monopoly in the supply of arms and war materiel, which could only be shipped to Afghanistan by way of India; the treaty now opened a new avenue for materiel purchased in Europe. King Amanullah was able to crush the Khost Rebellion (q.v.) in summer 1924, with the assistance of several aircraft from the Soviet Union and a number of foreign pilots, including several Russians. In spite of the friendly rhetoric, differences existed between the two countries: King Amanullah wanted Khiva and Bukhara to be free from Soviet control, possibly associated with Afghanistan in a Central Asian confederation, but the "Young Khivan and Bukharan" revolted and opted for membership in the Soviet Union. The Soviet Union saw this as an expression of the "wishes of the people" and retained the czarist possession of Central Asia. A more serious crisis in Soviet-Afghan relations occurred in December 1925 when Soviet troops occupied the island of Darqad (also called Urta Tagai and Yangi Qal'a) on the Amu Daria (q.v.). At the turn of the century, the course of the Amu Daria had changed from south of the island to the north and, since the main stream was designated as the Afghan boundary, Kabul considered the island Afghan territory. After the Bolshevik Revolution, refugees from the Soviet Union settled on the island, including some Basmachi (q.v.) counterrevolutionaries, who made it a base for raids into Soviet Central Asia. The matter threatened to develop into an international conflict, but the Soviets apparently wanted good relations with King Amanullah and evacuated their troops on February 28, 1926. Moscow paid the promised subsidy only irregularly, and by the mid-1920s the Kabul government had expanded its diplomatic base to the extent that it did not need to maintain a special relationship with the Soviet Union.

During the 1929 civil war, the Soviet Union had maintained its embassy in Kabul and immediately recognized the government of Nadir Shah (q.v.). The new king sent Muhammad Aziz, his half brother, as ambassador to Moscow, to indicate the importance of the post, but he was determined to end Soviet influence in Afghanistan. One June 24, 1931 he renegotiated and signed the Treaty of 1921, with the inclusion of an article calling for the prohibition in both territories of activities that "might cause political or military injury" to the other. Nadir Shah was thinking of the followers of ex-King Amanullah who might attempt a return to power, and the Soviets were concerned about the Basmachi threat. A commercial treaty had to wait until 1936, and the Afghan government did not renew a Soviet airline concession and eventually dismissed all Soviet airline pilots and mechanics. The Afghan government turned increasingly to Germany for its technological and developmental needs, and a special relationship developed that greatly disturbed Moscow and was accepted in London only as the lesser of two evils. The outbreak of World War II and the temporary alliance between Germany and the Soviet Union resulted in fears in London and Kabul that the Soviets might support a pro-Amanullah coup. And, indeed, these worries were not unwarranted. The German foreign ministry considered Zahir Shah pro-British and toyed with the idea of supporting a coup against the monarch. Count Schulenberg, the German ambassador in Moscow, queried Vyacheslav Molotov whether the Soviet Union would permit the transit of Afghan forces into northern Afghanistan. But Molotov was noncommittal and the matter was dropped.

On June 22, 1941 Germany attacked the Soviet Union and Moscow joined the Western alliance. The alliance of Britain and the Soviet Union caused considerable anxiety in Kabul because Afghan foreign policy had been based on the premise that its territorial security depended on the continued rivalry between its imperialist neighbors. Concerted Allied action was soon to follow: In October 1941 the Allies presented separate notes to the Afghan government demanding the expulsion of all Axis nationals. Kabul was forced to comply, and the Afghan king convened a *Loya Jirga* (q.v.), Great Council, which gave retroactively its approval after the Axis nationals had left. The Afghan government insisted that they be given safe passage to a neutral country. From that time the Afghan government kept its northern border closed to nondiplomatic travelers, but trade continued between the two countries.

When India became independent in 1947 and the State of Pakistan was created, Afghanistan repudiated the treaties that accepted the Durand Line as an international boundary and demanded that the Afghans of the NWFP be given the choice of independence. Afghanistan was the only country voting against the admission of Pakistan to the United Nations. The cold war had begun and the Eisenhower administration sought to contain Moscow's expansionism by sponsoring alliances with states bordering on the Soviet Union. Washington supported the creation of the Baghdad Pact (later renamed CENTO), which united Britain, Turkey, Iraq, Iran, and Pakistan in a defensive alliance. This alliance guaranteed international borders but ignored irredentist and nationalist aspirations in the Middle East. As a result, relations between Afghanistan and Pakistan, a Western ally, turned increasingly hostile. The Afghan government "normalized" its relations with the Soviet Union and in 1946 agreed to accept the *thalweg* (middle) of the Amu Daria as the international boundary. A telegraph link was established with Tashkent in 1947, and in 1950 Afghanistan signed a four-year trade agreement with the USSR. The Soviet government praised Afghanistan's "positive" neutrality and, when in December 1955 Nikita Khrushchev and Nikolai Bulganin came to Kabul, the stage was set for a major rapprochement. The two countries renewed the Treaty of 1931 for 10 years, the Soviet Union granting Afghanistan a $100 million loan at two percent interest for projects selected by a joint USSR-Afghan committee. The Afghan national airline started flights from Kabul to Tashkent in 1965, which were subsequently extended to Moscow and other European countries.

The Afghan government wanted to purchase arms from the United States, and when it was unable to obtain what it wanted, Prime Minister Daud turned to the Soviet Union for help. In 1956 the first shipments of East Bloc weapons arrived and the Afghan armed forces began to be

Plate 11. Soviet "Stalin Organ." Source: Shah Bazgar

Plate 12. Burning Soviet Helicopter. Source: Mahaz

Plate 13. Mujahed Aiming a Stinger Missile. Source: S. Thiollier

Plate 8. Fort and Village of Mollah Abdul Guffoor, Captured and Destroyed by Brigadier-General Charles Gough. Source: ILN

Plate 15. Mujahedin Anti-Aircraft Unit. Source: E. De Pazzi

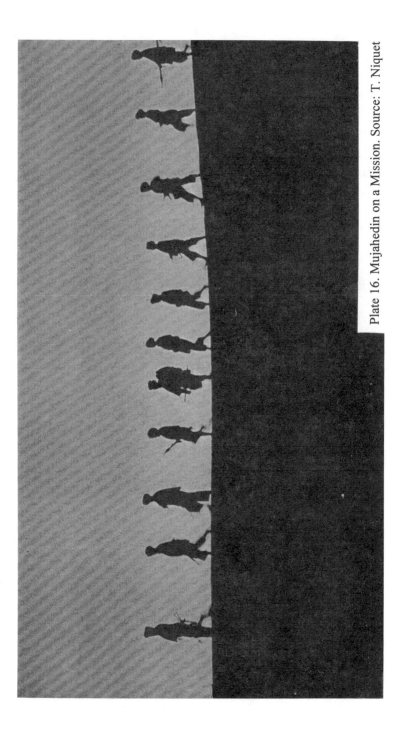

Plate 16. Mujahedin on a Mission. Source: T. Niquet

Plate 17. Destroyed Soviet Tank. Source: Jam'iat

Plate 18. Parade of Kabul Forces. Source: *Afghanistan Today*

Soviet-equipped. Thousands of Soviet advisers came to Afghanistan, and thousands of Afghan technicians and military officers went to the Soviet Union for training. The result was a growing cadre of military officers, students, and technocrats with leftist, if not pro-Russian, sympathies. When Muhammad Daud staged a coup with leftist support on July 17, 1973, the stage was set for the Saur Revolt (q.v.), which brought a Marxist government to power. The new Kabul government accepted Soviet advisers in virtually all its civilian and government branches and concluded a series of treaties that made the Soviet Union the dominant influence in Afghanistan. On December 5, 1978 the Taraki regime concluded a treaty of friendship, similar to the one the Soviet Union concluded with Vietnam, which also provided for military assistance and which became the basis for military intervention a year later. Resistance was growing against the Marxist regime, resulting in a civil war that turned into a war of liberation when Soviet troops tried to prop up a faltering regime. The war turned out to be costly to Afghanistan: *mujahedin* sources claim that as many as one million Afghans perished, whereas the Kabul government claimed that 243,900 soldiers and civilians were killed. After Soviet troops evacuated Afghanistan in February 1989, Moscow announced it had suffered about 13,000 deaths and another 35,000 wounded. *See also* AFGHAN FOREIGN RELATIONS.

SOVIET INTERVENTION/INVASION. The question as to the motive for Soviet intervention in Afghanistan was a matter of conjecture. Some saw it, as well as the Marxist coup in Afghanistan, as part of a master plan with the objective of gaining access to the resources and the warm water ports of the Persian/Arabian Gulf. But recent revelations of politburo notes indicate that it was to be a temporary effort to rescue a faltering Kabul regime from defeat by rebel forces. Recent disclosures of minutes of politburo meetings in March 1979 indicate that requests by Nur Muhammad Taraki (q.v.) for direct military assistance were at first not granted. Yuri V. Antropov, chairman of the KGB, is quoted as having said, "We can suppress a revolution in Afghanistan only with the aid of our bayonets, but that is for us entirely inadmissible. . . . Thus our army if it enters Afghanistan will be an aggressor." Prime Minister Alexei N. Kosygin added, "We cannot introduce troops. . . . There would be huge minuses for us. . . and no pluses for us at all." In a meeting with Taraki in which Defense Minister Dimitri F. Ustinov also participated, the Soviets pointed out that Vietnam never demanded

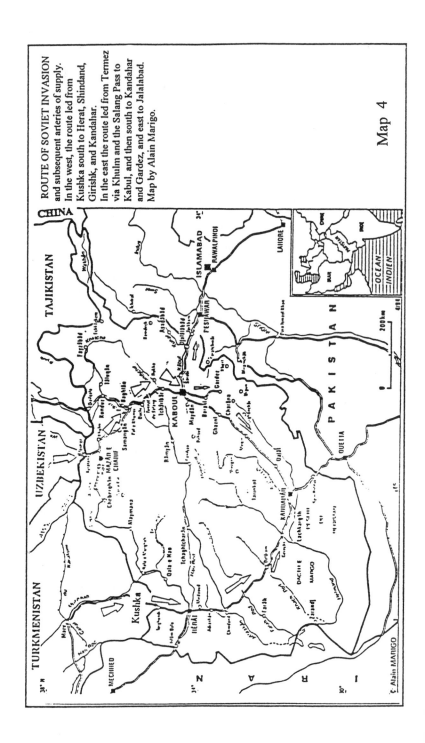

ROUTE OF SOVIET INVASION and subsequent arteries of supply. In the west, the route led from Kushka south to Herat, Shindand, Girishk, and Kandahar.
In the east the route led from Termez via Khulm and the Salang Pass to Kabul, and then south to Kandahar and Gardez, and east to Jalalabad.
Map by Alain Marigo.

Map 4

assistance of foreign troops. Taraki was told that he can expect considerable assistance, "You have working for you 500 generals and officers. If necessary we can send an additional number of party workers, as well as 150–200 officers," but, he was told,   the introduction of Soviet forces would alarm the international community and would involve the Soviets in a conflict with the Afghan people and "a people does not forgive such things." By the end of 1979, these prescient words were forgotten or the situation had deteriorated to a degree that the Kremlin agreed on intervention. Its legality was based on the Soviet-Afghan Treaty of Friendship and cooperation of December 5, 1978, which stated in Article 4

> The high contracting parties . . . shall consult each other and take
> by agreement appropriate measures to ensure the security,
> independence, and territorial integrity of the two countries.

The "temporary occupation" was legalized under a Status of Armed Forces Agreement signed in April 1980. The Kabul government claimed that the rebels were supported by foreign powers and that the Limited Contingent of Soviet Forces in Afghanistan (q.v. [LCSFA]) would withdraw at the end of foreign interference.

The reconnaissance for the intervention was said to have been carried out by General Ivan Pavlovski, a Soviet deputy defense minister, who spent three months in Afghanistan prior to the invasion. And the overall command was under Marshall Sergei Sokolov. By the time the Soviet 40th Army entered Afghanistan on December 27, 1979, two airborne assault brigades had already secured the Bagram (q.v.) air base, about 40 miles north of Kabul, and in 180 sorties of Antonov–12 and Antonov–22 transport aircraft, escorted by 100 combat aircraft, troops and munitions were brought in. The Salang Pass/Tunnel (q.v.), and the Kabul airport were secured by paratrooper and *Spetsnaz* (q.v.) units. Two motorized rifle divisions crossed the Amu Daria on pontoon bridges, and in a pincer movement the 357th proceeded from Kushka south to Herat and Shindand; and the 360th "Nevel-Polovsk" moved from Termez to Salang and to Kabul and Kandahar (Isby, 1989, 23). (Urban [42] gives the route to Kandahar via Herat) The Soviet forces were equipped for conventional war, including an SA-4 antiaircraft missile brigade and chemical warfare decontamination units. Within a week some 50,000 Soviet troops with some 350 tanks and 450 other armored vehicles had crossed the Amu Daria. (O'Ballance, 89) The objective was to secure the key cities and links of communication. The

Soviet armed forces were intended for the protection of major towns and lines of communication, leaving counterinsurgency tasks to the Afghan army, but they were inevitably drawn into search-and-destroy missions that cost 80 percent of its casualties. *See also* AFGANTSY.

SOVIET INVASION COMMAND. The Soviet invasion team consisted of Marshal Sergei Sokolov in overall command; General Valentin Varennikov in command of operational planning; Colonel General Yurii Maximov and Colonel General Petr Lushev in charge of Turkestan and Central Asian military districts; Lieutenant General Tukharinov in operational command.

The commanders of the 40th Army included Lieutenant General Tukharinov until Sept. 23, 1980; Lieutenant General B. I. Tkach until May 7, 1982; Lieutenant General V. F. Ermakov until Nov. 4, 1983; Lieutenant General I. E. Generalov until April 19, 1985; Lieutenant General I. N. Rodionov until April 30, 1986; Lieutenant General V. P. Dubyninun until June 1, 1987; and Lieutenant General B. V. Gromov until end of war. (Galeotti,1995, 174-75)

SOVIET OPERATIONAL AND STRATEGIC LESSONS OF THE WAR. Mark Galeotti, in his excellent study of the Afgantsy and the effects of the war on the former Soviet Union, *Afghanistan: The Soviet Union's Last War,* declares that the real importance of the war in wider military thinking is fourfold:

1.   It accelerated the rise of new commanders, a generation eager to make its presence felt in a time of change and with a different set of formative experience.
2.   It uncovered problems and identified weaknesses within existing thinking.
3.   It provided a new fund of combat experience at the very time when new-generation weapons, vehicles and communications systems were having their impact on Soviet doctrine.
4.   It forced the Soviets to come to terms with low-intensity warfare at the very time when perestroika was sparking such unrest within the USSR itself. (208) *See also* INTRODUCTION.

SOVIET OPERATIONS. Colonel Ali Ahmad Jalali (also Isby, 28) describes the inherent weakness of early Soviet military operations as follows: "Soviet troops, in the spring and summer of 1980, moved in heavy columns along the major roads. Closely supported by aircraft and helicopter gunships, these columns found comfort in technical superiority. Obsessed by massive firepower to support the advance, they fired to the front and flanks (sometimes at random) to suppress suspected *mujahedin* positions. The lack of troops patrols and the absence of tactical reconnaissance and security elements, especially on the ridges and high ground that so often dominate the roads, was exploited by the *mujahedin*, who on several occasions launched successful ambushes, despite being deployed where they could have been easily outflanked and routed. The inexperienced Soviet troops would not dismount and resort to close combat. Firepower could not produce results because it was not exploited at close quarters. The *mujahedin*, short of weapons, often defeated totally mechanized Soviet forces, unable to operate effectively in the rugged and close terrain where the guerrillas moved. In 1980, Soviet forces were unsupported by light infantry." In the following year, some modifications such as leap-frogged mechanized forces, were only partially successful. The change to an "air war" was equally unsatisfactory, and *spetsnaz* and other elite counterinsurgency forces supported by close air power were increasingly drawn into combat. When the *mujahedin* acquired surface-to-air missiles, including stingers in 1986, the war entered a new stage that put Soviet forces on the defensive. *See also* lessons of war in INTRODUCTION.

SPETSNAZ. Special Operations Forces (*Spetsnaz*) are an elite counter-insurgency force that, together with airborne, air assault/air mobile, and designated reconnaissance units, made up 10 percent to 20 percent of the Soviet forces deployed in Afghanistan. The elite force was created in 1941–42 during World War II and in the 1960s expanded to battalion size. In December 1978, *spetsnaz* forces were said to have been employed in securing airfields, communications centers, and other key points in Afghanistan prior to the invasion. They constituted the commando that was responsible for the assassination of Hafizullah Amin. *Spetsnaz* operated as raiders, sabotage teams, reconnaissance and intelligence commandos. According to McMichael (108), they operated in disguises such as shepherds, nomads, and itinerant traders. It is not clear how effective they could have been, since they were primarily of Slavic background, blond and blue eyed and not familiar with any Afghan languages. About nine battalions each with 250 men are said to have been active in Afghanistan. They were stationed at

Asadabad, Baraki-Barak, Ghazni, Shahjoy (about midway between Ghazni and Kandahar), Lashkargah, Farah, Kandahar, and Jalalabad. Brigade headquarters were at Lashkargah and Jalalabad.

STEWARD, GEN. SIR DONALD M. Commander in chief in India. Commanded the First Multan Division and subsequently the forces in southern Afghanistan, numbering 12,000 combatants and an equal number of camp followers, from the outbreak of the second Afghan war until April 1880. Advanced from Quetta and occupied Kandahar and Qalat-i-Ghilzai. Commanded the Ghazni Frontier Force in an advance on Ghazni and participated in the Battle of Ahmad Khel (q.v.) and in the action at Arzu. Was placed in command of the forces in northern Afghanistan from May 1880 until the evacuation of Kabul in August 1880. The evacuation by way of the Khaibar Pass was termed a success, because of the "patriotic co-operation, free from self-seeking motives of the two generals" [General Roberts, being the other]. (MR, 63)

STINGER. An American infrared, heat-seeking missile, with a high explosive warhead, capable of engaging low-altitude aircrafts, including high-speed jets, which has been credited in dipping the tactical balance in favor of the *mujahedin*. Long sought by the resistance, the first missiles were fired in September 1986 and became an immediate success. According to General Yousaf (q.v.), head of the ISI, the American government trained Pakistanis, who then trained Afghans. The first missiles were delivered to commanders of Hekmatyar and Yunus Khales, and possession of a stinger soon became the ultimate status symbol. The American government agreed to deliver 250 grip stocks with 1,000 to 2,000 missiles per year (Yousaf, 1992, 182). The missiles had been deployed by American forces first in 1981, but had never been used in combat. According to Yousaf, the *mujahedin* achieved a hit rate of 70 percent to 75 percent (68 percent, according to Isby, 1989), much better than the rate of their Pakistani or American teachers. To reward success, *mujahedin* commanders were given two stingers for each hit (Rubin, 1995, 196). As was to be expected, a *spetsnaz* (q.v.) commando was able to capture a number of missiles in an ambush, and one commander, Mulla Malang, boasted of having sold four launchers for $1 million each with 16 missiles to Iran (Rubin, 336, n. 45). Overby (115) claims that of 1,150 stingers originally sent, only 863 reached the *mujahedin*. China obtained several stingers and was said to be copying them (*Nouvelles*, No. 63). In 1987 the Soviet/Kabul forces had 150 to 200 air losses, and the much-feared Hind D helicopter never recovered its tactical preeminence. Isby (114) quotes Commander Ahmad Shah Mas'ud (q.v.), as saying, "There are only two things Afghans must have: the Koran and Stingers." *See also* ROKETI, MULLA SALAM.

STOLIETOFF, MAJ. GEN. Head of an uninvited Russian mission sent to the court of Amir Shir Ali by General Kaufman (q.v.) in 1878 to conclude an alliance against Britain. Stolietoff reached Kabul on July 22 at a time when General Kaufman was dispatching a force of 15,000 men to the upper reaches of the Amu Daria. Not being able to prevent the mission from reaching Kabul, the amir treated the Russian and his staff of six officers with curtesy. Stolietoff presented several "letters of friendship," in one of which Kaufman wrote:

> I have deputed my agent, Major-General Stolietoff, an officer high in the favour of the Emperor. He will inform you of all that is hidden in my mind. I hope that you will pay great attention to what he says, and believe him as you would myself.... The advantage of a close alliance with the Russian Government will be permanently evident." (Sykes, 97)

The draft of a treaty promised what Britain was not willing to offer: protection from foreign aggression and recognition of his son Abdullah Jan as heir apparent. Article 3 of the treaty stated:

> The Russian Government engages that if any foreign enemy attacks Afghanistan and the Amir is unable to drive him out, and asks for the assistance of the Russian Government, the Russian Government will repel the enemy either by means of advice or by such other means as it may consider proper. (Sykes, 107)

The fact that the type of Russian support was left to the discretion of the Russian government apparently did not occur to the amir. His refusal to permit a British mission under General Sir Neville Chamberlain to proceed to Kabul was taken as Lord Lytton's excuse for starting the second Anglo-Afghan war. *See also* ANGLO-AFGHAN WARS; and SHIR ALI, AMIR.

STRONGHOLD STRATEGY. Invaders of Afghanistan during the past two centuries never succeeded in pacifying the country; therefore, they had to rely on a stronghold strategy, holding large towns, key facilities, economic centers, and transportation links. Inevitably, these bases became the targets of guerrilla attacks, making it necessary to stage offensive sweeps that only provided temporary relief. Lines of logistics became vulnerable to attacks and the invaders became captives in their stronghold positions. Not much has changed in this respect, even at a time when Soviet/Kabul forces had aerial superiority.

SUPPLIES, COLLECTION OF. The British-Indian army depended on local supplies when it invaded Afghanistan, but the availability of supplies depended on a number of factors: When British prestige was high during a rapid campaign, there was little difficulty in purchasing supplies. But after a reverse on the battlefield, supplies immediately dried up. The British found that once established in the country, it was best to set up a free market where the natives could make a profit selling their goods. Another means was to requisition supplies but offer immediate payment. If the natives were unwilling to deliver supplies, requisitioning by force would be required. *The Handbook for the Indian Army* (66) suggests the use of "adequate force to seize state granaries, the inhabitants animals and stocks of grain, and the timber of their houses for fuel." It advised that

> strong mobile columns, of all arms, will be required for rounding up livestock, for the collection of supplies and for the removal of both to the collecting centre. . . . Foraging by Cavalry alone, possible in other countries, is seldom advisable in Afghanistan.

The overriding maxim was, "Soldiers must eat, even if villagers starve." *See also* FORAGING; and LOGISTICS.

- T -

TAKHT-I SHAH. A mountain on the south of Kabul, with which the Sher Darwaza heights are connected by a narrow ridge, and the most commanding point in the immediate vicinity of Kabul. The Afghans under Muhammad Jan captured it on December 11, 1879, and in a seesaw battle fought off British troops under Brigadier General Baker. It was one of the battles in which General Roberts decided to abandon Kabul and retreat into the Sherpur cantonment. The situation looked like a repeat of the defeat of December 1841, and a British historian commented, "It must never be forgotten that at this time our people in Afghanistan held no more territory than the actual ground they stood upon and the terrain swept by their fire." (Forbes, 246) The British forces remained under siege in Sherpur during the winter and recognized Sardar Abdur Rahman in July 1880, before evacuating their forces from Afghanistan. *See also* SHERPUR, SIEGE OF.

TALEBAN. A mysterious movement of "*Taleban*" students who attended religious schools in Pakistan and suddenly emerged as a politico-military force in Afghanistan. Headed by Maulawi Muhammad Omar, a Nurzai from Oruzgan, and his deputy, Maulawi Muhammad Hasan, the movement first came to public attention when it rescued from *mujahedin* captors a Pakistani truck convoy bound for Central Asia. The *Taleban* then captured the city of Kandahar and moved north against Kabul. On Monday, February 13, 1995, they captured Pul-i Alam and the next day Charasiab, the stronghold of *Hizb-i Islami* leader Hekmatyar. Hekmatyar (q.v.) was forced to flee to Sarobi, about 37 miles east of Kabul. It is still unclear who is supporting the "students" and how they were able to quickly defeat the supposedly battle-hardened *mujahedin*. According to recent reports, ex-army officers and *mujahedin* commanders defected to the *Taleban*, forcing Sayyaf (q.v.), leader of the *Ittihad-i Islami*, to take refuge in Jalalabad. In March 1995, the Shi'a *Hizb-i Wahdat* surrendered its enclave in Kabul to the *Taleban*, and Mazari (q.v.) was killed while in *Taleban* captivity. On September 3 the *Taleban* captured Shindand (q.v.), an important air base, and two days later the city of Herat. The *Taleban* claim not to be affiliated with any of the *mujahedin* groups and only desire to unite Afghanistan, end the power of the warlords, and create a "true" Islamic state.

TALEBAN ORGANIZATION. According to a table published in the *Frontier Post* by Ibrar Ahmad Qureshi, the *Taleban* political structure is as follow:

Maulawi Muhammad Omar
Amir

INNER SHURA

1. Maulawi Muhammad Rabbani - Chief of Staff
2. Maulawi Ehsanullah - Head of Administration

3. Maulawi Abbas - Political Spokesman
4. Maulawi Muhammad - Field Commander
5. Maulawi Pasani - Chief Justice

CENTRAL SHURA

1. Maulawi Bor Jan - Commander, Kabul Front
2. Maulawi Muhd. Hasan - Acting Governor, Kandahar
3. M. Nuruddin
4. Maulawi Wakil Ahmad
5. Maulawi Sher Muhd. Mulang
6. Maulawi Abdur Rahman
7. Maulawi Ibrahim
8. Maulawi Abdul Hakim
9. Sardar Ahmad
10 Haji Muhammad Ghaus
11. Masum Afghani

Liaison Officer for NWFP and Liaison Officer for Quetta
Abdur Rahman Zahid Muhammad Masum

Provincial Governors
Kandahar, M. Muhammad Hasan
Helmand, M. Abdul Muhammad
Oruzgan, M. Abdul Salam
Zabul, M. Abdul Ghani
Wardak, M. Turabi

(*Les Nouvelles*, 68, 17.)

TANAI, LT. GEN. SHAHNAWAZ. Member of the *Khalq* faction of the
PDPA, chief of general staff since 1986, and minister of defense from
1988 to 1990. A Pashtun born in Paktia Province of the small Tani
tribe. A captain major until the Saur Revolt, he was considered a rising
star in the PDPA, when on March 6, 1990, Tanai and several *Khalqi*
officers staged a coup against the Najibullah government from the
Bagram air force base. They attacked the presidential palace and key
government facilities in Kabul, but were unable to topple the

government. Tanai and some of his closest supporters escaped from the Bagram air base in three military aircraft and a helicopter and landed in Parachinar, Pakistan. Gulbuddin Hekmatyar, leader of the Islamist and most radical of *mujahedin* groups, gave the coup his support. This alliance of hard-line *Khalqis* and radical Islamists caused considerable consternation in Afghanistan. Tanai and Hekmatyar were seen as determined to win power, regardless of ideological considerations. Najibullah's control of the air force and scrambling of the communications network enabled him to rout the rebels. On March 16 Tanai made his appearance in the Hekmatyar camp in Logar Province, claiming to continue the campaign against Najibullah, but remaining a loyal member of the PDPA. After the fall of Najibullah in April 1992, many *Khalqi* officers also joined Hekmatyar's forces.

TARAKI, NUR MUHAMMAD. Leader of the *Khalq* faction of the PDPA and, after the Saur Revolt, president and prime minister of the Democratic Republic of Afghanistan. In the 1950s he became known as an author and a journalist. He convened the "founding congress" of the PDPA on January 1, 1965, which was attended by 27 persons. Taraki was elected secretary general, and his rival Babrak Karmal became secretary of the central committee. After the Saur Revolt, Taraki became the "Great Leader," and a personality cult prepared the way to legitimize his rule as the "teacher and great guide." His life was cut short when he was executed on order of Hafizullah Amin (q.v.) On October 9, 1979.

TEZIN, BATTLE OF. (34–21' N, 69–35' E) Tezin is a collection of settlements in the valley of the same name, lying near a pass on the Kabul-Jalalabad road. It was strategically important and therefore the scene of a number of engagements during the first Anglo-Afghan war. Brigadier Sale (q.v.), retiring from Kabul to Jalalabad, was able to defeat a body of Afghans on October 22, 1841. During the Death March in January 1842, the remnants of the retreating force took shelter in the valley, hoping to regain their energies.

General Pollock (q.v.), advancing on Kabul in September 1842, encountered strong Afghan resistance at the pass. Sardar Muhammad Akbar (q.v.) had occupied the heights, and Pollock approached the mouth of the pass, where he left two guns, two squadrons of Her Majesty's 3rd Light Dragoons, a party of the 1st Light Cavalry and of the 3rd Irregular Cavalry. An attempt by the Afghans to capture the baggage train was foiled by the Dragoons and Native Cavalry. British troops then mounted the heights, and the Afghans made the mistake of advancing to meet them, engaging in hand-to-hand combat. The Light Company of Her Majesty's 9th Foot, led by Captain Lushington, ascended the hills to the left of the pass and was able to dislodge the Afghans. "The slaughter was considerable, and the fight continued during a great part of the day, the enemy appearing resolved that the British should not ascent the Haft Kotal," but they succeeded, "giving three cheers when they reached the summit." A British historian described the capture of the heights, saying, "Broadfoot's bloodthirsty little Goorkas who, hillmen themselves from their birth, chased the Afghans from crag to crag." According to British estimates, General Pollock was opposed by some 15,000 men in the field, a large part cavalry, led by Sardar Muhammad Akbar and a number of other chiefs. Afghans lost their guns and three standards, and several hundreds were killed, as compared to British claims of 32 killed and 130 wounded. (40 killed and 91 wounded, according to MR)

THAL, SIEGE OF (1919). An action in the third Anglo-Afghan war that pitted General Nadir Khan the subsequent king of Afghanistan, against Major General Eustace and his garrison at the fort and village of Thal. Thal was of considerable importance for the control of the autonomous tribal belt in the North-West Frontier Province of India. It was where Waziristan, home of the Waziri tribes, impinged on the territories of the Shi'a Turis in the Kurram valley. It was an important staging area for an invasion of Afghanistan. A small-scale railroad and metaled roads led from Bannu and Kohat to the village. Nadir Khan moved from Khost with an army of 3,000 regular and about 6,000 tribal forces equipped with two 10cm Krupp howitzers and seven 7.5cm Krupp mountain guns. As he advanced some 30 miles toward Thal, the British withdrew from their small posts, which were quickly occupied by Afghan regular troops. Members of the British-led Waziristan Militia began to desert and turned against their British officers. Nadir Khan established his headquarters at Yusuf Khel on the Kurram River, about three miles from Thal, and on May 27 began to invest the fort. His artillery caused considerable damage, and the infantry advanced and occupied Thal village. The British mountain guns were outranged by the Krupp howitzers, and even attacks by two R.A.F. aircraft were not able to silence the Afghan guns. On May 28-29 the Afghans captured a tower from which they were able to dominate the fort's water supply. On May

30 an all-day bombardment cause additional damage to the fort. The "British" tribes were watching the situation, ready to join the Afghans if the fortunes of war should turn against India. The British had planned to follow up on their territorial gains at Dakka with a move against Jalalabad, but the danger of a tribal rebellion on the Frontier led them to dispatch the "Thal Relief Force," headed by Brigadier General R. E. H. Dyer (q.v.). After dispersing the tribal forces that threatened to block his advance, Dyer came to the rescue of the besieged fort. By May 30 he disposed of a force of 19,000 troops and 13 guns, as well as 22 "dummies," tree trunks covered with canvas to resemble guns. The next day Nadir Khan informed the British general that Amir Amanullah had ordered him to suspend hostilities because of the beginning of peace negotiations. On June 3 the armistice was signed and the Afghans withdrew. British casualties numbered 94, eight were killed, including one British officer and seven Indians, and four died later of wounds. The importance of the action at Thal was that it stopped British attempts to advance on Jalalabad, and fear of a general uprising of the tribes on the British side of the border made peace seem a preferable alternative to continuation of the war. *See also* THIRD ANGLO-AFGHAN WAR.

THIRD ANGLO-AFGHAN WAR (1919).   A short war between Afghanistan and British Indian forces, which lasted from May 4 until the conclusion of a cease-fire on June 3, 1919. Amir Amanullah (q.v.) had ascended the throne in February 1919, after the assassination of his father, Amir Habibullah. He was an ardent nationalist and reformer and was said to have been a member of the "war party" at the Afghan court, which favored an attack on India during World War I. Afghanistan had remained neutral in the "holy war" against Britain, and Amir Habibullah expected a generous financial reward and British recognition of Afghanistan's complete independence. But once the European conflict had ended, Britain showed no intention of freeing the country from its control.

Upon accession to power, Amir Amanullah demanded a treaty that would end Afghanistan's political dependence on Britain and establish normal, neighborly relations between the two states. Lord Chelmsford, the viceroy of India, however, suggested that no new treaty was required, despite the fact that previously India had held that the agreements with Afghan rulers were personal and therefore subject to renegotiation with each new ruler. He merely acknowledged Amaullah's

Plate 19. British Air Raid, 1919. Afghans soon learned to disperse
at the approach of an aircraft and seek shelter. Source: ILN

election as amir "by the populace of Kabul and its surrounding," implying that he was not in complete control of his country. The subsidy given to previous Afghan rulers was halted, and when Amanullah sent his new envoy to India, he was asked "what amir" he represented.

On the occasion of a royal *darbar* on April 13, 1919, Amanullah showed himself belligerent, announcing to an assembly of dignitaries:

> ... I have declared myself and my country entirely free, autonomous and independent both internally and externally. My country will hereafter be as independent a state as the other states and powers of the world are. No foreign power will be allowed to have a hair's breath of right to interfere internally and externally with the affairs of Afghanistan, and if any ever does I am ready to cut its throat with this sword. (Adamec, 1974, 47)

He turned to the British agent and said, "Oh Safir, have you understood what I have said?" The British agent replied, "Yes I have." (Adamec, 1967, 110)

To emphasize his demands, Amanullah sent three of his generals to the border: Saleh Muhammad, the commander in chief, arrived at Dakka, the border town, on May 3; Abdul Quddus, the prime minister (*sadr-i a'zam*), moved to the area of Qalat-i Ghilzai on May 5; and a day later Muhammad Nader, the commander in chief (and subsequent king of Afghanistan), moved to Khost with a tribal *lashkar* (army) of several thousand men in addition to his regular forces.

On May 5 the government of India stopped demobilization of all combatant forces in India and began to recall all British officers. India intended to confront the Afghans with an overwhelming force in the Khaibar to induce them to withdraw quietly.

Lieutenant General G. N. Molesworth described the Afghan regular forces as ill-trained, ill-paid, and probably under strength.

The cavalry was little better than indifferent infantry mounted on equally indifferent ponies. Rifles varied from modern German, Turkish, and British types to obsolete Martinis and Sniders. Few infantry had bayonets.

Artillery was pony drawn, or pack, and included modern 10cm Krupp howitzers, 75mm Krupp mountain guns, and ancient 7-pounder weapons. There were a few, very old, four-barrel Gardiner machine guns. Ammunition was in short supply and the Kabul arsenal inadequate.

The British North-West Frontier Force consisted of two cavalry brigades (1st and 10th), two infantry divisions (1st and 2nd), and three frontier infantry brigades (Kohat, Bannu, and Derajat). Each division had 18-pounder field guns, R.F.A., four 4.5" howitzers, R.F.A., and eight 2.75" mountain guns, R.G.A. Each cavalry brigade had four 13-pounder guns, R.H.A. The available striking force in the Khaibar area had six cavalry regiments, 24 infantry battalions, 40 pieces of artillery, and 48 machine guns. The forces in the Peshawar area were needed for internal security.

The superiority of the British-Indian forces was to a certain extent matched by the power of the Pashtun tribal *lashkars* (q.v.) from both sides of the border. They were aggressive fighters and operated in an inaccessible terrain that was well known to them. The Pashtun soldiers of the British Khaibar Rifles were not willing to fight their Afghan brothers, and, given the choice, 600 men out of 700 elected to be discharged, making it necessary for the British to disband the units. (OA 3, 22–23)

Lord Chelmsford was warned by the London government, "You will not have forgotten [the] lessons of history, that we have not so much to fear from [the] Afghan regular Army as from the irregular tribesmen and their constant attacks on our isolated camps and lines of communications." (Adamec, 1967, 116)

Hostilities began on May 4, 1919, when Afghan troops cut the water supply to Landi Kotal on the Indian side of the border and Britain retaliated by closing the Khaibar Pass. (*See* BAGH, BATTLE OF.) The Afghans wanted to make a concerted effort involving the frontier tribes and the people of Peshawar, but a Peshawar revolt was prevented when British forces cut the supplies of water, electricity, and food to the city. Saleh Muhammad's forces became prematurely engaged and had to give ground. It was primarily on the Waziristan front that the Afghans were able to break through the British defenses and lay siege to the British base at Thal. (See THAL, SIEGE OF.) The entire Northwest Frontier was in ferment, and Indian tribesmen were ready to rally to support the Afghans.

John Maffey, the chief political officer with the field force, indicated in a letter that the "threat to Thal has delayed the Jalalabad move, as the motor transport available does not admit of two simultaneous offensives." He also was afraid that British forces would have to push so far that there would be nobody to settle up with. (Adamec, 1967, 118)

Therefore, the Indian government permitted the Afghan envoy in India to proceed to Kabul to persuade Amanullah to end his hostile activities. Amanullah agreed, and a cease-fire was concluded leading to peace and the establishment of normal neighborly relations after long and heated negotiations at Rawalpindi, Mussoorie, and Kabul (qq.v.) On the southern front British forces captured Spin Boldak, but could not follow up on their conquest, and no major campaign occurred on the northern, Chitral, front. British casualties included 236 killed (49 British ranks), 615 wounded (133 British ranks), as well as 566 deaths of cholera and 334 of other diseases and accidents. British "ration strength" reached 750,000 British and Indian troops, and the animals involved numbered 450,000. (Molesworth, vii) No figures are available on Afghan casualties. (*See also* THAL, SIEGE OF; AFGHAN FOREIGN RELATIONS; MUS-SOORIE CONFERENCE; and ANGLO-AFGHAN TREATY, 1919; and 1921.)

THE THIRD ANGLO-AFGHAN WAR, AFTERMATH. Following the war, the autonomous tribes of the Frontier were in semirevolt, assuming that the cease-fire was only temporary, and that the Afghan government would continue the war if King Amanullah's demands were not met. Afridis, Wazirs, and Mahsuds continued their raiding of British positions, and the Indian government faced a slow process of reasserting its authority in the area. Sir Hamilton Grant recommended to the viceroy on October 9, 1919 the bombing of tribal villages without warning, reporting, "As the after-math of the Afghan war we have an outbreak of raiding such perhaps as has never before discredited our administration." Dealers and shopkeepers were holding up their stock, and there was an imminent danger of bread riots and disturbances in the Peshawar area. The viceroy answered, "I am up against a serious financial situation and an army which is tired of war." On December 13 he reported that the operation against the Afridis (q.v.) was so far successful,

> although I am sorry to say we have lost another aeroplane and the two airmen if alive are prisoners in the hands of the Afridis, I trust they will be given up unharmed. . . . The constant raiding by Afridi gangs into the Peshawar District is sorely discrediting our administration. It is astounding that such a state of affairs should be possible with the number of troops we have got in the Peshawar Valley and shows how very difficult it would be to make any military operation of trans-frontier areas really successful.

He felt that "the only real cure is the radical cure, namely, an Afridi war and the subjugation of the whole tribe, but this, unless we are forced to do it, would be a most formidable and undesirable undertaking."
On January 26, 1920 he reported on operations against the Mahsuds:

> The Mahsuds are putting up a good fight, and indeed the whole operations are very different from any I remember on the Frontier. The Mahsuds attack with extraordinary recklessness, and hand to hand fighting is quite common; but this is to our advantage, for it means very heavy casualties to them. These must tell in the end; and unless we suffer any serious reverses, I think the Mahsuds must chack up the sponge before very long. Force is expensive. It takes nearly a hundred thousand men with miles of mechanical transport, railway trains, camels, mule carts etc. to have about 18 battalions in the field, but such is modern war. (Hamilton Col. I.O. MSS Eur. D. 660)

The British eventually prevailed: some of the more militant members of the tribes withdrew into Afghanistan, and the rest made their peace with the British. Eventually, they intervened for their militant brothers, which enabled them to return to their homes.

THIRD ANGLO-AFGHAN WAR, BRITISH PLAN OF CAMPAIGN.

The British military command stated the following objectives:
"1. To undertake an offensive with the main striking force against Jalalabad with the object of dividing the Afridis and Mohmands, and strike at any Afghan concentration within reach, and to thus induce the withdrawal, for the purpose of covering Kabul, of Afghan forces from our borders elsewhere.
"2. To maintain an active defense on other portions of our front.
"3. In the Tochi and Derajat areas, we are prepared to evacuate temporarily, should the necessity arise, those portions of country held by Frontier Militias between the Administrative and Political borders, the retention of which would possibly result in a series of sieges necessitating relief measures and consequent dissipation of transport."
The operations were directed by General Sir Charles Munro, the commander in chief in India. Army headquarters were at Simla, and the army was first organized into two forces: 1. The North-West Frontier Force, commanded by General Sir Arthur Barrett. 2. The Baluchistan force, which included the troops guarding the Nushki-Duzdap Railway and the L. and C. through east Persia to Meshed, commanded by Lieutenant General R. Wapshare. Further decentralization developed by

formation of the "Waziristan Force" under the command of Major General S. H. Climo, consisting of the troops in the Bannu and Derajat area. The force comprising the East Persian Cordon under Major General W. Malleson, with headquarters in Meshed, was charged to intervene if Turkestan Bolsheviks were sending assistance to the Afghans.

The third Anglo-Afghan war differed from the previous wars is several respects. Before, the British made war when they were ready – this time the Afghans were the aggressors. Troops were engaged along the entire Afghan frontier from Chitral on the northeast to Seistan on the southwest, a distance of about 1,000 miles. Failure of the system of tribal militias, which necessitated their disbandment or serious reduction. The British realized that in a war with Afghanistan, they would always have the Afghan tribes on their side of the frontier turn against them.

THIRD ANGLO-AFGHAN WAR. FACTORS AFFECTING THE BRITISH CAMPAIGN. British forces faced the usual serious problems. Lack of communications, general sterility of the soil in the theaters of war and shortage of water, extremes of climate, epidemic diseases, the natural aptitude of the Afghan and Pathan for guerrilla warfare, the danger of a general conflagration along the frontier, and the uncertainty as to when and where such outbreaks would take place. (OA 3, 7)

THIRD ANGLO-AFGHAN WAR, LESSONS OF. Britain again learned the bitter lesson that her hold on the tribal territory on the north-west frontier of India was as tenuous as it had been in the past. The frontier militias had to be disbanded because they were unwilling to fight their Afghan brothers, and the entire tribal belt was preparing to obey the Afghan king's call to *jehad*. The British realized, "We must expect a portion, or all, of them to be hostile to us in the case of another war with Afghanistan." The extremes in temperature, lack of water and supplies, endemic disease, and the inhospitable nature of the territory proved to be serious problems in spite of the British advantage of superior weapons technology. The use of the Frontier Militias as a covering force behind which the Field Army was to concentrate proved a failure in the Khaibar and Waziristan. The lesson to be learned was that "irregular troops should not be left to meet the first onslaught of the invader." They should be replaced with strong, mobile columns of regular troops.

The British employed a system of troop movements whereby "the 1st Division was replaced at Peshawar and Nowshera by the 2nd Division, which in turn was pushed forward when relieved by the 16th Division." This caused the staff and transport to become disorganized, and the Field Army disintegrated. The tactical lesson of the value of pursuing a vigorous offensive was proven correct, because it kept the fence-sitting tribesmen out of the war; whereas inaction at Dakka and the Khaibar encouraged the tribesmen to join the Afghan forces. This was the first major use of aerial warfare and, although it had a great moral effect, there were limits to air power. Most of the British planes were obsolete, their climbing power was low, so that the tribesmen were able to shoot at them from the hilltops; but the bombing of Dakka, Jalalabad, and Kabul proved to have a great moral effect. In short-distance tactical reconnaissance, aircraft were of no value, because the tribesmen soon learned to break up into small groups and take cover at the sound of an approaching aricraft. The armored car possessed great fire power and was an invulnerable target. But its use was limited to patrolling roads, it was liable to engine trouble, and the heat in the turrets when closed became intolerable. Howitzers were employed with great effect, and machine guns were eminently suitable to the hilly terrain as they could be employed for direct overhead cover. Grenades were used to good effect, but many failed to explode or were thrown without the pin being removed. The British felt that permanent pickets proved to be preferable to temporary ones, although it deprived them of their mobility. The British felt a need for more effective training to "cultivate dash, and a desire to close with the enemy with the bayonet." Much more transport than in previous wars was needed because of the more extensive use of artillery and machine guns. (OA, 1919 War)

For the Afghan side, the lesson was clear that great efforts were needed for improving the effectiveness of the Afghan army. New weapons, more intensive training, and a rationalization of logistics were only some of the needs. As in the past, the tribesmen proved to be better fighters, but lacked staying power, having provisions for only a few days. They were prone to plunder, which they wanted to carry to their villages. They operated best in their own tribal areas and were good in short aggressive attacks. Afghan offensives on the Waziristan front were largely due to tribal support. The tribes on the British side of the border were ready to join the war against India, but they could not be mobilized and equipped before the short war was ended.

THIRD ANGLO-AFGHAN WAR. PHASES OF OPERATION. Phase 1. From May 6 to 25. Actions on the Khaibar front and attempted Afghan penetration through Mohmand country. Movements of British reserves to northern area and the formation of a further reserve by the creation of the 60th Brigade at Ambala, the 61st Brigade at Jubbulpore, the 62nd Brigade at Dhond, and the 63rd Brigade at Lucknow. During this period the border tribes were quiet.

Phase 2. From the May 26 to June 2. Invasion of the central area by Nadir Khan and siege of Thal. Evacuation of militia posts in Waziristan and mutiny of the North and South Waziristan Militias. Diversion of British reserves to Kohat and Bannu. The armistice. During this period the border tribes were showing signs of hostility.

Phase 3. From June 3 to August 8. Cessation of hostilities on the part of the Afghan regulars, but general activity on the part of the Afghan border tribes. (OA 3, 25)

THIRD ANGLO-AFGHAN WAR, PRESS REACTION. The British press complained about scandal and mismanagement in the war. One officer told the *Army and Navy Gazette* (Sept. 16, 1919) of a case of mismanagement: 300 horses were sent in corrugated iron trucks. Instructions to thatch the roofs and spray them with water at stops were ignored. Simla said not necessary! The result was that 150 horses died on the journey and 75 more on arrival.

Under the heading "Afghan Frontier Scandal," *The Englishman* (Sept. 13, 1919) reported that the army was not prepared. Transport was missing. "Airplanes available were all of an antiquated type, save the two Handley-Page machines, of which one flew once and the other not at all."

"British troops at Dakka for three weeks had no rations save bully beef, biscuits, tea and sugar." The troops never received more than half rations. Hospital conditions were a disgrace: "Cholera patients had to be put in tents at 115 degrees heat." "While Simla rewarded itself with a stream of foreign decorations. . . ."

"Mesopotamia was bad, but Afghanistan is worse, because it shows that the lesson of the former debacle was not learnt."

TIMUR SHAH (1773–93). One of Ahmad Shah's six surviving sons and governor of Herat at the time of the death of his father. He defeated his brother Sulaiman Mirza and quickly established himself as successor to the Afghan throne at Kandahar. To weaken the power of the Durrani chiefs, he moved his capital to Kabul, where he continued his father's policy of forging an alliance with the Barakzais, granting hereditary offices, and maintaining a strong army. He made alliances by marriage and further strengthened his power by creating an elite bodyguard of non-Pashtun soldiers. However, he was unable to create a centralized state. Afghan historians describe him as "humane and generous but ... more a scholar than a soldier." He appointed his sons Zaman, Huma-yun, Mahmud, Abbas, and Kohandil as governors of Afghan provinces, and upon his death in 1783, they started an internecine struggle for power that eventually cost the Sadozai rulers their throne.

TODD, ELLIOT D'ARCY (1808–45). A Bengal officer attached to the British legation with the Persian camp at Herat in 1838. He entered the besieged city, in which Eldred Pottinger (q.v.), another Englishman was helping in the defense of the city. The negotiations of the two men did not have any effect on the siege. Deputed to make a treaty with Shah Kamran at Herat, he remained as a political agent, from 1839 to 1841. Removed by Lord Auckland because of his independent actions.

TRANSPORT, MILITARY. Until the end of the Second World War, motorized transport was limited to the major roads, leading from Herat to Kandahar and from there to Kabul or south to Quetta. A road connected the capital over the Lataband, about 20 miles east of Kabul, with Jalalabad and the Indo-Pakistani subcontinent. From Kabul to Mazar-i Sharif a tortuous road led over the Salang Pass, which was not passable in the winter. The Hazarajat (q.v.) in the center of the country was closed to motorized traffic. Until the 1930s only a few landing strips existed for small aircraft. Therefore, invaders of Afghanistan depended on large numbers of animal transport. Bullocks, donkeys, ponies, horses, and camels were the major animals used; elephants and mules were less frequently employed. Donkeys were excellent for transport work: they could easily move in the mountainous terrain and carry loads up to 160 pounds. The Afghan camel was superior to camels from India; it was sure-footed and hardy, could travel with ease over mountain tracks, and was used for long-distance travel. The British army lost 20,000 camels during the first Anglo-Afghan war and 100,000 during the second (*Handbook*, 1933) and had difficulty in providing replacements by hire or confiscation from the Afghans. British lines of communication remained vulnerable to Afghan attacks. Overby (167) quotes Amir Abdur Rahman, as saying, "100,000 English soldiers require more transport animals than 1,000,000 Afghans, because they require so many kinds of provisions. . . The Afghans are such a strong, healthy people that they can run over the mountains nearly as fast as horses, carrying their guns and food on their backs."

In the 1980s no more than 3,000 miles of hard-surface roads existed, and many of those were severely damaged as a result of the war. The *mujahedin* employed contractors who used their own pack animals to transport supplies into Afghanistan. As animals died, horses and mules were imported from Argentina, China, and Pakistan. Mules would carry mortars, machine guns, and other heavy equipment, as well as ammunition, close to the firing points. Initially, convoys of pack animals traveled by night, but during the latter stages of the war they traveled unhindered even during the day. However, in many areas close to the enemy, the *mujahedin* had to carry their heavy weapons over paths that did not permit the use of pack animals. *See also* LOGISTICS.

TREATIES. *See also* **ANGLO-AFGHAN TREATIES.**

TREATY OF PESHAWAR, 1855. A treaty of friendship and alliance between Amir Dost Muhammad and the government of India, which stipulated "perpetual peace and friendship, that the British government should respect the territories in possession of the Amir, and the amir respect the territories of the British government. The Afghan ruler was to be the friend of Britain's friends and enemy of her enemies, and that the British should assist the amir against his enemies.

TREATY OF SIMLA. *See* **TRIPARTITE AGREEMENT.**

TRIPARTITE AGREEMENT. An agreement, also called Treaty of Simla, signed on July 16, 1838, among Ranjit Singh, ruler of the Sikh nation of the Panjab, Shah Shuja (qq.v.), the exiled king of Afghanistan, and the British government. It stipulated relations between the future Afghan ruler and Ranjit Singh and allied the three powers in an attempt to restore Shah Shuja and the Sadozai dynasty to the Kabul throne. Ranjit Singh was not required to commit his army and wisely left the task of invading Afghanistan to the British "Army of the Indus." He was thus spared the British defeat in the first Anglo-Afghan war. *See also* AFGHAN FOREIGN RELATIONS; ANGLO-AFGHAN WARS; and SIMLA MANIFESTO.

- U -

ULAMA. A collective term for the "doctors of Islamic sciences." They are graduates of *madrasas*, colleges of Islamic studies, or of private study with an *'alim* (pl. *ulama*, one who possesses the quality of *'ilm*, knowledge of the Islamic traditions, law, and theology). Commonly referred to as the Islamic clergy, they have been in the forefront of the struggle against non-Muslim invaders and have become a dominant class after the victory in the war against the Soviet forces.

- V -

VICEROYS AND GOVERNOR GENERALS OF INDIA.

Governor General:	
Hastings, Warren	1774–85
Cornwallis, Charles C.	1786–93
Wellesley, Richard Colley	1798–1805
Cornwallis, Charles C.	1805
Minto, Gilbert Elliot	1808–14
Marquis of Hastings	1813–23
Amherst of Arakan, William P.	1823–28
Bentinck, William Henry C.	1834–39
Auckland, George Eden	1836–42
Dalhousie, James Andrew	1848–56
And Viceroy:	
Canning, Charles John	1858–62
Elgin and Kincardine	1862–63
Napier, R. off.	1863
Denison, W. off.	1863
Lawrence, John Laird Mair	1864–69
Mayo, Richard Southwell B.	1869–72
Strachey, John off.	1872
Lord Napier off.	1872
Northbrook, Thomas George B.	1872–76
Lytton, Edward Robert B.	1876–80
Ripon, George Frederick R.	1880–84
Dufferin and Ava, Frederick T.	1884–88

Lansdowne, Henry Charles K.	1888–93
Elgin and Kincardine, Victor	1894–99
Curzon, George Nathaniel	1899–1905
Baron Ampthill off.	1904
Curzon, G. N.	1904
Minto, Gilbert John Murray	1905–10
Hardinge of Penshurst	1910–16
Chelmsford, Frederic John	1916–21
Reading, Rufus Daniel I	1921–26
Earl of Lytton actg.	1925
Baron Irwin	1926
Viscount Goschen actg.	1929
Willingdon, Earl of	1931
Sir G. F. Stanley actg.	1934
Linlithgow, Victor Alexander	1936–43
Baron Brabourne actg.	1938
Wavell, Viscount	1943
Sir John Colville actg.	1945
Mountbatten, Viscount	1947

(Incomplete list, IO)

VITKEVICH, CAPT. IVAN (VICKOVICH). A Russian agent, or adventurer, of Lithuanian descent who came to Kabul in December 1837 for the purpose of establishing commercial relations with Afghanistan. He had a letter from Count Simonich, the Russian ambassador to Tehran, and an unsigned letter purported to be from the czar. Alexander Burnes (q.v.) was also at Kabul on a similar assignment for the British-Indian government. Consulted by the amir, Burnes told him to receive Vitkevich and inform the British of his objective. Dost Muhammad wanted to regain Peshawar from Sikh control, but Burnes told him that he must surrender all claims to Peshawar and make his peace with the Sikh ruler. Having gotten no help from the British, Amir Dost Muhammad negotiated with Vitkevich for Russian support. Vitkevich was later repudiated by the Russian government and, upon his return to St. Petersburg, committed suicide. The mission aroused fears in Britain that Dost Muhammad would ally himself with Russia, and the decision was made to depose the Afghan ruler. *See* ANGLO-AFGHAN WARS; ALEXANDER BURNES; and DOST MUHAMMAD.

- W -

WAHDAT. *See* **HIZB-I WAHDAT.**

WAPSHARE, LT. GEN. R. Commanded Baluchistan force in the third Anglo-Afghan war. Attacked and captured Spin Boldak at the cost of 18 killed and 40 wounded. British counted 170 bodies and captured 169 of the 600-man garrison.

WATANJAR, MUHAMMAD ASLAM. Held positions as minister of communications, interior, and, finally, defense in Prime Minister Khaliqyar's government of May 1990. A member of the *Khalq* faction of the PDPA, he had a leading role in the coup of Muhammad Daud (1973) and the subsequent Saur Revolt (1978). In both events he rode the lead tank in the assault on the palace, and his tank was placed on a pedestal in the square facing the presidential palace in commemoration of the '78 coup. In April 1978 he and General Abdul Qadir headed the Revolutionary Council, which formed the government until Nur Muhammad Taraki was installed as president.

WEAPONS BAZAAR. *See* **ARMS BAZAAR.**

WYMER, SIR GEORGE PETRE (1788–1868). Served under General Nott at Kandahar during the first Anglo-Afghan war and relieved Qalat-i Ghilzai. Commanded the First Brigade of the Kandahar Force and participated in other engagements.

- Y -

YAQUB KHAN, AMIR MUHAMMAD (Feb. – Oct. 1879). Born about 1849, the son of Amir Shir Ali (q.v.) and his governor of Herat. Yaqub Khan also coveted Kandahar and was greatly disturbed when in 1868 the amir gave his favorite son Abdullah Jan that post. In 1871 Yaqub Khan revolted and marched on Kabul but was forced to retreated to Herat. Amir Shir Ali forgave Yaqub Khan and reappointed him governor of Herat. Yaqub Khan came to Kabul under a promise of safe conduct, which the amir did not keep, holding him in confinement until December 1878, when British troops invaded Afghanistan. Amir Shir Ali fled to northern Afghanistan and appointed Yaqub his regent. The latter proclaimed himself amir in February 1879, after he learned of the sudden death of his father. Hoping to save his throne, Yaqub concluded the Treaty of Gandomak with Britain and accepted a mission under Sir Louis Cavagnari (qq.v.) at Kabul. When the latter was assassinated during an insurrection of troops, the British took control of government powers and Yaqub was forced to abdicate in October 1879. He went to India and lived there until his death in 1923. *See also* ANGLO-AFGHAN WARS; and GANDOMAK, TREATY OF.

YAR MUHAMMAD, WAZIR. Wazir (prime minister) of Prince Kamran (1829–41) who ruled Herat as an independent principality. Yar Muhammad is said to have been an able but cruel man who eventually became the virtual ruler of Herat. He ably withstood Persian attempts to capture Herat and led the defenses in two sieges in 1833 and 1837–38 in which the Russian general, Berovski participated on the Persian side and Eldred Pottinger on the side of the defenders. Yar Muhammad had Prince Kamran assassinated in 1841 and embarked on an ambitious plan of conquest. He allied himself in marriage with Akbar Khan, son of Amir Dost Muhammad (qq.v.), and conquered the western Uzbek khanates of Afghan Turkestan. He died in 1851.

YAZDAN-BAKHSH, MIR. Born in 1790, the son of Mir Wali Beg, the chief of Behsud, Hazarajat. He expelled his older brother, Mir Muhammad Shah, who had become chief of Behsud after his father was assassinated by a minor chief. Mir Yazdan-Bakhsh consolidated his power to become the undisputed chief of the Hazaras (1843–63). Amir Dost Muhammad Khan called him to Kabul and had him imprisoned. He escaped and fled to Bamian, where he was assassinated. *See also* HAZARA; and HAZARAJAT.

- Z -

ZAHIR SHAH, MUHAMMAD. King of Afghanistan, 1933–73. Born on October 15, 1914, the only surviving son of Nadir Shah (q.v.), he was educated in Kabul and in France. He was proclaimed king on November 8, 1933, within a few hours after his father's assassination, and adopted the title *al-Mutawakkil Ala'llah, Pairaw-i Din-i Matin-i Islam,* (Confident in God, Follower of the Firm Religion of Islam). During the early period of his reign (1933–46), the young king reigned while his uncles Muhammad Hashim and Shah Mahmud Ghazi ruled, sucessively holding the powerful position of prime minister. His cousin Muhammad

Daud succeeded as prime minister from 1953 until 1963, when Zahir Shah forced his resignation. In 1964 he promulgated a new constitution that excluded members of the royal family from certain government positions (*see* CONSTITUTIONAL DEVELOPMENT), provided for a bicameral parliament, free elections, a free press, and the formation of political parties. He ushered in a period of unprecedented political tolerance, which was marred only by the intransigence of parliamentary representatives who could not establish a working coalition. The law on political parties was never ratified by the king, but parties were tolerated, although not legally permitted, and numerous groups published their manifestos in privately published newspapers and periodicals. Members of Parliament were elected as independents and not members of a party, but Parliament was stymied with political infighting. Foreign aid from East and West kept flowing into the country, and Kabul experienced considerable growth. However, not all sectors of Afghan society benefited from the economic development. Zahir Shah toured Afghanistan on several occasions and frequently traveled abroad. During one of his trips abroad, his cousin Muhammad Daud staged a coup and established a republican government with himself as president. Zahir Shah abdicated in August 1973 and has since lived in Italy. The impasse in the present war has led to demands by some that the ex-king return to serve as head of an interim government, which would end the war and establish a representative government in Afghanistan.

ZHAWAR, BATTLE OF. Zhawar is a village in Khost Province, south of Parachinar and about six miles from the Pakistan border. It was the major base along the *mujahedin* supply route for attacks on the Kabul garrison at Khost. The importance of the base can be seen from the fact that about 60 percent of *mujahedin* supplies passed through Zhawar and Ali Khel (Yousaf, 1992, 164). The base, built by a Pakistani construction company, had large underground facilities — seven tunnels housed living and medical quarters as well as depots of weapons and other facilities. Generators provided electricity and permitted radio communication. The base was defended by commanders of Khales, Hekmatyar, Nabi, and Gailani (qq.v.). Jalaluddin Haqqani was one of the major commanders. Some 400 men provided close protection and administrative support, and some additional 10,000 *mujahedin* controlled positions between Zhawar and Ali Khel. Because of Zhawar's proximity to the Pakistan border, reinforcements could quickly be obtained. The *mujahedin* had antiaircraft protection, including British Blowpipe missiles (q.v.), three Oerlikon guns, and shoulder-fired SA-7s. Anti-Tank minefields, mortars, and other heavy artillery provided for a formidable defense. Destruction of the base and closure of the supply line had long been an object of the Kabul government, and in early 1986 it started a major offensive. Major General Tanai (q.v.), who was a native of this area, was in tactical command, and Brigadier Abdul Ghafur led the Soviet/Afghan contingent. The Soviets deployed one air assault regiment of the 103rd Guards Airborne Assault Division, and the Afghan forces included units of the 7th and 8th Divisions in Kabul, the 12th Division of Gardez, and the 14th Division at Ghazni and Khost, numbering altogether about 12,000 men. After a slow and fiercely disputed advance, the Soviet/Kabul forces reached Zhawar on April 11, and during the coming week succeeded in isolating the base and destroying the underground structures with laser-guided bombs. A Soviet heliborne commando brigade, landing in an open area, was destroyed to a man. The *mujahedin* fired 13 Blowpipe missiles, without destroying an aircraft (Yousaf, 1992, 171); nevertheless, at the end of the battle, the *mujahedin* claimed to have downed 13 helicopters and aircraft. The Kabul government captured the base but withdrew shortly thereafter, and the *mujahedin* returned within 48 hours. The Kabul government claimed to have killed 2,000 and wounded 4,000, and the *mujahedin* claimed to have captured 100 Afghan soldiers and killed or wounded about 1,500. A *mujahedin* spokesman said only 300 *mujahedin* were killed. The Kabul campaign did not achieve its objective.

CHRONOLOGY

1747	Ahmad Shah crowned, begins 26-year rule during which he united Afghan tribes under the Sadozai dynasty.
1748	Durranis move against Lahore. In November Ahmad Shah begins third invasion of India.
1757	January. Khutba read in name of Ahmad Shah at Delhi, India, and coins are struck in his name, making him suzerain of India.
1761	Afghans defeat Maratha confederacy at Battle of Pani-pat, marking greatest extent of Ahmad Shah's empire, which included Kashmir, the Panjab, and parts of Baluchistan.
1769–70	Ahmad Shah moves into Khorasan.
1772	Oct. 16/17. Ahmad Shah died at Toba Maruf.
1773	Timur Shah begins 20-year rule. Moves capital from Kandahar to Kabul. Campaigns in Sind and Bukhara.
1793	Zaman Shah begins six-year rule.
1798	Britain, fearing Afghan invasions of India, initiates policy of containment, enlisting Persia to keep Afghanistan in check.
1799	Zaman Shah deposed by Mahmud and goes into exile in India.

1803   Shah Shuja deposes Shah Mahmud.

1805   Persian attempt to take Herat fails.

1807   At Tilsit, Alexander II and Napoleon plan joint Russian-French invasion of India through Persia.

1809   British envoy Mountstuart Elphinstone and Shah Shuja sign defensive alliance in first official contact between Afghanistan and a European power. Shah Mahmud defeats Shah Shuja at Gandomak and rules until blinding of Fateh Khan, his Barakzai wazir, causes Barakzai revolt and Shah Mahmud's downfall in 1818.

1816   Persian attempt to capture Herat fails.

1818   Civil war results in division of Afghanistan into virtually independent states until 1835.
                Ranjit Singh seizes Peshawar.

1819   Ranjit Singh conquers Kashmir.

1826   Dost Muhammad, ruler of Ghazni, takes Kabul.

1833   Persians besiege Herat.

1834   Dost Muhammad defeats Shah Shuja and captures Kandahar.

1835   Dost Muhammad begins his first rule of Afghanistan.

1837   Lord Auckland appointed governor general.
                Akbar Khan, son of Dost Muhammad, defeats Sikhs at Jamrud.
                Aug. Eldred Pottinger arrives at Herat.
                Sept. 20. Alexander Burnes arrives in Kabul on a diplomatic mission for British.
                Nov. 23. Commencement of second siege of Herat.

| 1837 | Dec. 19. Ivan Vitkevich (Witkiwicz), emissary from Russia, arrives in Kabul. |

1838   Apr. 26. Burnes leaves Kabul.
            June 26. Tripartite treaty signed by Ranjit Singh, the British East India Company, and Shah Shuja to restore the latter to the Afghan throne.
            Sept. 9. Siege of Herat raised.
            Oct. 1. British break relations with Dost Muhammad and declare war.

1839   **First Anglo-Afghan War**
            Jan. 14. "Army of the Indus" enters Sind.
            Jan. 21. Shah Shuja's contingent at Shikarpur.
            Feb. 20. Cotton reaches Shikarpur.
            Mar. 26. Cotton reaches Quetta.
            Apr. 6. Sir John Keane assumes command.
            Apr. 25. Force arrives at Kandahar.
            July 21. Arrival at Ghazni.
            July 22. Afghan Ghazis attack.
            July 23. British capture Ghazni.
            Aug. 2. Amir Dost Muhammad flees.
            Aug. 7. Kabul occupied by the "Army of the Indus."
            Sept. 3. Prince Timur arrives at Kabul.
            Sept. 18. Part of British-Indian army leaves Kabul.
            Oct. 2. Orders received for the greater part of Bengal Division to remain in Afghanistan.
            Oct. 15. Bengal troops begin return march to India.
            Oct. 18. Bombay troops begin return march to India.

1840   Mar. 13. News reaches Kabul of the failure of the Russian expedition to Khiva.
            May 7–17. Anderson moves against Ghilzais.
            June. British disaster a Bajgah.
            Aug. Dost Muhammad escapes from Bukhara.
            Aug. 30. Attack on Bajgah.
            Sept. Rising in Afghan Turkestan.
            Sept. 14. Dennis reinforces Bamian.
            Sept. 18. Defeat of Uzbeks near Bamian.
            Oct. 3. Sale attacks Julga.

1840   Oct. 11. Dost Muhammad reaches Ghorband.

Oct. 11. Withdrawal of Bamian detachment.

Nov. 2. Action at Parwan Darra.

Nov. 2. Surrender of Amir Dost Muhammad.

Nov. 12. Dost Muhammad leaves for India.

Nov. The court moves to Jalalabad for the winter.

1841   Jan. 3. Farrington's action near Kandahar.

Jan. Todd's mission leaves Herat.

Apr. 7. Action near Kalat-i Ghilzai.

May. Wymer's action at Asiya-i Ilmi.

July 3. Action at the Helmand.

Aug. 5. Chamber's expedition against the Ghilzais.

Aug. 17. Action at Girishk.

Sept. Expedition to Tarin and Derawat.

Sept. Capture of Akram Khan.

Oct. Nott returns to Kandahar.

Oct. 9. Attack on Monteith's camp at Butkhak.

Oct. 12. Affair of Khurd-Kabul. March to Gandomak.

Nov. 2. Assassination of Burnes.

Nov. 2. Shelton arrives at the Bala Hisar.

Nov. 3. Arrival of the 37th Native Infantry at Kabul.

Nov. 3. Macnaghten writes to recall Sale's force and the troops returning to India.

Nov. 3. Abandonment of Mackenzie's post.

Nov. 4. Fort containing commissariat stores abandoned.

Nov. 6. Capture of Muhammad Sharif's fort.

Nov. 6. Action by Anderson's Horse.

Nov. 7. Return of Akbar Khan to Bamian.

Nov. 9. Shelton returns to cantonments.

Nov. 10. Affair of Rikab Bashi's fort.

Nov. 10. News of Kabul outbreak reaches Sale.

Nov. 11. March to Jalalabad commenced.

Nov. 12. Rearguard action.

Nov. 12. Arrival at Jalalabad.

Nov. 13. Fighting begins at Bemaru Hills.

Nov. 15. Arrival of Pottinger after Charikar defeat.

Nov. 16. First action at Jalalabad.

1841	Nov. 18. Macnaghten recommends holding out.
	Nov. 23. Second fight on the Bemaru Hills.
	Nov. 25. Macnaghten interviews the chiefs.
	Nov. Massacre at Ghazni and capitulation.
	Dec. 1. Second action at Jalalabad.
	Dec. 6. Abandonment of Muhammad Sharif's fort.
	Dec. 8. Macnaghten consults Elphinstone on question of retreat. Discussion of treaty. Return to Kandahar of Maclaren's brigade.
	Dec. 13. Evacuation of Bala Hisar.
	Dec. 22. Orders issued for the evacuation of Ghazni, Kandahar, and Jalalabad.
	Dec. 23. Assassination of Macnaghten.
	Dec. 26. Encouraging letters from Jalalabad.
	Dec. Mutiny of *Janbaz* at Kandahar.
1842	Treaty ratified.
	Jan. 4. First brigade of the Relief Force crosses the Sutlej.
	Jan. 6. Retreat from Kabul commences.
	Jan. 7. Skinner proceeds to Akbar with truce flag.
	Jan. 8. Sale receives letter from Pottinger.
	Jan. 8. Kabul force marches to Tezin.
	Jan. 9. Orders received at Jalalabad for the evacuation. The reply.
	Jan. 12. Action at Arghandab. The end of the Kabul force.
	Jan. 13. British last stand at Jagdalak.
	Jan. 13. Arrival of Brydon at Jalalabad.
	Jan. 26. Sale convenes council of war.
	Feb. 10. Governor general issues order to Relief force.
	Feb. 13. Earthquake at Jalalabad.
	Feb. 19. British disaster at Ali Masjid.
	Feb. 21. Order for evacuation reaches Kabul.
	Feb. 23. Evacuation of Ali Masjid.
	Mar. 7. Action near Kandahar.
	Mar. 10. Attack on Kandahar.
	Mar. 25. Wymer's action near Kandahar.
	Mar. 28. England's defeat at Haikalzai.
	Mar. 31. Pollock reaches Jamrud.

1842	Apr. 1. Death of Shah Shuja.
	Apr. 5. General Pollock forced the Khaibar Pass.
	Apr. 7. Battle at Jalalabad.
	Apr. 25. King Shaha Shuja assassinated at Kabul.
	Apr. 30. Passage of the Khojak.
	May. Pollock at Jalalabad. Relief of Qalat-i Ghilzai. Akbar Khan captures Bala Hisar.
	May 29. Action near Kandahar.
	June. Operations in Shinwari valley.
	June-Oct. Fath Jang becomes amir.
	Aug. 7. Evacuation of Kandahar.
	Aug. 20. Pollock sets out from Jalalabad. Action near Gandomak.
	Aug. 28. Cavalry action near Mukur.
	Aug. 30. Battle of Karabagh.
	Sept. 5. British reenter Ghazni.
	Sept. 8. Action in Jagdalak Pass.
	Sept. 12. Action at Sayyidabad.
	Sept. Progress of M'Caskill's Division.
	Sept. 13. Action at Tezin.
	Sept. 15. Pollock arrives at Kabul.
	Sept. 19. Nott arrives at Kabul.
	Sept. 29. Action at Istalif.
	Oct. 12. British force leaves Kabul.
	Oct. 14. Action at Haft Kotal.
	Dec. 17. British forces arrive at Ferozpur.
	End of First Anglo-Afghan War
	Dec. Most Muhammad returns to Kabul and rules for 21 years.
1855	Treaty of Peshawar reopens diplomatic relations between Britain and Afghanistan.
1856	Oct. Persians capture Herat.
1857	Jan. Anglo-Afghan Treaty signed in Peshawar provides subsidy for Dost Muhammad.

1863	Dost Muhammad takes Herat and dies. Shir Ali ascends Afghan throne. During next two years Shir Ali puts down revolts by half brothers, Azim and Afzal, and his brother Muhammad Amin. Abdur Rahman and his uncle Azim attack Kabul and liberate Afzal, Abdur Rahman's father.
1866	Afzal becomes amir. Shir Ali flees to Kandahar.
1867	Afzal dies.
1868	Azim becomes amir.
1869	Shir Ali defeats Azim. Abdur Rahman goes into exile in Russia. British recognize Shir Ali as amir but refuse to recognize his son, Abdullah Jan, as successor. March. Ambala Conference held between Amir Shir Ali and Lord Mayo, viceroy of India.
1872	In Granville-Gortchakoff Agreement, Russia assures Britain that Afghanistan is outside Russia's sphere of influence. British commission marks Sistan boundary.
1873	Abdullah Jan named heir to Afghan throne. Shir Ali's oldest son, Yakub Khan, revolts, flees to Herat. Russia takes Khiva.
1874	Yakub Khan imprisoned in Kabul.
1876	British occupy Quetta.
1878	July 22. Russian mission under General Stolietoff arrives in Kabul. **Second Anglo-Afghan War** Sept. 21. General Faiz Muhammad, commander of Ali Masjid, denies the British envoy, General Sir Neville Chamberlain, passage into Afghanistan. Amir Shir Ali is given an ultimatum to apologize for this "insult" and to meet certain conditions lest he be

1878   treated as an enemy. Lord Lytton denounces alliance
                   with Amir Dost Muhammad.
                   Nov. Colonel Grodekoff arrives in Herat from
                   Samarkand.
                   Nov. 21. Sir Samuel Brown attacks the fort of Ali
                   Masjid, General Roberts crosses the frontier at Thal,
                   and an advance guard of General Donald Steward
                   marches from Quetta against Kandahar.
                   Nov. 22. Fort Ali Masjid is captured.
                   Dec. 2. General Roberts defeats an Afghan force at
                   the Paiwar Kotal Pass.
                   Dec. 20. General Brown occupies Jalalabad.
                   Dec. 23. Amir Shir Ali leaves Kabul and appoints his
                   son Yaqub Khan governor of Kabul.

1879   Jan. 2 – 30. General Roberts moves into the Khost
                   valley.
                   Jan. 12. General Steward occupies Kandahar and
                   takes Qalat-i Ghilzai on January 21.
                   Feb. 21. Amir Shir Ali dies at Mazar-i Sharif, Yaqub
                   Khan proclaimed king.
                   Apr. 2. General Charles Gough defeats the Khugianis
                   at Fathabad.
                   May 26. Treaty of Gandomak signed by Sir Louis
                   Cavagnari and Amir Yaqub Khan.
                   July 24. Cavagnari arrives in Kabul to assume post of
                   British envoy to amir.
                   Sept. 3. Cavagnari and his staff are killed.
                   Sept. 11. Brigadier General Massey occupies the
                   Shuturgardan Pass with the advance guard of General
                   Roberts's force.
                   Oct. 6. General Roberts's "Avenging Army" wins
                   Battle of Charasia.
                   Oct. 12. General Roberts occupies Kabul.
                   Oct. 14 – 19. Afghan forces unsuccessfully attack
                   British troops as Ali Khel and Shuturgardan.
                   Oct. 16. Explosion of the ammunition depot at Bala
                   Hisar.
                   Oct. 28. Amir Yaqub abdicates, British take over the
                   government of Kabul.

1879   Dec. 10. General Macpherson defeats Kohistani force at Karez Mir.

Dec. 11. General Massey fails in attack on Muhammad Jan and his forces advancing from Ghazni.

Dec. 12. Macpherson's brigade under Colonel Money fails in attack on Takht-i Shah.

Dec. 13. General Baker drives Afghans from Takht-i Shah.

Dec. 14. General Baker driven from Asmai hills with losses. General Roberts abandons Bala Hisar and Kabul city and stations his forces at Sherpur.

Dec. 15 – 22. Muhammad Jan cuts Roberts's communications and lays siege to Sherpur.

Dec. 23. Muhammad Jan's forces are defeated and Roberts returns to Bala Hisar the next day.

1880   Apr. 1. Sir Donald Steward begins his march from Kandahar to Kabul.

Apr. 19. Battle of Ahmad Khel.

Apr. 21. Steward defeats Afghan forces at Ghazni.

May 2. Steward arrives at Kabul.

June 15 (about). Sardar Ayub Khan moves from Herat against Kandahar.

July 10. A brigade under General Burrows moves against Ayub.

July 22. Sardar Abdur Rahman recognized by Britain as Amir of Kabul and its Dependencies.

July 27. General Burrows is totally defeated in Battle of Maiwand and the remnant of his brigade forced to seek security in Kandahar.

Aug. 6. Ayub Khan invests Kandahar.

Aug. 8. General Roberts begins march from Kabul to Kandahar.

Aug. 11. General Steward withdraws from Kabul and Amir Abdur Rahman moves in.

Aug. 16. Sortie of the British garrison of Kandahar is repulsed with great losses.

Aug. 31. Sir Roberts arrives at Kandahar and on Sept. 1 defeats Ayub Khan at Baba Wali Kotal.

1880   Sept. 9. British troops return to India from the Paiwar
                       Kotal and the Kurram valley and begin withdrawal
                       from Jalalabad.

1881   Apr. 21. British troops withdraw from Kandahar.
                       End of Second Anglo-Afghan War.

1882   Muslim agent appointed to represent British in Kabul.

1883   Russia occupies Tejend oasis. Britain annexes Quetta
                       district. Abdur Rahman occupies Shignan and
                       Roshan. Britain grants Abdur Rahman subsidy of 12
                       lakhs (1,200,000) rupees.

1884   Britain and Russia open negotiations on northern
                       boundary of Afghanistan. Sir Peter Lumsden leads
                       British mission to Herat. British again start building
                       Quetta railroad. Russians occupy Pul-i-Khatun.

1885   Russians occupy Zulfikar and Akrobat and take
                       Panjdeh.

1886   British construct Bolan railway to Quetta.
                       Oct. British boundary mission returns to India by way
                       of Kabul.

1887   Russia occupies Karki. Britain and Russia make final
                       settlement and demarcation of Afghan-Russian
                       frontier. Ayub Khan escapes from Persia, but
                       rebellion in Afghanistan fails and he surrenders at
                       Mashhad and is exiled to India.

1888   Jan. British extend Quetta railway to Kila Abdullah.
                       July. Ishaq Khan, son of Azim, revolts in Turkestan,
                       retreats to Samarkand.

1891   Abdur Rahman introduces oath of allegiance to the
                       Koran among his councillors.

1892   Uprising of Hazaras suppressed.

1893   Nov. 12. Afghanistan and Britain sign Durand
                Agreement, which sets eastern and southern borders.
                British increase Amir Abdur Rahman's subsidy by six
                lakhs and permit Afghanistan to import munitions.
                British occupy New Chaman as railway terminus.

1895   Abdur Rahman abolishes slavery in Afghanistan.
                Abdur Rahman accepts oaths of allegiance from
                whole state of Afghanistan and adopts title *Zia ul-
                Millat wa ud-Din*. Sardar Nasrullah, second son of
                Abdur Rahman, visits England. Russia and Britain
                agree on Wakhan border.

1896   Kafiristan brought under Afghan control by Amir
                Abdur Rahman, renamed Nuristan.

1900   Russia presses for direct Afghan-Russian relations
                along northern Afghan border in memorandum of
                Feb. 6 to Britain.

1901   Oct. 1. Abdur Rahman dies.
                Oct. 3. Habibullah proclaimed amir, rules for 18
                years.

1902   British envoy, Sir Henry Dobbs, supervises reerection
                of boundary pillars on Afghan-Russian border during
                1902 and 1903.

1903   A. H. McMahon leads British mission in demarcating
                Sistan boundary. Habibia College, first secular high
                school, opened in Kabul. British begin construction of
                Quetta-Nushki railroad.

1905   British agreements of 1880 and 1893 with Abdur
                Rahman confirmed by treaty with Amir Habibullah.

1906   Shah of Iran rejects McMahon arbitration award.

1907   Jan. Habibullah visits India.

1907	Aug. 31. Britain and Russia sign convention concerning spheres of influence in Afghanistan, Persia, and Tibet.
1909	Plot on Amir Habibullah's life fails.
1910	First telephone line in Afghanistan built between Kabul and Jalalabad.
1914	General Muhammad Nadir Khan named commander in chief of the Afghan army. Habibullah declares Afghanistan's neutrality in World War I.
1915	Sept. Hentig-Niedermayer mission from Germany arrives in Kabul and remains for nine months.
1919	Feb. 20. Amir Habibullah assassinated in Laghman. Nasrullah Khan named amir in Jalalabad.

1919

Feb. 20. Amir Habibullah assassinated in Laghman. Nasrullah Khan named amir in Jalalabad.
Feb. 25. Amanullah proclaimed amir in Kabul.
Feb. 28. Nasrullah arrested.
Mar. 3. Amanullah suggests new Anglo-Afghan agreement to viceroy of India.
Apr. 13. Amanullah proclaimed Afghanistan independent.
May 1. Saleh Muhammad Khan, the commander in chief, moves to the Indian border with two companies of infantry and two guns, for the ostensible purpose of inspecting the border.
Beginning of Third Anglo-Afghan War
May 3. An escort of British Khaibar Rifles accompanying a caravan was stopped in the disputed area between Landi Khana and Torkham.
May 4. Afghan uniformed troops occupied Bagh and began to cut the water supply to Landi Kotal. A *fatwa* proclaiming *jihad*.
May 7. Afghan forces at Bagh strengthened and Nadir Khan moves to Khost.
May 8. Peshawar uprising suppressed.
May 9. First Battle of Bagh, British forces stopped.
May 11. Second Battle of Bagh.

1919   May 12. On the Chitral front, Afghan troops occupy
                       Arnawai.
                       May 23. Afghans driven from Arnawai.
                       May 13. British occupy Dakka.
                       May 24. Kabul bombed by Royal Air Force.
                       May 21. General Nadir Khan crosses Indo-Afghan
                       boundary, marches on Thal. Decision made to
                       evacuate the militia posts on the Waziristan front.
                       May 27. Battle of Spin Boldak.
                       May 28. Wali Muhammad Khan arrives in Tashkent
                       on way to Moscow and Europe as Amanullah's envoy.
                       Jun. 1. General Dyer occupies Thal.
                       June 2. Armistice.
                       Aug. 8. Preliminary Anglo-Afghan Treaty signed at
                       Rawalpindi peace conference.
                       End of Third Anglo-Afghan War
                       Sept. Soviet envoy arrives in Kabul.
                       Oct. 10. Muhammad Wali Khan arrives in Moscow.

1920   Apr. 17. Mussoorie Conference opens. Mahmud
                       Tarzi represents Afghanistan and Henry Dobbs,
                       Britain.
                       July 18. Mussoorie Conference ends.

1921   Amir of Bukhara seeks asylum in Afghanistan.
                       Jan. 20. Kabul conference between Afghanistan and
                       Britain opens.
                       Feb. 28. Treaty of Friendship signed by Afghanistan
                       and the Soviet Union.
                       Mar. 1. Treaty of Friendship signed by Afghanistan
                       and Turkey.
                       May 30. Fundamental law of government of
                       Afghanistan goes into force.
                       June 3. Treaty of Friendship signed by Afghanistan
                       and Italy.
                       June 22. Treaty of Friendship signed by Afghanistan
                       and Persia.
                       Dec. 2. Kabul Conference ends. Britain recognizes
                       Afghanistan as independent in internal and external

1921   relations. Diplomatic relations established between
              the two states.

1922   Apr. 28. Treaty establishes diplomatic and
              commercial relations between France and
              Afghanistan.
              Sept. 9. Agreement gives France rights to conduct
              archaeological excavations in Afghanistan.

1923   Apr. 10. First constitution adopted.
              June 5. British-Afghan trade convention signed.
              Sept. French legation opened in Afghanistan.
              Oct. Criminal code adopted.
              Nov. Statute governing marriage issued.
              Dec. Statute on civil servants confirmed.
              Dec. German legation opened in Afghanistan.

1924   Jan. Amani (Najat) high school founded. First
              hospital for women and children opened in Kabul.
              May. Uprising of tribes in Khost.

1925   Khost rebellion defeated.

1926   Afghani introduced as new monetary unit. Ten
              afghanis equal 11 Kabuli rupees.
              Mar. 3. Treaty of Friendship signed by Afghanistan
              and Germany.
              June 7. Amanullah adopts title of king.
              Aug. 15. Soviet Union agrees to cede Urta Tagai
              Islands in Amu River to Afghanistan.
              Aug. 31. Treaty of neutrality and mutual non-
              aggression signed by Afghanistan and Soviet Union.

1927   *Anis* founded as fortnightly, later major national daily,
              newspaper.
              Nov. 27. Treaty of neutrality and mutual
              nonaggression signed by Afghanistan and Persia.
              Dec. 1927. King Amanullah visits India, Egypt, and
              Europe.

1928	May 25. Treaty of Friendship and Collaboration signed by Afghanistan and Turkey.
	July. King Amanullah returns to Afghanistan.
	July – Sept. Amanullah introduces reforms in dress.
	Nov. Uprising of Shinwari near Jalalabad.
	Dec. Habibullah Kalakani leads uprising in Kohistan.
1929	*Islah* newspaper founded.
	Jan. 14. Amanullah renounces throne. His brother, Inayatullah, abdicates after three days.
	Jan. 18. Habibullah Kalakani proclaimed amir.
	Oct. 14. Kabul seized by Nadir Khan's troops.
	Oct. 17. Nadir Khan proclaimed king.
	Nov. 3. Habibullah Kalakani caught and shot.
1930	May. Nadir Shah confirms validity of 1921 and 1923 Anglo-Afghan Agreements and other international treaties.
	Sept. 20. Nadir Shah confirms statute governing elections of members of National Assembly.
1931	June 24. New treaty of neutrality and mutual nonaggression signed by Afghanistan and Soviet Union.
	July. Nadir Shah opens National Assembly session.
	Oct. 31. New constitution confirmed by Nadir Shah.
1932	Medical school founded and other schools closed by Habibullah Kalakani reopened.
	May 5. Treaty of Friendship signed by Afghanistan and Saudi Arabia.
	Aug. 24. Statute setting up new administrative divisions issued. Five major and four minor provinces formed.
	Oct. Uprising begins in Khost.
	Nov. 8. Ghulam Nabi executed on charge of complicity in Dari Khel Ghilzai revolt.
1933	Road over Shibar Pass to north completed.

1933   June 6. Muhammad Aziz, Afghan minister to
                             Germany, assassinated in Berlin.
                             Nov. 8. Nadir Shah assassinated. His son,
                             Muhammad Zahir, becomes king, and brother of
                             Nadir Shah, Muhammad Hashim, becomes prime
                             minister.

1934   Feb. 16. Zahir Shah orders general election for
                             National Assembly.
                             Aug. 21. The United States formally recognizes
                             Afghanistan.
                             Sept. 25. Afghanistan joins the League of Nations.

1935   April–May. W. H. Hornibrook accredited as non-
                             resident American minister to Kabul.
                             May. Turkey arbitrates Afghanistan's boundary
                             dispute with Persia.
                             June 8. National Assembly session opened by Zahir
                             Shah.
                             Sept. Mohmand uprising.

1936   March. Treaty on commerce and noninterference
                             signed by Afghanistan and Soviet Union.
                             Mar. 26. Treaty of Friendship signed by Afghanistan
                             and United States.

1937   Lufthansa starts weekly service between Berlin and
                             Kabul; first regular air link between Afghanistan and
                             Europe.
                             Turkish military mission arrived in Kabul.
                             July 7. Treaty of Saadabad signed by Afghanistan,
                             Iran, Iraq, and Turkey.

1938   May. Afghan air force expanded by purchase of
                             planes from Italy and Britain. Officers sent to Britain,
                             Soviet Union, and Italy for training. Arms bought
                             from Britain and Czechoslovakia.

1939   Sept. 3. Beginning of World War II and Afghan
                             armed forces mobilized as precautionary measure.

1940	Jan. 12. All men over 17 obliged to do national service. Special taxes imposed to pay for arms, build radio station. Radio Kabul gets 20-kilowatt medium-wave transmitter. July 29. Trade agreement by Afghanistan and Soviet Union signed. Aug. 17. Zahir Shah declares Afghanistan's neutrality in World War II in statement to National Assembly.
1941	July 28. Afghanistan reaffirms its neutrality in World War II. Oct. 19. Afghanistan agrees to expel German and Italian residents at demand of Britain and the Soviet Union.
1942	Apr. 27. Cornelius van Engert, consul general in Beirut, named resident U.S. minister to Afghanistan. Nov. 5. Afghanistan reaffirms neutrality in World War II.
1943	May 16. Afghan consulate opened in New York. June 5. Abdul Husain Aziz, first Afghan minister to United States, presents credentials. Dec. 28. Saadabad Pact reported automatically renewed after five years.
1944	Mar. 5. Treaty of Friendship signed by Afghanistan and China.
1946	Kabul University established by combining already existing faculties, such as medicine and law. Jan. 22. King Zahir orders election of deputies for session of National Assembly to meet on April 21. May 9. Muhammad Hashem Khan resigns as prime minister, citing poor health as reason. Mahmud Khan, minister of defense, asked to form new government. June 13. Boundary treaty signed with Soviet Union. Soviet Union gets Kushka River water rights.

1946   Nov. 9. United Nations General Assembly approves
                entry of Afghanistan.
                Nov. 19. Abdul Husain Aziz, Afghanistan's first
                representative to the United Nations, takes seat.

1947   Apr. 24. Afghan delegation arrives in Tashkent to
                start demarcation of Afghan-Soviet border.
                June 13. Afghanistan sends note to British and Indian
                governments saying that inhabitants of region
                between Afghan-Indian border and Indus River are
                Afghans and must decide themselves whether to join
                Afghanistan, Pakistan, or India or become inde-
                pendent.
                July 3. Britain replies it holds to the Treaty of 1921 by
                which boundary was recognized by both nations and
                asks Afghanistan to abstain from any act of inter-
                vention on northwest frontier at time of transfer of
                powers to Indian government.
                July 10. Afghanistan reiterates views on Pashtuns in
                second note to Britain.
                July 26. Prime Minister Mahmud arrives in London.
                Aug. 3. Prime Minister Mahmud arrives in New York
                City.
                Sept. 18. Iran says diversion of Helmand waters in
                Afghanistan causes crop failures in Sistan.
                Sept. 30. Afghanistan casts only vote against admit-
                ting Pakistan to the United Nations on grounds that
                Pashtuns have not had fair plebiscite.

1948   Apr. 1. Muhammad Naim named Afghan ambassador
                to the United States.
                Apr. 23. Sir Giles Squire named British ambassador
                to Afghanistan.
                May 6. Faiz Muhammad named Afghan ambassador
                to Britain.
                June 5. U. S. legation elevated to status of embassy.
                Ely E. Palmer presents credentials as first U.S. am-
                bassador.
                June 16. Pakistan arrests Abdul Ghaffar Khan and
                other *Khuda-i Khetmatgar* leaders. Afghanistan

1948   begins press and radio campaign for independent Pashtunistan.

Sept. 29. Afghan-Soviet mission completes demarcation of border. Agreement signed fixing revised boundary.

1949   Mar. 24. Foreign ministry says statement of Pakistani governor general that tribal territory is integral part of Pakistan is contrary to pledges of Jinnah in 1948.

Apr. 2. Chargé d'affaires in Karachi recalled after Pakistani bombing in Waziristan.

Apr. 20. Louis G. Dryfus named U.S. ambassador to Afghanistan.

June 4. Afghanistan restricts movement of vehicles along border with Pakistan.

June 12. Pakistani plane bombs Moghalgai (inside Afghan territory), killing 23.

June 20. Alfred Gardener named British ambassador to Afghanistan.

June 30. Afghan National Assembly opens 7th Session, known as "Liberal Assembly."

July 11. Pakistani foreign minister says Pakistan will discuss economic cooperation with Afghanistan, but rejects Afghanistan's claims to tribal territory.

July 26. Afghan National Assembly repudiates treaties with Britain regarding tribal territory.

1950   Jan. 4. Treaty of peace and friendship signed by Afghanistan and India.

Jan. 13. Afghanistan recognizes the People's Republic of China.

Mar. 8. Zahir Shah begins visit to Europe.

May 26. Recall of Pakistan embassy staff member for violating Afghan laws requested by Afghanistan.

July 18. Four-year trade agreement signed by Afghanistan and Soviet Union.

Oct. 14. New cabinet announced by Prime Minister Shah Mahmud.

1951   Feb. 9. Agreement for technical assistance under
                    Point Four program signed by Afghanistan and the
                    United States.
                    Mar. 19. George R. Merrell appointed U.S.
                    ambassador to Afghanistan.
                    Apr. 25. Prime Minister Shah Mahmud arrives in
                    United States.
                    May 28. The United Nations assists in drilling explor-
                    atory oil wells in the north.

1952   Jan. 15. United States suspends economic and
                    technical aid to Afghanistan until bilateral agreement
                    under the Mutual Security Act is signed.
                    Sept. 23. Soviet note expressing concern over
                    activities of United Nations' technical assistance
                    experts in areas near Afghan-Soviet border rejected
                    by Afghan government.

1953   Jan. 8. United States extends loan of $1.5 million for
                    emergency purchase of wheat and flour from the
                    United States.
                    Mar. 18. Sultan Muhammad named foreign minister
                    to succeed Ali Muhammad, who remains deputy
                    prime minister.
                    Sept. 6. Shah Mahmud resigns as prime minister,
                    citing poor health. Zahir Shah asks cousin,
                    Muhammad Daud, present defense and interior
                    minister, to form new cabinet.
                    Sept. 20. Prime Minister Daud announces cabinet
                    members.
                    Oct. 26. Muhammad Hashem, prime minister from
                    1929 to 1946, dies.
                    Nov. United States Export-Import Bank makes loan
                    of $18.5 million for development of Helmand valley.
                    Dec. 30. Prime Minister Daud describes proposed
                    U.S. military aid to Pakistan as a "grave danger to
                    security and peace of Afghanistan."

1954

Jan. 27. Soviet Union makes loan of $3.5 million for construction of two grain mills and two silos. Soviet technicians to help carry out projects.

Sept. 17. Foreign Minister Naim arrives in Karachi to continue talks begun in Kabul on improving relations between Afghanistan and Pakistan.

Nov. 7. Foreign Minister Naim says Pashtunistan issue is not question of territorial adjustment but of giving Pashtuns an opportunity to express their wishes.

1955

Jan. 14. Former Prime Minister Shah Mahmud meets Pakistan prime minister.

Jan. 19. Afghanistan and the People's Republic of China establish diplomatic relations at embassy level.

Jan. 25. Legislation strengthening armed forces approved by upper house of Parliament.

Mar. 29. Prime Minister Daud warns Pakistan of "grave consequences" if Pashtun areas of the North-West Frontier Province are included in unified West Pakistan.

Mar. 30. Demonstrators march on Pakistani embassy and ambassador's residence in Kabul.

Mar. 31. Demonstrators march on Pakistani consulate in Kandahar.

Apr. 1. Demonstrators march on Pakistani consulate in Jalalabad. Afghan consulate in Peshawar attacked.

Apr. 4. Britain, Turkey, and United States protest attack on Pakistan embassy in Kabul.

Apr. 12. Pakistan rejects Afghan replies to its protests, evacuates families of diplomats and nationals, closes Jalalabad consulate.

Apr. 18. Foreign Minister Naim goes to Bandung Conference.

Apr. 29. Colonel Gamal Abdul Nasser, prime minister of Egypt, visits Afghanistan.

Afghanistan says it is willing to apologize, pay compensation for damage, and make amends for 1955 the insult to Pakistani flag if similar amends are made for the insult to its flag.

1955   May 1. Pakistan demands closing of all Afghan consulates in Pakistan, says it will close its consulates in Afghanistan.

May 4. Afghanistan mobilizes troops.

May 13. Afghanistan and Pakistan accept Saudi Arabian offer of mediation.

June 21. Five-year agreement signed with Soviet Union allowing goods of each nation free transit across territory of other.

June 28. Saudi Arabian mediator announces his proposals have been rejected.

July 5. Thin Kuo Yu, ambassador to Afghanistan from the People's Republic of China, presents credentials.

July 14. Afghanistan tells Pakistan it will be held responsible for any loss or damage to goods held up in transit to Kabul or Quetta.

July 14. Afghanistan becomes member of International Monetary Fund and International Bank.

July 28. State of emergency ended; Afghan army demobilized.

Aug. 14. Postal agreement signed by Afghanistan and Soviet Union.

Aug. 17. India agrees to export four Dakota planes to Afghanistan for internal service.

Sept. 9. Foreign Minister Naim and Pakistan ambassador negotiate agreement to stop hostile propaganda.

Sept. 13. Pakistan flag raised over Pakistani embassy in Kabul.

Sept. 15. Afghan flag raised over consulate in Peshawar.

Oct. 11. Afghan leaders request meeting with Pakistani leaders on condition one-unit act can be postponed. Pakistan says postponement is impossible.

Oct. 17. Afghanistan recalls ambassador from Karachi.

Oct. 18. Pakistan recalls ambassador from Kabul.

Nov. 8. Afghanistan protests further restrictions by Pakistan on transit of goods to Afghanistan.

1955

Nov. 20. During five-day session, Loya Jirgah gives its approval to resolutions calling for plebiscite to decide future of Pashtun area disputed with Pakistan, recommending government find means to reestablish balance of power upset by Pakistan's decision to accept arms from the United States, and refusing to recognize Pashtunistan as part of Pakistan.

Dec. 6. Defense Minister Muhammad Arif resigns.

Dec. 15–18. Soviet Prime Minister Bulganin and Soviet Communist Party Secretary Khrushchev make official visit to Kabul.

Dec. 16. Soviet Union backs Afghanistan in Pashtunistan dispute.

Dec. 18. Three agreements signed by Afghanistan and Soviet Union: a loan of $100 million, a protocol extending 1931 treaty of neutrality and nonaggression, a statement of foreign policy matters. Foreign Minister Naim says agreements do not weaken Afghan determination to remain neutral.

Dec. 21. United States confirms it has offered to mediate Pashtunistan dispute between Afghanistan and Pakistan.

1956

Jan. 8. Afghan consul in Quetta recalled at request of Pakistan. Pakistan military attaché requested to leave Afghanistan.

Jan. 24. Soviet economic delegation begins talks with Afghan government on use of $100 million loan.

Jan. 30. Soviet Union presents Ilyushin 14 to Zahir Shah.

Feb. 18. Technical cooperation agreement signed by Afghanistan and the United States for 1956.

Mar. 1. Technical assistance agreement signed by Afghanistan and the Soviet Union for building of hydroelectric plants, highway through Hindu Kush, air fields, motor repair shop, and reservoirs.

Mar. 6. SEATO powers declare region up to Durand Line is Pakistani territory and within treaty area.

1956   Mar. 21. Afghanistan formally protests SEATO
              decision to uphold Durand Line as Afghan-Pakistani
              border.

              Mar. 26. United States International Cooperation Ad-
              ministration announces grant of $997,000 to Teachers
              College of Columbia University to set up English
              language program for Afghan secondary schools and
              train English teachers.

              Mar. 31. Gift of 15 buses and equipment for 100-bed
              hospital to Kabul municipality from Soviet Union
              arrives.

              Apr. 4–18. Afghan military mission visits Czecho-
              slovakia.

              June 27. Agreement for $14 million to develop
              Afghan civil aviation signed by Afghanistan and the
              United States.

              July 26. Soviet Union agrees to carry out Nangarhar
              irrigation project.

              Aug. 7–11. Pakistan President Iskander Mirza visits
              Kabul.

              Aug. 25. Prime Minister Daud announces military
              arms agreements with Czechoslovakia and Soviet
              Union.

              Sept. 12. Pan American Airlines to supervise pilot
              and ground crew training of Ariana Afghan Airlines.
              A $2.5 million contract to be part of $14 million
              program announced earlier, which also includes $5.5
              million for Kandahar airport.

              Sept. 24. Air service to Iran inaugurated.

              Sept. 27. First installment of arms from Soviet Union
              and Czechoslovakia arrives.

              Oct. 17–30. Prime Minister Daud visits Soviet Union.

              Oct. 28. Afghan air force receives 11 jet planes from
              Soviet Union.

              Nov. 24. Prime Minister Daud discusses Pashtunistan
              question with Pakistani leaders during visit to
              Karachi.

1957

Jan. 8. Trade protocol signed with Soviet Union.

Jan. 19–23. Chou En-lai, prime minister of the People's Republic of China, visits Afghanistan.

Jan. 27. M. C. Gillett named British ambassador to Afghanistan.

Feb. 10. Radio Moscow inaugurates Pashto program.

Apr. 27. Agreement for increased aid from Czechoslovakia signed by Afghanistan.

June 8–11. Pakistani Prime Minister Suhrawardy visits Kabul. Afghanistan and Pakistan agree to restore diplomatic relations.

June 30. United States makes loan of $5,750,000 for Helmand Valley Authority and $2,860,000 for building roads and training personnel.

July 17–31. Communiqué says Soviet Union will aid Afghanistan in prospecting for oil, that a special commission to regulate boundary questions will be created, and that an agreement was reached regarding use of waterways crossing the two countries.

Aug. 31. Foreign Minister Naim says Afghanistan to receive about $25 million in military assistance under arms agreement signed with Soviet Union in 1956.

Oct. 22. Prime Minister Daud begins visit to the People's Republic of China.

Dec. 21. Andrei Gromyko, Soviet foreign minister, meets Afghan mission in Moscow to negotiate new frontier agreement.

1958

Jan. 8. Soviet Union agrees to survey oil deposits in Afghanistan.

Jan. 18. Treaty regulating Afghan-Soviet border signed by Afghanistan and Soviet Union.

Feb. 1–5. Zahir Shah visits Pakistan.

Feb. 11–26. Zahir Shah arrives in India for two-week visit.

June 26. Cultural agreement signed by Afghanistan and the United States.

Protocol on utilization of Amu Daria signed by Afghanistan and Soviet Union.

June 30. Prime Minister Daud begins U.S. visit.

1958   The United States agrees to help Afghanistan improve highway from Spin Boldak to Kabul and makes $7,708,000 grant to Pakistan to improve its transport lines with Afghanistan.

July 17. Agreement on transport of goods by road signed by Afghanistan and Pakistan.

Oct. 1–5. Marshal Voroshilov, president of the Supreme Soviet of the Soviet Union, visits Afghanistan.

Nov. 18. Foreign Investment Law promulgated.

1959   Jan. 1–6. Foreign Minister Naim visits Soviet Union.

Jan. 12. The United States agrees to ship 50,000 tons of wheat to Afghanistan.

Jan. 20. Henry A. Byroade named U.S. ambassador to Afghanistan.

Feb. 5–13. Prime Minister Daud visits India.

Mar. 9. Prime Minister Daud calls Baghdad Pact aggravation of international tension.

Apr. 23. Afghanistan and Soviet Union sign protocol on exchange of goods.

May 18–22. Prime Minister Daud visits Soviet Union.

May 28. Afghanistan and Soviet Union sign agreement on building of 750 km Kandahar- Herat- Kushka Highway.

July 15. Afghan military mission visits Turkey and the United Arab Republic.

Aug. 23. Soviet Union agrees to provide assistance to complete Nangarhar irrigation project.

Aug. 31. Afghan women appear unveiled in public at Jashen celebration.

Sept. 14. Indian Prime Minister Nehru visits Afghanistan. Afghan women appear without veils at dinner for Nehru. Henceforth veil no longer obligatory.

Oct. 28. Afghan-Soviet Friendship Society founded.

Dec. 9. U.S. President Eisenhower spends six hours in Kabul. Assures Afghanistan of continued economic support.

1959   Dec. 21. Police and army units suppress rioting in Kandahar. No official figure of casualties given. Radio Kabul blames rioting on elements trying to evade payment of overdue taxes. Other reports say religious leaders oppose government measures of allowing women to remove veil and accepting Soviet assistance.

1960   Jan. 19. Afghanistan and Soviet Union sign agreement for construction of irrigation and power project on Kabul River.

Mar. 2–5. Soviet Prime Minister Khrushchev visits Kabul. Inspects Soviet aid projects, signs cultural cooperation agreement, assures Afghanistan of support on Pashtun question.

Mar. 6. Pakistan calls Soviet support of Afghanistan on Pashtun question interference in Pakistan's internal affairs.

Mar. 7. Prime Minister Daud says Pakistan is putting out propaganda against reforms in Afghanistan such as the emancipation of women. Says Afghan monarchy has decided to give Afghans complete freedom to choose form of government and to organize political parties.

Apr. 3. Construction work begins on Kandahar-Herat-Kushka Highway.

Apr. 26. Former King Amanullah dies in Switzerland.

May 13. Prime Minister Daud meets Soviet Prime Minister Khrushchev while in Moscow for medical treatment.

May 18. Foreign Minister Naim protests to Pakistan and the United States the violation of Afghan airspace by U.S. U-2 plane.

July 15. Soviet prospecting team announces discovery of petroleum and natural gas deposits in northern Afghanistan.

Aug. 4. Czechoslovakia announces a £100,000 technical assistance grant to Afghanistan.

Aug. 10. Two-year Afghan-Soviet barter agreement signed.

1960

Aug. 18. Darunta Canal opened. Built with Soviet assistance.

Aug. 21–26. Chen Yi, foreign minister of the People's Republic of China, visits Afghanistan.

Aug. 26. Treaty of friendship and nonaggression signed by Afghanistan and the People's Republic of China. Commercial and payment agreement renewed.

Dec. 3. Agreements on trade and transit signed with Iran during visit of Iranian prime minister to Kabul.

1961

Apr. 5. Prime Minister Daud confers with Soviet Prime Minister Khrushchev in Moscow on return from Rome, where Daud underwent a spinal operation. *Pravda* article says Pashtun situation is not a matter of indifference to Soviet Union.

May 19. Afghanistan denies Pakistani reports that Afghan soldiers are taking part in border fighting.

June 6. Prime Minister Daud says Pakistan has savagely bombarded Afghan populations with aid of arms furnished by the United States and has confined more than 1,200 leaders of Pashtunistan in Peshawar in the past five days. Denies that Afghanistan has pushed Pashtun tribes to revolt.

June 15. Pakistan protests acts of provocation and aggression in note to Afghan government.

June 22. Pakistan says nomads will no longer be allowed to enter Pakistan without valid passports, visas, and international health certificates.

June 23. Pakistan says friendlier atmosphere should exist between Afghanistan and Pakistan before any summit meeting can be held.

June 26. Prime Minister Daud confers with British Foreign Secretary Home and is received by Queen Elizabeth during visit to London.

July 23. During a meeting with President Kennedy, Muhammad Hashem Maiwandwal, ambassador to the United States, expresses his government's grave concern over Pakistan's use of American arms against Pashtun tribes.

1961

Aug. 23. Pakistan announces it is closing Afghan consulates and trade offices in Pakistan and is considering prohibiting transit facilities given to Afghanistan.

Aug. 30. In reply to Pakistani note of August 23, Afghanistan says it considers decision to close consulates an inimical act and threatens to break diplomatic relations.

Prime Minister Daud leaves for Belgrade Conference of Nonaligned Nations.

Sept. 3. Afghanistan seals border. Transfer of merchandise suspended between Afghanistan and Pakistan.

Sept. 6. Afghanistan breaks diplomatic relations with Pakistan.

Sept. 18. Pakistan accepts Iranian offer of mediation in dispute.

Sept. 19. Saudi Arabia agrees to look after Pakistani interest in Afghanistan.

Sept. 21. The United Arab Republic agrees to look after Afghan interest in Pakistan.

Sept. 27. Foreign Minister Naim says Afghanistan will not allow its transit trade to pass through Pakistan unless its trade offices and consulates in Pakistan are reopened.

Sept. 29. Pakistani President Ayub Khan rejects possibility of reopening Afghan consulates and trade offices, says they were used for subversive activities.

Oct. 11. Soviet army delegation arrives in Kabul for 11-day visit.

Oct. 16. Afghan-Soviet technical and economic cooperation agreement signed.

Oct. 24. Soviet deputy minister of public works arrives in Kabul to inspect projects carried out with Soviet assistance.

Nov. 19. Supplementary transit agreement, providing expansion of facilities for Afghan foreign trade, signed with Soviet Union.

1962   Jan. 24. John M. Steeves named U.S. ambassador to Afghanistan.

Jan. 29. Afghanistan opens border with Pakistan for eight weeks to allow entry of U.S. aid goods.

Apr. 14. Prime Minister Daud announces Second Five-Year Plan. Calls for spending Afs. 31.3 billion for economic development.

Apr. 20. Five-year transit agreement signed by Iran and Afghanistan.

May 6. Pul-i Khumri power station opened. Built with Soviet assistance.

July 1. Pakistan accepts shah of Iran's offer to mediate its dispute with Afghanistan.

July 12. Afghanistan accepts shah of Iran's offer to mediate its dispute with Pakistan.

July 27–31. Formal talks held in Kabul between shah of Iran and Zahir Shah and in Rawalpindi between the shah and President Ayub Khan in efforts to settle Afghan-Pakistani dispute.

Aug. 6. During meeting in Quetta, Pakistani President Ayub Khan suggests a confederation of Afghanistan, Iran, and Pakistan.

Aug. 6–15. Zahir Shah makes visit to Soviet Union.

1963   Feb. 12. The United States decides to ship all its foreign aid goods to Afghanistan via Iran because of the continuing dispute between Afghanistan and Pakistan.

Feb. 25. Trade and assistance agreement signed by Afghanistan and Soviet Union.

Mar. 10. Resignation of Prime Minister Daud announced.

Mar. 14. King Zahir Shah asks Muhammad Yusuf, former minister of mines and industries, to form new government.

Apr. 26. The United States grants loan of $2,635,000 for purchase of a DC-6 and two Convairs for Ariana Afghan Airlines. Purchase will bring Ariana's fleet to nine planes.

1963

Apr. 29. Cultural cooperation agreement signed by Afghanistan and Soviet Union.

May 11–15. Indian President Radhakrishnan visits Afghanistan.

May 25. Afghan and Pakistani representatives begin meetings in Tehran to resolve dispute over Pashtunistan.

May 28. Shah of Iran announces that Afghanistan and Pakistan have agreed to reestablish diplomatic and commercial relations.

May 29. Joint Afghan-Pakistani communiqué confirms reestablishment of relations.

July 20. Afghan consuls reopen consulates in Peshawar and Quetta. Communication reestablished on Afghan-Pakistani border.

July 25. First trucks cross Afghan-Pakistani border in 22 months. Ariana Afghan Airlines resumes flights halted at same time.

Aug. 12. Afghanistan and Pakistan exchange ambassadors.

Aug. 15. Shah of Iran says confederation of Afghanistan, Iran, and Pakistan is good idea but cites many obstacles.

Sept. 2–19. Zahir Shah and Queen Homaira visit the United States.

Sept. 6. Afghanistan and Soviet Union sign agreement for construction of atomic reactor in Afghanistan and training of specialists in peaceful use of atomic energy.

Oct. 12–17. Soviet President Leonid Brezhnev visits Afghanistan; lays cornerstone for new polytechnic institute in Kabul.

Oct. 16. Agreement signed with Soviet Union for technical assistance in extraction and exploitation of natural gas in northern Afghanistan.

Dec. 2. Border treaty signed by Afghanistan and the People's Republic of China..

1964

Feb. 29. Consultative Constitutional Commission, headed by Abdul Zahir, begins sessions that last through May 14.

May 31. Zahir Shah opens new Aliabad campus of Kabul University, built with U. S. assistance.

June 29–July 14. Afghan military delegation visits Soviet Union.

July 1. During one-day stay in Kabul, Pakistani President Ayub Khan discusses ways to improve Afghan-Pakistani relations with King Zahir Shah and Prime Minister Yusuf.

July 4-5. Anastas Mikoyan, deputy prime minister of Soviet Union, visits Kabul.

July 13. Soviet Union makes loan of $25.2 million for Pul-i Khumri-Mazar-i Sharif-Shiberghan Highway.

July 27. Cabinet approves new constitution.

Aug. 4. Proposed content of new constitution announced in press. It allows freedom of speech and press and formation of political parties, calls for two-house parliament and independent judiciary, and bars members of royal family from serving as prime minister, cabinet members, chief justice, or parliament members. King appoints prime minister and commands armed forces.

Sept. 3. Zahir Shah and Soviet Deputy Prime Minister Alexei Kosygin open Kabul-Doshi Highway over Salang Pass. Built with Soviet assistance.

Sept. 6. Delegation returns from demarcating 90 km border with the People's Republic of China.

Sept. 9–19. Loya Jirga debates and approves constitution after adding that members of royal family cannot become members of political parties nor renounce their titles to participate in politics.

Oct. 1. Zahir Shah endorses new constitution. National Assembly dissolved. Transitional government to govern for a year.

Oct. 27. Soviet Union agrees to loan $6.2 million to build polytechnic institute in Kabul.

1964	Oct. 29–Nov. 12. Zahir Shah, accompanied by Queen Homaira, makes first visit to the People's Republic of China by any Afghan head of state.
1965	Jan. 1. Founding of the PDPA.

Jan. 12. The United States agrees to loan $7.7 million for construction of the 121 km Herat-Islam Kala Highway.

Jan. 18. Soviet Union agrees to loan Afghanistan $11.1 million over three years for import of consumer goods.

Feb. 15. Protocol on exchange of goods and prices for 1965 signed by Afghanistan and Soviet Union. Increase of 20 percent expected in reciprocal goods deliveries.

Mar. 11. Zahir Shah and Soviet Prime Minister Dimitri Polyansky open Nangarhar irrigation and power project, built with Soviet assistance.

Mar. 22–25. Chen Yi, deputy prime minister and foreign minister of the People's Republic of China, confers with Zahir Shah and Prime Minister Yusuf during a three-day visit. Boundary protocol, cultural agreement, and economic and technical cooperation agreement signed.

Apr. 21–30. Prime Minister Yusuf makes official visit to Soviet Union. Gets assurance of Soviet help with Third Plan.

Apr. 28. Kunduz airport completed. Built with U.S. assistance.

May 11. New electoral law, providing for universal, direct vote by secret ballot for all Afghan men and women over 20, goes into effect.

May 23. Ariana Airlines begins weekly flight to Tashkent, its first to Soviet Union.

June 5. Mazar-i Sharif airport completed. Built with U.S. assistance.

June 22. Jangalak smelts its first iron ore mined in Afghanistan.

July 7. King Zahir Shah announces plan to rebuild old city of Kabul.

1965

July 24. Soviet Union agrees to build 97 km pipeline from Shiberghan gas fields to Soviet border and 88 km line from fields to fertilizer and power plants in Balkh Province.

July 28. Soviet Union agrees to extend payment on loans to Afghanistan by 30 years and provide teachers for Afghan Polytechnic Institute.

Aug. 3–14. Zahir Shah and Queen Homaira visit Soviet Union. Afghanistan and Soviet Union agree to extend treaty of neutrality and mutual nonaggression of 1931 for 10 years.

Aug. 8. First census of Kabul finds population of 435,203.

Aug. 26–Sept. 28. Election of Parliament members held. Over 1,000 run for 216 seats in Wolesi Jirga (House of the People) and 100 for 28 elective seats in Meshrano Jirga (House of Elders). All run as independents.

Sept. 9. New press law goes into effect allowing Afghan citizens freedom of expression while safeguarding the fundamental values of Islam and the principles embodied in the constitution.

Oct. 12. Dr. Abdul Zahir elected president of Wolesi Jirga. Zahir Shah names Abdul Hadi Dawai president of Meshrano Jirga.

Oct. 13. Zahir Shah's appointees to Meshrano Jirga announced.

Prime Minister Yusuf presents report of interim government and offers resignation. King asks him to form new government.

Oct. 14. Parliament officially opened by King Zahir Shah.

Oct. 19. Wolesi Jirgah decides proposed cabinet members should submit lists of property they hold before vote of confidence is taken.

Oct. 24. Prime Minister Yusuf's presentation of his cabinet to Wolesi Jirgah postponed when spectators crowd into deputies' seats and refuse to leave.

Oct. 25. Wolesi Jirgah decides 191-6 to hold vote of confidence in secret session.

1965

Student demonstrators are dispersed by police and army; three persons are killed. Schools are closed and public meetings banned.

Wolesi Jirgah approves Prime Minister Yusuf's cabinet. Vote reported to be 198 in favor and 15 abstaining.

Oct. 27. King Zahir Shah receives cabinet.

Oct. 29. In wake of demonstrations, Prime Minister Yusuf resigns, giving poor health as reason. King Zahir Shah asks Muhammad Hashem Maiwandwal to form cabinet.

Nov. 4. Prime Minister Maiwandwal makes unexpected appearance at condolence ceremony on Kabul University campus for those killed during Oct. 25 demonstrations. Brings king's message of sympathy and promises to consider student demands.

Toryalai Etemadi elected president of Kabul University by university senate.

Nov. 6. Ministry of interior announces three people died during demonstrations on October 25.

Nov. 7. List of property belonging to ministers debated and accepted by Wolesi Jirgah members.

Nov. 27. Kabul University senate refuses to accept student demands for a lower passing grade and postponement of exams.

Dec. 13. Kabul University's college of science closed because of continued disturbances.

Dec. 14. Ministry of interior forbids public gatherings after two days of demonstrations.

1966

Jan. 1–2. President Ayub Khan of Pakistan makes stop in Kabul on way to Tashkent talks.

Jan. 14–15. Soviet Prime Minister Alexei Kosygin stops in Kabul for talks on way from Delhi to Moscow.

Feb. 1–10. Prime Minister Maiwandwal visits Soviet Union.

Mar. 2. New Kabul University constitution approved by cabinet.

1966   Apr. 4–9. Liu Shao-Chi, president of the People's
                Republic of China, makes official visit to Kabul.

                Apr. 11. *Khalq*, a Pashto and Dari newspaper
                published by Nur Muhammad Taraki, puts out first
                issue.

                Apr. 13. Wolesi Jirgah begins consideration of
                political parties' draft law.

                May 4. After debate on *Khalq*, Meshrano Jirgah
                passes resolution saying any publication against
                values of Islam should be halted.

                May 22. Wolesi Jirgah passes resolution, asking
                government to take action against *Khalq* for not
                following values of constitution.

                May 23. Government bans distribution of *Khalq*
                under Art. 48 of the press law.

                July 19. Wolesi Jirgah approves political parties'
                draft law.

                Aug. 20. Supreme judiciary committee set up as
                foundation of future supreme court.

                Sept. 20. Abdul Rahman Pazhwak, Afghan
                representative to the United Nations, elected
                president of the United Nations General Assembly.

1967   Mar. 25–Apr. 9. Prime Minister Maiwandwal visits
                the United States.

                May 10. Protocol on export of natural gas signed by
                Afghanistan and Soviet Union. Afghanistan expected
                to earn over $320 million in next 18 years from
                export of gas, which is to reach 3 bil. cubic meter a
                year by 1971.

                May 30–June 2. Nikolai Podgorny, chairman of the
                Presidium of Supreme Soviet of Soviet Union, visits
                Afghanistan.

                Aug. 20. Direct telephone link between Kabul and
                Herat completed.

                Oct. 11. Prime Minister Maiwandwal resigns because
                of poor health. King Zahir Shah names Abdullah
                Yaftali acting prime minister.

                Oct. 15. Zahir Shah inaugurates supreme court.

1967   Nov. 1. Zahir Shah asks Nur Ahmad Etemadi to form new government.

Nov. 15. Prime Minister Etemadi gets vote of confidence, 173 to 7 with 6 abstentions after three-day debate in which 183 deputies spoke. Entire proceedings broadcast over radio. Etemadi pledges to work against bribery and corruption.

1968   Jan. 31. Soviet Prime Minister Kosygin stops in Kabul to discuss economic questions.

Feb. 20. Afghan Polytechnic Institute, built with Soviet assistance, completes first year of instruction. Has 224 students in first class.

Apr. 21. Indian Airlines introduces weekly jet service between Delhi and Kabul.

Apr. 22. Shiberghan gas pipelines officially opened by Second Deputy Prime Minister Yaftali and Skachkov, president of the Soviet Union's Council of Ministers Committee of External Affairs.

1969   May 25. U.S. Secretary of State Rogers paid a brief visit to Kabul for talks with government leaders.

June 10. Indian Prime Minister Indira Gandhi ended a five-day official visit.

June 22. Afghan government ordered closing of all primary and secondary schools in Kabul, after a wave of student unrest and a student boycott of Kabul University.

July 17. A Soviet military delegation led by Marshal of the Soviet Union, Ivan Bagramyan began a visit.

Dec. 25. A Soviet military delegation led by Defense Minister Grechko arrived for an official visit.

1970   Jan. 21. The USSR signed a protocol for the export of 2.5 billion cubic meters of Afghan natural gas in 1970.

Jan. 26. Defense Minister Khan Mohammed began an official visit to the United States.

1971   May 17. It was announced that the government of
                Premier Nur Ahmad Etemadi resigned. King Zahir
                Shah accepted the resignation and requested that the
                premier stay in office until a new government could
                be formed.
                June 8. Former Ambassador to Italy Abdul Zahir was
                asked to form a new cabinet.
                July 26. The National Assembly gave Abdul Zahir a
                vote of confidence after a 17-day debate, and he took
                office along with his cabinet.
                Aug. 22. Afghanistan is suffering the worst drought in
                its recorded history.

1972   Jan. 3. The USSR signed an agreement for expanding
                natural gas refining and collection centers in the
                north.
                Jan. 11. Pakistan President Zulfikar Ali Bhutto
                arrived in Kabul for official talks.
                Apr. 3. Indian Foreign Affairs Minister Swaran Singh
                left after a three-day visit and talks on economic aid
                and cooperation.
                May 16. Kabul Radio broadcasts a demand for
                Pashtunistan's independence from Pakistan.
                July 21. U.S. special envoy John Connally told the
                government that the United States could not make any
                further commitment of aid.
                Aug. 25. A natural gas discovery at Jarquduq was
                estimated to be the second largest in the country.
                Dec. 5. Muhammad Zahir Shah accepted the
                resignation of Premier Abdul Zahir, who agreed to
                remain in office until a new premier could be
                appointed.
                Dec. 9. Musa Shafiq was appointed to form a new
                government.
                Dec. 11. A new cabinet was announced with
                Muhammad Musa Shafiq as premier and foreign af-
                fairs minister.

1973   Jan. 17. It was announced that diplomatic relations
                would be established with East Germany.

1973

Mar. 13. Iranian Prime Minister Amir Abbas Hoveyda and Prime Minister Muhammad Musa Shafiq of Afghanistan signed a formal settlement of the Helmand River dispute.

Apr. 21. A royal decree was issued setting general parliamentary election dates.

May 11. The border with Pakistan was ordered closed for two weeks for "administrative reasons."

July 8. Zahir Shah arrives in Italy for a vacation.

July 17. **Sardar Muhammad Daud deposed his cousin, the king, and proclaimed a republic.**

July 18. Muhammad Daud proclaimed president and defense minister.

July 19. The Soviet Union and India extend diplomatic recognition of the new government.

July 27. President Daud abrogated the Constitution of 1964 and dissolved Parliament.

Aug. 2. New cabinet announced.

Aug. 24. Deposed King Muhammad Zahir announced his abdication.

Sept. 23. It was announced that a plot to overthrow the government was discovered and a number of senior army officers arrested. Pakistan was accused of supporting the group.

Oct. 30. Indian Foreign Minister Swaran Singh arrived for an official visit.

1974

Apr. 5. It was reported that a new trade and payments agreement between Afghanistan and the Soviet Union was concluded after Minister of Trade Muhammad Khan Jalallar visited Moscow.

July 7. A trade protocol was signed with India.

July 19. Soviet assistance in the development of the Jarquduq natural gas field and in oil exploration was reported.

July 24. Iran and Afghanistan signed a protocol for cooperation in a large-scale development program in the "joint region of the Helmand River."

Nov. 1. U.S. Secretary of State Henry Kissinger arrived and met with Premier Muhammad Daud.

1975

Feb. 26. The government issued a statement protesting the U.S. decision to lift the arms ban on Pakistan.

Mar. 13. President Muhammad Daud concluded an official visit to India.

May 1. The government announced the nationalization of all banks and banking affairs.

July 11. Deputy Foreign Minister Wahid Abdallah flew to Saudi Arabia to attend the Islamic Foreign Ministers Conference.

July 28. Afghan security forces captured a "terrorist" group in Panjshir, which was allegedly armed by Pakistan.

Oct. 17. Iran signed an agreement to provide aid and technical assistance to construct a railroad system and Kabul airport and to build a meat processing plant.

Nov. 21. New cabinet was appointed in October.

Dec. 2. Afghanistan denied Pakistani charges that it had mobilized troops along its border with Pakistan.

1976

Jan. 2. An agreement was concluded with the Soviet Union for the development of the Jarquduq gas fields and the provision of gas production and processing facilities.

June 7. Pakistani President Zulfikar Ali Bhutto began a visit to Afghanistan.

June 8. Pakistani President Bhutto met with President Muhammad Daud.

July 4. Indian Premier Indira Gandhi arrived in Kabul for a three-day visit.

Aug. 8. U.S. Secretary of State Henry Kissinger met with President Daud in Kabul.

Dec. 9. According to reports, more than 50 people had been arrested and accused of a plot to overthrow the government.

1977

Jan. 30. President Muhammad Daud convened the Loya Jirga, or Grand Assembly, to approve the draft of a new constitution.

1977

Feb. 14. The new constitution was approved by the Loya Jirga.

Feb. 15. Muhammad Daud was sworn in and the Loya Jirga was dissolved.

Feb. 24. President Muhammad Daud promulgated a new constitution.

Feb. 26. President Daud disbanded the cabinet and the central revolutionary committee.

Mar. 13. The Afghan government announced formation of a new government.

Mar. 23. A Soviet trade delegation began a trip to Afghanistan to hold talks on bilateral trade.

Mar. 29. An agreement had been reached in Kabul to resume air links between Pakistan and Afghanistan.

June 22. Pakistani Premier Zulfikar Ali Bhutto arrived in Kabul for talks with President Muhammad Daud.

July 29. Afghanistan and the USSR concluded a six-year consumer goods agreement in Kabul.

Oct. 11. Pakistani Chief Martial Law Administrator Muhammad Zia-ul-Haq met with President Daud at the Presidential Palace.

Nov. 16. Minister of Planning Ali Ahmad Khurram was assassinated in Kabul.

1978

Feb. 19. Sayyid Abdulillah was appointed vice president.

Feb. 21. President Muhammad Daud left Kabul for Belgrade on an official visit to Yugoslavia.

Feb. 24. A trial of 25 people accused of plotting to assassinate President Daud had begun in Kabul.

Mar. 4. President Daud met with Indian Premier Morarji Desai in New Delhi.

Apr. 17. Mir Akbar Khaibar, one of the founders of the PDPA, was assassinated in Kabul.

Apr. 20. Thousands turn Khaibar's funeral into an antigovernment demonstration.

Apr. 26. President Daud has PDPA leaders arrested.

1978

Apr. 27. **Communist Coup**. Members of the PDPA gained power in a coup led by insurgents in the armed forces. The military revolutionary council formed a new government.

Apr. 29. The government radio reported that Defense Minister Ghulam Haidar Rasuli, Interior Minister Abdul Qadir Nuristani, and Vice President Sayyid Abdulillah had been killed in the coup along with President Daud and his brother Muhammad Naim.

Apr. 30. A "Revolutionary Council" was proclaimed. Nur Muhammad Taraki was named president and premier of the Democratic Republic of Afghanistan. The Revolutionary Council selected the following leading ministers:

Babrak Karmal	Deputy Premier
Hafizullah Amin	Deputy Premier and Foreign Minister
Muhd. Aslam Watanjar	Deputy Premier and Communications
Abdul Qadir	National Defense
Nur Ahmad Nur	Interior

May 1. Shah Muhammad Dost and Abdul Hadi Mokamel were named deputy ministers of foreign affairs.

May 6. Premier Taraki said Afghanistan was "non-aligned and independent."

May 18. Foreign Minister Hafizullah Amin left Kabul for Havana for a meeting of nonaligned countries.

May – June. First *mujahedin* camp set up in Pakistan.

July 5. Kabul Radio said that Interior Minister Nur Ahmad Nur had been named ambassador to Washington and that Vice President and Deputy Premier Babrak Karmal had been named ambassador to Czechoslovakia.

Aug. 17. The central committee of the People's Democratic party decided that President of the Revolutionary Council Nur Muhammad Taraki would assume the duties of minister of defense.

Aug. 18. Kabul Radio announced that a plot to overthrow the government had been foiled and

1978

Defense Minister Abdul Qadir had been arrested for his role in the plot.

Aug. 23. The politburo of the PDPA ordered the arrest of Planning Minister Sultan Ali Keshtmand and Public Works Minister Muhammad Rafi'i for their parts in the conspiracy.

Sept. 9. Pakistani Chief Martial Law Administrator Muhammad Zia-ul-Haq met with Chairman of the Revolutionary Council Taraki at Paghman, near Kabul.

Sept. 17. The government announced it was breaking diplomatic relations with South Korea.

Sept. 19. Indian External Affairs Minister Anal Bihari Vajpayee met with Taraki in Kabul.

Sept. 22. Taraki dismissed six ambassadors who had been appointed in July. All were members of the Parcham section of the PDPA.

Oct. 19. Afghanistan adopted a red flag as its new national emblem.

Dec. 3. President Nur Muhammad Taraki arrived in Moscow for talks with Soviet leaders.

Dec. 5. Afghanistan and the Soviet Union signed a 20-year treaty of friendship and cooperation in Moscow.

1979

Jan. 28. Guerrillas were fighting government troops in the eastern provinces bordering Pakistan.

Feb. 2. It is reported that Afghan dissidents are undergoing guerrilla training at a Pakistan military base north of Peshawar.

Feb. 14. U.S. Ambassador to Afghanistan Adolph Dubs was taken hostage by terrorists in Kabul. Afghan forces rushed the building in which he was being held and he was slain.

The United States protested against the use of force by the Afghan government to free the U.S. ambassador.

Feb. 19. Foreign Minister Hafizullah Amin rejected a U.S. protest over the incident leading to the slaying of the U.S. ambassador as "completely baseless."

1979   Feb. 22. U.S. President Jimmy Carter ordered U.S.
                aid to Afghanistan to be reduced.
                Mar. 16. Revolt and uprising in Herat with the
                participation of the military garrison. Thousands were
                said to have been killed in recapture of town by
                government troops.
                Mar. 23. A U.S. spokesman said the United States
                expected that the "principle of noninterference " in
                Afghanistan 1979would be respected by all parties in
                the area, "including the Soviet Union."
                Mar. 27. Foreign Minister Hafizullah Amin was
                named premier.
                Apr. 1. The new Afghan government was announced:
                Hafizullah Amin, premier and foreign affairs;
                Shah Wali, deputy premier.
                Apr. 2. Washington denies Soviet charges that
                America is arming Afghan guerrillas.
                Apr. 8. Soviet Vice Minister of Defense Aleksey
                Yepishev met with President Nur Muhammad Taraki
                in Kabul.
                Apr. 30. Taraki said Pakistani President Muhammad
                Zia-ul-Haq was "involved" with attacks on border
                positions in eastern Afghanistan.
                June 13. Afghanistan accused Pakistan of involve-
                ment in a rebellion against the Afghan government.
                June 23. Kabul Radio reported that antigovernment
                demonstrators (Hazaras) in Kabul had been
                "annihilated and arrested" during the day.
                June. Soviet special forces occupy Bagram air force
                base.
                July. 28. The cabinet was reshuffled:
                Hafizullah Amin, premier and vice president of the
                Revolutionary Council; Shah Wali, deputy prime
                minister and foreign affairs minister.
                Aug. 5. Heavy fighting broke out in Kabul between
                loyal troops and a rebellious army unit at the Bala
                Hisar Fort. The rebellion was crushed and a curfew
                was imposed on the city.
                Aug. 19. Premier Hafizullah Amin said there were
                "no more than 1,600 Soviet advisers" in Afghanistan.

1979

Sept. 15. Kabul Radio reported that Interior Minister Aslam Watanjar and Frontier Affairs Minister Sherjan Mazduryar had been removed from their posts.

It was reported that gunfire and explosions had occurred in Kabul following the announcement of the cabinet dismissals.

Sept. 16. Kabul Radio reported that President Taraki had asked to be relieved of his government positions because of "bad health and nervous weakness."

Premier Amin assumed the additional post of president.

Sept. 23. President Amin said that former President Taraki was "alive but definitely sick."

Oct. 8. Kabul announced that President Amin had commuted death sentences of former Defense Minister Abdul Qadir and former Planning Minister Sultan Ali Keshtmand to 15 years' imprisonment.

Rebel tribesmen said they had cut the road leading from Kabul to Gardez during fighting with government troops.

Oct. 9. Kabul Radio announced that Taraki had died. President Amin publishes a list of 12,000 killed by Taraki regime.

Oct. 14. Heavy fighting took place at Rishkur barracks southwest of Kabul.

Oct. 16. It was reported that the government had crushed an army mutiny near Kabul.

Soviet forces take command of Shindand air force base.

Nov. 9. It was reported that several ambush attacks had been launched on government troops near Kabul, killing 200 persons.

Dec. 21. U.S. officials said that the Soviet Union had moved three army divisions to the border with Afghanistan and had sent about 1,500 combat soldiers to an air base near Kabul.

Dec. 26. A U.S. government spokesman said that in the past 24 hours there has been "a large-scale Soviet airlift" to Kabul, raising Soviet military involvement in Afghanistan to "a new threshold."

1979

Dec. 27. Fighting broke out in Kabul and President Hafizullah Amin was overthrown and assassinated. Former Deputy Premier Babrak Karmal assumed the post of president.

Dec. 28. President Karmal said the Soviet Union had agreed to supply Afghanistan "urgent political, moral and economic aid, including military aid."

U.S. President Jimmy Carter called the Soviet military intervention "a grave threat to the peace" and a "blatant violation of accepted rules of international behavior."

A cabinet was formed as follows:

Babrak Karmal, premier, chairman, Revolutionary Council, and secretary general, central committee; Asadullah Sarwari, deputy premier; Sultan Ali Keshtmand, deputy premier and planning; Rafi'i, national defense; Sayyid Muhd. Gulabzoi, interior; Shah Muhammad Dost, foreign minister.

1980

Jan. Carter administration requests about $30 million in covert aid to the Afghan guerrillas.

The United States begins covertly channeling Soviet-made weapons, including Kalashnikov AK-47 automatic rifles to the rebels in Pakistan.

Jan. 1. Afghanistan said it had invited Soviet troops into the country "in view of the present aggressive actions of the enemies of Afghanistan."

Jan. 2. Karmal addressed government leaders near Kabul and called on the Afghan people to "come together and support our glorious revolution."

Jan. 5. The Security Council opened debate on Afghanistan.

Jan. 7. The Soviet Union vetoed a UN resolution that called for the immediate withdrawal of "all foreign troops in Afghanistan." The vote was 13 to 2 in favor of the resolution.

Jan. 9. The Security Council voted 12 to 2 with 1 abstention for a resolution to move the issue of Afghanistan to the General Assembly.

1980

Jan. 14. The General Assembly voted 104 to 18 with 18 abstentions for a resolution which "strongly deplored" the "recent armed intervention" in Afghanistan and called for the "total withdrawal of foreign troops" from the country.

Jan. 23. President Carter announces sanctions against the Soviet Union, including a grain embargo.

Jan. 27. A conference of Islamic Foreign Ministers opened in Islamabad to consider the situation in Afghanistan.

Jan. 29. The conference in Islamabad adopted a resolution which condemned "the Soviet military aggression against the Afghan people."

Feb. 13. Egyptian Defense Minister Kamal Hasan 'Ali said that Egypt was providing assistance to Afghan rebels and was "training some of them."

Feb. 14. The UN Human Rights Commission voted by 27 to 8 with 6 abstentions to condemn the Soviet intervention in Afghanistan as "an aggression against human rights."

Feb. 15. The New York Times cited "White House officials" as saying the U.S. had begun an operation to supply light infantry weapons to Afghan insurgent groups.

Feb. 19. Foreign ministers of the European Economic Community (EEC) proposed that Afghanistan be declared a neutral country under international guarantees if the Soviet Union would withdraw its troops.

Feb. 22. Soviet President Leonid Brezhnev said that the Soviet Union would withdraw its troops from Afghanistan "as soon as all forms of outside interference" were "fully terminated."

Demonstrations and rioting against the government and the Soviet Union took place in Kabul.

Feb. 25. Shops remained closed in Kabul.

Feb. 26. It was reported that mass arrests had been made in Kabul during the day.

1980

Feb. 28. Almost all shopkeepers had opened for business in Kabul. It was reported that striking civil servants had returned to work.

Mar. 3. The *Hizb-i Islami* of Hekmatyar, one of six Afghan insurgent groups negotiating an alliance, said it had withdrawn from the alliance.

Mar. 7. Soviet soldiers appeared on the streets of Kabul. Soviet fighter planes and helicopter gunships flew over the city.

Mar. 10. Justice Minister Abdurrashid Arian said that 42 associates of former President Hafizullah Amin were being held for trial.

Mar. 13. Foreign Minister Shah Muhammed Dost arrived in Moscow on a "friendly visit."

Apr. Status of Soviet Armed Forces Agreement signed.

May 18. Indian Foreign Secretary R. D. Satha met with President Babrak Karmal in Kabul.

May 22. A conference of Islamic foreign ministers, meeting in Islamabad, adopted a resolution that demanded the "immediate, total and unconditional withdrawal of all Soviet troops from Afghanistan" and decided to establish a committee that would open "appropriate consultations" to seek a solution to the crisis in Afghanistan.

May 24. Demonstrators protesting the Soviet presence in Afghanistan marched in Kabul.

June 8. Kabul Radio announced that 10 supporters and aides of slain former President Hafizullah Amin had been executed.

June 14. Kabul news service reported that former Communications Minister Muhammad Zarif, former Frontier Affairs Minister Sahibjan Sahra'i, and former Planning Minister Muhammad Siddiq Alemyar had been executed.

July. Sixty countries boycott the Moscow Olympics in protest of the invasion of Afghanistan.

July 2. The Soviet Communist party newspaper *Pravda* said that for a political settlement of the situation in Afghanistan to take place, armed

1980

incursions by the "mercenaries of the imperialist and reactionary forces from the territory of neighboring states" must first be ended.

Aug. 16. Kabul Radio reported that Justice Minister Abdurrashid Arian had been named to the additional post of deputy premier.

Sept. 14. Frontier Affairs Minister Faiz Muhammad was killed earlier in the week while trying to enlist the support of Afghan tribes.

Oct. CIA provides some SAM-7 portable surface-to-air missiles to Ahmad Shah Mas'ud.

Oct. 15–Nov. 5. President Karmal and other high officials left Kabul on a visit to the Soviet Union.

Nov. 13. President Karmal said that those who were not working for the good of the party would be expelled "even if they had been heroes in the past."

Nov. 20. The United Nations General Assembly voted 111 to 22 with 12 abstentions for a resolution that called for the "unconditional" pullout of "foreign troops" from Afghanistan.

Nov. 21. Foreign Affairs Minister Shah Muhammad Dost said the UN resolution was "a flagrant interference in Afghanistan's internal affairs."

Dec. 25. Egyptian President Anwar al-Sadat said that he had "sent weapons" and would "send more weapons" to Afghan insurgents.

Dec. 27. Deposed King Muhammad Zahir said in exile that he prayed to God "to aid the Afghan people in its heroic struggle and its legitimate war for independence."

1981

Pakistan government declares that henceforth it will recognize only six Pakistan-based resistance organizations.

Feb. 18. President Babrak Karmal arrived in Moscow for talks with Soviet leaders.

Mar. 9. U.S. President Ronald Reagan said that if Afghan "freedom fighters" who were fighting Soviet forces asked for weapons, it would be something "to be considered."

1981

Apr. 7. Saudi Arabia announced it was severing diplomatic relations with "the current illegal regime" in Afghanistan.

May 9. Pakistani officials estimated the number of Afghan refugees in Pakistan at 2 million.

May 11. Sultan Ali Keshtmand becomes prime minister.

June 11. President of the Revolutionary Council Babrak Karmal turned the post of premier over to Sultan Ali Keshtmand and removed Abdul Rashid Arian as deputy premier.

June 13. The Revolutionary Council elected as its vice presidents Nur Ahmad Nur and Abdul Rashid Arian.

July 12. Member of the national committee of the National Fatherland Front, General Fateh Muhammad was killed by rebels.

July 22. Diplomatic sources in Kabul reported heavy fighting between the rebels and Soviet forces in Paghman, 16 miles from the capital.

Aug. 6. Foreign Minister Shah Muhammad Dost met with UN Representative Javier Pérez de Cuellar.

Aug. 12. Kabul Radio announced changes in the land distribution program that lifted restrictions on acreage held by religious and tribal leaders.

Aug. 22. Five Afghan resistance groups formed an alliance and created a 50-member advisory council.

Sept. 9. Foreign Minister Dost met with Prime Minister Indira Gandhi in New Delhi.

Sept. 22. Egyptian President Anwar al-Sadat said in a U.S. television interview that the United States had been buying old Soviet-made arms from Egypt and sending them to rebels fighting Soviet forces in Afghanistan. U.S. officials had no comment.

Nov. 18. By a vote of 116 to 23 with 12 abstentions the United Nations General Assembly voted for the third time that the Soviet Union must withdraw its troops from Afghanistan.

Dec. 15. President Babrak Karmal began a visit to Moscow.

1982

Jan. 6. In Washington, military analysts said Soviet troops in Afghanistan had grown to 110–120,000.

Feb. 20. The Afghan government rejected the appointment of Archer K. Blood, designated U.S. chargé d'affaires to Kabul. In response, the U.S. State Department imposed travel restrictions on Afghan diplomats in Washington.

Mar. 10. President Reagan proclaims March 21 as "Afghanistan Day."

May 16. A two-day PDPA conference ended in Kabul with the 841 delegates endorsing resolutions aimed at purging dissidents and continuing a program of land reform.

June 8. Soviet and Afghan troops regained control of the key Panjshir valley in a major offensive against mujahedin forces.

June 16–25. The first UN-sponsored direct talks between Afghanistan and Pakistan begin in Geneva.

Aug. 2. The Afghan government amended the conscription law, lengthening the term of service.

Oct. 30. An explosion in the Salang tunnel north of Kabul kills more than 1,000 people, including 700 Soviet troops.

Nov. The United Nations General Assembly approves a resolution demanding " the immediate withdrawal of foreign troops from Afghanistan" by a vote of 114 to 21 with 13 abstentions.

Dec. It is reported that the CIA was ordered to provide the Afghan insurgents with bazookas, mortars, grenade launchers, mines, and recoilless rifles.

1983

Jan. 19. UN Deputy Secretary-General Diego Cordovez began a peace mission to Geneva, Tehran, Islamabad, and Kabul to resolve the Afghan crisis.

Feb. 16. The UN Human Rights Commission voted 29 to 7 with five abstentions for an immediate Soviet withdrawal from Afghanistan.

June 15. The foreign ministers of Afghanistan and

1983
Pakistan arrived in Geneva for a third series of talks on the withdrawal of foreign troops.

June 24. UN-sponsored talks on Soviet troop withdrawal ended in Geneva without progress.

Nov. 23. The United Nations General Assembly called for the immediate withdrawal of Soviet troops by a vote of 116 to 20 with 16 abstentions.

Dec. 27. The Afghan government said it would request the departure of 105,000 Soviet troops if it received international guarantees that all opposition would end.

1984
Jan. 24. President Karmal had his three top military advisers replaced. Chief of Staff General Baba Jan was replace by Lieutenant General Nazar Moham-mad, Deputy Defense Minister Major General Khalilullah by Major General Muhammad Nabi Azami, and Chief of Operations General Nuristani by Major General Ghulam Qadir Miakhel.

Mar. 21. A bomb exploded in a Kabul mosque, killing four people and injuring seven.

Apr. 11. The Kabul government ordered the expulsion of Third Secretary Richard S. Vandiver of the U. S. embassy in Kabul on charges of espionage. The United States denied the charge.

May 14. The National Olympic Committee announced Afghanistan would boycott the 1984 Summer Olympics in Los Angeles.

May 17. U. S. Vice President George Bush visited the Khaiber Pass, where he condemned the Soviet invasion and expressed support for the Afghan resistance.

July 26. The U. S. House of Representatives Appro-priations Committee approved $50 million in covert aid to Afghans, according to intelligence sources.

Aug. 27. The foreign ministers of Afghanistan and Pakistan met separately in Geneva with a UN intermediary to discuss a political settlement to the Afghan war.

Aug. 30. The third round of talks between

1984 Afghanistan and Pakistan adjourned in Geneva with no sign of progress.

Nov. 4. Nine people were executed for the August 31 bomb explosion at Kabul airport.

Dec. 3. Radio Kabul reported that President Karmal had appointed Army Chief of Staff Brigadier General Nazar Muhammad to replace Lieutenant General Abdul Qadir as defense minister.

1985 Jan. 18. The United States announced it would increase its aid to Afghan *mujahedin* in 1985 to approximately $280 million. Saudi Arabia, Israel, and China were also reportedly assisting the rebels.

Jan. 26. The Afghan *mujahedin* leader Khan Gul was sentenced to death in Paktia Province.

Jan. 29. Zabiullah, a leader of the *Jam'iat-i Islami*, was killed when his jeep hit a mine.

Mar. 3. According to reports from Iran, four Shi'a *mujahedin* groups merged: the *Sazman-i Nasr*, the *Pasdaran*, Guards; the Islamic Movement of Afghanistan; and the United Front of the Islamic Revolution.

Apr. 23. President Karmal opened a grand tribal assembly (Loya Jirga) in Kabul in an effort to gain popular support in the government's war against the *mujahedin*.

May 10. Leaders of three of the main *mujahedin* groups in Peshawar denounced the attempt by Abd al-Rasul Sayyaf to appoint himself for another term as head of the seven-member Alliance of Afghan *Mujahedin*.

June 17. U. S. and Soviet officials met in Washington to discuss the war in Afghanistan.

June 20. UN-sponsored "proximity talks" began in Geneva between Afghan and Pakistani governments regarding the war in Afghanistan.

June 25. Afghan-Pakistani talks ended in Geneva, and were described as "intense and fruitful."

1985   Aug. 26. UN-sponsored indirect talks on Afghanistan between Pakistani and Afghan officials opened in Geneva.

Aug. 30. UN mediator Diego Cordovez said progress had been made on three of four points in the UN plan for ending the Afghan war. The two sides remained divided on the question of withdrawing Soviet troops.

Oct. 23. Afghan authorities ordered all males up to 40 years of age to enlist for three years of military service.

Oct. 23. Afghan Foreign Minister Shah Muhammad Dost said Afghanistan could not reach agreement on the withdrawal of Soviet troops unless Pakistan enters direct negotiations.

Nov. 2. Afghan troops ringed the U. S. embassy in Kabul in an effort to force the release of a Soviet soldier who walked into the embassy on Oct. 31, reportedly seeking help to return to the USSR.

Nov. 13. By a vote of 122 to 19 with 12 abstentions, the United Nations General Assembly adopted a Pakistani resolution calling for the immediate withdrawal of Soviet troops from Afghanistan.

Dec. 6. Radio Kabul announced that Ghulam Faruq Yaqubi had been named director of the KHAD, Afghanistan's secret police.

Dec. 13. The State Department notified the United Nations that the United States was ready to act as guarantor of a peace settlement in Afghanistan that would involve a Soviet troops withdrawal and an end to U.S. aid to the *mujahedin*.

Dec. 19. In Geneva, Afghanistan and Pakistan suspended their latest round of peace talks to study new UN proposals for a timetable for Soviet withdrawal.

Dec. 31. The Afghan government presented an informal timetable for the withdrawal of Soviet troops as part of an overall accord, during UN-sponsored Geneva talks Dec. 16 to 19, according to the State Department.

1986

Jan. 11. President Babrak Karmal rejected the U. S. offer to serve as guarantor of a peace settlement.

Feb. 4. Guerrilla activity near Kandahar had reportedly declined in recent days after former rebel leader Asmatullah Achakzai Muslim and his militia decided to back the Kabul government.

Feb. 20. The Revolutionary Council Presidium 1996 appointed a 74-member commission to draft a constitution.

Mar. 17. The Foreign Ministry rejected a UN report on human rights violations in Afghanistan as "a collection of groundless slanders and accusations."

Mar. 20. Pakistan lodged a "strong protest" over Afghan attacks on a border post and refugee camp in Khurram Agency that killed six people on March 16 and 18.

Apr. 2. The United States reportedly agreed to supply hundreds of stinger missiles to Afghan *mujahedin*.

Apr. 6. Kabul Radio said that rebels detonated a car bomb in Kabul that wounded 22 people.

Apr. 11. Soviet/Kabul forces start campaign against Zhawar.

May 4. Babrak Karmal resigned as secretary-general of the PDPA because of "ill health," according to Kabul Radio. He was replaced by Najibullah, former head of KHAD, the secret police. Babrak retained the post of chairman of the Revolutionary Council and a seat in the seven-member politburo.

May 5. The seventh round of peace talks between the foreign ministers of Afghanistan and Pakistan opened at UN headquarters in Geneva.

May 15. Najibullah announced a collective leadership, including himself as party leader, Babrak as head of the Revolutionary Council Presidium, and Sultan Ali Keshtmand as prime minister.

May 19. The seventh round of UN-sponsored indirect talks between Afghanistan and Pakistan resumed in Geneva.

May 28. Najibullah announced that a bicameral parliament would be established "within a few

1986

months," on the basis of "free and democratic elections."

June 16. President Reagan met with Afghan *mujahedin* in Washington and promised an "unshakable commitment" to their cause.

June 17. *Mujahedin* leaders Gulbuddin Hekmatyar and Rasul Sayyaf criticized the four other Peshawar leaders for the Washington visit.

1987

Feb. 18. Prime Minister Sultan Ali Keshtmand arrived in Moscow for talks.

Feb. 23. Pakistan's Foreign Minister Yaqub Khan met with Soviet Foreign Minister Shevardnadze in Moscow to discuss Afghanistan.

Feb. 26. The tenth round of negotiations aimed at ending the war in Afghanistan opened in Geneva.

Mar. 4. *Mujahedin* stage rocket attacks into Soviet territory from Imam Sahib in Kunduz Province.

July 20. Afghan leader Najibullah met with Soviet leader Mikhail Gorbachev.

Aug. 11. Felix Ermacora, the UN special human rights investigator, was allowed to visit three Afghan prisons and interview political prisoners.

Oct. 10. Najibullah authorized the purchase of weapons from *mujahedin* who put down their arms.

Oct. 13. Yunus Khales, leader of the *Hizb-e Islami*, denied reports that his commanders had sold stinger missiles to Iranian Pasdaran.

Oct. 18. Maulawi Yunus Khalis was elected spokesman of the seven-party *mujahedin* alliance.

Oct. 24. Shi'a groups headquartered in Iran announced a new coalition of *mujahedin* groups headquartered in Iran.

Nov. 10. Kabul Radio announced that the Revolutionary Council Presidium endorsed a decree providing for the formation and registration of political parties.

Nov. 24. Lieutenant General Muhammad Nabi Azimi, first deputy of defense, was reported to have

1987

committed suicide after an offensive he led ended in failure.

Nov. 29. A Loya Jirga had been called to approve a new constitution.

Nov. 30. The Loya Jirga confirmed Najibullah as president under the new "Islamized" constitution.

Dec. 6. *Mujahedin* leader Yunus Khales said the seven-party alliance would not accept Communist participation in any future Afghan government.

Dec. 10. UN envoy Diego Cordovez was reported to have opened negotiations between exiled King Muhammad Zahir and *mujahedin* leaders regarding formation of a transitional coalition government.

1988

Jan. Soviet Foreign Minister Shevardnadze arrived in Kabul for an "official working visit."

Jan. 6. In an interview with Afghan News Agency, Shevardnadze said the Soviet Union hoped to be out of Afghanistan by the end of 1988 regardless of the type of rule established there. He, however, linked troop withdrawal to the cessation of U. S. aid to the *mujahedin*.

Jan. 12. Pakistani President Zia-ul-Haq and Prime Minister Muhammad Khan Junejo said in separate interviews that members of the pro-Moscow government must be allowed to participate in any future government as a condition for the withdrawal of Soviet troops from the country.

Jan. 17. *Mujahedin* leader Yunus Khalis rejected statements by Pakistani leaders that the *mujahedin* would have to "coexist with remnants of a communist regime."

Jan. 20. At a press conference Najibullah stated that his government would be committed to nonalignment, following the withdrawal of Soviet forces and that Kabul was willing to accept aid from any country willing to give it.

Jan. 22. In Jalalabad at least 17 people were killed when two bombs exploded at the public funeral of Khan Abd al-Ghaffar Khan, who died on Jan. 20.

1988   Feb. 8. Soviet leader Mikhail Gorbachev said Soviet
            troops would begin pulling out of Afghanistan on May
            15 if a settlement could be reached by mid-March.

            Feb. 10. Reagan administration officials said a U. S.
            commitment was made in 1985 to end military aid to
            the *mujahedin* at the start of Soviet withdrawal. This
            commitment was made by Michael Armacost without
            the knowledge of the president. The official U. S.
            position is that the cutoff of aid would occur 60 days
            after a peace settlement and concur with a
            simultaneous withdrawal.

            Feb. 11. Sayyid Bahauddin Majruh, head of the
            Afghan Information Office in Peshawar, was
            assassinated in Peshawar city.

            Feb. 23. The *mujahedin* alliance announced the
            formation of an interim government.

            Mar. 4. The Reagan administration said it would not
            halt aid to the *mujahedin* until Moscow stopped its
            supply to the Afghan government.

            Mar. 14. Gulbudin Hekmatyar was reported appoint-
            ed spokesman of the *mujahedin* alliance.

            Mar. 23. Nikolai Egorchev (?) was reported to have
            replaced Pavel Mojayev as Soviet ambassador to
            Afghanistan after Mojayev suffered a heart attack.

            Mar. 24. U. S. officials reported that Pakistan with-
            drew its demand that an interim government be
            formed to oversee the Soviet withdrawal.

            Mar. 26. The Reagan administration was reported
            ending its supply of stinger missiles to the *mujahedin*
            in anticipation of a Geneva settlement.

            Mar. 29. President Najibullah promised opposition
            groups 54 of the 229 lower house seats and 18 out of
            62 in the Senate if they would participate in the
            coming parliamentary elections.

            Mar. 30. The *mujahedin* rejected President Najib-
            ullah's offer to form a coalition government.

            Apr. 9. A *mujahedin* leader said that the *mujahedin*
            "would not be bound by the outcome of the Geneva
            agreements."

1988

Apr. 14. Afghanistan, Pakistan, the Soviet Union, and the United States signed the Geneva Accords. Under the agreement the Soviet Union would withdraw its troops within nine months. The United States and the Soviet Union would be the guarantors of the agreement, which also provided for the return of Afghan refugees and a halt to military aid by both sides.

Apr. 21. President Najibullah said that 1.55 million voted in the Afghan elections.

Apr. 25. A UN "implementation assistance group," headed by Finnish Major General Rauli Helminen, arrived in Islamabad to monitor the Geneva Accord. Minister of Defense Major General Muhammad Rafi was promoted to lieutenant general as was Armed Forces Chief of Staff Shahnawaz Tanai. Minister of Communications Muhammad Aslam Watanjar was promoted to major general.

Apr. 28. President Najibullah said that Soviet military advisers would remain after the Soviet troop withdrawal.

May 4. President Najibullah arrived in New Delhi for three days of talks.

May 11. The United Nations appointed Sadruddin Agha Khan as coordinator for relief and resettlement in Afghanistan.

May 15. The Soviet Union began withdrawing troops from Afghanistan.

May 19. Major General Fazil Ahmad Samadi of the Afghan army defected to the *mujahedin*.

May 25. The Soviet Union announced the following casualties in the Afghan war: 13,310 dead, 35,478 wounded, and 311 missing.

May 26. Muhammad Hasan Sharq was appointed prime minister, replacing Sultan Ali Keshtmand, who became secretary of the PDPA central committee.

May 31. A State Department official said U. S. aid to the *mujahedin* would continue because the Soviet Union planned to leave $1 billion worth of equipment in Afghanistan.

1988   June 7. President Najibullah addressed the United
                               Nations General Assembly, complaining that Pak-
                               istan continued to violate the Geneva Accords.
                               June 9. President Najibullah said, according to the
                               Bakhtar News Agency, that 243,900 soldiers and
                               civilians had died in 10 years of war.
                               June 15. Pir Sayyid Ahmad Gailani, head of the
                               National Islamic Front, became spokesman for the
                               seven-member *mujahedin* alliance.
                               June 16. President Najibullah announced the
                               formation of a new government:

Prime Minister	Muhammad Hasan Sharq
Foreign Affairs	Abdul Wakil
Internal Affairs	Sayyid Muhammad Gulabzoi
State Security	Ghulam Faruq Yaqubi
Finance	Hamidullah Tarzi
Justice	Muhammad Bashir Baghlani

July 18. Sebghatullah Mujaddidi's National Front for
the Liberation of Afghanistan joined Sayyid Ahmad
Gailani's National Islamic Front of Afghanistan in
expressing support for UN envoy Diego Cordovez's
peace plan to establish a neutral government.
July 27. The Kabul government announced the
permission for formation of a new party, the Union of
God's Helpers (*Ittehadia-ye Ansarullah*).
Aug. 1. The Constitution Council was set up to
examine the constitutionality of laws and compliance
of treaties and laws.
Aug. 8. Soviet troops began the withdrawing from
Kabul.
Aug. 17. Lieutenant General Shahnawaz Tanai was
appointed defense minister, and Major General
Muhammad Asef Delawar was appointed chief of the
armed forces general staff.
Sept. 25. Edmund McWilliams, Jr., was appointed
special envoy to the *mujahedin*.
Oct. 5. Maulawi Zahir, a commander of Burhanuddin
Rabbani, was killed in Nejrab by Hekmatyar's forces.
Oct. 13. Yuli Vorontsov, Soviet first deputy foreign
minister, was appointed ambassador to Kabul.

1988

Oct. 17. Burhanuddin Rabbani, head of the *Jam'iat-i Islami*, became spokesman for the seven-member *mujahedin* alliance.

Nov. 17. Deputy Foreign Minister Abdul Ghafur Lakanwal and Sayyid Kamaluddin, deputy director in the foreign ministry, were reported to have defected.

Nov. 19. Soviet military command in Afghanistan warns if guerrillas escalate the war, they will jeopardize the withdrawal of Soviet troops.

Nov. 28. Muhammad Gul, a KHAD brigadier general and cousin of Najibullah, was reported to have defected.

Dec. 3. Alliance leaders, headed by Burhanuddin 1988 Rabbani, met in Ta'if, Saudi Arabia, for talks with Soviet Deputy Minister Vorontsov.

Dec. 25. Soviet Deputy Vorontsov met with ex-King Muhammad Zahir in Rome (at the request of Moscow).

1989

Jan. 2. Sebghatullah Mujaddidi succeeded Rabbani as spokesman for the alliance.

Jan. 13. Soviet Foreign Minister Edward Shevardnadze arrived in Kabul.

Jan. 18. Sebghatullah Mujaddidi returned from Iran, where he unsuccessfully tried to invite the Shi'a *mujahedin* groups to join an interim government.

Jan. 21. West Germany's diplomatic staff left Kabul.

Jan. 25. The United States decided to close its embassy.

Jan. 26. A *mujahedin* delegation, headed by Gulbuddin Hekmatyar, met with Iranian Foreign Minister Ali Akbar Velayati in Tehran.

Jan. 27. Britain, France, Japan, and Italy announced their decision to withdraw their diplomats from Kabul.

Jan. 28. Soviet Defense Minister Dimitri Yazov ended two days of talks with President Najibullah. He said Moscow would "not abandon its friends."

Jan. 30. The United States formally closed its embassy.

1989

Feb. 2. President Najibullah denounced the closing of Western embassies as "psychological war."

In Peshawar some 500 Afghans demonstrated for the return of ex-King Muhammad Zahir.

Feb. 7. A *mujahedin* commander said that the "Pakistanis are pushing us now to do an all-out attack on Jalalabad," but the *mujahedin* want to wait to prevent a bloodbath.

Feb. 13. President Bush signed a National Security Directive pledging continued financial and military support.

Feb. 14. The last Soviet soldier left Kabul airport.

Feb. 15. The United States rejected a Soviet call for an end to arms shipments to Afghanistan.

Feb. 18. The government declared a nationwide state of emergency.

Muhammad Nabi Muhammadi became spokesman for the *mujahedin* alliance.

Feb. 20. Prime Minister Sharq resigned

Feb. 21. Sultan Ali Keshtmand was appointed chairman of the executive committee of the council of ministers.

Feb. 23. *Mujahedin* leaders elected Abdul Rasul Sayyaf as acting prime minister and Sebghatullah Mujaddidi as acting president of the interim government.

Pir Sayyid Gailani challenged the legitimacy of the government.

Mar. 5. The *mujahedin* launched an offensive against Jalalabad.

Mar. 16. Afghan Army Chief of Staff Lieutenant General Asef Delawar was reported in Jalalabad supervising its defense.

Mar. 20. *Mujahedin* attempt to capture Jalalabad failed.

Mar. 24. An 85-truck government convoy broke through to Jalalabad.

Mar. 27. President Najibullah offered *mujahedin* commanders autonomy if they ended the war. A council of 35 commanders rejected the offer.

1989

Apr. 6. U. S. Secretary of State James Baker III recommended Peter Tomsen as special envoy to the *mujahedin* with the rank of ambassador.

Apr. 12. The *mujahedin* cabinet began a three-day session in Afghan territory.

Apr. 23. The *New York Times* reported that the unsuccessful attack on Jalalabad was made by the Benazir government and U. S. Ambassador Robert Oakley against the advice of General Hamid Gul, director of Inter-Services Intelligence. No Afghan representatives were present.

Apr. 24. Afghan Foreign Minister Abdul Wakil accused Pakistan of aggression.

May 6. Valentin I. Varennikov, Soviet deputy minister of defense, ended a four-day visit to Kabul.

May 9. Sayyid Ahmad Gailani challenged the legitimacy of the interim government.

May 16. KHAD chief Abdul Rahman is said to have defected to Yunis Khalis's *mujahedin* group.

May 17. Government troops reopened Jalalabad-Kabul road.

May 18. President Najibullah invited *mujahedin* leaders and commanders to take part in the Loya Jirga.

May 24. President Najibullah offered regional autonomy to *mujahedin* commanders if they agreed to stop fighting.

May 24. A convoy of Soviet-made tanks and artillery arrived in Kabul.

June 24. President Najibullah appointed Mahmud Baryalai first deputy prime minister.

July 5. Government troops recaptured Tor Kham.

July 19. Units of Burhanuddin Rabbani and Muhd. Nabi Muhammadi were fighting over turf in Helmand Province.

July 24. Defense Minister Shahnawaz Tanai said to be under house arrest.

July 26. Najmuddin Kawiani, head of foreign relations committee of the National Assembly and politburo member, reported secret peace talks with the "opposition."

Aug. 1. Defense Minister Tanai reported to be implicated in coup attempt.

Aug. 11. Abdul Rasul Sayyaf, prime minister, rejected Gulbuddin Hekmatyar's suggestion that the rebels should take control by backing an army coup.

Aug. 14. Government spokesman Muhammad Nabi Amani said 183 civilians were killed in Kabul by rockets in one week.

Aug. 20. Major General Muhammad Faruq Zarif, head of Najib's security force, announced his defection.

Aug. 25. *Jam'iat-i Islami* Commander Mas'ud accused *Hizb-i-Islami* of collusion with Kabul government.

Aug. 29. Fighters of Sayyaf and Muhammadi battle over control of a bridge in Helmand Province that produced lucrative tax and toll revenues.

Aug. 30. Gulbuddin Hekmatyar's *Hizb-i Islami* withdrew from the *mujahedin* alliance.

Oct. 17. Boris Nikolayevich Pastukhov, Soviet ambassador, presented his credentials.

Nov. 7. Lieutenant General Ali Akbar killed in fighting in Kandahar.

Nov. 14. *Mujahedin* launched a three-pronged attack on Jalalabad, which was repulsed.

Nov. 21. President Najibullah extended the state of emergency for another six months.

Nov. 30. *Mujahedin* leaders Burhanuddin Rabbani and Gulbuddin Hekmatyar announced a cease-fire and exchange of prisoners and captured land.

Dec. 2. The Kabul government arrested 127 people suspected of plotting a coup.

Brigadier General Ghulam Haidar was killed in fighting at Jalalabad.

Dec. 21. *Jam'iat* executed four members of Hizb, including Sayyid Jamal, who had ambushed Jam'iat commanders.

Dec. 31. President Najibullah called for PDPA to change its name.

1990

Jan. 24. President Najibullah said that he would step down if his government was defeated in UN-supervised elections.

Feb. 2. Some 10,000 refugees demonstrated in favor of the return of Zahir Shah in Quetta.

Mar. 5. Trials began of some 124 Afghans arrested in December and charged with plotting a coup.

Mar. 6. Defense Minister Shahnawaz Tanai launched a coup against President Najibullah.

Mar. 7. Gulbuddin Hekmatyar said his forces were supporting the Tanai coup.

Mar. 9. Government troops recaptured the Bagram air base.

Other *mujahedin* groups refused to support the Tanai coup.

Mar. 18. The PDPA plenum expelled 24 members for "treachery" against the party and country.

Apr. 6. Two generals and 11 other people were killed at a ceremony when a *mujahedin* group who promised to surrender opened fire on government troops. Fazl Haq Khaliqyar, governor of Herat, was wounded.

Apr. 14. The Kabul government accused the United Nations of failing to monitor alleged violations of the Geneva Accords.

May 21. Prime Minister Khaliqyar presents his new cabinet.

May 28. Kabul government convenes a *Loya Jirga* in preparation for amending the constitution.

June 16. Nine Shi'a *mujahedin* parties unite in the *Hizb-i Wahdat*, Party of Unity.

June 22. Conference of *mujahedin* commanders in Paktia Province.

June 27. Opening of the second party congress, which reelects Dr. Najibullah and changes the name of the party to "Homeland Party" (*Hizb-i Watan*).

July 18. Italian embassy reopened in Kabul.

July 25. Beginning of UN-assisted repatriation of refugees from Pakistan.

July 29–Aug. 25. Najibullah visited the Soviet Union; Abdur Rahim Hatef is acting president.

1990   Sept. 30. Alliance of democratic parties of the Left
                        dissolves itself.
                        Oct. 5. Tirin Kot, administrative center of Oruzgan
                        Province, captured by *mujahedin* forces.
                        Oct. 15. Mas'ud, the *Jam'iat* commander, visits
                        Islamabad, where he meets the Pakistani head of state
                        and Gulbuddin Hekmatyar.
                        Oct. 25. The U.S. Congress reduces its aid to the
                        Afghan resistance.
                        Nov. 19. President Najibullah arrived in Switzerland
                        for discussions with Afghan personalities.

1991   Jan. 9. Afghan General Hashim was captured by the
                        resistance and executed.
                        Jan. 23. Professor Rabbani opens embassy of the
                        resistance in Khartum.
                        Feb. 8. Afghan resistance sends 300 *mujahedin* to
                        Saudi Arabia in war with Iraq. Sayyaf and Hekmatyar
                        protest.
                        Mar. 31. Khost captured by *mujahedin* forces headed
                        by Commander Haqani: 2,200 prisoners taken and
                        seven generals (including Colonel General Muham-
                        mad Zahir Solamal, deputy minister of defense; Major
                        General Ghulam Mustafa, chief of political affairs of
                        the armed force; Major General Muhammad Qasim,
                        commander of artillery, special guards; Major
                        Muhammad Azam, an air force commander;
                        Lieutenant General Shirin, commander of the Khost
                        militia units).
                        Apr. 2. Kabul government declares a "Day of
                        Mourning."
                        Apr. 10. Vice President Sultan Ali Keshtmand was
                        dismissed.
                        Apr. 16. President Najibullah offers a new amnesty to
                        all Afghans living abroad who agree to return to
                        Afghanistan.

1991

Apr. 20. Explosion at Jamilurrahman's Asadabad (Wahhabi) headquarters in Kunar Province results in some 500 killed and 700 wounded. According to eyewitness accounts, the explosion occurred at the Dawa (formerly Asadabad Hotel) and a number of Arabs and 63 Pakistanis were among the killed. Some sources suspect a car bomb for the explosion, whereas the "Wahhabis" claim it was the result of a SCUD missile attack.

Apr. 26. Representatives of the Pakistani military intelligence service (ISI) meet in Geneva with representatives of the Kabul government.

May 21. Javier Pérez de Cuéllar, U. N. secretary-general, issued a five-point proposal for a political settlement in Afghanistan.

May 27–28. Soviet-Pakistan talks in Moscow about Afghanistan.

May 31. Explosion of ammunition depot in Nowshera, Pakistan.

June 20. Babrak Karmal returned to Afghanistan from exile in the Soviet Union.

July 1. The Kabul regime omits all references to the Saur Revolution from official documents .

July 22. Ahmad Shah Mas'ud takes Ishkashem and shortly thereafter the Wakhan Corridor.

Aug. 30. Assassination in Pakistan of Jamilur Rahman, chief of the Kunar "Wahhabi" Republic.

Sept. 13. The USSR and the United States agreed to end delivery of weapons to the Afghan combatants as of January 1, 1992.

Oct. 14. The supreme justice of Kabul declared that all legal decisions must conform to Islamic law.

Nov. 4. Former King Zahir was slightly wounded in an assassination attempt.

Dec. 5. The United Nations agrees on solution for transfer of government.

Dec. 15. The Soviet Union stops arms deliveries to Afghanistan.

1992   Jan. 14. Najibullah annuls decree 14, depriving the royal family of its property.

Feb. 6. Generals Dostum, Naderi, and Momen revolt against Najib government.

Mar. 15. *Mujahedin* seize Samangan Province.

Mar. 18. President Najibullah agreed to resign as soon as interim government was installed.

Mar. 29. Wahdat party takes Sar-i Pol.

Apr. 8. General Dostum takes over Mazar-i Sharif.

Apr. 12. Mas'ud takes control of Salang tunnel.

Apr. 15. Dostum Militia takes Kabul airport.

Apr. 16. Najibullah takes refuge in UN compound. Ghazni and Gardez taken by the resistance.

Military junta holds Kabul, consisting of Baba Khan, Asef Delawar, Abdul Momin, and Nabi Azimi, supported by party people Abdul Wakil, Farid Mazdak, and two other civilians.

The resistance controls Herat.

Apr. 18. Kunduz and Jalalabad fall to the resistance. Rahim Hatef nominated as interim president.

Apr. 21. Pul-i Alam in Logar taken by *Hizb-i Islami*.

Apr. 22. Gardez taken by Jalaluddin Haqani.

Apr. 24. Resistance leaders set up interim Islamic council of 51 members. Mujaddidi assumes provisional control.

Jalalabad taken by *mujahedin*.

Apr. 25. Resistance enters Kabul, partisans of Mas'ud and Hekmatyar fight.

Apr. 26. Mas'ud takes Presidential Palace and also takes barracks from *Hizb-i Islami*.

Shi'a *Harakat-e Islami* takes missile base of Darulaman.

Apr. 28. Mujaddidi arrives in Kabul, proclaims Islamic State of Afghanistan, and announces general amnesty.

Apr. 29. *Hizb-i Islami* fighters ejected from interior ministry. Ahmad Shah Mas'ud arrives in Kabul.

May 3. Egypt recognizes Islamic State of Afghanistan.

1992 Hekmatyar threatens to attack if Dostum does not leave Kabul.

May 6. First session of the Jehad Council under the presidency of Professor Rabbani.

May 10. Sayyid Ahmad Gailani arrives in Kabul.

May 21. Mas'ud and Hekmatyar conclude cease-fire. Yunus Khales arrives in Kabul.

May 24. Mujaddidi nominates Dostum general (*setar genral*) and Naderi (*dagar genral*).

May 30. Dostum and Hekmatyar fight for control of Karte Nau district.

June 19. Dostum Militia and Mas'ud's forces clash.

June 28. Mujaddidi surrenders presidency to Rabbani.

July 4. Violent artillery combat between forces of Dostum and Hekmatyar.

Aug. 2. Yunus Khales resigns from Jehad Council.

Aug. 15. Twenty-seven members of UN staff leave Afghanistan.

Aug. 27. Cease-fire concluded between Rabbani and Hekmatyar.

Sept. 5. Uzbek Militia quits Kabul.

Sept. 17. Agreement of Paghman between Rabbani and Hekmatyar, designation of an assembly for choosing Rabbani's successor.

1993 Feb. 3. The United Nations suspends its aid shipments by way of south and eastern Afghanistan.

Feb. 5. India evacuates its diplomats from Kabul.

Feb. 6. General Dostum is nominated deputy minister of defense.

Feb. 7. Government forces and *Wahdat* fight in the Soviet embassy compound.

Feb. 8. Turkey closes its embassy at Kabul.

Feb. 11. The *imam* of al-Azhar University call on the *mujahedin* to stop fighting and direct their efforts to areas where Muslims are still oppressed. Chinese diplomats leave Kabul.

Feb. 16. The firing in Kabul has stopped for the first time since January 19.

1993

March 7. The Islamabad Accord between Afghan parties (except Khales and Dostum) nominated Rabbani president for 18 months and Hekmatyar prime minister. A defense council of all parties is to be in charge of the ministry of defense; all heavy weapons are to be removed from the capital; a council to be elected in eight months, and presidential and legislative elections to be held in mid-1995. The Organization of Islamic Conference, the Afghan parties, and Pakistan should supervise the cease-fire.

Mar. 8. *Hizb-i Islami* and *Wahdat* fire 70 missiles on Kabul.

Mar. 11. The leaders assemble at Mecca to fix the details of the prerogatives of the prime minister, the control of the defense council, and the power of the Uzbek Militia. The accord was countersigned by King Fahd.

Mar. 19 and 20. Reunion at Jalalabad failed to achieve agreement.

Mar. 22. Fighting between *Wahdat* and *Ittihad* continues in Kabul.

Mar. 23. *Hizb-i Islami* captures Naghlu Dam from *Harakat-e Inqilab-i-Islami*.

Pakistani Militia seize stinger missiles from Mulla Abdul Salam (Mulla Roketi) and the mulla takes 27 hostages in reprisal.

Mar. 28. General Fauzi, a spokesman for Dostum, declares that there will not be any peace without representation of Dostum in the Kabul government.

Apr. 1. *Jam'iat* and *Hizb* form a committee to resolve their problems.

Apr. 2. *Jam'iat* and *Wahdat* agree to release prisoners and restore quiet.

Apr. 7. Afghan defense minister claims that Hekmatyar and Sayyaf supply weapons to Tajik Islamists.

Apr. 9. First break in the cease-fire between *Jam'iat* and *Wahdat*.

1993

Apr. 15. The governors of Herat and Khorasan, Iran, sign an accord of cooperation against drug trafficking

Mar. 25. Kabul blockaded by the forces of Hekmatyar.

May 3. More than 50 Islamists were killed fighting in Tajikistan.

May 9 and 10. Heavy fighting between forces of *Ittihad* and *Wahdat* in Kabul.

May 11. Kabul Museum burns.

May 12. Bombardment of Kabul resumed.

May 13. Mas'ud gains help of Dostum against *Hizb-i Islami* forces.

May 19. Rabbani and Hekmatyar agree to a cease-fire.

May 20. Mas'ud resigns as defense minister.

June 6. Hekmatyar presides at the first meeting of his government at Charasiab.

June 17. Government meets in Paghman.

June 21. Council of ministers meets in Darulaman.

June 23–28. Fighting between *Wahdat* and Mas'ud forces.

July 3. President Rabbani receives General Dostum.

July 12. Dostum and Hekmatyar meet and agree to a cease-fire.

July 15. Mas'ud and Hekmatyar forces fight near airport.

July 26. Mas'ud's forces take Bagram air base from *ittihad*.

Aug. 31. Cease-fire between *Ittihad* and *Wahdat*.

Sept. 14. *Hizb-i Islami* bombards eastern Kabul.

Sept. 15. The Afghan Communist party is said to have had a meeting in Microrayon and elected Mahmud Baryalai to head the party.

Oct. 2. A group of about 300 Tajik and *mujahedin* fighters carried an attack into Tajikistan.

Oct. 19. Kabul-Jalalabad Highway has been reopened for traffic.

Oct. 24. Afghanistan and Tajikistan sign an agreement to export natural gas to Tajikistan.

1993   Nov. 2. A Russian plane bombards Badakhshan.
              Nov. 9. Ms. Robin Raphel, American undersecretary
              of state for South Asia, visits Kabul regarding
              economic and humanitarian aid. She met Rabbani,
              Hekmatyar, Mas'ud, and Dostum.
              Nov. 21. Islamist ideologue Hasan Al-Turabi visits
              Kabul.
              Nov. 28. Arrival at Kabul of French Chargé d'Affaires
              M. Didier Leroy.
              Dec. 3. Telephone connection with Kabul restored.
              Dec. 23. General Dostum regains Sher Khan Bandar
              without a fight.

1994   Jan. 1. Forces of Dostum and Hekmatyar attack Kabul
              forces.
              Jan. 5. Rabbani forces take Kabul airport.
              General Momen killed in helicopter accident.
              Jan. 6. Fighting around Bala Hisar and Microrayon.
              Mujaddidi supports Dostum-Hekmatyar alliance.
              Jan. 10. Pul-i Khishti mosque destroyed.
              Apr. 2. M. Mestiri, UN emissary, arrived in Kabul
              and met with Rabbani, Mas'ud, and Hekmatyar.
              Apr. 4. Mas'ud's forces attack Pul-i Khumri held by
              Dostum and Ismaili forces.
              Apr. 6. Mestiri leaves Kabul without obtaining a
              cease-fire between the belligerents.
              Apr. 10. End of two-week cease-fire.
              Apr. 19. Rabbani announces his intention to prolong
              his mandate until December 1994, because his
              adversaries did not respect the accords of Jalalabad.
              Apr. 24. Mulla Salam, also called Mulla Roketi,
              holds two Chinese engineers and 10 Pakistanis 1994
              and demands that Pakistan free his brother and return
              the three stingers captured from him.
              Apr. 27. According to Red Cross International, the
              civil war in Kabul has resulted in 2,500 deaths,
              17,000 wounded, and 632,000 refugees from Kabul
              since January 1, 1994. At least 20,000 houses were
              destroyed.

1994

May 1. Offensive of Hekmatyar forces against Kabul is stopped.

May 7. Grand reunion of Ghazni commanders, Haqani and Ismael Khan participate.

May 9. Kabul air force bombards Mazar and Pul-i Khumri.

May 13–14. Dostum bombards the 10th Division at Qargha near Kabul.

May 17–18. Sayyaf takes Maidan Shahr from Hekmatyar forces.

May 21–22. General Dostum indicates having used six stinger missiles to down two aircraft of Rabbani. Dostum's head of the air force, General Jalil, claims to have 32 operational planes, more than 22,000 bombs, and 100 pilots.

May 28. Conflict within *Wahdat* between supporters of Akbari and Mazari.

June 3. Dostum and Ismail Khan forces clash in Shindand. Dostum bombs Herat.

June 8. Rabbani proposes that his successor be chosen by a Loya Jirga.

June 10. Fighting resumes in Kabul.

June 15. Rabbani extends his "mandate," which was to expire in June, for another six months.

June 17. Yunus Khales declares himself interim president.

June 19. Ismail Khan escapes an assassination attempt.

June 25. *Harakat* recaptures control of Darulaman Palace from *Hizb-i Islami*.

June 26. Rabbani's forces expel Dostum's forces from Bala Hisar and Maranjan Hill.

July 8. The parties of Gailani, Hekmatyar, Mujaddidi, Muhammadi, Muhseni, Mazari, and Dostum form a commission to negotiate with Rabbani and Sayyaf.

July 14. The Pakistani minister of foreign affairs threatens to close the offices of Sayyaf's party, if Mulla Roketi does not liberate his hostages. They were freed on July 21.

1994

July 20. Official opening of the Herat assembly in the presence of 700 participants.

July 24. Rabbani arrived at Herat, but did not participate in the assembly.

July 29. BBC correspondent Mir Wais Jalil was killed in an area controlled by Hekmatyar.

Aug. 7. Rabbani receives Muhammadi, Muhseni, and Gailani at Kabul.

Aug. 16. Pakistani authorities prevent Ariana from flying over Pakistani territory, because it does not observe international rules.

Sept. 8. *Hizb-i Islami* takes control of Khenjan north of the Salang Pass.

Sept. 12. Fighting breaks out between *Wahdat* and Harakat for control of Darulaman. Akbari defects from *Wahdat*.

Sept. 25. Iranian intermediaries help in establishing a cease-fire between the Shi'a parties.

Oct. 2. Pakistan holds goods destined for Afghanistan in Karachi.

Oct. 11. According to Red Cross International, 1,100 people were killed and 23,000 wounded in Kabul in September.

Nov. 2. A Pakistani convoy of goods destined for Turkmenistan was stopped by commanders between Spin Boldak and Kandahar. Taleban clash with commanders.

Nov. 5. The Taleban capture Kandahar, the commander of the Muslim group is hanged.

Nov. 7. A spokesman for Rabbani accuses Uzbekistan of interference in Afghan internal affairs for having delivered 30 Russian tanks to Dostum.

Nov. 8. Visit to Kabul by a UN delegation for the first time in seven months.

Nov. 13. Having repelled the commanders Lalay (Mahaz) and Sarkateb (*Hizb-i* Hekmatyar), the Taleban take control of Kandahar.

Nov. 17. The Pakistani minister of interior announced that Pakistan would start to repair the route from

1994

Kandahar to Herat. Kabul calls this an invasion of Afghanistan.

Dec. 5. Arrival in Kabul of the first aid convoy in six months, 32 trucks for Rabbani and 32 for his opponents.

Dec. 6. Return to Pakistan of the convoy from Turkmenistan.

Dec. 12. Departure of Rabbani for Morocco to participate at a meeting of the Organization of the Islamic Conference.

Dec. 13. Arrival of a UN aid convoy in Kunduz, the first in two years.

Dec. 19. Arrival in Kabul of an Indian delegation to prepare reopening of the embassy.

Dec. 20. Dostum arrives in Islamabad.

Dec. 28. Mestiri arrives in Islamabad to restart his peace effort.

Dec. 30. Arrival in Afghanistan of a Sudanese delegation for talks with Hekmatyar.

1995

Jan. 1. M. Mestiri arrives in Kabul during an unofficial cease-fire.

Maulawi Yunus Khales returns to Jalalabad after an absence of 19 years.

Jan. 4. Mestiri opens a new UN office in Jalalabad and meets with Hekmatyar. The American ambassador to Pakistan meets Rabbani in Kabul.

Jan. 17. Seven trucks with UN aid were plundered in Sarobi in the area controlled by Hekmatyar.

Jan. 22. The access roads to Kabul were again closed by the *Hizb-i* Hekmatyar.

Jan. 24. The Taleban take Ghazni.

Jan. 30. Dostum's forces capture Kunduz.

Feb. 4. The Taleban have deposed Qari Baba and replaced him with Maulawi Ihsanullah as head of Ghazni Province.

Feb. 10. Taleban capture Maidan Shahr. Mestiri announced a power transfer for February 20, at which Rabbani was to transfer power to a committee of 20 persons.

1995

Feb. 11. The Taleban claim capture of Pul-i Alam and control of the entire Logar Province.

Feb. 14. Hekmatyar retires his forces from the Kabul area to Sarobi, abandoning his heavy weapons.

Feb. 15. The Taleban occupy Pul-i Charkhi and expel the *Hizb-i Islami* from Khost.

Feb. 16. Rabbani' forces have retaken Kunduz.

Feb. 17. Kabul airport reopens after being closed for more than a year.

Feb. 19. The Taleban take Sharan, center of Paktika, and Gardez, center of Paktia.

Feb. 20. *Jam'iat* forces fight *Wahdat*. Mestiri admits failure of his plan for transfer of power in Kabul.

Feb. 25. The Taleban threaten to attack Kabul if Rabbani does not lay down his arms.

Mar. 5. Mazari declares his readiness to recognize the Kabul government if the Hazara get 25 percent representation.

Mar. 6. *Jam'iat* forces attack the positions of *Wahdat* at Kabul.

Mar. 7. Mazari threatens to use SCUD missiles if Rabbani's forces won't stop their attacks.

Mar. 9. *Wahdat* surrenders its position south of Kabul to the Taleban. Qazi Humayun, the new Pakistani ambassador, arrives in Kabul.

Mar. 10. Nabi Muhammadi deserts Rabbani for the Taleban. Sayyaf sells his arms depot at the Pakistani border to a Trimangal tribal chief.

Mar. 11. Kabul forces capture all the territory held by *Wahdat*, including the SCUD base at Darulaman and Kabul Museum.

Mar. 13. Mazari and a number of *Wahdat* leaders are killed while in Taleban captivity.

Mar. 14. The Taleban claim conquest of Nimruz and Ghor provinces.

Mar. 19. Mas'ud's forces take Charasiab from the Taleban.

Mar. 26. Mazari is buried in Mazar-i Sharif.

Mar. 30. A common grave of 22 executed Hazaras was found at Charasiab.

1995

Apr. 1. Mujaddidi replaces Hekmatyar as head of the four-party opponents of Rabbani.

Apr. 4. Taleban attack the Shindand air base and Herat. Also fight *Jam'iat* forces in Maidan Shahr.

Apr. 7. Iran prohibits commercial transit to Afghanistan.

Apr. 12. *Jam'iat* emissary Abdur Rahman meets Dostum in Tashkent.

Apr. 13. Taleban demand that foreign states not reopen their embassies in Kabul.

Apr. 19. The Taleban block the delivery of fuel to Kabul. *Hizb* and Taleban establish contacts.

Apr. 27. The Taleban free 300 captives of Dostum's forces.

Apr. 28. Taleban defeated in the Farah area.

May 3. India reopens its embassy in Kabul.

May 6. American diplomats visit Kabul University.

May 9. The Pakistani ambassador returns to Kabul. Forces of Ismael Khan take Farah.

May 14. Arrival in Kabul of delegations of the government of Tajikistan and the opposition.

May 15. Forces of Rabbani capture Zaranj from the Taleban.

May 17. M. Nuri and M. Rahmanov hold talks at Kabul.

May 24. Continuation of stalled negotiation between representatives of Dostum and Rabbani. Questions raised were opening of the Salang route and lifting of the *fatwa* proclaiming holy war against Dostum.

May 29. Arrival of Prince Turki al-Faisal, chief of the Saudi secret service, in Kabul.

June 20. *Jam'iat* forces take control of Bamian from the Shi'a *Wahdat*.

June 29. Sardar Abdul Wali, son-in-law of ex-King Zahir Shah, arrived in Islamabad at invitation of Pakistan government.

Aug. 20. Abdul Wali returns to Rome.

Aug. 26. Taleban take Girishk.

Aug. 31. Taleban take Delaram.

Sept. 2. Taleban take Shindand

1995   Sept. 5. Taleban take Herat and Islam Qala.

Sept. 6. Kabuli crowds attack Pakistan embassy, one person is killed and 20 are wounded, including the ambassador.

Sept. 7. Taleban take Ghor Province.

Sept. 15. Explosion in Herat by enemies of Taleban.

Sept. 24. Another explosion and sabotage.

Nov. 10. UNICEF suspends educational assistance to Taleban-controled areas because of the closing of girls' schools.

Nov. 14. It is reported that "Mulla Roketi" was killed.

1996   May 13. Hekmatyar concludes an anti-Taleban treaty with Rabbani.

Hekmatyar rejoins Kabul government as prime minister; upon arrival in Kabul orders all cinemas closed and forbids music to be broadcast on Kabul Radio and Television. He advises women to observe Islamic code of dress and orders government officials to perform their noon prayers in their places of work.

July 6. Prime Minister Hekmatyar forms new cabinet: Wahidullah Sabawun (of *Hizb*), minister of defense; Abdul Hadi Arghandiwal (of *Hizb*), minister of finance; Muhammad Yunus Qanuni (of *Jam'iat*), minister of interior; Ahmad Shah Ahmadzai (of *Ittihad*), minister of education; Qiyamuddin Kashaf (of *Ittihad*), minister of Information and Culture; Sayyid Ali Javid (*Harakat* of Muhsini), minister of planning; Sayyid Husain Anwari (of *Harakat*), work and social affairs; Maulawi Samiullah (of Kunar *Jama'at Tauhid*), minister of martyrs and disabled; Alimi Balkhi (of Akbari *Wahdat*), minister of commerce; and Qutbuddin Helal (faction not known), deputy prime minister.

BIBLIOGRAPHY

The sources presented in the following sections are a representative selection of books and articles in English with just a few titles in French and German.

The reader who desires a comprehensive survey may refer to the bibliographies listed below, especially the somewhat dated one by Kith McLachlan and William Whittaker (1983). Other bibliographies include the two-volume *Bibliographie der Afghanistan-Literatur* (1968 and 1969), which also lists sources in Dari and Pashtu. The most recent bibliographical source is the work by Muhammad Akram (1990), which is available on microfiche at the Bibliotheca Afghanica in Liestal, Switzerland.

No reference works dealing specifically with Afghan military history from 1747 to the 1990s exist. Standard reference works such as *Brassey's Battles*, by John Laffin; *A Dictionary of Battles*, by David Eggenberger; and *The Encyclopedia of Military History: From 3,500 B.C. to the Present*, by Ernest R. Dupuy and Trevor N. Dupuy are too large in scope to be useful for Afghan military history.

However, there are a good number of excellent sources examining various periods of Afghan military history, most of them produced by Englishmen for the period from 1747 to the early twentieth century. They include official accounts of Anglo-Afghan wars, such as *The First Afghan War and its Causes*, by Sir Henry M. Durand; *The Afghan Wars 1839–42 and 1878–80*, by A Forbes; *History of the War in Afghanistan*, by Sir J. W. Kaye; *Signal Catastrophe: The Story of the Disastrous Retreat from Kabul, 1842*, by Patrick A. Macrory; *The First Afghan War, 1838–42*, by James A. Norris; and *Journal of the Disasters in Afghanistan, 1841–2*, by Lady F. Sale.

Major works on the second Anglo-Afghan war include *The Second Afghan War, 1878–80*, an abridged official account by F. G. Cardew; *Recollections of the Kabul Campaign, 1879 and 1880*, by Joshua Duke; *The Second Afghan War, 1878–79–80, Its Causes, Its Conduct, and Its Consequences*, by Henry B. Hanna; *The Afghan War of 1879–80*, by

Howard Hensman; *The Second Afghan War*, 1878–80 Official Account by the Indian Army Intelligence Branch; *Kurum, Kabul & Kandahar, Being a Brief Record of Impressions of Three Campaigns Under General Roberts*, by Charles G. Robertson; and finally *The Afghan Campaigns of 1878–80, Compiled from Official and Private Sources*, by Sydney Shadbolt. Numerous military officers published books on their exploits.

For the short, third Anglo-Afghan war, the reader will have to rely on *Afghanistan, 1919: An Account of Operations in the Third Afghan War*, by George N. Molesworth, and on the official account of *The Third Afghan War, 1919*, by the General Staff Branch of Army Headquarters in India.

An excellent account of all three Anglo-Afghan wars was produced by T. A. Heathcote, entitled *The Afghan Wars, 1839–1919*. The most recent period, including the Soviet intervention in Afghanistan and the Afghan civil war, is discussed at great length by participants, journalists, world travelers, and others. Major works dealing with the technical aspects of the war are *Russia's War in Afghanistan*, by David C. Isby, as well as several of his other publications; *The Stumbling Bear: Soviet Military Performance*, by Scott McMichael; *The Bear Trap: Afghanistan's Untold Story*, by Mohammad Yousaf and Mark Adkin; and *War in Afghanistan*, by Mark Urban. An excellent work that deals with the *Afgantsy* (Soviet veterans) and the political impact of the war on the Soviet Union is *Afghanistan: The Soviet Union's Last War*, by Mark Galeotti.

Many other excellent works, too many to list here, will be found in this select bibliography dealing with the social, economic, and political aspects of the war. *Islam and Resistance in Afghanistan*, by Olivier Roy; *Afghanistan and the Soviet Union*, by Henry S. Bradsher; and *Afghanistan's Two Party Communism*, by Anthony Arnold have become classics. An excellent recent addition to the literature is Barnett R. Rubin's *The Fragmentation of Afghanistan*.

General works by Banuazizi et al., Dupree, Fraser-Tytler, Sir Percy Sykes, Gregorian, Halliday, Harrison, Kakar, Khalilzad, Poullada, Shahrani, and several volumes by this writer may be consulted for background information. *The Historical Dictionary of Afghanistan* is a handy reference source on Afghanistan, describing major events, important places, leading personalities — up to 1990 — and significant aspects of culture, religion, and economy.

CONTENTS

1. References

Adamec, Ludwig W. *Biographical Dictionary of Afghanistan.* Graz: Akademische Druck u. Verlagsanstalt (ADEVA) 1987.

————. *Historical Dictionary of Afghanistan.* Metuchen: Scarecrow Press, 1991.

————. *Historical and Political Gazetteer of Afghanistan.* 6 vols. Graz: ADEVA, 1972–85.

————. Historical and Political Who's Who of Afghanistan.. Graz: ADEVA, 1974.

Banks, Arthur. *A World Atlas of Military History, 1861–1945.* New York: Hippocrene Books, 1973.

Black, J. L. *The Soviet Union and Afghanistan.* Institute of Soviet and East European Studies, Bibliography No. 2. Carleton University, 1983.

Bonarjee, Pitt D. *A Handbook of the Fighting Races of India.* Calcutta, 1899.

Brereton, John M. *The Horse in War.* New York: Arco, 1976.

Davis, Anthony. "The Afghan Army." *Jane's Intelligence Review* 5, no. 3 (March 1993).

Dupuy, R. Ernest, and Trevor N. Dupuy. *The [Jane's] Encyclopedia of Military History: From 3,500 B.C. to the Present.* London: Harper and Row, 1970 and 1986.

Eggenberger, David. *A Dictionary of Battles.* New York: Crowell, 1967.

Farrow, Edward S. *Farrow's Military Encyclopedia.* 3 vols. New York: The Author, 1885.

General Staff, India. *Military Report, Afghanistan.* Pt. 1, *History.* Simla: General Staff, 1940.

Harbottle, Thomas B. *Dictionary of Battles from the Earliest Date to the Present Time*. London: Gale Research Co., 1904.

Hayward, P. H. *Jane's Dictionary of Military Terms*. London: Macdonald, 1975.

Hogg, Oliver F. G. *Artillery: Its Origin, Heyday, and Decline*. Hamden, Conn.: Archon Books, 1970.

Intelligence Branch, Chief of Staff. *Frontier and Overseas Expeditions from India*. Vol. 3 Calcutta: Government of India Press, 1910.

Katz, David J. "Afghanistan Biographic Database Comprehensive List." Washington, D.C.: Department of State, 1989.

Keegan, John. *A History of Warfare*. London: Hutchinson, 1993.

Keegan, John, and Andrew Wheatcroft. *Who's Who in Military History*. London: Weidenfeld and Nicolson, 1976.

Knollys, William W. *A Handy Dictionary of Military Terms*. London, 1873.

Luttwak, Edward. *Dictionary of Modern War*. New York: Harper and Row, 1971.

Maguire, Thomas M. *A Summary of Modern Military History with Comments on the Leading Operations*. London, 1887.

Maksey, Kenneth. *The Penguin Encyclopedia of Weapons and Military Technology from Prehistory to the Present*. London, 1993.

McLachlan, K., and William Whittaker. *A Bibliography of Afghanistan*. London: Menas Press, 1983.

Military Thought, 1937–1973. *Chronological, Author, and Title Index*. Washington, D.C.: Defense Intelligence College, 1981.

Nicolls, Sir Jasper. Commander-in-Chief, India. *Private Papers*. London: India Office Library.

Pant, G. N. *Studies in Indian Weapons and Warfare*. New Delhi: 1970.

Parkinson, Roger. *Encyclopedia of Modern War*. New York: Stein and Day, 1977.

Polmar, Norman et al. *Dictionary of Military Abbreviations*. Annapolis: Naval Institute Press, 1994.

Ridgway, R. T. I. *The Pathans*. Calcutta: Government of India Press, 1910.

Scott, Harriet Fast, and William F. Scott. *The Armed Forces of the USSR*. Boulder: Westview Press, 1984.

Spaulding, Oliver L. et al. *Warfare: A Study of Military Methods from the Earliest Times*. Washington, D.C.: Infantry Journal Press, 1957.

U. S. Army Field Manual 100-2-3. *The Soviet Army: Troops, Organization and Equipment*. Washington, D.C.: U. S. Government Printing Office, 1984.

Wilhelm, Thomas. *A Military Dictionary and Gazetteer*. Philadelphia: L. R. Hamersly, 1881.

Wragg, David W. Dictionary of Aviation. Reading: Osprey Publishing, 1974.

2. General

Adamec, Ludwig W. *Afghanistan 1900–1923: A Diplomatic History*. Berkeley: University of California Press, 1967.

———. *Afghanistan's Foreign Affairs to the Mid-Twentieth Century: Relations with the USSR, Germany, and Britain*. Tucson: University of Arizona Press, 1974.

Ahady, Anwar-ul-Haq. "Afghanistan: State Breakdown." In *Revolutions of the Late Twentieth Century,* by Jack A. Goldstone et al.

Al-Amri, Abdullah Sager. "The Doctrine of Jihad in Islam and its Application in the Context of the Islamic Jihad Movement in Afghanistan, 1979–1988." Master's Thesis, University of Idaho, 1990.

Anglesey, Marquess of. *A History of the British Cavalry: 1816 – 1919*. London: Shoe String Press, 1973.

Argyll, George. *The Afghan Question from 1841 to 1878*. London: Strahan, 1879.

Banuazizi, Ali, and Myron Weiner, eds. *The State, Religion and Ethnic Politics: Afghanistan, Iran and Pakistan*. Syracuse: Syracuse University Press, 1986.

Barton, Sir William. *India's North-West Frontier*. London: J. Murray, 1939.

Caroe, Olaf K. *The Pathans, 550 B.C.–A.D. 1957*. London: Oxford University Press, 1958.

Cohen, Stephen P. *The Indian Army: Its Contribution to the Development of a Nation*. Berkeley: University of California Press, 1971.

Colton, T., and T. Gustafson, eds. *Soldiers and the Soviet State*. Princeton: Princeton University Press, 1990.

Cotton, Sydney J. *Nine Years on the North-west Frontier of India from 1854–63*. London: Bentley, 1868.

Dupree, Louis. *Afghanistan*. Princeton: Princeton University Press, 1973.

Elliot, James G. *The Frontier 1839–1947: The Story of the North-West Frontier of India*. London: Cassell, 1968.

Elphinstone, Mountstuart. *An Account of the Kingdom of Caubul, and Its Dependencies in Persia, Tartary, and India; Comprising a View of the Afghaun Nation, and a History of the Dooraunee Monarchy*. London, 1815; Graz: ADEVA, 1969.

Fraser-Tytler, W. K. *Afghanistan, A Study of Political Development in Central Asia*. London: Oxford University Press, 1958.

Galeotti, Mark. *The Age of Anxiety: Security and Politics in Soviet and Post-Soviet Russia*. London: Frank Cass, 1994.

Gaury, Gerald de, and H. V. F. Winstone. *The Road to Kabul*. London: Quartet Books, 1981.

Goddard, E. "The Indian Army; Company and Raj," *ASA* 63 (Oct. 1976).

Gregorian, Vartan. *The Emergence of Modern Afghanistan: Politics of Reform and Modernization, 1880–1946*. Stanford: Stanford University Press, 1969.

Groetzbach, Erwin. *Afghanistan*. Darmstadt: Wissenschaftliche Buchgesellschaft, 1990.

Heathcote, T. A. *The Afghan Wars, 1839–1919*. London: Osprey, 1980.

Holden, G. *Soviet Military Reform*. London: Pluto Press, 1991.

Kakar, Hasan. *Afghanistan: A Study in Internal Political Developments, 1880–1896*. Lahore: Punjab Educational Press, 1971.

———. *Government and Society in Afghanistan: The Reign of Amir 'Abd al-Rahman Khan*. Austin: Texas University Press, 1979.

Keppel, Arnold. *Gun-Running and the Indian North-West Frontier*. Quetta, Pakistan: Gosha-e-Adab, 1977.

Lala, Mohana. *Life of the Amir Dost Mohammed Khan of Kabul*. Karachi, Pakistan: Oxford University Press, 1846.

Lockhart, L. *The Fall of the Safavi Dynasty and the Afghan Occupation of Persia*. Cambridge: Cambridge University Press, 1958.

Malleson, George B. *Decisive Battles of India, 1746–1849*. London: W. H. Allen, 1883.

———. *History of Afghanistan from the Earliest Period to the Outbreak of the War of 1878*. London: W. H. Allen, 1879.

Miller, Charles. *Khyber: The Story of an Imperial Migraine*. New York: Macmillan, 1977.

Morison, Frederick. *From Alexander Burnes to Frederick Roberts: A Survey of Imperial Frontier Policy*. London, 1936.

Nabi, Eden. *The Modernization of Inner Asia*. 1991.

Nevill, Hugh L. *Campaigns on the North-west Frontier*. London, 1912. Reprint, Lahore: Sang-e Meel Publication, 1977.

Nichols, Robert. *The Frontier "Tribal" Areas, 1840–1990*. New York: Afghanistan Forum, 1995.

Nyrop, Richard F., and Donald Seekins, eds. *Afghanistan: A Country Study*. Washington, D.C.: American University Press, 1986.

Orywal, Erwin. *Die Ethnischen Gruppen Afghanistans*. Wiesbaden: Ludwig Reichert Verlag, 1986.

Poullada, Leon B. *Reform and Rebellion in Afghanistan, 1919–1929*. Ithaca: Cornell University Press, 1973.

———. "Afghanistan and the United States: The Crucial Years." *Middle East Journal* 35 (1981).

Raverty, H. G. *Notes on Afghanistan and Baluchistan*. London, 1888. Reprint, Quetta: Gosha-e Adab, 1976.

Richards, D. S. *The Savage Frontier*. London: Macmillan, 1990.

Rodenbough, Theodore F. *Afghanistan and the Anglo-Russian Dispute: An Account of Russia's Advance toward India*. New York: G. P. Putnam, 1885.

Shahrani, M. Nazif. "State Building and Social Fragmentation in Afghanistan: An Historical Perspective." In *State, Religion and Ethnic Politics*. Edited by A. Banuazizi and M. Weiner. Syracuse: Syracuse University Press, 1986.

Singh, Ganda. *Ahmad Shah Durrani*. Bombay: Asia Publishing, 1959.

Swinson, Arthur. *North-West Frontier: People and Events, 1839–1947*. New York: Praeger, 1967.

Sykes, Sir Percy. *A History of Afghanistan*. London: Macmillan, 1940.

Tarzi, Nanguyalai. *Les Relations Afghano-Russe*. Paris: Université de Paris, 1970.

Wylly, Col. Harold C. *From the Black Mountain to Waziristan, being an Account of the Border Countries and the More Turbulent of the Tribes Controlled by the North West Frontier Province, and of Our Military Relations with Them in the Past*. London: Macmillan, 1912.

3. War of Independence to First Afghan War

Abbott, Augustus. *The Afghan War, 1839–42: From the Journal and Correspondence of Major-General Augustus Abbott*, edited by Charles Low. London: Richard Bentley, 1879.

Allan, J. "The Strategic Principles of Lord Lytton's Afghan Policy." *Journal of the Royal Central Asian Society* 24 (1937).

Allen, Isaac N. *Diary of a March Through Sinde and Afghanistan with the Troops under the Command of General Sir William Nott and Sermons Delivered on Various Occasions during the Campaign of 1842*. London: Hatchard, 1843.

Atkinson, James. *The Expedition into Afghanistan: Personal Narrative of the Campaign, 1839–40, Up to the Surrender of Dost Muhammad Khan*. London: W. H. Allen, 1842.

Barr, William. *Journal of the March from Delhi to Caubul with the Mission of Sir C. M. Wade*. London: James Madden, 1844.

Barthrop, Michael. "The Sorties from Jellalabad 1842." *Journal of the Society for Army Historical Research* (JSAHR) 56 (summer 1976).

Bellew, Henry W. *Afghanistan and the Afghans*. London: Sampson Low Maiston, 1979.

Buist, George. *Outline of the Operations in Scinde and Afghanistan*. Bombay: Times Office, 1843.

Colonial Society, East India Committee. *Report of the East India Committee of the Colonial Society on the Causes and Consequences of the Afghan War*. London: James Maynard, 1842.

Dennie, William H. *Personal Narrative of the Campaigns in Afghanistan*. Dublin: W. Curry, 1843. Compiled and arranged by William E. Steele.

Diver, Katherine H. M. *Kabul to Kandahar*. London: John Murray, 1935.

Diver, Maud. *The Hero of Herat*. London: John Murray, 1924.

———. *The Judgment of the Sword*. London: John Murray, 1913.

Dupree, Louis. "Afghan and British Military Tactics in the First Anglo-Afghan War (1838–1842)." *Army Quarterly and Defence Journal* (AQ) 107 (April 1977).

———. "The Retreat of the British Army from Kabul to Jalalabad in 1842: History and Folklore." *Journal of the Folklore Institute* (1967).

Dupree, Nancy H. "The Question of Jalalabad during the First Anglo-Afghan War." *Asian Affairs* (ASA) 62 (Feb. and June 1975).

Durand, Sir Henry M. *The First Afghan War and its Causes*. London: Longmans, Green, 1879.

Eyre, Vincent. *The Military Operations at Caubul*. London: W. H. Allen, 1843.

Fane, Henry E. *Five Years in India: Comprising a Narrative of Travels in the Presidency of Bengal, a Visit to the Court of Runjeet Sing, a Residence in the Himalayah Mountains, and Account of the Late Expedition to Kabul and Afghanistan*. London: Henry Colburn, 1842.

Forbes, A. *The Afghan Wars 1839–42 and 1878–80*. London: Seeley, 1892.

Gleig, G. R. *With Sale's Brigade in Afghanistan*. London: John Murray, 1846.

Greenwood, J. *Narrative of the Late Victorious Campaign in Afghanistan*. London: H. Colburn, 1844.

Havelock, Henry. *Narrative of the War in Afghanistan. In 1838–39*. 2 vols. London: Henry Colburn, 1840.

Heathcote, T. A. *The Afghan Wars, 1839–1919*. London: Osprey, 1980.

Holdsworth, T. W. E. *The Campaign of the Indus*. London: T. C. Saville, 1840.

Hough, William. *A History of British Military Exploits*. London: W. H. Allen, 1853.

———. *Narrative of the March and Operations of the Army of the Indus*. London: W. H. Allen, 1841.

Jacob, John. *Memoir of the First Campaign in the Hills North of Cutchee, under Major Billamore, in 1839–40, by One of His Surviving Subalterns*. London, 1852.

James, David. *Lord Roberts*. London: Hollis and Carter, 1954.

Kaye, Sir J. W. *History of the War in Afghanistan*. London: W. H. Allen, 1890.

———. *The Lives of Indian Officers*. London: A. Straham, 1867.

———. *Long Engagements: A Tale of the Afghan Rebellion*. London, 1846.

Kennedy, Richard H. *Narrative of the Campaign of the Army of the Indus, in Sind and Kabool in 1838–39*. 2 vols. London: Richard Bentley, 1840.

Low, C. R. *The Life of Sir George Pollock*. London: W. H. Allen, 1873.

———. *The Afghan War 1838–42: From the Journal and Correspondence of Major-General Augustus Abbott*. London: Richard Bentley, 1879.

Lunt, James. "Bokhara' Burnes." *History Today* (HT), 14 October 1964.

———. "The Illustrious Garrison." *HT*, 16 July 1966.

———. "Lady Sale in Kabul, 1842." *HT*, 9 October 1959.

Mackinnon, Daniel H. *Military Service and Adventures in the Far East: Including Sketches of the Campaigns Against the Afghans in 1839, and the Sikhs in 1845–6*. 2 vols. London: John Oliver, 1847.

Macrory, Patrick A. *The Fierce Pawns*. Philadelphia: J. B. Lippincott, 1966.

———. *Signal Catastrophe: The Story of the Disastrous Retreat from Kabul, 1842*. London: Hodder and Stoughton, 1966.

Martin, Denyse R. *The Postal History of the First Afghan War, 1838–1842*. London: Bath, 1964.

Melville, William H. *Remarks on the War in Afghanistan*. Edinburgh, 1842.

Neill, John M. B. *Recollections of Four Years' Service in the East with His Majesty's 40th Regiment: Comprising an Account of the Taking of Kurachee in Lower Scinde, in 1839; Operations of the Candahar Division of the Avenging Army of Afghanistan in 1841 and 1842; Under Major General Sir W. Nott*. London: R. Bentley, 1845.

Norris, James. A. *The First Afghan War, 1838–42*. London: Cambridge University Press, 1967.

O'Ballance, Edgar. *Afghan Wars 1839–1992*. London: Brassey's, 1993.

Outram, James. *Rough Notes of the Campaign in Sinde and Afghanistan*. London: J. M. Richardson, 1840.

Pearse, H. W. "First Forcing of the Khaibar Pass, 1838–39," *Journal of the Royal United Service Institution* (JRUSI) 41 (April 1897).

Pottinger, George. *The Afghan Connection*. Edinburgh: Scottish Academic Press, 1983.

———. *The Ten-Rupee Jezail: Figures in the First Afghan War 1838–1842*. Norwich: M. Russell, 1993.

Rawling, Gerald. "Afghan Disaster." *British History Illustrated* (BHI), 4 September 1977.

Roberts, F. S. *Forty-One Years in India*. 2 vols. London: Richard Bentley, 1900.

Sale, Lady F. *Journal of the Disasters in Afghanistan, 1841–2*. London: John Murray, 1843.

Sale, Robert H. *The Defence of Jellalabad*. London: W. L. Walton, 1846.

Stocqueler, J. H. *Memorials of Afghanistan*. Calcutta, 1843. Reprint, Peshawar: Saeed Jan Qureshi, 1983.

Taylor, William. *Scenes and Adventures in Afghanistan*. London: Luzac, 1847.

Trotter, Lionel. *The Earl of Auckland*. Oxford: Clarendon Press, 1890.

Urquhart, David. *The Edinburgh Review and the Afghan War: Letters Reprinted from the Morning Herald*. London: Diplomatic Review Office, 1843.

Vigne, Godfrey T. *A Personal Narrative of a Visit to Ghuzni, Kabul, and Afghanistan, and of a Residence at the Court of Dost Muhammad: With Notices of Runjit Sing, Khiva, and the Russian Expedition*. London: Whitaker, 1843.

Waller, John H. *Beyond the Khyber Pass: The Road to British Disaster in the First Afghan War*. New York: Random House, 1990.

4. Second Afghan War to 1901

Adye, John. *Indian Frontier Policy: An Historical Sketch.* London: Elder, 1897.

———. *Sitana: A Mountain Campaign on the Borders of Afghanistan in 1863.* London: Richard Bentley, 1867.

Ali, Mohammad. "The Battle of Maiwand." *Afghanistan,* 2 October 1955, 26–38.

Anderson, J. H. *The Afghan War: 1878–1880.* London, 1905.

Ashe, Waller, ed. *Personal Records of the Kandahar Campaign, by Officers Engaged Therein.* London: David Bogue, 1881.

Bajwa, Fauja S. *The Military System of the Sikhs During the Period 1799–1849.* Delhi: Motilal Banarsidas, 1964.

Bellew, Henry W. *Journal on a Political Mission to Afghanistan in 1857.* London: Smith Elder, 1862.

Brereton, John M. "Maiwand." *Blackwood's Magazine* (BLM), July 1976, 320.

———. "The Panjdeh Crisis, 1885." *HT.* 29 January 1979.

Brook, Henry F. *Private Journal of Henry Francis Brooke.* Dublin, 1881.

Brown, R. H. "Account of the Construction of Bridges Over the Kabul River, Near Jalalabad, During the Operations in Afghanistan, 1880," Ordnance Note No. 325. In United States, Ordnance Department, *Ordnance Notes* 12 vols. Washington, D.C., 1873–84.

Bruce, G. *Retreat from Kabul.* London: Mayflower-Dell, 1967.

Cardew, F. G. *The Second Afghan War 1878–80.* London: J. Murray, 1908. (Abridged official account)

Colquhoun, James A. S. *With the Kurram Field Force, 1878–79*. London: W. H. Allen, 1881.

Combe, Boyce A. *Letters from B.A.C.: Afghanistan, 1878*.

Cotton, Sydney J. *Nine Years on the North-west Frontier of India from 1854–63*. London, 1868.

Davies, C. C. *The Problem of the North-West Frontier 1890–1908*. London: Cambridge University Press, 1932.

Diver, Katherine H. M. *Kabul to Kandahar*. London: P. Davies, 1935.

Duke, Joshua. *Recollections of the Kabul Campaign, 1879 and 1880*. London: W. H. Allen, 1883.

Durand, Henry M. "Reminiscences of the Kabul Campaign, 1879–1880." *BLM*, April and May 1917, 201.

Eastwick, William J. *Lord Lytton and the Afghan War*. London: R. J. Mitchell, 1879.

Elliott, William J. *Victoria Cross in Afghanistan, and the Frontiers of India During the Years 1877, 1878, 1879, and 1880*. London: Dean, 1882.

Gillham-Thomsett, Richard. *Kohat, Kuram, and Khost*. London: Remington, 1884.

Great Britain, War Office. *Military Operations in Afghanistan Commencing 7th June 1880*. Simla, 1881.

Hambly, Sir E. "Russia's Approaches to Indian." *Journal of the Royal United Service Institution* 28 (1884).

Hamilton, Angus. *Afghanistan*. New York: Charles Scribner's Sons, 1906.

Hamilton, Lillias. *A Vizier's Daughter: A Tale of the Hazara War*. London: 1900.

Hanna, Henry B. *Lord Roberts in War*. London: Simpkin, 1895.

————. *The Second Afghan War, 1878–79–80; Its Causes, Its Conduct, and Its Consequences.* 3 vols. London: Constable, 1910.

————. "India's Scientific Frontier: Where Is It? What Is It?" *Indian Problems.* Westminster, Indian Problems, No. 2 (1895).

Haughton, J. C. *Chareekar and Service There.* London: Provost, 1879.

Hensman, Howard. *The Afghan War of 1879–80.* London: W. H. Allen, 1881.

Hills, John. *The Bombay Field Force 1880.* London: R. B. Johnson, 1900.

"Historic Reverse in Afghanistan: Maiwand, 1880." *Journal of the Royal United Service Institution* 78 (November, 1933).

Hopkins, Adrian E. *Post Offices of the Second Afghan War 1878–1881.* London, 1965.

Hoskyns, C. "A Short Narrative of the Afghan Campaigns of 1879–80–81, from an Engineer's Point of View," Ordnance Note No. 219, September 22, 1882. In *Ordnance Notes.* Washington, D.C.: 1873–84.

India, Quartermaster-General's Department. *Photographs of Types of Native Arms; Views in Afghanistan, Taken During the War of 1879; Northwest Frontier of Hindustan, Burma, during the British Operations in that Country.* N.p., 1895.

Intelligence Branch, Army Headquarters, India. *The Second Afghan War, 1878–80.* (Abridged official account, compiled by S. P. Oliver) London, 1908.

Kakar, Hasan K. *The Pacification of the Hazaras of Afghanistan.* New York: The Asia Society, 1973.

Khalfin, N. A. *Afghan War of 1879–80 and the Afghan Victory of Maiwand.* Moscow: Akademia Nauk, 1980.

Lawrence, Sir George. *Reminiscences.* London: John Murray, 1875.

Le Messurier, Augustus. *Kandahar in 1879: Being the Diary of Major Le Messurier*. Reprinted with corrections and additions from the *Royal Engineer's Journal*. London: W. H. Allen, 1880.

MacGregor, Charles M. *The Defense of India: A Strategic Study*. Simla, 1884.

————. *The Life and Opinions of Major-General Sir Charles Metcalfe MacGregor, K.C.B., C.S.I., C.I.E., Quartermaster-General in India*. Edited by Lady MacGregor. 2 vols. London, 1888.

————. *The Second Afghan War: Compiled and Collated by and Under the Orders of Major-Genl. Sir C. M. MacGregor, K.C.B., C.S.I., C.I.E., Quartermaster-General in India*. 6 pts. Simla, 1885.

Mackenzie, Colin. *Storms and Sunshine of a Soldier's Life*. London, 1884.

Male, Arthur. *Scenes Through the Battle Smoke*. London: Dean, 1890.

Martin, Denys R. *Further Postal History of the Second Afghan War, 1878–81. With Kandahar and Baluchistan, 1881–87; A Review in the Light of Contemporary Records*. London: Bath, 1961.

Marvin, Charles. *Reconnoitring Central Asia: Pioneering Adventure in the Region Lying between Russia and India*. London: Swan Sonnen-schein, 1884.

Maxwell, Leigh. *My God Maiwand! Operations of the South Afghanistan Field Force, 1878–80*. London: Cooper, 1979.

Mitford, Maj. R. C. W. *To Cabul with the Cavalry Brigade: A Narrative of Personal Experiences with the Force under General Sir F. S. Roberts, G.C.B.* London: W. H. Allen, 1881.

Mohl, Raymond A. "Confrontation in Central Asia, 1885." *HT,* 19 March 1969.

Northbrook, The Earl of. *A Brief Account of Recent Transactions in Afghanistan*. London: Private Printing, 1880.

Owen, Col. Edward. "The Maiwand Disaster and the Investment of Kandahar." *Army Quarterly and Defence Journal*. 114, no. 2 (1984): 202–7.

Roberts, Frederick S. *Afghan War, 1879–80. Despatches of Lieutenant-General Sir Frederick Sleigh Roberts*. Lahore, 1880.

———. *Forty-One Years in India: From Subaltern to Commander-in-Chief*. London: Richard Bentley, 1897.

Robertson, Charles G. *Kurum, Kabul & Kandahar, Being a Brief Record of Impressions of Three Campaigns Under General Roberts*. Edinburgh: David Douglas, 1881.

Robson, Brian. *The Road to Kabul: The Second Afghan War, 1878 – 1881*. London: Arms and Armour, 1986.

———. "Maiwand, 27th July, 1880." *Journal of the Society for Army History Research* 51 (winter 1973).

Shadbolt, Sydney H. *The Afghan Campaigns of 1878–80, Compiled from Official and Private Sources*. 2 vols. London: Sampson Low Marston, 1882.

Sobolev, Leonid N. *Anglo-Afghan Struggle: Sketch of the War of 1879–80*. Translated by Walter Gowan. Calcutta: Government Printing Press, 1885.

Swinnerton, Charles. *The Afghan War: Gough's Action at Futtehabad, April 2, 1879*. London: W. H. Allen, 1880.

Thackeray, Edward T. *Reminiscences of the Indian Mutiny and Afghanistan*. London: Smith and Elder, 1916.

Thomsett, Richard. *Kohat, Kuram, and Khost: Or Experiences and Adventures in the Late Afghan War*. London: Remington, 1884.

Throusdale, William. *War in Afghanistan, 1879–80*. Detroit: Wayne State University Press, 1985.

Willcocks, Brig. Gen. Sir James. *From Kabul to Kumassi: Twenty-four Years of Soldiering and Sport*. London: John Murray, 1904.

Wynne, Maj. A. S. "Heliography and Army Signalling Generally." *Journal of the Royal United Service Institution* 24 (1880): 235–58.

Yapp, M. E. *British Strategies of British India*. London: Oxford University Press, 1980.

5. From 1901 to the Third Afghan War

Ali Mohammad. *Afghanistan, the War of Independence, 1919*. Kabul, 1960.

Barrow, George. *The Life of General C. C. Monro*. 1931.

Cadell, P. *History of the Bombay Army*. London: Longmans, Green, 1938.

General Staff Branch, Army Headquarters, India. *The Third Afghan War 1919*. (Official account) Calcutta, 1926.

Mills, Chris P. *A Strange War*. Wolfeboro, N.H., 1989.

Molesworth, George Noble. *Afghanistan, 1919: An Account of Operations in the Third Afghan War*. Bombay: Asia Publishing House, 1962.

Niedermayer, Oskar von. *Im Weltkrieg vor Indiens Toren*. Hamburg: Hanseatische Verlagsanstalt, 1936.

Taniguchi Masaru. *The Soldier's Log: 10,000 Miles of Battle*. Translated by R. T. Fincher and Tashi Okada. [Tokyo, 1940].

6. Soviet Intervention and the Afghan Civil War

"Afghan Militiamen Defect with Government Weapons." *Jane's Defence Weekly*, 9 January 1988.

"The Afghanistan Air War." *Warplane* 1, no. 1 (1985).

"Afghanistan: the Soviet Army Will Stay." *Army Quarterly and Defence Journal* (July 1986).

Ahady, Anwar-ul-Haq. "Afghanistan: State Breakdown." In *Revolutions of the Late Twentieth Century*. Edited by Jack A. Goldstone et al. Boulder: Westview, 1991.

Alexiev, Alexander. *Inside the Soviet Army in Afghanistan*. Santa Monica: Rand Corporation, 1988.

———. *The United States and the War in Afghanistan*. Santa Monica: Rand Corporation, 1988.

———. *The War in Afghanistan: Soviet Strategy and the State of the Resistance*. Santa Monica: Rand Corporation, 1984.

Alexievich, Svetlana. *Zinky Boys: Soviet Voices from a Forgotten War*. London: Chatto and Windus, 1992.

Allan, Pierre, and Albert Stahel. "Tribal Guerrilla Warfare Against a Colonial Power." *Journal of Conflict Resolution* (Dec. 1983).

Amin, A. Rasul. "The Sovietization of Afghanistan." In *The Great Game Revisited*. Edited by Klass. New York: Freedom House, 1987.

———. "Unity is the Remedy." *Writers Union of Free Afghanistan* 1, no. 2 (1985).

———. "A General Reflection of the Stealthy Sovietization of Afghanistan." *Central Asian Survey* (1984).

Amstutz, J. Bruce. *Afghanistan: The First Five Years of Soviet Occupation*. Washington, D.C.: National Defense University Press, 1986.

Anwar, Raja. *The Tragedy of Afghanistan: A First-Hand Account*. London: Verso, 1988.

Arnold, Anthony. *Afghanistan: The Soviet Invasion in Perspective*. Stanford: Hoover Institution Press, 1985.

—————. *Afghanistan's Two Party Communism: Parcham and Khalq*. Stanford: Hoover Institution Press, 1981.

—————. *The Fateful Pebble: Afghanistan's Role in the Fall of the Soviet Empire*. Novato, California: Presidio Press, 1993.

—————. "The Ephemeral Elite: The Failure of Socialist Afghanistan." *The State and Social Transformation in Afghanistan*. Edited by A. Banuazizi and M. Weiner. Syracuse: Syracuse University Press, 1986.

Ashrati, Abdul Ahad. "Soviet Influence on the Afghan Judiciary." In *A Decade of Sovietization*. Peshawar: Elmi, 1988.

Banuazizi, Ali, and Myron Weiner. *The State, Religion and Ethnic Politics: Afghanistan, Iran and Pakistan*. Syracuse: Syracuse University Press, 1986.

Baumann, Robert. *Russian-Soviet Unconventional Wars*. Fort Leavenworth, Kans.: 1993.

Belitsky, S. "Authors of USSR's Afghan War Policy." Radio Liberty Report on the USSR, 28 April 1989.

Bennigsen, Alexandre. *The Soviet Union and Muslim Guerrilla Wars, 1920–1981: Lessons for Afghanistan*. Santa Monica: Rand Corporation, 1981.

Bennigsen, Alezandre et al. *Afghanistan: Dix Ans Terribles, 1977–1987*. Paris, n.d.

Bergmann, Ernest. *The Soviet Adventure in Afghanistan*. 1988.

Bernstein, Carl. "Arms for Afghanistan." *New Republic*, 18 July 1981.

Bertin, Giles. "Stingers Change the Face of War in Afghanistan." *Jane's Defence Weekly*, 10 October 1987.

Blank, Stephen. *Afghanistan and Beyond: Reflections*. 1983.

———. "Imagining Afghanistan: Lessons of a 'Small War." *Journal of Soviet Military Studies* 3, no 3 (1990).

Bocharov, G. *Russian Roulette: Afghanistan through Russian Eyes*. New York: Amish Hamilton, 1990.

Bodansky, Yossef. "Afghanistan: the Soviet Air War." *Defense and Foreign Affairs*, September 1985.

———. "Soviets Testing Chemical Agents in Afghanistan." *Jane's Defence Weekly*, 7 April 1984.

———. "Soviets Use Afghanistan to Test 'Liquid Fire." *Jane's Defence Weekly*, 26 May 1984.

———. "SAMs in Afghanistan: Assessing the Impact." *Jane's Defence Weekly*, 28 July 1987.

Bonner, Arthur. *Among the Afghans*. Durham, N.C.: Duke University Press, 1987.

Bonner, T. D. *Soviet Strategy Then and Now*. 1991.

Bonosky, Phillip. *Washington's Secret War Against Afghanistan*. New York: International Publishers, 1985.

Borovik, Artem. *The Hidden War: A Russian Journalist's Account of the Soviet War in Afghanistan*. Boston: Atlantic Monthly Press, 1990.

Bradsher, Henry S. *Afghanistan and the Soviet Union*. Durham, N.C.: Duke University Press, 1983.

———. "Afghanistan." *Washington Quarterly* (1984).

———. "Stagnation and C hange in Afghanistan." *Journal of South Asian and Middle Eastern Studies* (fall 1986).

Brigot, Andre, and Olivier Roy. *The War in Afghanistan*. New York: Harvester, 1988.

Broxup, J. M. "Then Soviets in Afghanistan: The Anatomy of a Takeover." *Central Asian Survey*. 1983.

Bruce, James. "Afghan Rebels 'Downing More Soviet Helicopters'." *Jane's Defence Weekly*, 15 November 1986.

Bucherer-Dietschi, Paul. *Afghanistan: Vom Königreich zur Sovietischen Invasion*. Liestal, 1985.

—————. *Afghanistan, 1985/86: The Effects of Soviet Occupation and Warfare*. Washington, D.C.: Congressional Research Service, The Library of Congress, 1987.

Canfield, Robert L. "Afghanistan: The Trajectory of Internal Alignments." *Middle East Journal* 43 (1989).

—————. "Islamic Coalitions in Bamyan: A Problem in Translating Afghan Political Culture." In *Revolutions and Rebellions in Afghanistan*. Edited by Shahrani and Canfield. Berkeley: Institute of International Studies, 1984

"Caravans on Moonless Nights: How the CIA Supports and Supplies the Anti-Soviet Guerrillas." *Time*, 11 June 1984.

Cardoza, Anthony A. "Soviet Aviation in Afghanistan." U.S. Naval Institute Proceedings, Feb. 1987.

Carpenter, Ted Galen. "The Unintended Consequences of Afghanistan." *World Policy Journal* 5, 11, no. 1 (spring 1994).

Centlivres, Pierre et al. *Afghanistan: La Colonisation Impossible*. Paris, 1984.

Chaliand, Gérard. *Guerrilla Strategies: An Historical Anthology from the Long March to Afghanistan*. Berkeley: University of California Press, 1982.

—————. *Report from Afghanistan*. New York: Viking, 1982.

Cherkasov, "Afghan War: The Beginning." *Soviet Soldier*, May 1990.

Cockburn, Andrew. *The Threat: Inside the Soviet Military Machine.* New York: Random House, 1983.

Cogan, Charles. *Holy Blood: An Inside View of the Afghan War.* Westport, Conn.: Praeger, 1993.

————. "Partners in Time: The CIA and Afghanistan." *World Policy Journal* (summer 1993).

————. "Shawl of Lead: From Holy War to Civil War in Afghanistan." Conflict 10, no. 3 (1990).

Coldren, Leo O. "Afghanistan in 1984: The Fifth Year of the War." *Asian Survey*, February 1985.

————. "Afghanistan in 1985: The Sixth Year of the Afghan War." *Asian Survey*, February 1985.

Collins, Joseph. *The Soviet Invasion of Afghanistan: A Study of the Use of Force in Soviet Foreign Policy.* Lexington: Lexington Books, 1986.

————. "The Soviet Invasions of Afghanistan: Methods, Motives and Ramifications." *Naval War College Review* (1980).

————. "Soviet Military Performance in Afghanistan." *Comparative Strategy* 4, no. 2 (1983).

Combined Arms Training Activity. *Light Infantry in Action.* Kansas: Fort Leavenworth, 1988.

Cordovez, Diego, and Selig S. Harrison. *Out of Afghanistan: The Inside Story of the Soviet Withdrawal.* Oxford: Oxford University Press, 1995.

Cordsman, A. H., and A. R. Wagner. *The Lesson of Modern War.* Vol. 3 *The Afghan and Falkland Conflicts.* Boulder: Westview Press, 1991.

Crisis and Conflict Analysis Team. *Report on Afghanistan.* Nos. 3, 4, 5, and 6. Islamabad, 1984.

Cronin, Richard. "Afghanistan After the Soviet Withdrawal: Contenders for Power." Washington, D.C.: Congressional Research Service, May 1989.

Dale, Tad. *Afghanistan and Gorbachev's Global Foreign Policy.* Santa Monica: Rand Corporation, 1989.

Day, Arthur R. *Escalation and Intervention: Multilateral Security and Its Alternatives.* Boulder: Westview Press, 1986.

Derleth, J. "The Soviets in Afghanistan: Can the Red Army Fight a Counter-insurgency War?" *Armed Forces and Society* 15, no. 1 (1988).

Dickson, Keith D. "The Basmachi and the Mujahedin: Soviet Responses to Insurgency Movements." *Military Review*, February 1985.

Dobbs, Michael. "Secret Memos Trace Kremlin's March to War." *Washington Post*, 15 November 1992.

Donnelly, C. "Afghanistan." Royal Military Academy Sandhurst SSRC Paper, 1981.

Dorn, Allen E. *Countering the Revolution: the Mujahedin Counter-revolution.* New York: Afghanistan Forum, 1989.

Dunbar, Charles. "Afghanistan in 1987: A Year of Decision." *Asian Survey*, February 1988.

———. "Afghanistan in 1986: The Balance Endures." *Asian Survey*, February 1987.

Dupree, Louis. "Red Flag over the Hindukush." Parts 2, 3, 4, 5, and 6. *American Universities Field Service Report.* New York: 1979–1980.

Edwardes, M. *Playing the Great Game: A Victorian Cold War.* London: Hamilton,1975.

Edwards, David Busby. "The Evolution of Shi'i Political Dissent in Afghanistan." In *Shi'ism and Social Protest.* Edited by Juan Cole and Nikki Keddie. New Haven: Yale University Press, 1986.

Eflein, Dennis. *A Case Study: Afghanistan - a Soviet Failure.* 1992.

Eflein, Dennis. *A Case Study: Afghanistan - a Soviet Failure*. 1992.

Emadi, Hafizullah. *State, Revolution, and Superpowers in Afghanistan*. New York: Praeger, 1990.

Eshaq, Mohammad. "Evolution of the Islamic Movement in Afghanistan." Pt. 1, "Islamists Felt Need for a Party to Defend Islam"; Pt. 2, "Daud's Hostile Attitude towards Islamists Led to Confrontation"; Pt. 3, "Panjshir Uprising of 1975"; Pt. 4, "Life in Exile from 1975 to 1978." *AfghaNews*, 1 and 15 January, 1 and 15 February 1989.

Evans, Richard. "The Battle for Paktia." *Far Eastern Economic Review*. 1991.

Farr, Grant M., and John G. Merriam. *Afghan Resistance: The Politics of Survival*. Boulder: Westview Press, 1987.

Fukuyama, Francis. *The Future of the Soviet Role in Afghanistan*. Santa Monica: Rand Corporation, 1980.

Fullerton, John. *The Soviet Occupation of Afghanistan*. Hong Kong: Methuen, 1984

Galeotti, Mark. *Afghanistan: The Soviet Union's Last War*. London: Frank Cass, 1995.

Gall, Sandy. *Afghanistan: Agony of a Nation*. London: The Bodley Head, 1988.

––––––. *Behind Russian Lines: An Afghan Journal*. London: Sidgwick and Jackson, 1983.

Galster, Stephen R. *Washington, Moscow and the Struggle for Kabul*. New York: Afghanistan Forum, 1990.

––––––. A Chronology of Events Relating to International Aid to the Afghan Resistance. Washington, D.C.: The National Security Archive, 1987.

Ghani, Ashraf. "Afghanistan: Islam and the Counterrevolutionary Movements." In John Esposito, *Islam in Asia*. New York: Oxford University Press, 1987.

Ghaus, Abdul Samad. *The Fall of Afghanistan*. Washington, D.C.: Pergamon-Brassey's, 1988.

Gibbs, David. "Does the USSR Have a Grand Strategy? Reinterpreting the Invasion of Afghanistan." *Journal of Peace Research*. 24, No. 4. Oslo: Norvegian University Press, 1987.

———. "The Peasant as Counterrevolutionary: The Rural Origins of the Afghan Insurgency." In *Studies in Comparative International Development*. 21, No.1. Brunswick, N. J.: Transaction, 1986.

Gille, Etienne. "'Accession au Pouvoir des Communistes Prosovietiques." In *Colonisation Impossible*. Paris, 1984.

Gille, Etienne, and Sylvie Heslot. *Lettres d'Afghanistan de Serge de Beaurecueil*. Paris, n.d.

Girardet, Edward R. *Afghanistan: The Soviet War*. London: Croom Helm, 1985.

———. "Afghan Guerrilla Leader Holds His Own Against Soviet Offensive." *Christian Science Monitor*, 2 October 1984.

———. "Arming Afghan Guerrillas: Perils, Secrecy." *Christian Science Monitor*, 20 November 1984.

Goldman, Minton F. "Soviet Military Intervention in Afghanistan: Roots and Causes." *Polity* (spring 1984).

Goodwin, Jan. *Caught in the Crossfire*. New York: Dutton, 1987.

Gregory, David C. *Soviet Invasion of Afghanistan: Causes and Future Options*. Air War College, Air University, 1986.

Grevemeyer, Jan-Heeren. "Religion, Ethnizität und Nationalismus im Afghanischen Widerstand." *Leviathan* 1 (1985).

Grevemeyer, Jan-Heeren, and Tahera Maiwand. *Afghanistan: Presse und Widerstand*. Berlin: Verlag Das Arabische Buch, 1988.

Gross, Natalie. "Soviet Press Review." *Jane's Soviet Intelligence Review*, July 1989.

———. "How Healthy Is the Soviet Soldier?" *Soviet Analyst*, 16 April 1986.

Gunston, John. "Afghans Plan USSR Terror Attacks." *Jane's Defence Weekly*, 31 March 1984.

———. "Soviets Using Su-25s in Attacks on Rebel Units." *Aviation Week & Space Technology*, 29 October 1984.

Gupta, Bhabani Sen. *Afghanistan Politics, Economics, and Society: Revolution, Resistance, and Intervention*. London: Frances Printer, 1986.

Hall, Jonnie H. "To Save the Pilot's Life - Soviet Air Rescue Service." *Air University Review* (May-June 1982).

Halliday, Fred. "Revolution in Afghanistan." *New Left Review*, 1978, 112.

———. "War in Afghanistan." *New Left Review*, 1978, 119.

———. "War and Revolution in Afghanistan." *New Left Review*, January–February 1980.

Hammond, Thomas. *Red Flag Over Afghanistan: The Communist Coup, the Soviet Invasion, and the Consequences*. Boulder: Westview Press, 1984.

Hansen, James H. "Afghanistan: The Soviet Experience." *Jane's Defence Review*, January 1984.

Haqqani. Hussain. "The Chinese Connection." *Far Eastern Economic Review*, 14 February 1985.

Harrison, Selig S. "Dateline Afghanistan: Exit Through Finland?" *Foreign Policy* (winter 1980–81).

———. "Inside the Afghan Talks." *Foreign Policy*, no. 72 (fall 1988).

Hart, Douglas M. "Low Intensity Conflict in Afghanistan: The Soviet View." *Survival*, March/April 1982.

Hauner, Milan. *The Soviet War in Afghanistan: Patterns of Russian Imperialism*. Lanham, Md.: University Press of America, 1991.

Hauner, Milan, and Robert Canfield. *Afghanistan and the Soviet Union*. Boulder: Westview Press, 1989.

Heinamaa, Anna. *The Soldier's Story: Soviet Veterans Remember the Afghan War*. Berkeley: University of California Press, 1994.

"Helicopter Protection from IR Missiles." *Jane's Defence Weekly*, 5 October 1985.

Herda, D. J. *The Afghan Rebels: the War in Afghanistan*. New York: F. Watts, 1990.

Holcomb, James F. "Recent Developments in Soviet Helicopter Operations." *Soviet Military Studies*, no. 3 (1989).

Holden, Constance. "Unequivocal Evidence of Soviet Toxin Use." *Science*, no. 216, April 1982.

Huldt, Bo, and Erland Jansen, eds. *The Tragedy of Afghanistan: the Social, Cultural, and Political Impact of the Soviet Invasion*. London: Croom Helm, 1988.

Hussain, Syed Shabbir. *Afghanistan: Whose War?* Islamabad: World Affairs Publications, 1987.

Huxley, Tim. *The War in Afghanistan*. Canberra, 1983.

Hyman, Anthony. *Afghanistan under Soviet Domination, 1964–81*. London: Macmillan, 1982.

———. "Politics and the Resistance." In *Afghans in Exile*. Conflict Studies, No. 202. London, 1987.

"Improvised Convoy Escort Vehicle." *Jane's Defence Review* 2, no. 2 (1982).

Information and Press Department, Ministry of Foreign Affairs. *The Undeclared War*. Kabul, 1984.

Isby, David C. *Russia's War in Afghanistan*. London: Osprey, 1986.

———. *The War in Afghanistan 1979–1989: the Soviet Empire at High Tide*. Hong Kong, 1990.

———. *War in a Distant Country, Afghanistan: Invasion and Resistance*. London: Arms and Armour, 1989.

———. "Soviet Special Operations Forces in Afghanistan, 1979–1985." Report of Proceedings: Light Infantry Conference, Seattle, 1985.

———. "Soviet Tactics in the War in Afghanistan." *Jane's Defence Review* 4 no. 7 (1983).

———. *Weapons and Tactics of the Soviet Army*. London: Jane's Publishing Company, 1988.

Jalali, Col. Ali. "The Soviet Military Operation in Afghanistan and the Role of Light and Heavy Forces at Tactical and Operational Level." Report of Proceedings: Light Infantry Conference, Seattle, 1985.

Jukes, Geoffery. "The Soviet Armed Forces and the Afghan War." Amin Seikal and William Maley, eds. *The Soviet Withdrawal from Afghanistan*. London: Cambridge University Press, 1989.

Kakar, Hasan Kawun. *Afghanistan: the Soviet Invasion and the Afghan Response. Berkeley*: University of California Press, 1995.

Kaplan, Robert D. *Soldiers of God: With the Mujahedin in Afghanistan*. Boston: Houghton Mifflin, 1990.

Karp, Aaron. "Blowpipes and Stingers in Afghanistan: One Year Later." *Armed Forces Journal International* (Sept. 1987).

Karp, Craig M. "The War in Afghanistan." *Foreign Affairs* (summer 1986).

Kemp, Ian. "Abdul Haq: Soviet Mistakes in Afghanistan." *Jane's Defence Weekly*, 5 March 1988.

Khalidi, Noor Ahmad. "Afghanistan: Demographic Consequences of War, 1978–1987." *Central Asian Survey* 10 (1991).

Khalilzad, Zalmay. "Moscow's Afghan War." *Problems of Communism*, Jan.- Feb. 1986.

———. "The Soviet Dilemma in Afghanistan." *Current History* (October 1985).

———. "Soviet-Occupied Afghanistan." *Problems of Communism*, 29 June 1980.

Khan, Riaz Muhammad. *Untying the Afghan Knot: Negotiating Soviet Withdrawal*. Durham: Duke University Press, 1991.

Klass, Rosanne T. *Afghanistan: The Great Game Revisited*. New York: Freedom House, 1987.

Konovalov, V. "Legacy of the Afghan War: Some Statistics." Radio Liberty Report on the USSR, 7 April 1989.

Koza, Catherine M. *Spoils of War: How International Assistance Can Influence Local Processes of Economic Change: The Case of Afghanistan*. Boston: M.I.T. Press, 1990.

"Kremlin Assails Its Afghan Role." *International Herald Tribune*, 24 October 1989.

Laber, Jeri, and Barnett Rubin. *A Nation Is Dying: Afghanistan Under The Soviets, 1979–87*. Evanston: Northwestern University Press, 1988.

Lajoie, Roland. *The 1979 Soviet Intervention in Afghanistan*. 1981.

Lohbeck, Kurt. *Jihad: Holy War*. Washington, D.C. 1984.

———. *Holy War, Unholy Victory*. Washington, D.C.: Regnery Gateway, 1993.

Mackenzie, Richard. "Afghan Rebels Never Say Die." *Insight*, 25 January 1988.

Magnus, Ralph H. *Afghanistan: Marx, Mullah and Mujahed*. Boulder: Westview Press, 1985.

————. *Afghan Alternatives: Issues, Options and Policies*. New Brunswick: Transaction Books, 1985.

————. "The Military and Politics in Afghanistan: Before and After the Revolution." In *The Role of the Armed Forces in Contemporary Asian Society*, by Edward A. Olsen and Stephen Jurika. Boulder: Westview Press, 1985.

————. "Tribal Marxism: The Soviet Encounter with Afghanistan." *Conflict*, 1983.

Majrooh, Sayd Bahauddin, and Sayyid Muhammad Yusuf Elmi, eds. *The Sovietization of Afghanistan*. Peshawar, 1986.

Male, Beverly. *Revolutionary Afghanistan: A Reappraisal*. London: Croom Helm, 1982.

Malhuret, Claude. "Report From Afghanistan." *Foreign Affairs* (winter 1983–84).

Marshall, William. *U.S. Policy Objectives in Aiding the Afghans*. 1991.

McDermott, David F. "The Invasion of Afghanistan." *Infantry*, January – February 1985.

McMichael, Scott. *The Stumbling Bear: Soviet Military Performance*. London: Brassey's, 1991.

Meschaninov, D. "A Powerful Blow by the Afghan Army: A Major Insurgent Base Destroyed." *Isvestiya*. Nov. 26, 1986 (FBIS translation JPRS-UMA-87-006, Jan. 30, 1987).

Mills, Chris P. *A Strange War*. Gloucester: Sutton, 1988.

Moorcraft, Paul L. "Bloody Standoff in Afghanistan." *Military Review*, April 1985.

Morozov, Alexander. "Our Man in Kabul." *New Times*, Moscow, 24 September, 1 October, 14 October, and 21 October 1991.

Moser, Charles. *Combat on Communist Territory*. Washington, D.C.: Regnery Gateway, 1985.

Naby, Eden. "The Afghan Resistance Movement." In *Afghan Alternatives: Issues Options and Policies*. New Brunswick, 1985.

Naqvi, M. B. "The Great Gamble." *The Herald*, Karachi, June 1988.

"New LAW Used in Afghanistan." *Jane's Defence Weekly*, 3 December 1988.

"New Mine Clearing Vehicle in Action." *Jane's Defence Weekly*, 16 January 1988.

"New Soviet Mine-Clearing Vehicle." *Jane's Defence Weekly*, 7 March 1987.

Newman, Joseph Jr. "The Future of Northern Afghanistan." *Asian Survey* (July 1988).

Niesewand, Peter. "Guerrillas Train in Pakistan to Oust Afghan Government." *Washington Post*, 2 February 1979.

O'Ballance, Edgar. *Afghan Wars, 1839–1992*. London: Brassey's, 1993.

O'Brien, Michael C. "Political Legitimacy and the Soviet War in Afghanistan." (Master's thesis) University of Virginia, 1989.

Operational and Strategic Lessons of the War in Afghanistan, 1979–90. Carlisle Barracks, Pa. 1991.

Ottaway, David B. "Stingers Were Key Weapon in Afghan War, Army Finds." *Washington Post*, 5 July 1989.

———. "What is 'Afghan Lesson' for Superpowers?" *Washington Post*, 12 February 1989.

Overby, Paul. *Holy Blood: The Afghan War from the Inside*. Westport: Praeger, 1993.

Owen, Richard. "The Afghan Cloud on Antropov's Horizon." *Times* (London) 3 March 1983.

Owens, Daniel E. *Assessment of Politico-Military Lessons Learned from the Soviet Intervention in Afghanistan*. Maxwell Air Force Base, AL, 1989.

Picolyer. "Caravans on Moonless Nights: How the CIA Supports and Supplies the Anti-Soviet Guerrillas." *Time*, 11 June 1984.

Pohly, Michael. *Krieg und Widerstand in Afghanistan*. Berlin: Das Arabische Buch, 1992.

Prokhanov, A. *A Tree in the Centre of Kabul*. Moscow: Progress, 1983.

Rees, David. *Afghanistan's Role in Soviet Strategy*. Conflict Studies, No. 118. London, 1980.

Reshtia, Sayed Qassem. *The Price of Liberty: The Tragedy of Afghanistan*. Rome: Bard Editore, 1984.

Richards, Martin. "Afghanistan: Stalemate or Climb Down." *The Army Quarterly and Defence Journal* (July 1983).

Ritch, John B. *Hidden War: The Struggle for Afghanistan*. Washington, D.C.: U.S. Government Publications Office, 1984.

Rogers, Tom. *The Soviet Withdrawal from Afghanistan: Analysis and Chronology*. Westport, CT.: Greenwood Press, 1992.

———. "Refugees, Afghans in Exile: A Threat to Stability?" *Conflict Studies*, No. 202, London, 1987.

Roy, Olivier. *Afghanistan: From Holy War to Civil War*. Princeton: Princeton University Press, 1994.

———. *Islam and Resistance in Afghanistan*. Cambridge: Cambridge University Press, 1990.

———. *The Lessons of the Soviet-Afghan War*. London: IISS Adelphi Papers No. 259, 1991.

———. "Le Facteur Massoud." Afghanistan Info., March 1992.

———. "War as a Factor of Entry into Politics." *Central Asian Survey* 8, no. 4 (1989).

Rubin, Barnett R. *The Fragmentation of Afghanistan: State Formation and Collapse in the International System*. New Haven: Yale University Press, 1995.

———. "Afghanistan: The Next Round." *Orbis* 33 (spring 1989).

———. "The Fragmentation of Afghanistan." *Foreign Affairs* (winter 1989–90).

Russo, Charles A. *Soviet Logistics in the Afghan War*. Carlisle Barracks, Pa. 1991.

Ryan, Nigel. *A Hitch or Two in Afghanistan: A Journey Behind Russian Lines*. London: Weidenfels & Nicolson, 1983.

Safi, Major Nasrullah. "The Different Stages of Afghanistan's Jehad." *Quarterly Journal of the Writer's Union of Free Afghanistan*. (Jan.-March 1988).

Safronchuk, Vasily. "Afghanistan in the Taraki Period" and "Afghanistan in the Amin Period." *International Affairs*. (Moscow, Jan-Feb. 1991).

Saikal, Amin. *Regime Change in Afghan Foreign Intervention and the Politics of Legitimacy*. Boulder: Westview Press, 1991.

Saikal, Amin, and William Maley. *The Soviet Withdrawal from Afghanistan*. Cambridge: Cambridge University Press, 1989.

Samimy, S. M. *Hintergründe der Sovietischen Invasion in Afghanistan.* Bochum: Brockmeyer, 1981.

Sarin, Maj. Gen. Oleg, and Col. Lev Doretsky. *The Afghan Syndrome: The Soviet Union's Vietnam.* Novato: Presidio Press, 1993.

Schultheis, Robert. *Night Letters: Inside Wartime Afghanistan.* New York: Orion Books, 1992.

Schwartzstein, Stuart J. D. "Chemical Warfare in Afghanistan: An Independent Assessment." *World Affairs* (winter 1982–83).

Scott, Harriet F. "Rise of the Afghantsi." *Air Force Magazine* 76, no. 8 (1993).

Shahrani, N. Nasif, and Robert L. Canfield, eds. *Revolutions and Rebellions in Afghanistan.* Berkeley: Institute of International Studies, University of California, 1984.

Shakaib, G. D. "Soviet Military Problems." *Quarterly of the Writer's Union of Free Afghanistan* (July-Sept. 1987).

Shansab, Nasir. "The Struggle for Afghanistan." *Combat on Communist Territory.* Lake Bluff, 1985.

Shroder, John F. "Afghanistan Resources and Soviet Policy in Central and South Asia." In *Afghanistan and the Soviet Union: Collision and Trans-formation.* Edited by Milan Hauner and Robert L. Canfield. Boulder: Westview Press, 1989.

Sikorsky, Radek. *Dust of the Saints: A Journey to Herat in Time of War.* New York: Chatto and Windus, 1990.

———. *Moscow's Afghan War: Soviet Motives and Western Interests.* London, 1987.

Sliwinski, Marek. "The Decimation of Afghanistan." *Orbis* 33 (winter 1988–89).

"Soviet Air Force in Afghanistan." *Jane's Defence Weekly,* 7 July 1984.

"Special Issue on Afghanistan." *World Affairs* (1982–83).

"Special Report: Afghanistan." *Aviation Week & Space Technology*, 29 October 1984.

Stahel, A. A., and Paul Bucherer. *Afghanistan, 1985/86: Besetzung und Kriegsführung der UdSSR.* Liestal, 1986.

————. *Afghanistan: 5 Jahre und Kleinkrieg.* Frauenfeld.

————. "Afghanistan, 1984/85; Bezetzung und Widerstand." In *Allgemeine Schweizerische Militärzeitschrift* 12 (1985).

Steele, Jonathan. "Moscow's Kabul Campaign." *Middle East Report* (MERIP) (July-Aug. 1986).

Storella, Mark C. *The Central Asia Analogy and the Soviet Union's War in Afghanistan.* New York: Afghanistan Forum, 1984.

Stork, Joe. "The CIA in Afghanistan." *MERIP* (July–Aug. 1986).

Strand, Richard F. "The Evolution of Anti-Communist Resistance in Eastern Nuristan." In *Revolutions and Rebellions.* Edited by N. Shahrani and R. Canfield. Berkeley: Institute of International Studies, 1984.

Suvorov, Viktor. *Spetsnaz.* Translated by David Floyd. London: Hamilton, 1987.

Tabibi, Abdul Hakim. *Afghanistan: A Nation in Love With Freedom.* Cedar Rapids: Ingram Press, 1985.

Taniwal, Hakim. "The Impact of Pashtunwali on Afghan Jihad." *Quarterly Journal of the Writers' Union of Free Afghanistan* 2 (Jan.-March 1987).

Taniwal, Hakim, and Ahmad Yusuf Nuristani. "Pashtun Tribes and the Afghan Resistance." *WUFA* 2 (Jan.-March 1987).

Tawana, Sayyid Musa. "Glimpses into the Historical Background of the Islamic Movement in Afghanistan." Pts. 1–5. *AfghaNews*, 1 April 1989 and 1 June 1989.

Thorne, Ludmilla. *Soviet POW's in Afghanistan*. New York: Freedom House, 1987.

Turbiville, Graham H. *Ambush! The Road War in Afghanistan*. Fort Leavenworth, Kans. 1988.

———. *Soviet Combat Engineers in Afghanistan*. Washington, D.C.: National Defense University Press, 1989.

Umnov, Alexander. "Afghanistan: What Price Dogma?" *New Times*, no. 19, May 9–15.

Urban, Mark. *War in Afghanistan*. 2nd. ed. New York: St. Martin's Press, 1990; London, 1988.

———. "The Limited Contingent of Soviet Forces in Afghanistan." *Jane's Defence Weekly*, 12 January 1985.

———. "A More Competent Afghan Army?" *Jane's Defence Weekly*, 23 November 1985.

———. "Soviet Army Turns Its Back on the War It Never Tried to Win." *Independent*, London, 14 February 1989.

U.S. State Department. *The Kidnapping and Death of Ambassador Adolph Dubs: Summary Report of an Investigation*. Washington, D.C.: Government Printing Office, 1980.

Vollmann, William T. *An Afghanistan Picture Show*. New York: Farrar, Straus, and Giroux, 1992.

Wilkins, Jacob. *The Soviet Invasion of Afghanistan*. 1986.

Wimbush, S. Enders, and Alex Alexiev. *Soviet Central Asian Soldiers in Afghanistan*. Santa Monica: Rand Corporation, 1981.

Winchester, Mike. "Night Raiders on Russia's Border." *Soldier of Fortune*, September 1984.

Woodward, Bob. *Veil: The Secret Wars of the CIA*. New York: Simon and Schuster, 1987.

Yarushenko, A. "A Bright Hour: Even Today There Is a Place for Heroic Deeds." *Soviet Patriot*, 15 October 1986.

Yermakov, Oleg. *Afghan Tales*. London: M. Secker and Warburg, 1993.

Yousaf, Mohammad. *Silent Soldier: The Man Behind the Afghan Jehad*. Lahore: Jang Publishers, 1991.

Yousaf, Mohammad, and Mark Adkin. *The Bear Trap: Afghanistan's Untold Story*. Lahore: Jang Publishers, 1992.

Zaloga, Steven. *Armor of the Afghanistan War*. London: Arms and Armour Press, 1992.

———. *Red Hammer*. Presidio, 1995.

ABOUT THE AUTHOR

Ludwig W. Adamec (B.A., political science; M.A., journalism; Ph.D., Islamic and Middle East studies, University of California at Los Angeles), is a professor of Middle Eastern studies at the University of Arizona and was director of its Near Eastern Center for ten years. Widely known as a leading authority on Afghanistan, he is the author of a number of reference works on Afghanistan and books on Afghan history, foreign policy, and international relations, including *Afghanistan 1900–1923: A Diplomatic History, Afghanistan's Foreign Affairs to the Mid–Twentieth Century*, a six-volume *Political Gazetteer of Afghanistan*, and the *Historical Dictionary of Afghanistan*.